JEWISH THINKERS
General Editor: Arthur Hertzberg

Elusive Prophet

Ahad Ha'am and the
Origins of Zionism

Elusive Prophet

Ahad Ha'am and the Origins of Zionism

Steven J. Zipperstein

PETER HALBAN
LONDON

FIRST PUBLISHED IN GREAT BRITAIN BY
PETER HALBAN PUBLISHERS
42 SOUTH MOLTON STREET
LONDON W1Y 1HB
1993

British Library Cataloguing-in-Publication Data.

A catalogue record for this book is available from the British Library

ISBN 1870015 54 1

Printed in the United States of America

For Sally, Max, and Sam

"And you're still teaching Bible there . . ."

"Yes, of course, only Bible."

"In that case"—still smiling—"everything's as usual."

"Yes, as usual"—and another long silence—"except of course for my pupils getting killed," I spit out in a whisper straight into his face.

He shuts his eyes. Then he sits up, huddled in his blanket, his beard wild, picks up a pipe and sticks it into his mouth, and begins to muse, like an ancient prophet, to explain that the war won't go on, haven't I noticed the signs, can't go on any longer. And now his wife wakes up as well, sits up beside him, likewise drapes the blanket about her, sends me a smile full of light, ready to make contact, join the conversation, explain her viewpoint, straightaway, without going for a wash, coffee, her eyes still heavy with sleep, in the shimmer of spring twilight, in the littered room filled with their warmth.

A. B. Yehoshua, "Early in the Summer of 1970," *The Continuing Silence of a Poet*

Contents

Acknowledgments

When I first set out to write about Ahad Ha'am I envisioned a biographical sketch of modest length, an extended essay as proposed to me by the London publisher Peter Halban for his series "Jewish Thinkers." As the manuscript grew much longer than anticipated, Halban watched with bemusement and remarkable patience. I thank him for this and much more. I also thank him for persuading Stanley Holwitz of the University of California Press to share the burdens of publication. Mr. Holwitz proved to be a superb editor: gently prodding, patient, and encouraging.

This book was conceived in Oxford, researched and all-but-completed during my four years at the University of California, Los Angeles, and appears in print now that I am in my new home at Stanford. While working on it I benefited from the advice of many colleagues and friends in England, Israel, and the United States—alas, more than would be possible to thank here. I am very grateful to all those who were generous with their time and expertise. I shall mention only a few: David Patterson, President of the Oxford Centre for Postgraduate Hebrew Studies, Sir Isaiah Berlin, Tony Judt, Eli Lederhendler, Marcus Moseley, and Ada Rapoport Albert. Chimen Abramsky, now retired from the Chair in Jewish History at University College, London, was throughout a source of guidance and intellectual inspiration. A conversation I had with Arthur Hertzberg soon before completing the manuscript prompted me to rethink some of its assumptions. At UCLA I was privileged to work closely again with my former dissertation adviser Hans Rogger who commented on various sections of this book. I owe thanks to Arnold Band, David Biale, and Mitchell Cohen, Gina Morantz-Sanchez, and Chaim Seidler-Feller for judicious, learned comments on drafts of this manuscript. Arnold Band proved a much valued colleague; I hope I've answered some of the questions he posed during our lunchtime conversations. The members of my biographers' group in Los Angeles—Ellen Dubois, Nina Gelbart, Robert Rosenstone, Debora Silverman, and Alice Wexler—provided me with a stimulating intellectual community. At Stanford I learned from talks with my new colleagues, especially Arnold Eisen, Mark Mancall, and Aron Rodrigue. I thank my research assistants Nina Caputo, David Rechter, Mitch Hart, and Naomi Koltun. Edith Johnson provided editorial help as I readied the first draft. Margaret Mullen and Michelle Nordon at the University of California Press gave me patient and intelligent guidance as I saw the book through publication.

I wrote the bulk of the manuscript while the Marta Sutton Weeks Fellow at the Stanford Humanities Center during the academic year 1990–1991. This gave me the opportunity to write with few (but, fortunately, at least some) distractions. I thank the Center, its staff and fellows, and especially its now former director W. Bliss Carnochan for a memorable and happily taxing year. I am grateful for research assistance and travel grants to Jerusalem and New York from the Committee on Research of the Academic Senate at UCLA and in particular for the encouragement of Provost (now University of California, Riverside President) Raymond Orbach. The UCLA Center for Russian and East European Studies helped with research funds, and the School of Humanities and Sciences at UCLA made it possible for me to take a year's leave in 1990–1991 by supplementing the fellowship at the Stanford Humanities Center. Since joining Stanford's faculty in 1991 my research has been supported by the Koshland Fund for the Study of Jewish History and Culture, and by funds made available by the Dean of the School of Humanities and Sciences.

I wish to acknowledge the libraries, archives, and individuals that helped provide the materials for this study: the archivists and librarians of the Jewish National and University Library; the Central Zionist Archives and their erudite (now retired) director Michael Heymann; the Kressel Library and Archives of the Oxford Centre for Postgraduate Hebrew Studies; the YIVO Institute for Jewish Research and its librarians Dina Abramowicz and Zachary Baker; the University Research

Library at UCLA and, especially, its exemplary Judaica bibliographer David Hirsch; and the Green Library, Stanford, whose curator of the Taube-Baron Judaica collection, my new colleague Roger Kohn, helped during the final, hectic stages.

The intellectual with whom I found myself obsessed for the last few years insisted on subsuming all—family, too—under the demands of an abstract agenda. In this respect Ahad Ha'am provided me with little guidance. It was my wife Sally Goodis—and with considerably greater persistence and much less tact, my sons Max and Sam—who helped recall for me the world beyond my study. I thank her, and them, for this and so much more. I dedicate this book, and all that I hold dear, to them.

Stanford, California
September 1992

Note on Transliteration, Dates, and Terms

In transliterating Hebrew and Russian I have followed the Library of Congress rules except that I have eliminated most diacritical marks and have presented well-known names in their most familiar form. For Hebrew words I have not used diacritical marks to distinguish between letters *het* and *hei*. The Yiddish transliteration is based on the system devised by the YIVO Institute for Jewish Research. Personal names appear in different versions depending on the geographic or cultural context in which the individual was most active.

Dates, until 1908, when Ahad Ha'am left Russia for England, follow the Julian or Old Style calendar, which in the nineteenth century was twelve days behind the Gregorian. Thereafter dates follow the Gregorian calendar. The terms Palestine and the Land of Israel (Erets Yisrael) are both used here, as they were in pre-state Zionist circles.

Introduction

For good reason biographers of Theodor Herzl, and there have been many of them, have found it unnecessary to justify their preoccupation with the turn of the century Zionist leader. His impact on contemporary Jewish life—and, most importantly, on the shaping of the Jewish State—is so self-evident that attention to his upbringing, his fantasies, or his pre-Zionist journalism and play writing (most of the latter almost painfully stilted and dated) is recognized by common consensus as necessary to understanding the emergence of the Zionist idea. During his lifetime, and also after his death, Herzl opened up Jewish nationalism to a larger world: his standing in European letters, his cultivated demeanor, his insistence on couching arguments for Zionism in the context of European self-interest, all these helped reassure non-Jews and Jews alike that Jewish nationalism was unparochial, expansive, and compelling.

"He was fortunate in life and fortunate in death" is how Ahad Ha'am somewhat acidly reacted to Herzl's death at his prime, at the age of forty-four, and just as he was beginning to lose his grip on his movement. Before Herzl appeared on the Jewish scene, and for a good many years later, it was Ahad Ha'am who was the voice of ideology and principle, of consistency and clarity in Jewish nationalism. "It may be said without exaggeration that Ahad Ha'am is the national hero of Russian Jewry, at least as far as its intellectual elements are concerned," declared an American follower in 1906. Even those who repudiated him could not, at least during his lifetime, fail to acknowledge his pervasive presence, his ability to infect so much of the Jewish national enterprise with his mordant and uncompromising view of the world. By the time of his death in Palestine in 1927 Ahad Ha'am was adored and despised with almost equal measure and passion.[1]

It has nonetheless proved to be far more difficult for historians— considerably more so than for Herzl or Weizmann (who proudly declared himself Ahad Ha'am's disciple)—to explain Ahad Ha'am's impact. He shunned the larger European stage, he insisted on writing in Hebrew (though he had mastered several European languages, including Russian), he remained suspicious of gentile help, of grand plans, and most public gestures. Although Herzl's Zionist years were spent in furious negotiations in the public arena, Ahad Ha'am's time was spent in his study where he wrote (and not with particular fluency: his collected essays would be published in four, by no means bulky, volumes), paced, complained, and conspired with the small coterie that remained true to him and his ideals.

The object of enormous attention in the Jewish nationalist world in its formative stages, this intellectual whose real name was Asher Ginzberg (Ahad Ha'am, or "One of the People," was his pen name), was a slight, reclusive, somewhat bitter, taciturn, untalkative, and rather snobbish man. Though widely considered Zionism's greatest thinker, he attended few of the movement's international congresses (and never spoke at them), excused himself from most other public appearances, and savaged Zionism's established leadership whenever the spirit moved him. "Herzl was the leader of his generation; Ahad Ha'am was its teacher," wrote his first biographer in a deceptively symmetrical reconstruction of Zionism which saw its two major figures (who, in fact, met only twice and couldn't stand the sight of one another) as nicely complementing each other's achievements in the shaping of a movement that embodied the political savvy of one and the unyielding morality of his counterpart.[2]

Symmetrical or not, it is fair to say that these two leaders represented very different sides of their movement. To an extent they still do. Tellingly, in recent years Ahad Ha'am has been put to use by some on the Israeli liberal-left frustrated by the right's ability to usurp not only control of the government (beginning with Menachem Begin's election in 1977 and ending with the 1992 Israeli election) but classical Jewish nationalism as well. As an early observer in the Zionist camp of the Palestinian problem, as a critic of the use of aggression as a tool in the nationalist arsenal, as a foe of Jewish clericalism, Ahad Ha'am has been deemed symbolically useful as an emblem of liberal Zionism's often marginalized political culture. This remains true outside Israel, as well: hence when Herzl's most recent biographer, Ernst Pawel, sought to distance himself from the political legacy of Herzl apparently he could think of no better way to do so than by dedicating his book, *The Labyrinth of Exile*, to "The Spiritual Heirs of Ahad Ha'am."[3]

Beginning with his first appearance on the public scene in Odessa in the mid-1880s, Ahad Ha'am was seen by devoted intellectuals as personifying the successful integration of Jewish nationalism's complex commitment to secularity and Jewish continuity: they considered him the prime representative of a Judaism without the form but with the same substance that had characterized it throughout its history. He was "the only one of us," wrote the Hebrew poet Hayyim Nahman Bialik, "who can be said to be a true disciple of the patriarch Abraham." What he came to personify in Jewish nationalism was (what his ideological camp claimed to be) its quintessentially Jewish side: secular, liberal, but nonetheless embedded (as he argued) in the fundamental teachings of Judaism. From the vantage point of Herzlians, such a perspective was cloistered, impractical, and precisely the sort of inward-looking politics from which Zionism sought to escape.[4]

The biographical literature he inspired is deeply respectful, even reverential, but it has been written almost exclusively by devotees. True, Ahad Ha'am was also the object of furious criticism, especially in Hebrew literary circles where many found his designation of what was and what was not Jewish to be cramped, conservative, and arbitrary. Such modernist criticisms had an impact on his biographers only insofar as they became all the more protective of their unjustly embattled hero, whose suffering was not only tragic and excessive but also redemptive, contributing to lifting him to an even higher plane of disinterestedness and moral purity. He came to serve for them, in short, as a nationalist totem, an emblem of his movement's achievements and potential.*

At the same time, in these accounts he remains strangely elusive and even the most respectful of them differ in the most fundamental ways on how and why he reacted as he did: on who and what Ahad Ha'am

---

*The one major exception, published just as I put the final touches on this book, is Yosef Goldstein, *Ahad Ha'am: Biografiah* (Jerusalem, 1992). This meticulous, sober study examines Ahad Ha'am's life in great detail with special emphasis on his political career. Curiously it avoids discussing the existing secondary literature on him, preferring, it seems, that the archival sources tell their own story. To a large extent it avoids taking a position on this primary material, too, except to argue for Ahad Ha'am's undiminished political appetite.

was. He is judged in them alternatively as uncannily influential and uninfluential, successful and unsuccessful, politically dexterous and dense or indifferent. I, too—though eventually I became reasonably confident that I could visualize Ahad Ha'am as he sat at his desk or entered a room—found that as vivid as he was for me on one level he remained throughout much of the time I spent working on this biography surprisingly elusive. Biographers have, of course, come to take for granted the elusiveness of their subjects, their "multiple, shifting, and often self-contradictory"[5] identities; as one feminist theorist recently put it. Nonetheless, as I attempted to negotiate my way through the voluminous backdrop of existing work on him—scholarly, publicistic, as well as memoiristic—the images of him that emerged seemed characterized by such basic discrepancies as to render initially any semblance of coherence inconceivable.

Even when compared to the literature on Herzl, which itself differs widely on whether he should be seen as a romantic or pragmatist, as obsessively self-absorbed or possessing a coherent social vision, it becomes apparent on how little Ahad Ha'am's biographers agree in comparison with his otherwise keenly contested contemporaries. Ahad Ha'am himself recognized this during his lifetime, suggesting that such ambiguities could be traced to the extreme brevity of his more important prose, to his insistence on expressing himself in the form of hints, to his commitment to producing the sparest prose conceivable in Hebrew.

What I came to appreciate was that it was precisely his elusiveness that represents the key to understanding him and his politics which were themselves predicated on a commitment to concealment, dissimulation, and elitism. This will, as we shall see, help explain why even during his lifetime his contemporaries were often at a loss to explain his personal and ideological impact, which was for much of the period before World War I greater than that of any other Jewish nationalist ideologue. Few saw him as an original thinker, but rather as a bold and masterful synthesizer, and, above all, an extraordinary Hebrew stylist. But they attributed his great attractiveness instead to something other than his literary skill: it was his human attributes, his standing as a man who managed to capture in his life and writing the essence of what it meant to be a modern Jew, that was held up as his real, most formidable contribution. Indeed, even those who disagreed with him—at one time or another in his exceptionally contentious career most Jewish nationalists would—continued to see him as someone who embodied a rare Jewish authenticity. He was in the words of one of his foremost ideological opponents Micah Joseph Berdyczewski "more Jewish than me, more Jewish than any of us." What Berdyczewski found so paradoxical about Ahad Ha'am's impact on him and his generation others took for granted. As his close friend Bialik said: "Ahad Ha'am is the symbol of the great culture that will be built by the community of Jews in the Land of Israel and will unify all segments of Jewry throughout the world."[6]

The devotional tone to so much of the biographical literature about Ahad Ha'am came to make him seem less intriguing than he is: much of this work is also keenly defensive about his legacy owing to the political climate in Israel in the 1950s when the best of it was written. By then Ahad Ha'am's pessimism and his call for a more gradual pace to immigration to Palestine had rendered him an anachronistic, even slightly absurd figure in the Zionist world. With the emergence and consolidation of the State of Israel his stance seemed to be at odds with the state's heroic prerequisites. And those who seemed to be most comfortable with his teachings were associated with the small, beleaguered circle of intellectuals—Martin Buber was the best known of these—who advocated binationalism and claimed Ahad Ha'am (albeit on tenuous grounds) as an ideological precursor.[7] His prognosis—or, at least, what Israeli society came to associate with it—seemed wrong to the majority: his caution misguided, his pessimism idiosyncratic and perverse rather than prescient; indeed, in the wake of the Holocaust his caution seemed to some to skirt the bounds of morality.

In the process of defending him against charges of irrelevance or obtuseness, his champions portrayed a man who was considerably more priggish and far less complex than he is in my view: less ambitious, less cunning, less sardonic, and less intellectually dexterous. He appears in biographies, such as that of Simon and Heller, published in 1955,[8] as something of an inspirational statue: stolid, consistent, principled, and rather dry. This may have contributed to his equivocal standing in Israeli cultural life where, similar to Emerson's in the United States, his exemplary prose has been foisted upon schoolchildren who, as a matter of course, disparage it or avoid it afterwards. Moreover, once the Hebraists close to him passed from the scene there was no institution or party—except perhaps for the Writers' Association in Israel—that was devoted to sustaining his memory in the way in which such existed for Herzl, Vladimir Jabotinsky, or David Ben Gurion.

This biography seeks to reread Ahad Ha'am's life without the pieties of the past. This study seeks to recast his life by making better sense of the sources—his essays as well as his letters (those published as well as many unpublished ones), press (in Hebrew, Yiddish, Russian, and German), memoirs and diaries, and other secondary literature. In the process I have found it essential to contextualize the man and his achievements by examining his leadership patterns and his political style from the perspective of the East European Jewish milieu that spawned him. No doubt the figure who emerges from this inquiry will seem somewhat diminished for those who have preferred to see him in more universal terms. But he also emerges as immeasurably more interesting, I think, than in earlier, more appreciative accounts of his life, most of which were written by close friends and disciples and tended to reproduce faithfully the world as he saw it.

Clearly a central preoccupation of this book is Ahad Ha'am's vision of the Land of Israel, the main focus of his attention as a public intellectual: what should it, and should it not, look like, what ought to be the character of its political culture, its dominant symbols, its attitudes toward the world, its neighbors, the non-Jews in its midst?

A close reading of his work reveals a coherent picture of the Jewish future in Palestine and elsewhere. True, Ahad Ha'am wrote no utopia; in fact, it is the elaboration of anti-utopia (the inevitable "shadow of utopia" as Krishan Kuman puts it in his superb *Utopia and Anti-Utopia in Modern Times*) that best suited his temperament. "Now I have left the land for which I have yearned for so long with a broken heart and broken spirits," he writes after his first trip. "No longer are the land, its people and all that happens there mere dreams for me, but now what I have seen is the concrete truth . . . of which I wish to reveal a bit—the ugliest bit."[9]

This is his most familiar side: jaundiced, barbed, even obsessively cynical. But this, as we shall see, was embedded in a comprehensive vision of a future society, a vision of a "conservative utopia" to usurp Karl Mannheim's terminology in much the way that Andrzej Walicki did in his work on the nineteenth-century Russian Slavophiles, those curiously kindred spirits of Ahad Ha'am's.[10] In his Zionism he negotiated his way between what was a truly ambitious, holistic vision of Jewry redeemed and suspicions of plans that promised redemption too quickly, that skirted the bounds of the possible. On the one hand, his Zionism was uncompromising: it promised the realization of prophetic aspirations; it predicted a time when under the benevolent skies of Judea genius would once again flower, when centered once again in their ancient home, their true home, the Jews would be equipped to negotiate for themselves the conflicting demands of modernity and tradition with deftness and authenticity. On the other hand, he cautioned against excessive hope, haste, waste, boastfulness, egotism, pride, even (or so it sometimes seemed) against joy. But in his nationalism, and perhaps only here, he permitted himself to be expansive—though here, too, he consigned its greatest achievements to the distant future, with the passing of the present generation, the death of their Moses, and the sublimation of his people's uglier inclinations.

My decision to write yet another version of the life of the foremost exponent of a humanistic, liberal Zionism is influenced by extra-academic concerns, by more than a professional desire as a historian of modern Jewry to set the record straight and better contextualize Ahad Ha'am's life. As someone who evolved into a liberal out of a deeply traditional Jewish milieu where attitudes toward Israel, and much else, were deeply conservative, Ahad Ha'am has always represented for me a guide to a sensible, balanced approach to Jewish affairs. Few voices better captured my own sense of intense attachment mixed with misgiving; an empathy for Zionism's aspirations coupled with the recognition that if Israel were to be successful it would have to balance the demands of pragmatism with compassion and become better aware of the fundamental limitations of power. Ahad Ha'am's clarity, caution, and stringent ethical commitments moved me deeply. I looked to him for guidance or at least for moral validation.

As I followed Israeli events in the late 1980s with mounting unhappiness and some sense of tragedy, I was drawn back once again to this intellectual influence of my late adolescence whose work interested me now, as then, chiefly for its didactic purposes. My motivation at first was to reread Ahad Ha'am to test whether one of the seminal voices in Zionist thought might still have something useful to say about the Jewish state—to be sure, not directly for he had died some twenty years before it was created. Perhaps a reassessment of him and his work would provide some clue as to how its humanistic underpinnings might be recast to move them closer to the center of Israel's political culture.

The writing of this biography did not, in fact, point me in such a direction. How could the study of a late nineteenth-century liberal nationalist provide clues to the torturous politics of the contemporary Middle East? What I encountered was a thinker who drew his most important insights into politics and society from the standards of traditional East European Jewish society that he had first imbibed in his youth. These standards—secularized but replete, especially, with abiding hasidic influences—were seen by many even in his lifetime as having little relevance to the realities of turn-of-the-century Jewish Palestine. To use them as a guide to present-day Jewish affairs was clearly a pointless exercise. The more closely I studied him the less directly relevant he appeared to be today, and the more deeply embedded in that Russian Jewish intellectual world that he had so dominated once and whose strategies he had deftly mastered.

I soon discovered that the man I sought to portray was quite unlike the one others before me had described: more provincial and less philosophically compelling. I also found that through this research I gained a considerably more vivid sense of the meaning of intellectual engagement, of scholarship wedded to a nationalist agenda: its sacrifices, its limitations, and its fundamental integrity.

And here, I think, is a key to his standing in Jewish thought. He was able—by virtue of the curious forcefulness of his personality, the tautness of his prose, the hunger of a constituency faced with a particularly vulnerable moment of Jewish history—to persuade minds more impressive than his own (Bialik and Gershom Scholem, for instance) that his solutions were embedded in Jewish sources, that he had squared the circle, had reconciled the tension between an increasingly discredited tradition and modernity's moral anarchy. Never would he be, or at least seem to be, torn like, say, Vladimir Jabotinsky's *Samson,* between the allure of Philistinian Timnah and the austere standards of the tribe of Dan. Ahad Ha'am seemed altogether self-sufficient in his Jewishness (a key to that aura of priggishness that so characterized him—but it is also here that the notion of him as, in Judah Magnes's words, a uniquely "harmonious Jew" originated); this same self-sufficiency was free from parochialism, or so he managed to persuade some of Jewry's finest minds. Here was a Jew who had absorbed all that was essential from the larger European intellectual arsenal and yet who knew nothing of its assimilatory allure, who wanted nothing but to be a son of his people, who had chosen to embrace his Jewish milieu not because of his limitations or fears, but because anything else would be humanly inauthentic, intellectually deadening, itself a curious and perverse exercise in parochialism.

My chief interest here is his work—his essays, his public activity, and his status as an emblem among the Jewish nationalists and in the larger Jewish world as well. I examine his personal life only in relation to his work. During his lifetime, and later, much of his impact was fueled by the belief that he embodied the aspirations of a reconstructed Judaism, reconciling its complex commitment to Jewish tradition and radical change, cultural continuity and revival in Palestine. The consolidation of this image of Ahad Ha'am is at the center of this study but the details of his daily affairs proved less important in its formation than the needs of his East European Jewish constituency, its assumptions about the prerequisites of leadership.

This book is organized along chronological lines but each chapter has a thematic character of its own that traverses at times the strict boundaries of chronological sequence. There was a set of fairly discrete preoccupations—not static but still reasonably consistent—that dominated Ahad Ha'am's thinking from the 1880s to the end of his life. To chart these strictly along chronological lines, without a recognition of the ways in which over time his various themes tended to coalesce, would have rendered the reason for their impact obscure. At the same time, I show him as a social analyst, not a systematic thinker: despite his own aspirations and the desires of a constituency that hungered for a Maimonides of their own, he produced no systematic philosophy. To treat him, as have most of his biographers, as an original thinker is misleading. It is for this reason that it seemed to me unfruitful (and probably impossible) to sort out his various intellectual influences: the Jewish enlightenment (perhaps preeminently from Nahman Krochmal), the German enlightenment (Johann Gottfried Herder), English utilitarianism, Russian populism (Peter Lavrov). He drew from all these in various ways that are usually too transparent to require comment. It was precisely his indebtedness to these sources, most of which were well known in his Russian maskilic (or, Jewish enlightenment) milieu, that lent his work much of its power: this power was a by-product of their very familiarity with his prooftexts, the way in which he cleverly manipulated them, stretching their meaning—as his readers themselves were intended to recognize—so as to endow them with a Jewish nationalist content.

One final note: I call him in this book Asher Ginzberg before the publication of his first essay under the pen name Ahad Ha'am; thereafter I refer to him as Ahad Ha'am. Especially since this pen name, like so much else surrounding him, represented, as I argue, an exercise in mystification, this decision might seem odd. I am nonetheless convinced, particularly since my interest is his literary and public life, that calling him here Ahad Ha'am is appropriate. Naturally I do so with an awareness of what Asher Ginzberg meant the pen name to represent. It is precisely such self-mystification that, if he is to be understood, must be situated at the core of any study of his life.

1

His Father's Son

I, at least, have no need to exalt my people to Heaven, to proclaim its superiority over all other nations in order to justify its existence. I, at least, know "why I remain a Jew" or rather why I find no meaning in such a question any more than I would in the question why I remain my father's son.

Ahad Ha'am, "Slavery in Freedom"

I

Named for his paternal grandfather, Asher Ginzberg was born on 18 August in 1856 (or 7 Av according to the Hebrew calendar) in Skvire, a Ukrainian town of some two thousand inhabitants, half of whom were Jews, located fifty miles southeast of Kiev. Skvire was well known in the Jewish world because of its exceptionally active hasidic sector. It was, as Ginzberg glumly recorded as an adult, "one of hasidism's darkest Russian corners." When asked to recall his earliest memory he said it was fear, "a frightening dream that awoke me from my sleep in the middle of the night. My parents came to soothe me as I cried loudly. I was, I think, three years old."[1]

Asher Ginzberg was one of the many talmudically adept and precocious youth so celebrated in East European Jewry; this aspect of his background was conventional. But from the outset his economic circumstances were remarkably comfortable for someone from this milieu. During his childhood his family, after a difficult stretch in his youngest years, was well-off; by the time of his adolescence they were by any standards quite rich. This wealth provided him with sufficient leisure to immerse himself in study. His parents supplied his scholarly needs: books, tutors, and a heavy-handed, stern, unrelenting encouragement. They took for granted that he would emerge as a prominent rabbinic figure.[2]

He was born into a family that placed a special premium on the acquisition of prominence—scholastic, financial, even familial. Neither side possessed the sort of unquestioned stature, or *yichus,* that set someone apart in East European Jewry, usually a combination of pedigree, learning, wealth, and personal character. Nevertheless, in the case of the Ginzbergs, their standing was solid and respectable: Asher's father's family had produced their share of rabbis of local reputation and had been wealthy for a time, which singled it out for special attention. His mother's family, which came from Skvire, was less prominent; they were wealthy merchant stock, in Ahad Ha'am's rather acidic description, "simple people without distinctions of any kind." The sole exception was her multilingual father, a confidant of one of the outstanding religious leaders of East European Jewry—the hasidic *rebbe* Israel Ruzhin—a charismatic, organizationally adept presence on the hasidic map and a great-grandson of Dov Baer, the Maggid of Mezhirech. Asher's grandfather was not especially learned (it was his Russian fluency that brought him to the hasidic leader's attention); when the rebbe was forced to abandon Russia for Galicia nearly two decades before Asher's birth, his grandfather lost whatever influence and also whatever source of financial security he had.[3]

In short, it was a family that had rubbed shoulders with the prominent but was not quite one of them and had on his father's side enjoyed briefly the prerogatives of the wealthy. It was perhaps because of this background that his parents were, as even Asher's sister Esther admits in an otherwise highly sympathetic portrait, keenly preoccupied with yichus, willful and very ambitious; both of them—strikingly attractive people judging from pictures of them in middle age—were taken with their good looks, something rarely expressed openly (by males at least) in traditional circles. Asher's own descriptions of them were almost entirely uncomplimentary. He described his mother as vain and hot-tempered, his father as uncompromising, rigid, and well-learned, but humorless.

The death of Asher's two younger brothers, born when he was three, also embittered his father who mourned their passing for years. It was an unpleasant household, and he was happiest when he was someplace else. This was rarely the case though; he remained at home, with only a few fairly brief excursions until he was twenty-nine.[4]

Russian and Polish Jewish history in the second half of the nineteenth century has come to be rightfully associated with poverty, misery, and with mass flight across the borders of the Russian empire. It was the dank and crowded Jewish quarters of such cities as Vilna, Warsaw, and Odessa, or the Pale of Settlement's hundreds of *shtetlach*—the very term already in midcentury a synonym for inexorable decline—that constituted the spawning ground for Ginzberg's generation. Jewish Skvire was such a place: isolated and introverted, poor or lower-middle class.

When Asher was twelve, his father, Isaiah—an enterprising businessman despite bouts of bad health—managed to acquire a remote rural leasehold called Gopchitse in the Berdichev region. He rented it despite the objections of his wife, Golda, for whom the move meant isolation in rural territory relatively uncharted by Jews some seven hours by wagon from the nearest rail stop. Isaiah elicited the recommendation of his rebbe, Israel Ruzhin's son Abraham Yaakov, who urged him to take the chance. Isaiah was further persuaded since the rental of Gopchitse represented a way for him to acquire far more than mere smalltown respectability.[5] It was a risky and ultimately very successful venture.

Asher left Skvire without regrets. He remembered a childhood of unhappiness mitigated only slightly by the solitary joys of learning. Many years later, when asked to describe childhood toys, he could think only of his annual Hannukah games. His time was spent almost entirely with books, first exclusively with sacred ones, and then, by his early adolescence, with a medley of sacred as well as those considered vaguely profane by the austere hasidic standards of his circle. The youngest student in the *heder* (a privately run traditional Jewish primary school) he attended from the age of three, he was remote and bookish and he left no record of intimacy with another student. His teachers were conventional; he later implied that he was wholly self-educated and, although this is untrue, prior to his move to Gopchitse he does not seem to have encountered a teacher who could truly inspire him.[6]

In Gopchitse, with private tutors hired to guide him in the intricacies of Jewish law and without the intrusive camaraderie of the heder, Ginzberg worked hard at making himself into a talmudic master. He described himself spending his days "wandering about always with his books, alone." He spent most of this time in a suite of rooms adjacent to the living room where he read, paced (a habit that proved to be lifelong), and entertained two close friends—probably his first—both sons of employees on the estate, whose admiration helped sustain him. He also confided in his sister Chana, who was four years younger. Otherwise daily life was dull and uneventful; his visitors were mostly those sent by his father to test him on the progress of his studies. In the morning when he was most alert, he studied the Talmud and rabbinic commentaries: he would complete, as was the custom among young scholarly adepts, at least one (and usually more than one) talmudic tractate each year, beginning each at the time of the early spring festival of Purim and finishing the next spring just before Passover. During less retentive times of his day, he read hasidic tracts, medieval biblical commentaries, and rabbinic responsa. Maimonides' *Guide to the Perplexed*, along with an array of medieval Spanish-Jewish philosophers, were his favorites. He appeared to be well on the road to becoming an accomplished Talmud scholar.[7]

The bucolic wonders of Gopchitse did not entice him, or so he claims in his memoirs. His sister Esther recounts that he learned to ride a horse and that he was once saved by the family dog while swimming in the estate's river. Later he would describe Gopchitse as his spiritual prison, as an isolated and intellectually barren spot. Immune as he may well have been to the estate's natural beauty, the fact that he spent his youth in the improbable role of a Jewish nobleman—celebrated by servitors, fawned upon by a doting staff, with a very small but loyal retinue of obviously subordinate friends who were themselves the children of staff, and with as much money as he could ever want—all this left its imprint.

Gopchitse was surrounded by dense forests and dominated by a manor house of fifteen rooms accompanied by several other buildings used by staff and visitors. A river flowed through the estate, a garden (serviced by a full-time gardener) encircled the house, which was shaded by massive old trees. The estate's four- or five-room guest cottage housed a steady stream of visitors, mostly relatives of the Ginzbergs and devotees of the Ruzhin hasidic dynasty. The staff was extensive and exceptionally handsome; Esther recalls that her mother chose them as much for their pleasing looks as for their expertise. Esther, who was nineteen years younger than Asher, remembered the estate's lushness, serenity, and overwhelming beauty:

The [main] building was one story and very old; in those days it was said to be one hundred years old. Carriages, upon reaching the house, would come by way of the large garden that surrounded it on all sides, and would travel alongside a double column of ancient and very tall trees lining the driveway on both sides up until the very entrance of the house. Here there was a wide thatched porch with pillars leading to an antechamber and then on to my parents' rooms.[8]

Rarely did the larger world impinge on Asher's cloistered world. At odd moments, such as Friday evenings after prayers, *hasidim* at the Skvire *shtibl* (a small synagogue) would sit and chat about provincial or national politics. "They would tell of what they had heard about national politics, and various people would talk about all this, until the time came to return home," recalled Ginzberg.[9] The family came into more frequent contact with non-Jews at Gopchitse, but found them inextricably alien, culturally inferior, and frequently the source of amusement. Once when a visiting nobleman asked Isaiah what occupied his son all day in his rooms and was told that he studied Jewish books, the nobleman said that if the boy was really talented he should be sent to a Russian school and eventually to university where his learning would be put to good use. Isaiah found the conversation very amusing: "Go and explain something like this to a *goy!*" he exclaimed to Asher later. A favorite story of Asher's grandfather, who enjoyed telling tales of his travels with Israel Ruzhin, was when his *tsadik* (holy man, or rebbe) explained why it was proper to lie to gentiles: "Don't you understand? For them it is lies that are truths and truths that are lies. So, the more you lie to them the more persuaded they are that you are telling the truth!"[10]

It was hasidism, above all the cult of the Sadagora rebbe, that dominated the lives of the Ginzbergs. "I learned to respect the Sadagora rebbe with the reverence of God," wrote Ahad Ha'am. The close association between his mother's father and Israel Ruzhin was the family's greatest distinction. Isaiah, whose veneration for the rebbe could only have been enhanced once Gopchitse prospered under his stewardship, spent Sukkoth at the cult's imposing Italian, neo-Gothic Bukovina center and it was here that he negotiated the terms of his son's betrothal to the daughter of another Sadagora hasid.

Sadagora hasidism, built around its founder, Israel Ruzhin, had survived the removal of the sect's leader to Galicia from its original center in Podolia and Kiev; in the 1840s the Russian government implicated the rebbe in the killing of Jewish informers. Israel Ruzhin had enjoyed great opulence in the Ukraine, and when he moved abroad a huge building was acquired for him to accommodate the throngs who continued to seek his counsel and blessing. Tales of the dynasty's opulence were related by followers proud of its grandeur, influence, and power;

opponents saw it as among the more vivid examples of unchecked decadence in the hasidic world.[11]

In Skvire Isaiah was already a prominent member of the Sadagora community but once he established himself as someone capable of running a large estate and a sizable staff, his own home came to take on some of the trappings of his rebbe. Often fifty guests at a time gathered at his Sabbath or festival table; Isaiah sat at the head sternly directing the proceedings, his brother Leib who came to work on the estate close at hand, and with Asher, his only son, at his right. Beggars came for doles at arranged times. On Purim they sat with family and other guests at a massive table loaded down with delicacies. On trips back to her native Skvire, Golda was treated akin to royalty, and rumors of her wealth provided relatives and friends with a powerful incentive to view her with awe. Esther relates that when they would arrive in Skvire on rather frequent excursions back home, the shtetl would literally echo with the cry: "Golda Ginzberg of Gopchitse has come!" as if a Rothschild had stumbled into town. The Ginzbergs spent lavishly. Esther tells of frequent shopping trips to Kiev or Odessa. During one trip, when Golda expressed her displeasure at her husband's unwillingness to buy a piece of jewelry priced (or so their daughter Esther later recalled) at thousands of roubles, he immediately rushed back to purchase it for her.[12] In no respect did their opulent style of life conflict with their hasidism since they were modeling their behavior after that of their master.

At the age of twelve it was at the rebbe's court that Asher, then a conventionally pious prodigy brought by his father for a blessing before his thirteenth birthday (and so that his father could seek the rebbe's advice on his move to Gopchitse), was transformed into a critic of hasidism and, eventually, traditional Judaism in general. The particular incident that he later identified which served to alienate him had nothing to do with the intellectual underpinnings of hasidism. Rather, what the prudish, cloistered adolescent found troubling was the coarseness of the rebbe's family and its entourage. Ginzberg recalls:

We spent the entire [Sukkoth] festival at Sadagora in the company of the Rebbe and his children. . . . One evening . . . there was no feast at the Rebbe's house, and so my father went to a feast of his children and took me with him. We arrived at the *Sukkah,* which was full of people, and one old man, a Galician, stood beside the table and diverted the children (specifically the rebbe's eldest son and his better-known brother-in-law) with gross stories full of coarse language. The stories were so gross that I, a child of twelve, understood practically everything in them. Everyone there laughed with all their heart. Suddenly one of the rebbe's children closed his eyes tightly and with great fervor exclaimed, "Where is

Yoshke?" (a famous Sadagora cantor who had also come for the festival). When they found Yoshke the son said, "Sing 'Let the Rock Command His Loving-kindness.'" The cantor began to sing and the young *tsaddik* listened with his eyes closed, his devotion increasing all the time until he seized the salt shaker, which was close to me, and used it to beat time on the table. The salt shot far and wide across the whole sukkah while the cantor finished his song. The scene, particularly the sudden transition from dirty stories to pious fervor, made a very bad impression on me.[13]

The rebbe himself, Abraham Yaakov, Asher found thoroughly impressive. Precisely what it was that moved him he did not say. His veneration for the rebbe would remain intact for some time though, and when writing his memoirs half a century later, Ginzberg would recall vividly the salutary impressions that the rebbe had made on him—of his "splendid appearance, actions, and teachings."[14]

As a youth he witnessed an even more telling incident of charismatic leadership and its impact. His maternal grandfather adamantly refused to ally himself with the competing Chernobyl hasidic master who had inherited much of the Ruzhin's rebbe's abandoned flock at Skvire; even when the town became a center for this dynasty, Asher's grandfather refused to place himself at the feet of another tsaddik. A clever man, warmhearted and witty, he was capable (as Asher would later tell it) of impressive displays of irony when debating followers of the town's master; indeed, he was the only adult relative about whom Asher Ginzberg would later reminisce with affection. It is likely that the battle in Skvire between those loyal to the Ruzhin rebbe and the devotees of Rebbe Isaac Twersky—which was so fierce that it culminated in denunciations to the authorities—shaped Ginzberg's earliest understanding of the costs of loyalty, leadership, and religious politics.[15]

In addition to the way in which his experience with an embattled hasidic background might have introduced the meaning of loyalty to a great leader, hasidism also gave him insight into the importance of self-effacement in the name of a higher ideal. He tells, in his memoirs, of a tutor, a Sadagora hasid who taught him at Gopchitse, who insisted upon walking to the ritual bath some two miles away in the worst weather, even in the deepest snow. Never again did he encounter such devotion: "Several times I have reflected that if a similar sense of obligation existed in the Zionist camp, it would take on a completely different character, one far more appropriate."[16] By the time Ahad Ha'am had fashioned his own coherent Jewish nationalist ideology, self-effacement would be among its fundamental underpinnings—a central feature (he was convinced) of the culture of the Jewish past and one that needed to be salvaged and also redefined for the sake of the future.

Asher may have discarded his hasidic beliefs with brisk efficiency but his odyssey into a Westernized, self-consciously modern *maskil* (a follower of the Jewish enlightenment, or *Haskalah*) was to be prolonged, deeply painful, and full of compromises, both petty and profound. He moved rapidly from hasidism to a commitment to mitnagdic Judaism with its classical rabbinic disdain for the revivalist hasidic movement. Within a year he then embraced Haskalah, and its call for a break with the most socially and intellectually cloistered features of Jewish life. Yet his rebellion was also timid and hesitant and it extended well into his twenties and perhaps even until he and his family abandoned Gopchitse for Odessa when he was twenty-nine. Even then, Ginzberg first moved with his immediate family for a tentative stay in Odessa but, after a few months there in 1884, returned home. When he settled permanently in the city two years later, he remained in business with his father. In his late twenties he stayed bound up to a traditional regimen, less because of religious devotion than because of his relationship with his father. Their relationship was an intense and difficult one: Asher, the child prodigy, disappointed his father whose ambitions for him were excessive, unrealized, and perhaps incapable of ever being satisfied.

As an adult Ahad Ha'am wrote of his father, particularly of his treatment of him as a child, with a fierce pain seemingly unaffected by the passage of time:

It was the habit in our house when sitting down to a meal at table that each one would bring a book to read between courses. My father usually brought the *Midrash Rabbah,* while I would choose various books from my father's library. Once father saw what my book was, and after inspecting it he said, "Do you know that the author of this book wrote it before he was eighteen?" "I know," I answered. "As for you," he went on, "when you're eighteen you won't even be able to understand what he has written." This annoyed me very much for I did understand everything in it perfectly well, despite all its complex dialectics, and though I was only eleven at the time. But that was a basic feature of his educational technique—to lower me in my own eyes. But I don't know what his goal was in doing this.[17]

No matter how well he performed when tested weekly by his father on Saturday afternoons, he was beaten until his mother demanded that

Isaiah stop. Asher later claimed that his father's most enduring legacy was his son's lifelong lack of self-assurance. He described Isaiah as remote, scornful, and dogmatic, yet also recalled the way in which he sometimes accompanied his father on trips to the estates of local nobles. Such pleasant memories were, however, rare and remained overshadowed by his father's dismissive, even abusive treatment. His mother, Golda, beautiful but rather frivolous, did not have much of a hold on Asher's emotional life, at least once he reached adulthood. Only on occasion would he speak of her with affection: he remembered her reading aloud a Yiddish translation of the weekly Bible selection while he sat nearby in rapt attention. In contrast, his father's hold on his emotional life was firm, and his death in 1899 grieved Asher to the point of distraction and contributed toward breaking his health.[18]

By then, as we shall see, it was apparent that his relationship with his father inspired both his radicalism (e.g., his contempt for the role played by the rich in Jewish communal affairs, which marginalized what he believed to be a previously potent scholarly elite), and also his lifelong anxiety about the need for moderation—his sense that forces obstructing change were all but insurmountable, that they must be finessed with consummate discretion. At times he veered with what seemed an erratic abandon from one stance to the other: from an uncompromising fury against every injustice to what amounted to a horror at the thought of any action that challenged the status quo without sufficient preparation and foresight.

His father, a powerful, self-confident, rich man fed Asher's huge ambitions that he too would grow up a genius, adored in much the way that Isaiah was by the guests at his generous table. Isaiah's, and his wife's, preoccupation with a somewhat ambiguous standing in an intensely status-conscious Jewish milieu, Isaiah's restlessness, his unfocused but (at least at one time) impressive scholarship, and, above all, his dissatisfaction with his accomplished son who suffered from the full weight of his father's expectations because of the loss of his younger brothers—all this inspired Asher to believe himself destined for greatness but at the same time doubtful of his ability. He emerged as a consummate peacemaker—aware of the value of all sides, able to satisfy the needs of even the most obdurate—and also the most severe of radicals, unyielding and principled. This meant that Asher was both evasive and hateful of dissimulation, hungry for adoration and doubtful that he merited it, confident of his place in the world and anxious of crossing some elusive line for fear of being humiliated much as he was at the wretched family meals of his childhood. It was there too, though, that he was celebrated. It was only when he lost his father that he could admit, and only then in passing, that he loved him.

II

In the wake of his visit to the Sadagora court, Asher's daily routine changed little. For a time, he led the life of a *mitnaged* and discarded some hasidic practices (for instance, hasidism's lax attitudes toward the rabbinically designated times for prayer) but little else. From the vantage point of the world in which he lived, he remained a talmudic prodigy with grand rabbinic aspirations. By the age of seventeen, he had acquired something of a local reputation and rabbis sometimes solicited his opinion on religious law. By that time he had completed a reading of the entire talmudic corpus, a considerable accomplishment marked by his father with a celebration in his honor. Apparently Asher thought of himself as a maskil, but he nonetheless remained in the traditional orbit and gave those around him little reason to believe that he had strayed.

His father knew that he had dipped into some questionable litera-ture—the medieval philosophy of Maimonides, for instance, widely considered by traditional Jews to be off-limits to the young and im-pressionable. Sadagora hasidim on the recommendation of Israel Ruzhin shunned philosophical literature entirely, but in this respect Isaiah Gin-zberg was lax by hasidic standards and his library was well stocked with such literature, which he made available to his inquisitive son and which he permitted him to store in his rooms. Asher was also allowed to buy, with his father's money, other less traditionally acceptable books and he built up a fine collection of philosophy and Hebrew grammar. His library included even some maskilic classics by Kalman Schulman, for instance, a special favorite of both father and son; Schulman's Hebrew translation of *Mystères de Paris* scandalized and intrigued a generation of cloistered readers in the Russian Pale. An occasional visitor and friend of Asher's father, Shalom Rapoport, brought Asher some books such as maskilic poetry which his father permitted in the house as long as they contained no outright heresy.[19]

Asher's passionate interest in the Bible was also slightly off the beaten track. Its importance was generally minimized in the traditional Jewish regimen of those with serious scholastic potential. He particularly enjoyed studying the Bible with the expositions of Yitzhak ben Aramah's *Akedat Yitzhak,* a warmly conversational work whose rambling, casual prose he admired but which had no apparent impact on the development of his own terse, highly disciplined style. (He imitated the style of *Akedat Yitzhak* in several exegetical sermons and he was sufficiently proud of them to save them for many years.) He devoured historical works such as *Yossippon* and *Shevet Yehudah,* and a tutor introduced him to musar literature, whose severe moralism attracted the introspective adolescent. By his late teens he had studied the classic thinkers of the Haskalah: Moses Mendelssohn, Nahman Krochmal, Samuel David Luzzatto, and Abraham Geiger. When Isaiah discovered in Asher's room a copy of a book by Naphtali Herz Wesseley, a particularly hated maskil in traditionalist eyes, he warned that if Asher ever brought home any similar books he would never again be permitted to use his father's library. Soon afterwards, when Asher chanced upon still another controversial book hawked by an itinerant bookseller, he bought it and with enormous trepidation spent the night reading it. He burned it before morning.[20]

For most of his adolescence, then, Asher combined a penchant for marginally suspicious literature and a continued interest—and mounting expertise—in the sacred works of Judaism. Eventually he crossed the line separating innocent syncretism from real heterodoxy, but only with cautious deliberation and secrecy.

Hasidim was particularly disdainful of the philosophical and belletristic literature that Asher now devoured. Elsewhere, in the mitnagdic circles of the East European Jewish world, an acquaintance with Haskalah was frequently viewed as an acceptable part of an educated man's syllabus. What distinguished the well-read mitnaged (or hasid like Asher's father) from a maskil was subtle, but essential: for the literate traditionalist Jew, secular literature served an auxiliary function, a way of imposing clarity onto sacred texts, which remained the sole source of truth. Hence it was for the sake of such knowledge that the exemplar of mitnagdic Judaism, the eighteenth-century Elijah the Gaon of Vilna, permitted the study of geography or science books that he felt illuminated otherwise opaque passages of the Talmud. For the maskil, however, secular books represented in themselves an alternative avenue to truth, a fundamental source of authority. Hence, a conservative maskil (like Kalman Schulman) and a reasonably tolerant mitnaged had a good deal in common; they were acquainted with the same literature and frequently practiced a similarly punctilious Judaism. They differed in their attitudes on the self-sufficiency of the Torah.[21]

The Haskalah, the focal point of much of Asher's attention after he reached his mid-twenties, was characterized by the belief that the fundamental features of Judaism were entirely reconcilable with the modern world and that Jewish life could be judged by outside standards. It was pedagogic in character and optimistic in tone and tended to stress the centrality of those aspects of Jewish life that non-Jews were believed to consider positive: the purity of biblical Hebrew, the stability of Jewish family life, Jewry's financial aptitude, its agricultural past, and Judaism's philosophical legacy. It denounced aspects of contemporary Jewish life at variance with the beliefs of the larger society, such as mystical speculation, disdain for secular study, and ignorance of the vernacular. In Russia in particular, in the absence of emancipation or the somewhat closer social contact with non-Jews that characterized nineteenth-century Western or Central European Jewish life, the Haskalah offered a haven for Jews caught between an inaccessible, larger cultural world and an unacceptable, Jewish one.[22]

As Asher came to see himself as a maskil and grew eager to expand his intellectual horizons beyond the confines of knowledge available in Hebrew, he laboriously taught himself to read other languages. Much earlier he had learned the Cyrillic alphabet by deciphering Skvire's street signs; his father apparently forbade his heder from teaching him the alphabet even though some of the children studied it with a special teacher because the Sadagora rebbe had decreed that the letters of foreign alphabets were cursed. This seems out of character for Isaiah, whom even Ahad Ha'am calls something of a maskil and who hired Russian-language tutors for his daughters Esther and Chana; Ginzberg recalled in his memoirs that Reuven Braudes, the well-known Hebrew writer, was brought to their home for this purpose but stayed only briefly and was followed by others. Perhaps Isaiah assumed that Asher, unlike his classmates at the heder who required training in clerical skills for the sake of their future careers, was destined for rabbinic greatness and could be spared learning any mundane knowledge that would distract him from Torah. Once Asher reached adolescence he devoured, even memorized, Russian books that came his way—including odd volumes of the *Proceedings of the St. Petersburg Academy of Sciences*. Soon he turned his attention to German and Latin; when he moved to Odessa he studied English and French.[23]

But Asher, because of filial attachment, material comfort, or timidity, seems to have been suspended for some time between a way of life that was publicly observant and privately, behind the doors of his study, maskilic, intellectually daring, and even heretical. He hungered for new horizons (and especially for new books), yet entered into a prearranged marriage when he was seventeen to a pious girl closely related both to the Lubavitcher and Cherkassy rebbes. For his parents, eager to enhance their yichus, the match was heaven sent; Asher himself seems to have entered into it sullen and unhopeful:

During the last few years before I became a bridegroom, two fathers-in-law were in competition for me. One was a wealthy ignoramus, and the other belonged to a well-pedigreed family into which I eventually married. The girl of that family had been orphaned by her father, the Rabbi of Zhitomir, who died while still a young man. Naturally she had no dowry. The other man was then well known in our area as a very wealthy man who was ready to give his daughter a large dowry. My father wanted to proceed with things properly and decided that I must be asked which I preferred. The matter was given over to my tutor; he was told to talk with me and did so. I was very puzzled and did not know how to answer. In my heart I was inclined to prefer the match with the wealthy one because I feared the other family's piety and hasidism. But I was embarrassed to admit this openly to my tutor and instead of a direct answer, I reminded him of the talmudic saying: "Let a man sell all that he possesses . . ." without finishing the quote, for I expected my teacher would understand. I wanted to indicate that the sages of the Talmud had not thought it essential to marry the daughters of scholars, since one version of the phrase ends "and marry the daughter of a scholar" while the other ends "and buy shoes for his feet." My teacher, though, did not grasp my intention and thought, quite simply, that I was referring to the first one. In this way my fate was sealed.[24]

Why he felt constrained at the age of fourteen (he was betrothed long before his marriage) to acquiesce to an arranged marriage is not difficult to understand. What remains surprising though is the evasive and self-lacerating game that he employed which, as he admits, helped determine the course of his life. Surprisingly, what he appears to regret most on this score is not that he failed to answer his parents' question in a forthright manner but rather that those around him—particularly a literalistic tutor—lacked the cleverness or the textual dexterity to discern his true desires. In recalling the incident, he represents himself as virtually powerless, in the hands of forces bigger than himself which left him angry but resigned. The adolescent's elitism, his desire to appear unin-terested in the worldly benefits of a rich match (which he will not acknowledge even in retrospect), his evasiveness and the resignation that he displayed when his wishes didn't prevail, all prefigure characteristics of the more mature Ginzberg.

Here as elsewhere, the way he told the truth was veiled, inaccessible (as it was meant to be) to most listeners, hidden conveniently behind biblical allusion or rabbinic text. That he spoke in this way, and despite his later reputation for clarity, was a by-product of his elitism; that others were unable to understand him testified, in his mind, not to his lack of clarity but rather to the unsophistication and shortcomings of those to whom he was compelled to speak. He spoke here in a time-honoured scholarly discourse whose decline in his age, as he would later complain, was one of the trademarks of Jewry's collective decline as a people. He meant himself to be frank but in a manner that few understood or, for that matter, were meant to understand.[25]

He was barely seventeen when he was married to Rivka, a pious girl of exemplary hasidic lineage. She soon discovered that her severe, scholarly husband, despite his impeccable traditional bearing, was an enlightened man of the sort whom she had been taught to fear and avoid. Asher claimed that his parents chose her without bothering to find out how she looked. According to his sister, one of Isaiah's staff was sent to see her, though (in a domestic drama, replete with biblical associations) it is not clear that it was Rivka he was shown. He writes sardonically of his bride: "The young lady was neither blind nor one-armed but was a normal Jewish girl who had been strictly brought up and knew her prayers and all the other things that a Jewish girl has to know. And what more could one want?"[26]

She proved to be an unfailingly adaptable, loyal, and affectionate wife, and their relationship was, despite intermittent periods of indifference on Asher's part, warm and supportive. From the outset, Rivka was forced to adapt to the religiously more lax environment of the Ginzbergs' rural home where, for instance, in contrast to the regimen to which she was accustomed in Berdichev, Asher's sister Chana walked about in shirt sleeves. Here, also, Golda's religiously prescribed wig was made with human hair unlike those used by Berdichev fundamentalists. She adjusted to her new surroundings with good humor; eventually of course she was compelled to make much greater adjustments for the sake of her secularist husband. Before coming to Gopchitse the couple attempted, as was the custom for newlyweds when the groom was an aspiring Talmud scholar, to move in with Rivka's family; when his in-laws objected to Asher's unorthodox reading habits Rivka sided with her husband and they abandoned her family for Gopchitse after only three or four months.[27]

Asher and his bride moved into an apartment of three rooms at the manor house which—in addition to Asher's study—were put at their disposal. Eager to see the larger world and to meet some of the *maskilim* whom he had read so assiduously, at the age of twenty-two he made trips to seek them out at the two major centers of Eastern European maskilic life, Warsaw and Odessa. In Warsaw the unknown provincial found himself patronized by local maskilim: when a host at a maskilic gathering introduced him for want of any better description as a reader of Hebrew, the writers in the room chuckled at the description, commenting how such readers were a rare breed. This bruised the status-conscious visitor. By the time he left Warsaw, he was disillusioned with the efficacy of Haskalah, oddly, for reasons similar to those that had caused him to turn away from hasidism: the squalid working conditions of Warsaw's maskilim had the greatest impact on him. He was most upset by his encounter with the eminent maskilic editor of *Ha-Boker Or,* Abraham Ber Gottlober, whose editorial office he was invited to visit. Ginzberg found that the journal was edited in a one-room flat, which was also the editor's apartment, where he entertained company on his unkempt bed. Asher had imagined him commanding a staff in appropriately impressive surroundings.[28] Once again, essentially aesthetic shortcomings led him to question ideological commitments.

In Odessa, which he visited after Warsaw, he avoided looking up local maskilim and spent much of his time with a Jewish student who talked to him about European literature. He was introduced to the work of the Russian social and literary critic Dmitri Pisarev, the leading nihilist thinker of the time, who helped confirm for him that Haskalah was merely a way station on the path toward much greater knowledge outside Judaism. Thus he was persuaded that he should now prepare himself for a university education. He spent the next year or two studying Latin and mathematics without a tutor in an attempt to qualify for entrance into a Russian university—in examinations comparable to the German *Arbitur*—but without success. The prospect of studying at his age in a secondary school was, in his mind, unthinkable, a humiliation he felt he could not endure.[29]

He decided to try his luck abroad at a German or Austrian university where entrance requirements were less rigorous. But his stays in Vienna, Breslau, and Leipzig each lasted for no more than a few weeks and on every occasion he returned home more dispirited than when he had left.

Suffering from chronic insomnia and complaining of the antisemitism he encountered, he concluded that he could not remain abroad as a student surrounded by mere schoolchildren, far from his family and their emotional support. He had delayed his trips to Central Europe for so long—his first attempt to attend a university was in 1882—that by the time he left he was twenty-six, married, and the father of a baby girl, Devorah-Leah (Rachel would be born in 1885, Mordecai Zalman, but known as Shlomo was born in 1889). He felt unprepared for the rigors and loneliness of student life. His delays had resulted from various family illnesses, the pogroms of 1881–1882, and his abiding ambivalence about leaving home which led him to lie to his parents about the trips—he told them, or so he recalled years later, that he was off to St. Petersburg to study Russian. He cursed his lack of self-confidence and blamed his father for his decision to abandon a university education and return home to the familiar monotony of the family estate.[30]

What he found most unsettling about his brief forays abroad was the experience of living unknown and uncelebrated like one of thousands of other university youth and rather less prepared than most. He craved attention and recognition even if these were only available in rural Gopchitse where he remained, on and off, until 1886. At least here his specialness was acknowledged: "It was very difficult for me to sit on a student's stool once I was already a man of great learning [talmid hakham gadol] and was even considered something of a genius in the area where I lived." Back here, though, he languished without direction, prospects, or meaningful fellowship:

But when I returned home, I fully realized how utterly I loathed this village life. It had sucked me dry; it had consumed the best years of my young life. . . . I had no rest day or night; I walked around like a shadow, wrapped up in my thoughts and dreams with nobody to confide in, nobody who could help me in the least with my troubles. Surrounded by happy and cheerful people who enjoyed every day of their lives, I alone was miserable in the midst of wealth and plenty, and nobody took any notice of me. How could practical Jewish folk understand that the only son of rich parents was eating his heart out in absolute wretchedness while he had plenty of money and wanted for nothing?[31]

Clearly Asher was disinclined or incapable of cutting himself off from a parental home he found restrictive (his "crucible of affliction" he later called it) and from parents he found not only excessively pious but also frivolous, materialistic, and often abusive: "On the whole, life in my [family] house was unpleasant and I was happy whenever I was able to spend any time outside of it."[32] Yet, until only a few years before his permanent move to Odessa in 1886, he conducted himself with a caution comparable to that of his adolescence when he burned suspicious literature before daybreak. By the time he abandoned Gopchitse for Odessa (where he hoped to proceed informally with his education) he had come to feel, despite the active role he now played in his father's business, that insurmountable, obdurate obstacles blocked his movements and that change was inexorably slow, deliberate, and painfully wrought. No doubt the surreptitiousness and prolonged character of his own rebellion contributed to his particular understanding of change—one of the central features of his thinking once he emerged as a public figure.

In 1886 Isaiah was forced to give up his leasehold because the May Laws made the renewal of such arrangements for Jews in rural areas next to impossible. Two years earlier Asher had spent a few months in Odessa where he was courted by local Jewish intellectuals and other leaders who invited him to serve on the newly formed Palestinophile Hovevei Zion (Lovers of Zion) executive committee, a far cry from his dispiriting experience in Warsaw. He found the city exciting and decided that, short of a university education, he could acquire many of the skills he sought by living there and mixing with its intelligentsia. He saw to it that his extended family would move with him once they abandoned Gopchitse; Odessa's business prospects were in any event alluring for his father. Isaiah had considered seriously settling in Palestine, but Asher dissuaded him with the use of rather uncompromising but apparently persuasive arguments: "Asher insisted," recalled Esther, "that we would not depend upon foreign labor in our agricultural work in Palestine, but would have to become a family of true farmers."[33] Apparently unable to imagine settling in Odessa without his parents—despite his move there without them two years earlier—and unwilling to follow them to Palestine and abandon his dream of living in the midst of the vibrant intellectual culture he had encountered in Odessa, his arguments may have been designed to manipulate them into cooperating with a decision that suited him particularly well.

On the eve of his departure for Odessa, Asher Ginzberg was twenty-nine years old, reasonably rich, a good talmudist (though no talmudic master, as his friend Chaim Tchernowitz later observed), and a self-taught, well-read, "Westernized" Jew.[34] He had by now, or would soon in Odessa, read David Hume, Mill, John Locke, Peter Lavrov, Nicholas Mikhailovsky, and the Spencerian psychologist Frédéric Pauhlan. Above all, Herbert Spencer was a key inspiration to the intellectually ambitious, restless autodidact eager to construct himself a system since he had at last openly broken with traditional Judaism.

Ginzberg charts his intellectual trajectory from haskalah to Jewish nationalism in a semiautobiographical piece (billed by him as fiction) that was probably written in 1888. The article, "Kesavim balim" ("A Tattered Manuscript") was very different from the better-known essays that Ginzberg would soon produce. It ends, for instance, on a plaintive and inconclusive note—so unlike the memorable conclusions of Ahad Ha'am's later essays—and it is infused with explicitly autobiographical ruminations of the sort that the mature Ahad Ha'am would transform into depersonalized philosophical statements.

"Kesavim balim" records the spiritual odyssey of a poor Jew without the benefits of yichus; indeed, Ginzberg shows himself here to be acutely aware of the dynamics of social status in traditional Jewish society. The narrator lamely attempts to establish some semblance of standing by recalling that a well-known scholar—whom he calls, rather grandly, a "beloved friend"—once acknowledged him as they passed on the street. Recognizing that he is grasping at straws, he admits that he can lay no claim on the Jewish reading public who care only about the stature of the authors whom they read and not what they read. He tells of his hasidic upbringing and of his disenchantment with hasidism in favor of mitnagdic Judaism which he quickly discarded in turn for Haskalah, whose pretensions he satirizes mercilessly. Before launching into the satire, though, he questions whether he could ever have been considered a maskil since his attachments to more traditional Jewish forms have always remained resonant and compelling. In a passage that examines more poignantly than any other in Ginzberg's writings the anguish and beauty of such abiding attachments, he writes:

But what am I now? A maskil? I cannot say that with certainty. Still now, in the moments before the end of the Sabbath, between the time that the sun sets and one begins lighting candles once again, I love to sit in a corner in the dark and examine the range of my feelings. In such moments I feel my soul rising heavenward, as if my spiritual elation has emerged from within me to the sound of heavenly voices, and I recall various memories from my youth, memories that make me laugh, pleasant recollections—recollections that please me very much. . . . Sometimes my lips will open as if by themselves and I find myself chanting some well-known melody in a hushed voice. . . . During those long winter evenings, at times when I'm sitting in the company of enlightened men and women, sitting at a table with *tref* food and cards, and my heart is glad and my face bright, suddenly then—I don't know how this happens—suddenly before me is a very old table with broken legs, full of tattered books (sefarim balim), torn and dusty books of genuine value, and I'm sitting alone in their midst, reading them by the light of a dim candle, opening up one and closing another, not even bothering to look at their tiny print . . . and the entire world is like the Garden of Eden.[35]

Soon he abandoned the designation maskil for *ohev yisrael* (lover of Israel), which seemed to him less cumbersome, more authentic. Once done, he finds it easier to write. With great fluency (if not with particular insight) he emerges as a public figure in the self-important and rather tiny world of Hebrew letters. In the Hebrew periodicals of the day he denounces the policies of Otto von Bismarck and the antisemitism of Adolf Stoecker, and he behaves as if such attacks in Hebrew will have an impact on their treatment of Jews. Ahad Ha'am shows the narrator participating in a series of meaningless, demeaning literary battles, heaping praise on literary mediocrities (Hebrew literary circles are inundated by such fulsome praise, he writes), and attacking the lethargy of the Jewish poor and the parsimony of the rich.[36]

Not even the fury of the 1881 pogroms can derail his career as a liberal literary pundit and he manages to reconcile them with a maskilic *Weltanschauung*, seeing them merely as an albeit excessive gentile response to Jewish exploitation. Indeed, he contends, in contrast to the anti-Jewish violence of the fanatical middle ages, Jews are now being attacked for rational, if misguided, reasons. No longer are they hated because they are unbelievers; rather, today's hatred is secular and consequently amenable to change.

But when he finds his wife's shop sacked by pogromists (it is she who supports his writing) and his family's finances in ruins, he is forced to reconsider his priorities. He then decides to devote himself to agricultural labor in Palestine and begins to follow avidly the greatly exaggerated reports of the land's economic potential; when more realistic news reaches him, he is crushed. He does not know what to think nor whom to believe, and then recalls a scene from his childhood: the town fool, Abraham, was seen dashing down the street one day, stick in hand, ready to beat someone whom Abraham thought had spoken badly of him. He refused to stop despite reasonable advice and assurances that his suspicions were unfounded. How fortunate, writes Ginzberg, are those like Abraham who feel free to act without constraint. Only someone prepared to act, free from paralyzing doubts and indecision, is capable of heroism: "Abraham, Abraham, it is best that he be a fool" he concludes.[37]

Much of what he had to say in "Kesavim balim" would soon find its way into Ahad Ha'am's oeuvre: the denunciation of maskilic half-measures and deluded optimism; the criticism of unrealistic expectations fanned by Jewish nationalists; and complaints about the pathetic bombast of Jewish literary and communal life. Yet Abraham's uninhibited willpower that Ahad Ha'am praises in this early piece of writing is precisely what he attacks within the next few years with the greatest ferocity. Here it is Abraham's quite literally insane self-confidence that he finds so compelling, so impossible to emulate, and, in the public sphere, so commendable. Soon, however, Ahad Ha'am emerged as the preeminent exponent of a self-consciously modulated Jewish political strategy, one that would embrace, contrary to his admiration for Abraham's impetuousness, indefinite inaction to haste. His complex feelings for those like foolish Abraham, who embodied a spontaneity that he lacked and loathed but also somehow admired, he subsumed as he reshaped himself into a nationalist totem. Nonetheless, he would remain more ambivalent on this score than he cared to admit.

"I took my family to Odessa in the month of Nissan 5644 [March–April 1884], and there I began a new life."[38] In fact, his new life wouldn't begin for another two years, until Isaiah Ginzberg abandoned his estate. Once settled in Odessa Asher quickly climbed the rungs of an urban milieu wholly different from and immeasurably more receptive than rural Gopchitse. He did so with surprising ease and emerged very quickly as a nationalist leader. Soon a small cadre of maskilic nationalists in the Odessa-based Hovevei Zion acclaimed him as their mentor, as someone who could provide them, and the rest of a bewildered and beleaguered Jewry, with a coherent guide to the future.

2

A Ring of Conspirators:
The Bnei Moshe Society

Not the life of the ghetto in its despicable and harrowing form, which leaves its stamp on body and soul, but rather a healthy life of study and civility, of agriculture and industry.

Joshua Rawnitsky, *Pardes*, volume 3

I

The Hovevei Zion was to be the focal point of Asher Ginzberg's political life, even after the group all but dissolved with the advent of Herzlian Zionism in 1897. When the Russian-based Jewish nationalist movement was still reasonably active in the 1880s and early 1890s, Ginzberg was its most relentless internal critic; once it fell into a state of terminal decline, he spoke proudly if somewhat improbably as its heir in opposition to Theodor Herzl's political Zionism. It was foremost as a Hovev Zion that he represented himself until his death.

Palestinophilism gained its first following and a coherent leadership in the wake of catastrophe: the pogroms of the 1880s, which were the first serious wave in imperial Russian history. Immediately after the pogroms, the probably mistaken but widespread belief that they were organized by the government, the assertions of government officials that the attacks resulted from Jewish exploitation of peasants, and word of new anti-Jewish regulations undermined the maskilic conviction that Russia would follow in the liberalizing course of the West. Maskilic strategy, previously the chief way in which self-consciously modern Jews of the region had understood Jewish society and politics, was based on the assumption that Russia would move in the direction of Western Europe—its politics would be liberalized and its minorities emancipated. In the wake of the pogroms many maskilim concluded that this prognosis was naive, dated, and perilously optimistic.[1]

The political focus of the Hovevei Zion, its hope to establish by worldly means a self-governing community of Jews in Zion, distinguished it from classical Jewish messianism with its reliance on divine redemption. At the same time, it was energized in its quest by a host of messianic associations that were biblical in origin and intuitive rather than rational. The call to abandon exile for the Land of Israel could not be separated wholly from its ancient (its critics would say atavistic) origins. Branches were given biblically evocative names, for example, the Odessa branch was called Zerubabel. Much of the membership, if only a rather small proportion of the leaders, were recruited in synagogues where the Hovevei Zion also conducted its most efficient fundraising. Jewish nationalism from its beginnings walked a thin line between secular and religious revivalism, progressivism and nostalgia, postliberalism and dreams of a Davidic return.

Palestinophilism was only one of several new political currents vying in the 1880s for the allegiance of a highly volatile Russian Jewish intelligentsia and *folk*. It was far from the most successful. The movement's focal point, Palestine, was distant from the locus of East European Jewish misery and its success was predicated upon a host of unpredictable forces: Turkish cooperation, the availability of good land in Palestine, and the readiness of Jewish emigrants to move there. Even when Herzl appeared on the scene in the mid-1890s and lent the movement considerably greater visibility, Zionists found it difficult to compete with socialists and others who sought to solve East European Jewry's dilemmas without recourse to the primitive and remote margins of the Ottoman Empire.[2]

The leadership of the Russian-based movement was drawn from a medley of provincial rich and free professionals, rabbis, and maskilim who led a haphazardly organized network based in Odessa and devoted mostly to collecting money for the settlement of Jews in Palestine. Lacking any official recognition from the government until 1890, it was chaired by a humane, intuitive, but phlegmatic Odessa physician, Leon

Pinsker, whose visionary pamphlet, *Autoemancipation* (1882), played an important inspirational role. Once the Hovevei Zion coalesced into a coherent movement, however, it all but abandoned the politicized messianism embodied in *Autoemancipation* for a considerably less sweeping and essentially philanthropic agenda that Pinsker himself then embraced.[3]

Somewhere between 80 and 140 branches of the Hovevei Zion existed by the late 1880s, with a total membership of 14,000 at its height. The organization raised 40–50,000 roubles annually, which did not go very far since the average cost of settling a family in Palestine was 3,000 roubles. As David Vital writes: "The movement was a grey affair, well-meaning but generally unimaginative, honest but at the same time somewhat fearful. All-in-all, even in retrospect, it was disappointing."[4]

Even in its first years and before its first major conference held in Kattowitz in November 1884, its political focus was narrow: the meetings of its Odessa Zerubabel branch, whose executive committee Ahad Ha'am joined in 1884, dealt mostly with acquiring new farm animals for Palestinian colonies, constructing sheds, and providing subsidies for emigrants. As the maskilic nationalist Mordecai Ben Hillel Ha-Cohen, who attended a meeting of the Odessa Hovevei Zion executive around the time of the Kattowitz conference, described the discussion:

Middle-class merchants, all more-or-less rich, came and they read a letter or two from Palestine, heard reports from various places near Odessa. . . . There was no real order to the meeting, and bits and pieces of all sorts of information were mentioned.[5]

Underlying this well-intentioned if seemingly unfocused activity were, of course, larger concerns: the fierceness of Russian Judeophobia, the socioeconomic decline of Russian Jewry, and the seemingly irreversible misery of Jewish life under the tsars. But the gap between what was required by Russian Jews and what the Hovevei Zion could provide was recognized—and frequently bemoaned—by its leaders. They could only hope that once their movement was legalized, Turkish emigration laws liberalized, and Western Jews attracted to the cause, Jewish nationalism's impact would be enhanced. What to do in the meantime became a topic of heated controversy, especially in the months before the Kattowitz conference.[6] In the midst of these discussions Asher Ginzberg arrived on the scene.

It requires, or so it would seem, a leap of imagination to connect the taciturn, unadventuresome, very bright, but essentially untutored, and apparently unsociable, Asher Ginzberg with Jewish Odessa's enfant terrible of the late 1880s. When seen from this perspective his rapid ascent was remarkable; Ahad Ha'am himself later described it as all but inexplicable.

In fact, at the time of his arrival in Odessa, Ahad Ha'am's hebraist, Palestinophile circle (which soon coalesced around him in the Bnei Moshe) was neither as distinguished nor as celebrated as history has made it out to be. It was a circle of young, communally disenfranchised, politically powerless maskilim. By and large patronized or ignored by those who controlled Jewish communal life and those who set the agenda for local Jewish intellectual concerns, it was in one another's presence that they felt at home. In retrospect it seems of self-evident importance that Ahad Ha'am, Rawnitsky, Bialik, and others sat in living rooms in Odessa and mapped out ideologies that would later transform contemporary Jewish life. But theirs was a world of rather unfrequented Jewish libraries and unclubbable intellectuals—a world dominated not by them but by local grain exporters, retailers, upper-middle-class salons and cabarets. The misplaced priorities of the Hovevei Zion mirrored, in Ahad Ha'am's view, this lamentable social reality.

As a member of the executive committee, he was privy to its pre-Kattowitz deliberations in which the draft of Pinsker's conference address elicited sharp criticisms. The draft brought tensions to the surface that had plagued the group since its beginnings, torn as it was between a majority favoring its philanthropic agenda and a minority that opposed it, preferring to emphasize cultural renewal as a prerequisite for national reconstruction.

What this alternate agenda meant in concrete terms was unclear, even to its advocates. Joshua Rawnitsky's call at the close of an article in 1883 was typical: "Here is not the place to elaborate on how to awaken love of one's nation in the youth of our generation; Jews must do all that is possible to bring back those who have strayed and then . . . nationalist tasks will come to be seen as praiseworthy and glorious and the enemies of Israel will be vanquished."[7] The partisans of cultural politics, led at this juncture by Zvi Zev Frankfeld and Zalman Epstein, established in 1884 a branch of the Hovevei Zion, called Nehemiah, something of a loyal opposition that announced its intention to start under its aegis a journal. Der Yidisher Veker was not published until three years later, and only one issue appeared. Nehemiah accomplished next to nothing. It was this Hovevei Zion circle—ambitious, unfocused, and dissatisfied—that would constitute the core of Ginzberg's political support; Rawnitsky, Frankfeld, and Epstein would be among his first disciples.[8]

From the outset, Ginzberg was one of two members of the executive committee who supported the culturalist line—the other was the acerbic and widely disliked bibliophile and local bookseller, Ephraim Deinard. The dissidents placed great hope in the provincial newcomer from Gopchitse. Debates within the committee continued for some three weeks, and apparently Ginzberg played a key role in them. He writes:

We used to meet every Tuesday in Pinsker's house to discuss Palestinian colonization. These meetings made a profound impression on me, especially at first. I had never before been privileged to spend hours every week in such enlightened company. Naturally I was very shy at first, being a mere "rustic," and was all ears for what my colleagues had to say; but gradually I lost my nervousness and came to realize that even so simple a person as myself might at times have a useful contribution to make, and that the "townsmen" did not necessarily always talk sense. From this point on, I became one of the vocal members and sometimes had a real impact.[9]

Ginzberg failed to win over the majority. But the controversy was far from resolved and even escalated over the next few years. At issue, particularly in the minds of the culturalists, was much more than the priorities of their still rather small group. What they saw themselves debating—in a movement that they believed was the vanguard of a reconstructed Jewish civilization—were the prerequisites of leadership in modern Jewry. They argued that the philanthropic agenda of the Hovevei Zion was itself a symptom of a larger problem, namely the enhanced importance of the rich in an Eastern European community in decline. The provincial bankers and merchants who dominated the Hovevei Zion were unable to appreciate the national goals of the Hovevei Zion and viewed the group merely as a vehicle for the retraining of poor Jews bound for Palestine. Pinsker's *Autoemancipation* had, they argued, envisioned so much more, and they cited it as a prooftext. The tract (which Pinsker never disavowed but whose recommendations he came to believe were too radical to impress Western Jews whose support he sought) was, indeed, studded with exhortations of a culturalist mold: "National self-respect! Where can we obtain it? It is truly the greatest misfortune of our race that we do not constitute a nation, that we are merely a people." Or: "More efficient than anything else will be the resolution of the first and most essential condition—the national resolution."[10]

It is one of the ironic features of this debate that the Hovevei Zion's marginalized radicals called for what seemed to be less activity rather than more. They shunned philanthropy, the one clear avenue open to Jewish nationalism, and promoted instead a gradual reeducation of Jewry, which they claimed embodied vast ambitions but that seemed rather benign, even bloodless. But an emphasis on fundraising consigned them to the margins of communal life, whereas a culturalist agenda did exactly the opposite, drawing heavily on the Haskalah, whose pedagogical emphasis and cultural politics they still embraced even if they rejected its emancipationist goals. At the same time their arguments reflected a keen antagonism toward the rich. It is hardly surprising, in view of Asher Ginzberg's hostility toward his parents' frivolities and his rich father's tempestuousness, that he found the culturalist argument congenial. Ironically, his own wealth lent his views formidable authority. The awkward provincial was well positioned for leadership.

Before his move to Odessa—when he encountered Warsaw's maskilim for instance—he came off, as he relates, as tongue-tied and morbidly silent. No one he met during his trips mentions him; he does not seem to have stood out sufficiently for anyone to take notice. He then lacked the verbal dexterity, the worldliness, the prerequisite hunger for power necessary for leadership or prominence. His situation in Odessa was quite different. Soon after he settled there in 1886 he played a central role in breaking up one of the city's Jewish intellectual circles. A new one was established which was promptly built around him.

Along with other local maskilic nationalists, Ginzberg had attended Friday evenings at the home of Shimon Aryeh Schwabacher. This erudite man, Odessa's official rabbi since 1860, provided his guests with summaries of his synagogue sermons of the next day. From the time of his arrival in the city opinions regarding Schwabacher were mixed. Some saw him as eloquent; others claimed that he was vacuous and unimaginative, a cultural anachronism. Ginzberg agreed with the detractors and persuaded others to join him in starting a new circle, which gathered at first in the library of the Jewish clerks' association. Eventually it moved to Ginzberg's home. Schwabacher's star was beginning to dim (his successor, M. Pomerantz, would also on occasion host Ahad Ha'am's circle) and, within a year, Schwabacher would be toppled from his post as official rabbi; perhaps Ginzberg sensed this vulnerability.[11]

This breakaway circle was quite homogeneous. It consisted mostly of underemployed Hebrew tutors, bookkeepers who worked for the Hovevei Zion, or journalists who eked out a living by writing for what was then a small cluster of Hebrew, Yiddish, and Russian-language Jewish periodicals. None had secular training; only one, Rawnitsky, had been born in Odessa. Nearly all of them had been drawn to Odessa from Ukrainian hasidic-dominated townlets and came because of the city's reputation for freedom, culture, and wealth. Several were religiously observant but they all saw themselves as maskilim, as "modern"—committed to a transformation of Jewry's cultural mores. At the same time, their pious backgrounds, their poverty, and their lack of formal European education set them apart from the vast majority of Odessa's Jewish intelligentsia who were secularly sophisticated, fluent in Russian, cultivated in ways that such newcomers would never be, and considerably farther from the rhythm of traditional Jewish life. The russified intellectuals ignored or at best patronized them, and the Hebraists knew this and resented it deeply. [12]

These *batlanim melamdim* (idlers and tutors), as Chaim Tchernowitz called them affectionately, were all the more resentful of such treatment in light of their considerable political ambitions and an arsenal of resentments fanned by the prolonged and unsuccessful pre-Kattowitz debates. By the time the circle came to meet at Ginzberg's house, it counted among its members Epstein and Frankfeld, who both served in menial clerical posts for the Hovevei Zion; Rawnitsky, who made a meager living as a Hebrew tutor; Abraham Elijah Lubarsky; and his brother Jacob. [13]

Theirs was one of several overlapping local maskilic circles that met on Friday evenings with the participants alternating between various homes. Those who frequented Ginzberg's on occasion met at the home of Yiddish writer Mendele Mocher Seforim (pen name for Shalom Jacob Abramowitsch) or at the Zionist publicist Moses Leib Lilienblum's. Mendele entertained guests in his spartan home adjacent to the *talmud torah* (a communally funded school for indigent children) that he ran in Moldavanka, one of the city's poor neighborhoods. Lilienblum, who himself was very poor and lived in a series of wretched apartments, nonetheless maintained an occasional salon.

Each stamped evenings at his home with a particular style: Mendele entertained guests with elaborate monologues, sometimes lasting four or five hours, in which he frequently related in humorous detail conversations he overheard on the streets of Odessa. In contrast, Lilienblum was glumly uncommunicative but those who sat at his feet respected his publicistic skill as the author of the autobiography *Hata'ot Neurim,* one of the more influential Hebrew books of the 1870s which had inspired a generation of maskilim. Relations between the heads of these circles were at first strained. Both Lilienblum and Mendele found Ginzberg overbearing; once the Bnei Moshe was established with Ginzberg as its totem, the mordant Mendele referred to its members as "the ten lost tribes." Both found the veneration by local maskilic nationalists of the otherwise unknown, unpublished, and untested Ginzberg to be inexplicable.[14]

What most clearly distinguished Ginzberg was his wealth, his yichus (former hasidim could not but be impressed with his relations to two hasidic dynasties), the range of his learning, and his coveted membership on the Hovevei Zion executive committee. There were other factors as well: his Victorian-like rigidity—the same rigidity that Mendele found so jarring—impressed his circle who saw it as a sign of European sophistication. They spoke admiringly of his exceptionally rigid schedule, the way in which he divided his time between the business office that he maintained with his father where he spent his mornings—they opened in Odessa a liquor distillery, an olive-oil factory, and were engaged in wheat speculation—and his study where he would not permit himself to be disturbed, except on Friday evenings and Saturdays when he entertained guests. Chaim Tchernowitz wrote of their first encounter when he was told by Ginzberg on his doorstep that he did not have the time to speak with him but would set an appointment: "Jews talk even when they don't have the time; he seemed like a gentile [*goy l'havdil*]." Simon Dubnow recalled in his autobiography that his personal demeanor was severe, his movements spare and deliberate.[15]

For his admirers this self-discipline was inspiring. Even his coolness and apparent lack of intimacy they considered indicative of a European sensibility free from the burdens of Russian tempestuousness and impracticality. He was viewed as both practical and intellectually expansive, a sober visionary, an authentic Jew who eschewed all parochialism. This perspective on him as a European was influenced by the fact that he was the only one of his circle seen by the russified Jewish intellectuals at Odessa, who dominated the Jewish cultural scene, as a worldly, unparochial, and uncharacteristically cultivated Hebraist. Even before meeting him, Dubnow, a regular writer for the St. Petersburg Russian Jewish monthly *Voskhod,* had heard good things about him and intended to seek him out. The view of him as a European originated in part because of his Hebraist circle's need for an emblem, a source of legitimization, and Ginzberg fit the bill.

Thus he was transformed from a brooding and isolated maskil into a celebrated intellectual leader of a small but ambitious entourage. Ginzberg's ascendancy owed much to the initiative of Joshua Eisenstadt, better known as Barzilai. He came to Odessa from Palestine as a self-appointed emissary for Jewish Palestine in the winter of 1887 and remained for several months hoping to revive the fortunes of the Hovevei Zion movement. Few branches had opened since the congress at Kattowitz, and Pinsker, who even at his most vigorous had failed to be an inspirational leader, was ailing and would soon step down.[16]

The maskilic nationalists close to Ginzberg meanwhile were enjoying a shortlived prominence because of the publication of their long-awaited *Der Yidisher Veker*. The volume was ambitious and impressive: it drew on the most talented Yiddish writers of the period—Abraham Goldfaden, Sholem Aleichem, Eliakum Zunzer, and Abraham Ber Gottlober, along with lesser-known talents with a local reputation in Odessa and nearby Kherson. It appeared in Yiddish and, preoccupied as it was with the need to address the masses, it employed an explicitly populist tone markedly different from the elitist one that would later characterize the Bnei Moshe. Lilienblum's introductory essay was a refutation of the traditionalist criticisms of Jewish nationalism; Rawnitsky explained, in a very straightforward fashion, why Jews possessed the attributes of a nation. The journal was clearly intent on nationalist consciousness-raising and soon, with Barzilai's prompting, its editors and writers found other ways to channel their political commitments.[17]

There seemed at first few ready options. The Hovevei Zion was cramped by its unofficial standing, by a shortage of funds with which to aid Palestinian colonization, and by the lack of a network of agents either in Russia or Palestine; the group was also dominated by mostly unimpressive leaders at war with one another over who would inherit Pinsker's role. Religious activists maligned secularists who in turn held the traditionalists in contempt. Religious tensions were quelled by the respect felt for Pinsker; his death or resignation was expected to unleash a terrible battle.

Barzilai's idea was the creation of a league of elite nationalists headed by an exemplary leader to "work for the revival" of Jewish nationalism. With a mystic, even anarchist, bent—he dreamed, according to Shmuel Tchernowitz, about anti-Turkish rebellions and the establishment of a new Jewish kingdom—and inspired by already existing, secret nationalist societies in Palestine, Barzilai sought in Odessa a leader for one that would thoroughly reinvigorate the movement. He had already searched for a suitable candidate in Palestine without success. One night, discussing the idea with Elijah Lubarsky, a lively and energetic member of Ginzberg's circle, Lubarsky leaped from his couch, and declared, "You will see, Israel is not bereft of such a man! With your own eyes you will see him and soon!" On an evening soon afterwards, as Barzilai relates:

> Lubarsky took me, without first telling me where we were going, into a neighborhood with beautiful streets, the likes of which I had never before seen [in Odessa], and we finally arrived at a large and beautiful house that, at least by the light of the lanterns reminded me of the palace of a baron. And Lubarsky walked with me up its wide and fine steps and escorted me into a marvelous hall, introducing me to the master of the house—a young gentleman of moderate height with a large and unusually shaped head . . . which alerted me to the fact that I was face to face with an *intelligent*.[18]

This, of course, was Asher Ginzberg. Barzilai engaged the young sage in conversation while the normally loquacious Lubarsky sat before Ginzberg in reverent silence. Barzilai left the house convinced that he had met an uncannily modest and impressive young man. Ginzberg in turn had found himself an agent who would soon devote himself tirelessly to promoting him.

Returning to Odessa in the summer of 1888, Barzilai urged members of Ginzberg's circle to constitute themselves formally as a nationalist league and appoint Ginzberg at its head. Neither Barzilai, nor any of its would-be members, yet had a clear idea of what such a group would do. His suggestion was, however, taken sufficiently seriously to inspire lengthy—and inconclusive—discussions that summer. Ginzberg was approached by Barzilai and Lubarsky and asked to assume formal leadership of the nationalist league. He resisted, but meetings continued to take place at his house with him as the dominant presence. By now the Friday evening gatherings had taken on a considerably less fluid character, drawing regularly on more or less the same group of men. At times, others thought to be potentially receptive to the group's message were invited to participate. The group met at Ginzberg's on Friday evenings and occasionally at Lilienblum's on Saturday afternoons.[19]

The discussions, as Moshe Pearlman later recalled, were devoted to politics: "We did not deal with small matters but with high politics, grand and deep as the waters of the ocean. We spoke about the conquest of the land (kibush ha-aretz), the situation in Turkey, relations between the states of Europe and Turkey."[20] The land's conquest meant its acquisition—through purchase, negotiation with the Turks, or the intervention of the Great Powers; the term "conquest" drew upon ancient associations linking the rather prosaic machinations of the present with the grandeur of the epoch of the biblical Joshua.

During these prolonged discussions Lilienblum was passed over as the potential leader in favor of Ginzberg. By no means was this inevitable. Lilienblum was one of Russian Jewry's preeminent maskilim whose fertile career had already by the mid-1880s spanned two decades, whereas Ginzberg had no standing outside the circle of Odessa Hebraists. No intellectual, except for Pinsker himself, was more closely associated in the public mind with the Hovevei Zion than Lilienblum; he ran its Odessa office and was chosen to write the lead articles for both of the first periodicals published by the Odessa culturalists—*Der Yidisher Veker* and later, in 1890, *Kaveret*.

Lilienblum's position on cultural nationalism was, however, equivocal, and though he never altogether dismissed the importance of a cultural transformation of Jewry, he insisted that the task take a backseat to the socioeconomic reconstruction of Jewish Palestine. Consequently, in the debate between a philanthropic and a cultural nationalism, he supported the majority line and would emerge as the most sustained critic of what came to be known as Ahad Ha'amism. The vehemence of his attacks on Ginzberg might well have been influenced by a residue of personal rivalry; in ideological terms, however, his stance was consistent with his thinking since the 1870s, predating his emergence as a Jewish nationalist. Nonetheless at first he saw the Bnei Moshe as a relatively benign collection of nationalist devotees; he explained to one member that he joined only because "they are all young men and the public doesn't know them and so I had to join the group." His attitude was that of an older, somewhat patronizing, and seasoned nationalist toward well-intentioned newcomers.[21]

Another reason why Lilienblum was passed over was, quite simply, because he was taciturn, uncommunicative, even wooden in his demeanor and consequently an unlikely choice for leader of a small group of inspired nationalists. Ginzberg, however, was seen as charismatic and cast in the mold of the hasidic rebbes only recently discarded by his maskilic entourage. His followers claimed that even the way in which he carried himself—distant, disapproving, cerebral, reclusive—represented proof of his authenticity as a leader.

A rare description of how this situation looked even before the establishment of the Bnei Moshe in February-March 1889 may be found in a letter Yehudah Leib Dawidowicz wrote to the Hebrew journalist Reuven Brainin in 1888.[22] Dawidowicz, also known by his pen name Ben David, gained entry into Ginzberg's circle (he knew the Ginzberg family and had tutored the sisters at Gopchitse) and observed it from an unusual perspective since he was neither a follower nor an outright critic. He would, in fact, soon embrace Ginzberg's teachings with much the same fervor that he had mocked in his letter. His comments reflect the condescension of a Vilna-born Jew for the excesses of former hasidim. More importantly, they show Ginzberg as having moved his followers to an extraordinary state of devotion:

Not long ago the metropolis Odessa was chosen as the home of a fine young gentleman; Asher Ginzberg is his name. Together with his father he settled here and opened up an olive-oil factory, and the owners themselves are both fine fellows, like pure olive oil. The father is a hasid and the only son is the son-in-law of the Admor; the Lubavitcher rebbe. [In fact the rebbe was his wife's uncle.] The bridegroom himself actually resembles the Admor, in that he too is a "rebbe" of another sort, of a European kind, a "rebbe" of the left. . . . He came from some village, as it were, and there in splendid isolation he prepared himself for the redemption that he as rebbe would bring about for the Jewish people—all this in the style of the Baal Shem Tov. The light of this new rebbe was revealed suddenly in our sinful Odessa, by his new devotees among our writers. And to this new rebbe (in these truly messianic days) were attributed coronets and legends. They associated him with miracles and great deeds: that he has mastered the seven wisdoms, that he has learned seventy languages, that he is a man of mighty wisdom (with money in his purse) and a fine character.

And this rebbe, Rebbe Asherl Ginzberg, oversees a hasidic-like table, just like a real hasidic master and on Sabbath eve his followers gather at his home, Hebrew writers and just plain maskilim, the chosen ones.

I am one of those who merited on several occasions an invitation (not all do—not a single one of my friends has been invited), and I don't know what good deed of mine might have caused this to happen, and I was permitted to sit at the table of Asherl on Sabbath eve. The rebbe sits surrounded by a "congregation" of hasidim, drinking boiling tea, treating him with fervent devotion and respect. The rebbe lights Sabbath cigarettes, and his hasidim follow suit. For if this is permissible for the rebbe—all the more so for his followers. His "assembly" is silent, endeavoring to hear what his holy mouth utters. But this rebbe of ours is a real quiet one whose very silence is golden [paraphrasing the Aramaic saying]. The rebbe, *Gospodin* [Mr.] Ginzberg, a red-headed man, short, modest, with a sharp and complex mind, gesticulates with the use of his bony hands in a manner that is vaguely hostile. And his followers examine his remarks eagerly, his hints and intimations. The rebbe, may he live a long life, is stingy, careful with words. . . . Not so his hasidim. The "assembly" devours tea, smokes cigarettes, slowly gets more and more heated, and then words begin to flow. . . . The rebbe maintains his distance, cool, chilly, and, like a real mitnaged, not an unbecoming word passes his lips.

Soon the circle was meeting daily at Ginzberg's house. Their discussions concerning the creation of a nationalist league continued only among those willing to commit themselves without reservation to the Palestinophile cause. Perhaps what finally persuaded them to move quickly was news of Pinsker's impending retirement (he first stepped down in the summer of 1889); however, they sought the Hovevei Zion's mantle with discretion, allowing ample room for retreat and denial that there had been any thought of pursuing power. When later accused of attempting to do this, its members, (especially Ahad Ha'am) acted as if the mere suggestion scandalized them, and they demanded apologies. Yet it was power that they sought and, in the first few years of the group's existence, they managed to garner, as we shall see, a fair measure of it.[23]

In the meantime, Ginzberg published two very short pieces—a birthday greeting for the distinguished Vilna maskil and Palestinophile Samuel Joseph Fin (which showed a keen awareness to court religious nationalists of Fin's ilk) and a call for an end to a vituperative literary quarrel between the Hebrew poet Judah Leib Gordon and the Hebrew newspaper *Ha-Melitz*'s editor, Alexander Zederbaum. By the winter of 1888, Ginzberg was at work on another, considerably longer piece written to disseminate some of the ideas formulated in his living room over the course of the last year or two. Indeed, in an exchange of letters by Barzilai and Elijah Lubarsky in November and December 1888 the two had agreed that the time was ripe for the writing of a "nationalist program." Barzilai recalls that Lubarsky rushed into his flat one evening late in 1888 and announced with great satisfaction, and trepidation, "Thank God he is finally writing! My only fear is that the Devil might interfere and ruin things!"[24] The essay, signed Ahad Ha'am, launched Ginzberg's political career and, in effect, that of the Bnei Moshe as well.

The piece's appearance—it was entitled "Lo zeh ha-derekh" ("This Is Not the Way")—was arranged behind the scenes by Lubarsky. He persuaded *Ha-Melitz*'s haughty editor Zederbaum during a visit to Odessa in the fall of 1888 to see Ginzberg and urge him to publish in his newspaper. Lubarsky told the Hebrew editor that Ginzberg was a *nistar*, literally a hidden holy man, and Zederbaum, who usually expected authors to court him, set out in pursuit of the talented newcomer.

Ginzberg agreed to write the article and Zederbaum, with considerable persistence and some finesse, managed to extract it from him. "Lo zeh ha-derekh" was sent to Zederbaum in November or early December 1888 (some accounts say that Ginzberg wrote it in one night) and it was published in March 1889, after being delayed and cut by the censor who thought it excessively nationalistic.[25]

In his correspondence with Zederbaum, Ginzberg already speaks with surprising authority and the self-possession of the mature Ahad Ha'am. For instance, in reply to an effusive letter from Zederbaum urging that he send his article quickly, Ginzberg admits that he had nearly despaired of writing the piece:

Despite the fact that it is my custom to guard my tongue, I will nonetheless admit that various difficulties that I have faced in my personal affairs, coupled with my recent frame of mind and fear of the reactions of the community and of writers . . . caused me to nearly abandon hope of writing anything for Ha-Melitz, as I had promised, Sir, when you were here.[26]

On many occasions in the past, he continued, he had planned to air his views but had hesitated, aware as he was of the inadequacies of the Hebrew literary world, its paranoia, and its probable reactions to his criticisms of it. But the calamitous reports he received almost daily from Palestine had strengthened his resolve to put pen to paper.[27]

Already he refers to his custom of guarding his tongue, his "personal difficulties," and his despairing "frame of mind": he gives the impression of a man struggling alone against hostile forces, though as Zederbaum knew Ginzberg's article sought to articulate the views of what was beginning to be an ideologically coherent group. The nature of the personal difficulties that had obstructed his writing of the essay are not specified and probably was an allusion to the depressions that would periodically intrude on his public activity.

Before sending the article, he set down conditions for its publication similar to those that he would later as an editor reject out of hand. He demanded that not a word be changed without his permission and, irrespective of its length, that it appear in one or at the most two, consecutive issues. Within less than two weeks of sending the article to Zederbaum, he wrote complaining that he had not heard from the editor (the maskilic press was notoriously lax about such things, as he must have known); Ginzberg insisted that the negligence was particularly galling since Zederbaum himself had invited him to write. Exasperated and furious, he added that there could be no reason, short of Zederbaum's hatred for the article, that could account for the delay, and he demanded an immediate reply.[28]

In this exchange of letters, which continued for several months, Ginzberg showed himself alternatively to be carping, imperial, touchy, and apologetic. He complained frequently of lack of time (a lifelong complaint), apologized when his suspicions proved unwarranted, and repeatedly demanded special treatment. Apparently Zederbaum did not feel such demands excessive for his first letter to Ginzberg began: "Beloved one of my soul, man of wisdom and might, man of great knowledge, modest one with numerous followers [hasidim], Mr. A. Ginzberg."[29] Even by the typically florid standards of contemporary Hebrew salutations, this was obsequious in a letter written by a well-established editor to a literary unknown. It bordered on prostration.

The vast ambitions of the author of "Lo zeh ha-derekh"—no less than to replace Judaism's theological foundations with national-cultural ones—were clear from the essay's first paragraph. The article constituted a blueprint for a thorough reassessment of the cultural legacy of the Jewish people. It begins:

After many centuries spent by the Jewish people in poverty and degradation, sustained only by faith and hope in divine mercy, the present generation has seen the birth of a new and far-reaching idea, one that promises to bring down our faith and aspiration from the heavens, and transform them into living and active forces, [one that] makes our land the object of our hopes, and our people the anchor of our faith.[30]

Leaning heavily on the ideas of Herbert Spencer, he explains that ideas originate only "when the time is ripe." At first they manage to win over only the most sensitive and receptive, not necessarily the brightest. Once their allegiance is secure however, they influence others. This is precisely what occurred in the early stages of Jewish nationalism, whose impact was felt by a small—but, as he adds, exceptionally influential—sector of maskilim who managed to spread the word by virtue of the sincerity of their convictions. In this period, the movement's growth was "natural, inevitable, and ethically sound."[31]

What occurred soon afterwards, however, was tragic. Contrary to the caution it first exercised, the movement began to promote rapid Palestinian colonization. For a short time this aim gave Palestinophilism a heightened stature, marking it off as a serious enterprise with concrete accomplishments. In the long run, though, that aim sapped the organization's vitality by forcing it to focus its attention prematurely on financial support for a handful of struggling agricultural colonies that were set up much too quickly and mainly for the sake of their dramatic impact. The result was neither dramatic nor inspiring, but, rather, "intrigues, quarrels, petitions." The chief reason that this occurred was Jewry's chronic impatience, its inclination—repeatedly the cause of tragedy in its history—to reap quick rewards before the time was ripe.

Had the Hovevei Zion remained on course and grown slowly by virtue of the influence of its small cadre of activists, it would have achieved a good deal. As Spencer teaches, the successful promotion of any idea is dependent upon three prerequisites: it must be necessary; it must be clear how its goals are achieved; and it must be within one's power to accomplish them. Individuals best suited to promote new ideas according to Ahad Ha'am are those whose

sensibilities are quick and who are governed by their feelings—they alone will listen. And for that reason the originators of the idea must themselves be, above all, men of keen sensibility, temperamentally equipped to concentrate their entire spiritual lives on a single point, on one idea and desire, capable of devoting their whole life to it and expending in its service their last ounce of strength. By doing their work competently and with absolute devotion, they show that they have boundless faith in the truth of their idea and infinite love in serving it. And that will constitute the only sure way of awakening faith and love in others. . . . In the course of time, as the idea takes root more and more firmly in the hearts of the people, making its way into every home and family, it will at last capture the allegiance of great men, the leaders and thinkers. They, too, will begin whether they like it or not, to feel the impact of the new forces which will envelop them on every side.[32]

Here, in brief, is the political strategy of the Bnei Moshe which set out to redress the errors of the Hovevei Zion and to put it back on its original course. Ginzberg's essay did not openly argue for the creation of a nationalist league but made it clear that Jewry's future was dependent upon precisely such an elite who would, by virtue of its commitment and activist élan, transform Jewish life.

The collective commitments of Jewry—dormant and awaiting renewal—would be reinvigorated by such an elite. In the past it was precisely such commitments that had constituted the glue of Jewish identity; their decline in modern times threatened the continued existence of the Jewish people. Religion had once played a central role in solidifying this identity and its prominence was itself a by-product of the disruptions of the first century CE when the Jewish state was destroyed and when theology replaced nationalism as Judaism's linchpin. Religion was created, then, for the sake of the Jews but it was nationalism that represented the original, and, according to Ginzberg, the basic category of Jewish society. It had been the original focal point of ancient Judea's cultural life and, as Jews refocused their attention on Zion, they must also reaffirm this central feature of their identity:

All the laws and ordinances, all the blessings and curses of the Law of Moses, have but one unvarying object: the well-being of the nation as a whole in the law of its inheritance. The happiness of the individual is not regarded in this context. The individual Israelite is treated as being a part of his people the same way that a single limb is part of the human body. . . . One long chain unites all the generations, from Abraham, Isaac and Jacob to the end of time.[33]

The vicissitudes of exile had required the creation of a theological buffer; with the coming of a secular age, if left unchanged, it could suffocate Jews. Weakened by medieval oppression (which Ginzberg never credited with having a salutary impact on Jewish self-awareness) and rendered all but obsolete by emancipation, religion constituted a profoundly unsteady foundation for Jewish life. It is "the heart of the people [that must serve as] the foundation" for a regenerative process and activists can contribute toward this renewal by cleansing Jewish sensibilities and reviving its collectivist sentiments. Ginzberg's platform represented a maskilic agenda in its emphasis on cultural renewal, collective reeducation, and enlightenment; the role provided for its maskilic nationalists was that of secularized rabbis, as their people's moral exemplars and teachers.

"Lo zeh ha-derekh" was published in its entirety in a single issue of *Ha-Melitz*, as Ginzberg had requested. It gave rise to a series of critical replies that ran for weeks on the newspaper's front page. In his reply to them Ahad Ha'am directs himself primarily to Lilienblum who accused him both of trying to check the movement's momentum and being blind to human nature and the primacy of self-interest. Perhaps it was his essay's brevity, wrote Ahad Ha'am, that caused Lilienblum to so misinterpret him. Having said this, he then went on to restate the arguments made in "Lo zeh ha-derekh," showing that Lilienblum had understood him perfectly well.[34]

In this instance, his excessive brevity might have contributed to attacks on him. (It would again in the future when Ginzberg came to favor extremely short essays, often no more than a few paragraphs in length.) Frequently he complained that he was misunderstood and that what was attributed to him was exaggerated and unfair. As much as he may have been misconstrued, however, the cause was probably deliberate concealment on his own part since, from the beginning of his public life, he had surrounded himself and his politics with a veil of secrecy, one that seemed all the more jarring since he was Jewish nationalism's chief advocate of truthfulness and candor. The fact that he acted as the head of a semisecret league whose very existence he denied to outsiders while arguing that Palestinophilism must speak without any concealment and ambiguity had a significant impact on both his political and publicistic career. True, what set his writing apart from the very beginning of his career was the unequaled clarity of his Hebrew philosophical prose, a clarity that, as he would later claim, was self-conscious and laboriously achieved and modeled after traditional sources he had devoured as a child. Admirably lucid as this prose was it nonetheless obscured at times nearly as much as it revealed with its various levels of meaning appreciated only by his devotees, and with some of these hotly disputed even by them.

His most prolific years as a publicist—between 1889 and 1896—coincided with the period during which he headed the Bnei Moshe. Not only did he fail to acknowledge the relationship between his journalism and politics—in truth, two sides of the same coin—but he was consistently evasive about the nature of Bnei Moshe's goals even once the group became an open secret in Jewish nationalist circles by the mid-1890s. He flatly denied, often with great indignation, the group's hunger for power and its grand aspiration to constitute itself as a secularized and resurrected Yavneh—the rabbinic center of Palestinian Jewish life credited with having sustained Judaism after the second temple's destruction. When challenged by critics who insisted that he answer their questions with complete candor, Ginzberg, although always acknowledging the importance of honesty in public life, rarely revealed more than what he absolutely had to.

This apparent contradiction between Ahad Ha'am as an exemplar of truthfulness and the head of the Bnei Moshe has even disturbed Leon Simon, his least critical biographer, who insisted that the group's secrecy, the dictatorial powers granted its leader, its masonic-like ritualism, and its pretensions were quite simply alien to its leader. They were, he wrote, imposed upon Ahad Ha'am despite his objections, and his term as head of the Bnei Moshe was the most puzzling period of his life and the least representative. As its leader, Simon believed, "he attempted to act in a way that was thoroughly alien to him, to pursue a path for which he was completely ill-suited."[35] This, of course, is how Ginzberg wished himself to be seen, as a man lacking in administrative aptitude, as one who deferred to others, even to his inferiors—in short, a man lacking the prerequisites of leadership.

Ironically, it was precisely these traits that helped to mark him as a leader with a devoted following. The Bnei Moshe, as Dawidowicz wryly observed, took on the characteristics of a secularized hasidic milieu, and Ginzberg's leadership strategies mirrored those of the world out of which he, and most of his closest devotees, emerged. A *nistar,* a hidden holy man, is how Lubarsky described him to Zederbaum, and his use of the term testifies to more than an adherence to abiding linguistic conventions.

For the rather provincial, traditionally attuned Jews closest to Ginzberg, his style of leadership was eminently recognizable, thoroughly Jewish, and yet also modern to them. From their perspective, charisma and leadership were the products of unrivaled learning and humility, and an unwillingness to assume leadership was frequently seen as a sign of authority. The great Lithuanian sage, Elijah of Vilna, an austere, socially reclusive and brilliant talmudic scholar who refused all communal posts, separated himself from local life and yet, when Lithuanian Jewry was threatened with the spread of hasidism, he assumed leadership and played a significant role in checking hasidism's advance beyond the Ukraine and Poland. The Gaon or "genius" of Vilna was referred to in his lifetime as a hasid despite his fiercely anti-hasidic stance, and the use of the term was less a reflection of denominational affiliation than of a spiritual style, a mode of conducting public affairs.[36]

Ginzberg's elitist political commitments, his grand aspirations for the Bnei Moshe, his belief in the need for secrecy to protect the rightful elite from the intrusive scrutiny of the mob were all drawn from that same traditional repertoire. Even his apparent unwillingness to assume the burdens of power and seeming disinterest in those mundane matters that so preoccupied worldly men (odd in light of his experience as a businessman) coupled with his insistence that leadership was thrust upon him against his will, were traits culled from the traditional leadership patterns he had admired since his childhood. Leaders rightfully hid their true aspirations from the larger public; their secrecy was essential for the well-being of their community. Particularly since Jewry had become more than ever dependent upon the ministrations of its secularized priests, politics had to be conducted in private and without fanfare. In short, what was to be made accessible to the public had to differ from what the elite knew to be true.

For his immediate entourage, the regimen of the Bnei Moshe and its veneration for Ginzberg represented something of an alternative for the rigors of traditional Jewish life. The ornate and ritualistic demands that the Bnei Moshe made were unsurprising and familiar. Ahad Ha'am's followers spoke of him in terms that were at once paternal and reverent describing him quite explicitly as a tsaddik: as a man of genius, charisma, and unmatched moral authority. The launching of his public career and the role Lubarsky played in the publication of "Lo zeh ha-derekh" involved much the same pious, backroom maneuverings that might have existed in the hasidic communities of their pasts.

In creating the Bnei Moshe, Ahad Ha'am attempted to translate into a Jewish political idiom methods used to inspire and rule traditional Jewry. It was to serve as a focal point, comparable to that of a hasidic court, that would inspire Jews elsewhere by virtue of the austere and exemplary behavior of its members, and especially its leaders. This is why he would later dismiss the criticisms of members who insisted on knowing what they were expected to do, what activities they should perform as members of this elite group. If, Ahad Ha'am felt, they didn't appreciate what was expected of an elite in times of cultural crisis and were unable to understand that their service to the community had less to do with concrete activity than with inspiration, they were unworthy of membership.

From the outset, then, at the heart of his politics was the redefinition of modern Jewish authority. Those exemplary men who had led the Jewish people in the past—Moses, Yochanan ben Zakkai, Maimonides— did so, first and foremost, by ensuring that it was they, not the masses, who defined the criteria for leadership. This too was the goal of the "Sons of Moses." Acting, as Ahad Ha'am piously intoned, in the absence of a leader of comparable stature to those of the past, his group sought to define the rules that would transform Jewry's political inclinations. To fight by any other standards would itself represent a victory of the enemy: it would place the Jewish people in danger of being overtaken by forces similar—despite superficial differences in time and place—to those that had conspired against it for centuries. Indeed, it had fought such adversaries successfully with the use of much the same arsenal now reemployed by the Bnei Moshe.

It is within this context that Ginzberg's choice of the pen name Ahad Ha'am must be understood. He first used it in "Lo zeh ha-derekh," and he claimed that he selected it to highlight his unprofessional standing, to explain that the essay was for him simply a casual excursion into literature: "The idea of this pen name was to make it clear that I was not a writer, and had no intention of becoming one, but was just incidentally expressing my opinion on the subject about which I wrote as 'one of the people' interested in the people's affairs."[37]

In fact, he was not "just incidentally expressing" his opinions; rather his essay encapsulated, as we have seen, many months of discussions and sought to serve as the public manifesto of a politically ambitious group of men. His explanation for the choice of the pen name is also, I think, less than frank. Here, too, what was visible mirrored only rather vaguely a hidden and immeasurably more significant reality. In all likelihood the choice of his pen name was made for very different reasons from the ones he gave.

In a culture where humility (in the right hands) implied greatness, a stated disdain for power was something of a prerequisite, and the pursuit of anonymity characterized true saintliness, someone who called himself "One of the People" did not necessarily intend to be seen in quite the way that the name might imply. A clue as to why Ahad Ha'am chose it may be gleaned from its use in the Pentateuch where it appears only once, in *Genesis* 26:10: "And Abilmelech said, 'What is this that you have done to us? One of the people (ahad ha'am) might easily have lain with your wife and you would have brought guilt upon us.'" Rashi, the seminal medieval exegete, whose commentary adorns the bottom of the standard Jewish bible, explicates the biblical words "one of the people," המיוחד בעם זה המלך as "the special one of the people, namely the king." Here Rashi draws on the second century exegete Onkelos whose Aramaic translation is identical.[38] In effect, then, his choice of this pen name—whose initials were identical to those of his Russian name (the Russian "G" transliterates as an "H")—was itself a bid for leadership, for primacy, perhaps even a form of contemporary kingship. At least his choice of Ahad Ha'am as a pen name implied ambiguity: a combination of modesty and ambition, anonymity and greatness, the pretence to blend into the folk with the recognition that this was inconceivable. Oddly, though his entourage included superb Bible scholars, like Rawnitsky and Bialik, who would later coauthor *Sefer Ha-Aggadah,* none mentioned the connection (if only to dispute it) between his name and the biblical passage. Nor for that matter, did any of them contradict him when he published a misrepresentation of the origins of the Bnei Moshe.[39] Here is how Ginzberg described his relationship with the group in an article written in 1913 which promised to speak frankly about the society, by then defunct for seventeen years:

My article, "Lo zeh ha-derekh," made a great impression on the community of Hovevei Zion followers, and some of my friends in Odessa attempted upon its publication to translate its ideals into reality. We met frequently to discuss how this might be done and after considerable and prolonged deliberations we established . . . the Bnei Moshe society. . . . The society existed for about eight years with most of the leading figures in Hovevei Zion counting themselves as members of it.[40]

Contrary to his account, however, the Bnei Moshe was founded a month before the appearance of "Lo zeh ha-derekh" and long after a draft of the article was first circulated among the society's devotees. The "prolonged deliberations" to which he refers took place before its publication. Ginzberg's revision was not only forgiven by his entourage but encouraged as part and parcel of what they believed was their responsibility to establish and maintain his authority. Never would Ahad Ha'am acknowledge this practice, but his comments about leadership—particularly those written in the 1890s when he was the Bnei Moshe's head—provide insights into what he considered the prerequisites of power and politics. He examines the political tactics of Bnei Moshe in a way that is at times remarkably frank for the leader of a secret society and someone so practiced in the art of political duplicity. Perhaps he felt shielded by their theoretical abstraction or was simply eager to share with a larger readership ideas that someone else in his position would have reserved for his closest confidants. His essays of the period are surprisingly, even self-destructively, candid.

II

By the time "Lo zeh ha-derekh" appeared in print, the Bnei Moshe was formally established, launched on Adar 7 in February 1889, the date believed by Jewish tradition to be the birthday of Moses. It was named Sons of Moses (Bnei Moshe) because, as Barzilai relates, "Moses is the outstanding symbol of the decency, the righteousness, and the justice of the people of Israel, and also a symbol of self-sacrifice." Barzilai adds that according to a popular Jewish legend, redemption will be ushered in by the intervention of the sons of the biblical Moses. Moreover, Moses was an important symbol in Jewish masonic lodges, and this was sustained by the Bnai Brith with whom the Hovevei Zion from the time of the Kattowitz conference had close contact. The dates of the birth and death of Moses were, in fact, frequently commemorated by Jewish masons. In this and other respects the Bnei Moshe was influenced by the masonic patterns of non-Zionist, Jewish fraternal societies.

The core membership of the original Bnei Moshe consisted of eight or nine men: Frankfeld, the two Lubarksy brothers, Epstein, Rawnitsky, Levi Vilensky (a friend and business associate of Ginzberg), Barzilai, Ahad Ha'am, and perhaps a ninth man; some recalled this was Lilienblum. According to one account, its founding meeting was called without telling Ginzberg of its purpose and only when he arrived was he informed of plans to start the group and urged to serve as its leader. Another memoirist relates that on the night of its establishment, a building owned by Ginzberg burned to the ground (which would signal a major decline in his family's finances) but he came to the founding ceremony, neither visibly ruffled nor shaken.[41]

Members were required to be twenty-five years old, to provide detailed information about themselves, including their source of livelihood, marital status, and their childrens' education. Ahad Ha'am had wished that membership be restricted to those fluent in Hebrew but was persuaded that this would prove unworkable: in the end, the founders stipulated that prospective members must be able to demonstrate that they were prepared to study Hebrew seriously. Those who joined were required to keep the group's existence a secret (even if they were to leave it), and they weren't permitted to circulate its literature to nonmembers. They were also forbidden from joining illegal organizations (especially radical political groups), but even membership in legal ones was to be disclosed to the Bnei Moshe leadership who would ascertain whether this clashed with the needs of the society. They were expected to visit Palestine and to instruct their children properly in Jewish studies. The Bnei Moshe's structure was unabashedly oligarchical, with the leader of the Odessa branch—*manhig lishkat alef,* leader of Branch Number One— granted all-but-unlimited powers. The only check on his authority were periodic elections that never, in fact, took place. Though Ahad Ha'am resigned from the day-to-day responsibilities of running the group in 1891, he never relinquished his role as *manhig.*[42]

Elaborate and repeatedly revised initiation oaths, symbolic greetings, and bylaws were formulated. New members were typically received in the following way: once tested and found acceptable, they were sent a letter written by Ahad Ha'am (signed "Maleh," an acronym for *Manhig lishkat alef*) describing the group's goals. They also received "Derekh he-hayyim" ("The Way of Life"), a privately circulated piece that Ahad Ha'am wrote expressly for Bnei Moshe members and a copy of "Lo zeh ha-derekh." Code names—usually drawn from letters in their names—were provided. Membership for all but those admitted to the secret society before its first congress in Odessa in the summer of 1890, was provisional and for an initial period of six months—during which time "important matters" were not revealed to recruits, except by the express permission of the society's leader—and only after this trial period was permanent membership conferred. Once recruited into the society, new members were informed of their financial, ethical, and educational obligations and were asked to prepare themselves to be called upon to act as Jewish nationalism's elite corps.[43]

There were several formative influences on the Bnei Moshe and its penchant for secrecy: clearly one was the masonic model with its stress on good works not politics (though in Russia and elsewhere a political dimension was often apparent), its elitism, and the promise of European, bourgeois conviviality. The desanctified ritualism of the masons also satisfied the needs of this medley of erstwhile yeshiva students and hasidic hangers-on. Secrecy remained an important component beyond masonic circles where nearly all public life in Russia, even an organization with an essentially philanthropic agenda like the Hovevei Zion, was technically illegal until nearly a decade after it was launched; after that it was closely monitored by the government to ensure that it did not overreach its officially stated goals. In this atmosphere secrecy was encouraged, spurred on by the mystique of the revolutionaries whose impact was felt from the late 1870s especially on politicized Jewish circles. Finally for those nationalists within the traditional Jewish world secrecy was also deemed necessary as a protection from the intrusiveness of the Orthodox. Indeed, in the yeshiva circles a network of small, secret nationalist societies was established who saw the Bnei Moshe as their successor; and in some respects it was.

Once the Bnei Moshe was established, Barzilai left Odessa to recruit members (Ahad Ha'am would later call him "a sort of apostle" for the group) mainly in his native region of Belorussia where a large and literate concentration of maskilim could be found. Without informing them that they were being tested for membership, he quizzed prospective members including the various local leaders of the Hovevei Zion. Clearly the Bnei Moshe hoped to infiltrate the movement and win over its most influential figures. "Our profound hope," Ahad Ha'am wrote in 1889 to a Bnei Moshe member in Kovno, "is to gather to our flag all of our nation's good young men." This, he observed, must be done gradually "without either thunder or noise." He paraphrased a rabbinic passage: "Abstinence or keeping silent is of greater value than being involved actively in making demands." Only once Jewry's leaders have been won over will the masses be attracted.[44]

In contrast to the homogeneity of its original membership, new recruits to the Bnei Moshe were a diverse lot. Religious as well as irreligious Jews were brought into the movement by Barzilai, a pious Jew himself, who attracted the faithful by relating, according to one source, "legend-like tales portraying [Ahad Ha'am] as their nation's authentic leader and genius." Barzilai described him as the leader most likely to revive Jewry's spiritual sentiments, though when the term *ruhaniyut,* or spirituality, was used in the inner circles of the Bnei Moshe its connotation was cultural and not religious. Recruits of a more secular bent were given a dramatically different spin on the Bnei Moshe's leader, whom they were told was a modernized sage.[45]

Ahad Ha'am himself also actively recruited, which was not surprising in view of the importance he placed on the selection of appropriate members. A. Friedenberg, an Odessa Jew, tells in his memoirs how, before the publication of "Lo zeh ha-derekh," Ginzberg and Rawnitsky came to a lecture he gave about Moses for a local Hovevei Zion group. He recalls his surprise when he saw Ginzberg in the audience since he was known to be a reclusive man who rarely ventured into public and socialized only with a small circle of intimates. Friedenberg was even more startled when he was approached by the two Hebraists after the lecture who handed him without explanation a document that they asked him to read and discuss with them later. It was the as-yet-unpublished "Lo zeh ha-derekh." They made no mention of their secret society and, once Friedenberg told them that he approved of it, he was invited to join the Bnei Moshe.[46]

The exhilaration and sense of purpose felt by recruits is captured vividly by one of its first Warsaw members, Elijah Zev Levin-Epstein, in a description of his initiation ceremony:

I remember the evening when we, the new members, were initiated into the branch. All five of us stood together in a room. The three documents [of the society] were read in the proper order. We swore to uphold them in a festive manner, all according to the society's accepted pattern. All of us were in a spiritually exalted state. Willingly, we accepted onto ourselves the rules of the society. . . . That night I walked with two other new members until very late at night, and the entire time we spoke to one another about our new tasks and the work that we would do, and when we parted to return home, two of them called out: "Today a new life has been given to us! Today we learned the true reason for our lives!"[47]

Soon the Bnei Moshe was an open secret in the small, rather self-contained hothouse of Russian Jewish nationalist politics, and its existence—about which there were many rumors but at first few hard facts—endowed Ahad Ha'am and his essays with a special mystique. From the outset, the group's members remained uncertain as to what they were expected to do. The movement's internal document that attempted to address this question was "Derekh he-hayyim." "Lo zeh ha-derekh" had set out to dictate what the Hovevei Zion should not do, while "Derekh he-hayyim"—whose very title ("The Way of Life") prefigured its inspirational character—provided more concrete and positive recommendations. Here Ahad Ha'am set out an agenda for his devotees which was reminiscent of the Russian populist Peter Lavrov whose work Ahad Ha'am read and admired and was designed to encourage Jews to transcend their personal needs for the sake of larger collective concerns. For both Western and Eastern European Jews—the former culturally bankrupt and devoid of national vitality, the latter faced with mounting misfortune of a more obvious kind—the essential aim was simple self-love, to adore their own people "with every fibre of their beings. Not a single Jew should be able to take delight in his personal happiness as long as his nation's fate hangs in the balance."[48]

In language that belied the image of him as distracted, skeptical, and unable either to inspire others or move himself to the point of inspiration, he outlined in "Derekh he-hayyim" a political program for the resurrection of Judaism:

"National" must be raised to the level of a moral concept, a designation so well-regarded in the eyes of [our] people, one which imposes an obligation to guard scrupulously the honor of our flag, to ensure that there is no danger of its being desecrated either by the person who bears it or by those outside its ranks. Little by little the society will enlarge its sphere of influence. It will include [among its tasks] the education of the young as well as measures to bring back to the fold the sons and daughters of our people whom we have lost to other nations. Whenever improvement is needed it will set about improving things. In the end, and it does not matter when this is achieved, the sort of revitalized generation that we are seeking will arise—a generation that will refuse to bow down before Baal and grovel in the dust before its enemies, that will take pride in its people, glory in the honor of its nation. . . . Such a generation will save Israel, it will carry it to Zion, it will act, it will succeed.[49]

He went on to describe the political tasks of his elite: "If men of character, wherever they may be, unite in one society so that each might be an inspiration to the other and help in communicating their own feelings to the people, then who knows but that, in the course of days or years, they might well succeed in infusing their spirit into the people as a whole, and in restoring those moral qualities without which a people cannot exist?"[50]

Elsewhere in his published pieces, although less explicit about such tasks, he nonetheless spoke through hints and intimations with sometimes surprising frankness. His best-known essays of the period were "Petsa'eh ohev" and "Ha-kohanim ve-ha-am." In the latter he posited a heroic ideal against the grey and mundane machinations of philanthropic nationalism. ("All new ideas, whether ethical or social ones, can only emerge by virtue of the work of a brotherhood of 'priests,'" he writes.) His call for a cadre of committed Jews prepared to suffer for the sake of the enlightenment of their people was intended to contrast vividly with the passive and marginal role relegated to all but the rich in a Jewish nationalist enterprise devoted to fundraising.[51]

"Petsa'eh ohev" was particularly explicit in its renunciation of the philanthropic priorities of the Hovevei Zion, these all the clearer once the movement was legalized in 1890. (He remained, despite his criticisms, one of the group's visible leaders.) In this essay, for the first time he cites in support of his culturalist agenda the historical precedent of Yochanan ben Zakkai who would soon play a central role in expositions of his ideology. A rabbinic legend told of Yochanan ben Zakkai who led the Pharisaic masters of Jerusalem out of the beseiged city and brought them to Yavneh where he established a religious legislative center credited by Jewish tradition with reviving Judaism once the Temple fell. Various motifs of the rabbinic version were easily reshaped by Ahad Ha'am: the fanaticism (and futility) of those who insisted on waging war against the Romans; the quiet wisdom of the Pharisees whose seemingly reclusive activity set the foundations for the continued existence of the Jewish people; the contention that the Pharisees, considered at the time to be obtusely indifferent to politics were actually, as later events showed, astute in their political judgments.[52]

The essay was prompted by Lilienblum's claim that Ahad Ha'am had not addressed the misery of East European Jewry—which he insisted must be the central concern of Jewish nationalism. Hungry, harassed, and desperate for refuge, the masses, said Lilienblum, are in immediate need of rescue, not cultural transformation. Ahad Ha'am responded that no one was more aware of Jewry's economic misery than he, but Jewish nationalism must come to terms with the fact that it cannot solve such problems. However sympathetic it might be, it had neither the influence nor the financial resources to put an end to those conditions endemic to the diaspora. Anyone who mistakenly looked to the Hovevei Zion for solutions—Ahad Ha'am categorized such problems as the "misery of the individual" (tsarat ha-perat)—will only turn against Jewish nationalism with disgust and disillusionment. Only more general and collective concerns can successfully be addressed by the movement. This might seem brutal, but a nationalist movement had an obligation to be brutally honest.

Jewish nationalism's natural constituency, in Ahad Ha'am's view, is consequently not the poor, and in an extraordinary call to arms he describes how only the middle class are likely to be truly receptive to the message of the Hovevei Zion:

There are still many Jews whose financial position hasn't deteriorated and who still share a love for their people in their hearts, and desire its collective existence. It is they, once they recognize that the very foundations of our solidarity are fast disappearing and without new foundations, and that religion can no longer serve to unify our hearts . . . once they come to see all this they will ask one another with broken hearts and aggrieved souls: Isn't there some way to gather together the banished ones, to unify once again those separated [from Jewry], to renew the spirit that escaped from its midst? . . . It is to them and only them we answer—there is no other answer: Hovevei Zion.[53]

By the early 1890s he had identified a potentially receptive constituency, designated their tasks, and set in motion a semisecret political league. His ideas were now widely disseminated, albeit in a veiled form, to large numbers of still-as-yet uninitiated Jews. He was also, as we shall see, one of a very small cluster of Hebrew writers familiar outside the maskilic circles that produced and devoured the region's Jewish press. As one reader, Moshe Smilansky, recalled—he read "Lo zeh ha-derekh" in his adolescence soon after he decided to settle in Palestine—as soon as he put the piece down he felt his "heart rip." Ahad Ha'am had called into question all his "Tolstoyan" beliefs regarding the rebuilding of Palestine. When he nonetheless immigrated to Palestine, via Odessa, he avoided Ahad Ha'am out of fear of his "withering" and "fierce" judgment. For him, Ahad Ha'am was a severe judge—powerful, dangerous and uncannily persuasive.[54]

Ahad Ha'am's message even found its way into the yeshiva world, where secularist literature like his was normally shunned. His writings, as one former yeshiva student recalled years later, were not read but studied much like sacred texts with the students in his Vitebsk province study hall each providing their own gloss. It was widely felt that their contents could not reasonably be seen as secularist: how, for instance, could "Ha-ohanim ve-ha-am"—with its call for Jewry's elite to live up to austere spiritual obligations—be described as having anything but religious implications? Indeed, this particular piece helped inspire the creation at the Volozhin yeshiva, the flagship of rabbinic Judaism, of a nationalist league called *Netsakh yisrael* (The Glory of Israel). No writer since the Haskalah was at its height had as great an impact on yeshiva circles, insists Chaim Tchernowitz, who discovered Ahad Ha'am while a student at the Kovno yeshiva. Tchernowitz recalls that debates raged in yeshiva corridors as to whether Ahad Ha'am was a religious or secular Jew. Studied by yeshiva students with the assiduousness usually reserved for a traditional religious authority, the rabbinic flavor of his prose lent support to those affirming his piety.[55]

Bialik, one of the founders of Netsakh yisrael, published an exposition in *Ha-Melitz* while still in yeshiva on the importance of the "spiritual component of Jewish nationalism," a good example of how Ahad Ha'am's secularist arguments were manipulated by some readers into a religious context. "There is no healthy body without a healthy soul," Bialik reminds his readers, and unless the Jewish people prepare themselves spiritually for rebirth in the Holy Land, they will fail in their effort. It is now the moment for "a renewal of their spirits . . . and fear of God." For many pious Jews, he continues, the slightest infraction of a traditionally sanctioned custom—let alone a biblical or rabbinic commandment—is assiduously avoided. But how many obey as carefully the biblical injunction "And you shall love your neighbor as yourself"? It is essential that such commandments achieve a new sanctity and prominence. This can be achieved, he says, on the basis of renewed commitment to Jewish education. He concludes: "If we pay attention only to improving our material conditions we will not have accomplished anything." At the very least what can be now achieved is that "out of Zion will come. . . . the spiritual salvation of the Jewish people." This will help ensure that we will be able to "observe the entire body of Jewish law" and live better than we do today.[56]

"Every word that Ahad Ha'am wrote," said Bialik many years later, "seemed addressed to me, to my innermost thoughts." His move to Odessa soon after the publication of his article in *Ha-Melitz* was prompted in no small measure by the fact that Ahad Ha'am lived in the city. Despite Bialik's mounting fame for most of his life his relationship with his mentor would remain that of a somewhat distant admirer, an awestruck child. Perhaps Bialik—orphaned, hungry for paternal guidance, and at odds with himself even after being dubbed the Jewish national poet—was more worshipful than most, but this was only a matter of degree. Never invited to join the Bnei Moshe (Bialik described himself in his early days in Odessa as "wild, shy, dumb, unmannered"), his attitude toward Ahad Ha'am was nonetheless characteristic of the group's early days when the single thread that bound together its widely disparate membership was veneration for the leader of Branch Number One.[57]

Ahad Ha'am relished at first his role as leader of a small group of intimates and carefully supervised all aspects of their lives: when Frankfeld's bride complained, for instance, that her husband, who had married late, found it difficult to break with old habits and stayed out late playing cards (a practice that was frowned upon by the Bnei Moshe), Ahad Ha'am intervened in the domestic dispute. One evening when Frankfeld was out, he sat in his living room awaiting his return. Frankfeld returned in the early morning to find Ahad Ha'am sitting in his house. Not a word was spoken; Ahad Ha'am simply looked at him and left, and Frankfeld changed his ways.[58]

When on another occasion his wife's uncle, the Lubavitcher rebbe, sent him a note during a visit to Odessa inviting Ahad Ha'am to see him, he told the rebbe that, instead, the hasidic leader ought to come to him because (paraphrasing a rabbinic text) whether judged on the basis of the number of one's followers or the extent of one's learning Ahad Ha'am was, arguably, the superior of the two. Needless to say, that meeting never took place.[59]

To devotees he could be abusive (he accused Barzilai of boundless vanity, adding "please excuse me for telling the truth"); but he could also be tactful and warm.[60] He was an exceptionally loyal friend and his correspondence with disciples who were also friends, which includes several of the Bnei Moshe's inner circle—was often playful, ironic, and gently mocking. Take, for example, a letter written in 1892 to one Bnei Moshe devotee, Levi Vilensky, to whom he extends the regards of "my entire household and also my father's house." He had received Vilensky's last letter some time ago, but

I hesitated to answer you since I arrived at this inference: If you are quite as preoccupied as you say with your "visits" [vizitim] so that you cannot find the time to pick up your hands and write me for many weeks, then certainly you are also busy with other matters and your eyes, no doubt, are so satiated that you must not have had the opportunity to read the letters that I already sent you.

Now I assume that your visits have ended and that you've seen all that you need to see. So the time is right for me to answer your letter. But before I answer your questions, I'll start with my own question, like all proper Jews [kederekh kol yehudi kasher].

My question is this: Why didn't you tell me anything about your private affairs? . . . This question can be subdivided into many specific questions; but, as you know, my way is to say things succinctly and to depend upon the reader's understanding to fill in the gaps.[61]

Few, however, saw this side of him. To most members of the Bnei Moshe what he projected—or, perhaps, what they preferred to see in him during the movement's first few, heady years—was not the vulnerable, affectionate, and untalkative man of Vilensky's acquaintance but rather an authoritative and judgmental leader. This certainly is the portrait of Ahad Ha'am that emerges in Ben Avigdor's pamphlet *Shene hezyonot* (Two visions) published in 1891 and dedicated to him: "The wise teacher, of great ability and knowledge, the superb writer."[62]

The dedication is benign compared to what Ben Avigdor (pen name for Abraham Leib Shalkowitz), an influential member of the group's Warsaw branch, attributed to Ahad Ha'am in the final section of the text, "Moshe o sheloshet ha-nevi'im" (Moses or the three prophets). Here the author portrays Moses at the foot of Mt. Sinai, echoing Odessa's nationalist sage: "'Arise my children from all across the land,' called Moses in a pleasant voice as he began to descend the mountain, 'I am not a man of God, just a man like the rest of you, like any other man of Israel.'" Moses then proceeds, "for the good of the nation," to preach to Israel the deeds that it must perform: "I will let it be known to you what road you should take and what deeds you must do: . . . Sons of Isaiah, even if your intentions are pure but your actions are not, this is not the way [Lo zeh ha-derekh]!"[63]

Ben Avigdor could not have been more explicit, particularly when he had Moses exclaim, "This is not the way"; no phrase in Hebrew letters was more intimately associated with Ahad Ha'am. Only slightly less obvious was Moses's admonition that the nation's dry bones must now be imbued with flesh and the breath of life. The responsibility before us, Moses declares, is nothing less than the nation's resurrection:

This task, the task of resurrecting a nation, is great and honorable work, hard and burdensome work, and you must not do anything to bring on resurrection before the time is ripe. It is incumbent upon you to move forward with slow but deliberate steps, it is incumbent upon you to keep in mind all relevant factors, because even the smallest error made in midst of work such as ours can damage everything.[64]

Not surprisingly, the pamphlet elicited a great stir: Lilienblum mocked it in a scathing attack that also implicated the Bnei Moshe, though his article never mentioned the group by name and he denied that it was ever meant to attack Ahad Ha'am. (As member he had promised never to divulge its secrets.) In his reply Ahad Ha'am claimed that Lilienblum had misinterpreted the work (it was merely a fantasy he insisted) while distancing himself from Ben Avigdor whom he portrayed as a youthful enthusiast and unrepresentative of his supporters. Lilien-blum, he says, is merely seeking to reopen his advocacy of "activity" over "thought" (the latter being the arena Ahad Ha'am and his supporters consider worthwhile), and he mistakenly pits rationality against confu-sion, careful planning against sheer chance. Here as elsewhere the dis-crepancy between the candor championed by Ahad Ha'am and the secrecy with which he enveloped his public life would, as we shall see, contribute toward demoralizing the group and had a direct bearing on its eventual unraveling.[65]

And unravel it would and rather soon. He remained unable to make it clear to its members what they were supposed to do. This was left intentionally ambiguous, probably an inevitable by-product of Ahad Ha'am's politics. He hoped that the group could shoulder the ambiguity; in the end, it buckled under its weight.

It was attempted in several addenda to "Derekh he-hayyim" to explain what activities members of the Bnei Moshe were to perform. One exclaimed that its main task was to uphold the following tenets: "The land of our fathers and its settlement, the Torah of Israel, our language and literature, the memory of our people's past, the fundamental customs of our fathers, and the nationalist customs of our lives over the gener-ations." Recited at initiation ceremonies, the statement continues,

If you understand—and this is not easy—if you feel, if you sense all of this, with all your heart, with all your soul, and throughout your life until your last drop of blood, then you are ours! Then, give us your hands and be blessed. And know today, as you stand here before us, that great and holy are such moments in one's life.[66]

How should this translate itself into day-to-day tasks? When first questioned on this score Ahad Ha'am urged members gently and pa-tiently that they must wait until the group grew in size and influence.

This growth was likely to be laboriously slow but essential. Later, when the same question was repeated—often with mounting impatience—he answered tartly that never had he promised that the Bnei Moshe would satisfy the desires of those requiring constant political engagement. Even if called upon to serve their movement once a year, he added, this should suffice to satisfy both the Bnei Moshe and the personal needs of its constituency. When in 1893 Eliezer Kaplan, leader of the Warsaw branch, expressed his misgivings about the group's lack of direction, the solution he proposed was more attention to the nationalist education of Bnei Moshe's members. Others mocked such proposals: it was, they said, the cream of the Hovevei Zion who joined the group; their further edification could not possibly be sufficiently important to justify spending Jewry's paltry resources.[67]

As one unhappy member wrote: if the Bnei Moshe was created simply for the sake of bringing together into one fraternal organization Jewish nationalists with good hearts, the enterprise was really rather ludicrous. Was such a group of any greater importance than one dedicated, say, to gathering together all blond or bearded men? All that the Bnei Moshe asked of its members was that they should declare to another, "I'm a good man and so are you, let us come together as two good men." Although cozy and self-satisfying, such a purpose did not amount to much.[68]

Tension was apparent from the group's very beginnings. In debates conducted soon after its founding—and in a series of meetings in Odessa and Warsaw in which its goals were defined—Ahad Ha'am's vision of a society devoted to "the preparation of hearts," as he called it, was pitted against other alternatives: Menachem Mendel Ussishkin, for instance, called for the creation within the ranks of the Bnei Moshe of a *Bnei Akivah* (Sons of Akivah), composed of hearty nationalists who would be taught self-defense and whose responsibility would be to defend Jews from physical attack. Other members called for an explicitly religious society that affirmed its commitment to the laws of the Torah. Lilienblum, however, tried to guide it in the direction of practical work in Palestine and, once this proved impossible, resigned his membership in it. Even some of those who supported Ahad Ha'am's emphasis on the spiritual reeducation of the Jewish people, tended to understand the process in religious rather than secular terms. (One of the society's key documents, entitled "Come in peace, brothers" and distributed to all new members, was, for instance, written in part by Barzilai and spoke quite clearly in religiously charged messianic terms.)[69] Divided over fundamental issues, unclear about its primary goals, most of the members of

the Bnei Moshe lacked a coherent understanding of what their participation in it meant.

By no means was Ahad Ha'am insensitive to the dilemma. When he
heard from Zederbaum in 1890 the rumor that the government would
soon permit throughout the empire the expansion of heders without
burdensome restrictions he declared, "Now we will be able to accomplish a good deal in the area of education."[70] Such moments of euphoria
were rare, however. His disdain for what he felt to be the excessive haste
of the Hovevei Zion, his interest in limiting his group exclusively to what
he deemed to be realistic goals, and his preoccupation with the Jews'
poverty, political inexperience, and vulnerability—all this influenced his
assumptions about what the Bnei Moshe could realistically do.

The Bnei Moshe was not as inactive as some of its detractors claimed:
it launched several important periodicals (*Kaveret, Pardes,* and, somewhat more indirectly, the distinguished *Ha-Shiloach*), the Hebrew publishing house Ahiasaf, libraries in Palestine and elsewhere, and the first
self-supporting agricultural colony in Palestine, Rehovot. It was responsible for setting up schools in Palestine and Eastern Europe and was
a pioneer in the education of women. To be sure, its interest in female
education was prompted mainly by an awareness that if they started boys'
schools they would likely run into spirited opposition from the *melamdim,* the private traditional teachers who dominated this sphere and were
known to guard their preserve vigorously, but who were largely indifferent to teaching females. Bnei Moshe schools (including kindergar-
tens) were opened in Warsaw, Poltava, Lublin, Dinaburg, and Vilna.
The society also helped to modernize, even to resurrect, otherwise
marginalized festivals like Hannukah, which it endowed with new nationalist content. It published regularly an invaluable fact sheet on
Palestinian affairs, entitled *Emet me-eretz yisrael* (Truth from Palestine),
inspired by Ahad Ha'am's muckraking piece of 1891.

An impressive record, but most of this activity was the work of a very
small group of devotees—the original core of the Bnei Moshe in Odessa
and a handful of others from Warsaw and Jaffa: Rawnitsky, Levin-
Epstein, Barzilai, and Eliezer Kaplan. The bulk of the Bnei Moshe's
approximately 150 members, however, were asked to wait patiently for
their marching orders.[71] As recruits, they had been promised great
personal engagement. In fact, they were given little to do.

The main reason for this inattention, however, was neither Ahad
Ha'am's reticence nor his caution. Rather it was an outgrowth of his far
from modest political goals: he envisioned the creation of a core of

receptive nationalists who would ensure that the Bnei Moshe's vision of the future had a sympathetic, ultimately decisive role in the Hovevei Zion. Its devotees, by virtue of their pristine personal behavior, their commendable activist élan, their integrated vision of the Jewish past and future, would make certain that the Jewish people were reschooled in its image. The tactics used to pursue these goals were themselves, he believed, imbued with authenticity and culled from the arsenal of traditional, especially hasidic, Judaism.

Ultimately, their goal was to replace the leadership of the Hovevei Zion with one receptive to Ahad Ha'am's priorities and with him as Pinsker's heir. This required the infiltration of the Hovevei Zion; the majority of Bnei Moshe could personally contribute little particularly since that aim was never stated explicitly. They could of course have an indirect influence by tacitly acquiescing to changes promoted by Bnei Moshe activists in the Hovevei Zion, or by electing its own members to positions of authority in the larger Palestinophile movement. But the crucial work was to be done behind the scenes by a handful of men.[72]

At first, this strategy was reasonably successful. In the spring of 1890 the Hovevei Zion held its first meeting as a legal organization. It was a large gathering in Odessa by Russian standards with sixty-three delegates in attendance. There Ahad Ha'am not only managed to fend off attacks by critics, but counterattacked with great skill. He rehearsed arguments similar to those used in the pre-Kattowitz debates but this time with greater success, no doubt because he had built a solid and committed block of support that was as loyal as any in the movement. In the end, three of the eight members elected to the executive committee board—Barzilai, Jacob Lubarsky; and Ahad Ha'am—belonged to the Bnei Moshe. (This amounted to less than Ahad Ha'am had expected—he hoped to walk away with control of the movement—but represented a considerable achievement.) Within a year of its establishment, the Bnei Moshe had scored an important political victory.[73]

The group was even more successful in establishing a power base in Palestine. When the staff of the newly opened Jaffa office of the Hovevei Zion was selected in 1890, all three of those named were members of Ahad Ha'am's group. The head of the Jaffa branch of the Bnei Moshe, Vladimir Tiomkin, a russified Ekaterinoslav engineer of a secularist bent, was picked to run the Palestinian Hovevei Zion along with two religious men, Yehiel Pines and Isaac Ben-Tovim. The appointment of this medley of religious and irreligious Bnei Moshe members was intentional and meant to underline the partnership, whether real or imagined, across the spectrum in the ranks of the movement. Not only was Ahad Ha'am responsible for selecting them, but when trouble broke out in the office in 1891 he rushed off to Palestine to handle the matter personally.[74]

For members of the Bnei Moshe who viewed their organization from afar, the group no doubt appeared to be rather whimsical, even naive. But its inner circle knew it to be fiercely political and doggedly seeking influence within the shifting sands of the Hovevei Zion. Only a small number were even aware of the fight; the rest had been recruited— though they were never told this—to serve as discreet and silent troops in maneuvers about which they were kept completely in the dark. Promised action and nationalist fervor, they waited as patiently as could be expected; soon they made it clear that their idealism was far from nourished by Ahad Ha'am's benign neglect.

By the time such criticisms were leveled, beginning in 1891–1892, Ahad Ha'am was already under attack from persons from across the political spectrum of East European Jewry. The attacks sprang from the dissatisfaction in his own ranks which owed much to the nearly impossible coalition of religious and secularists that he had cobbled together. The criticisms were also self-imposed. At the very height of his influence in 1891 he managed to alienate not only his religious allies (whose support was tenuous, at best) but many others whose support was considerably firmer. He claimed that his insistence on always speaking the truth was the cause. Nevertheless, as we have seen, when he found it necessary he could be less than candid and so subtle that he did not tarnish himself irrevocably. His political troubles were somewhat self-inflicted: the product of a combination of single-minded idealism and self-abasement, of a hunger for success and an overpowering and self-fulfilling pessimism. Much of this can be traced to the publication of "Emet me-eretz yisrael."

Ahad Ha'am's reputation as Jewish nationalism's major internal critic dates from the publication of this essay in 1891. Several of his earlier pieces were controversial but what made this article stand out was both its wealth of detail, marshaled during Ginzberg's first trip to Palestine, and its stark rejection of the emigrationist premises of the Hovevei Zion which he would soon counter with the idea of a "spiritual center." In his disavowal of emigrationist politics he even turned his back on the relatively modest tactics of his own Bnei Moshe; his members reacted with fury.

Oddly enough, when he had jotted down his impressions during his trip between February and May 1891, his comments were considerably less grim than those that found their way into "Emet." In his diary he wrote how moved he was wandering about on Passover in Jerusalem near the Temple Mount where he visited synagogues; the experience left him with a feeling that was both surprisingly pleasant and also menacing: "Holy feelings of this sort are very rare in one's lifetime." In a letter to Rawnitsky written during the visit he poked fun at diaspora Jews who tried to dictate to the Palestinian settlers how they ought to live their lives. He was particularly aware how patronizing and senseless such instructions were now that he had seen the colonists' hardships firsthand. Neither his lyrical reactions to the Temple Mount nor his self-deprecating acknowledgment of the limitations of advice from the diaspora found any echo in his article published on 1 June 1891. It contained only a fraction of his impressions of his trip which were presented in the form of a book-length oral report to the Hovevei Zion and transcribed, ironically, by its secretary, and his political nemesis, Lilienblum.[75] "Emet me-eretz yisrael" begins:

After many years of thinking about and imagining the land of our fathers and the rebirth of our people there, I finally succeeded in seeing with my own eyes the object of my dreams, this land of wonders which captivates so many from all nations and lands. I spent about three months there. I saw its ruins—the remnants of its past life, I studied its present wretched conditions, but I paid special attention to the future. Everywhere I went there was one question that most preoccupied me: to what extent is there hope here regarding the future? Is the land ready for Jewry's return, and is Jewry ready to return to the land? The question of the land's suitability is not difficult to answer: It is enough to go about and travel here for a few days and see its mountains and valleys, its fields and vineyards that yield fruit despite the laziness of the Arabs . . . to see that now as in the past it can provide countless numbers of its children with life and sustenance as long as they return with a true heart and are willing to diligently work the land. Despite this, it was not easy to answer whether Jewry itself is ready. Now I have left the land for which I have yearned for so long with a broken heart and broken spirits. . . . No longer are the land, its people, and all that happens there mere dreams for me, but now what I have seen is the concrete truth . . . of which I wish to reveal a bit—the ugliest bit.[76]

He tried, he told Rawnitsky, to write a more positive appraisal: "I want with all my heart—believe me—to tell my readers only good things. But I can't, my soul just isn't suited for that."[77] He had quite rightly anticipated that his report would meet with protest, particularly since it appeared at an uncharacteristically optimistic moment in Hovevei Zion circles. In 1891, the Turks had eased immigration restrictions to Palestine while the Russian authorities were expelling tens of thousands of

Jews from Moscow. The expulsion was seen by Russian Jews as another and particularly brutal indication that no improvement of their standing could be expected. Some of those expelled looked to Palestine as a prospective haven, including a handful of wealthy Jews and others who, although not rich, had enough money to purchase land, which immediately set them apart from the indigents normally handled by the Hovevei Zion. Land prices in Palestine soared; the Jaffa office of Hovevei Zion predicted, with glee and considerable apprehension, that some ten thousand settlers might descend on them in the near future. Suddenly the building of a substantial Jewish settlement in the Holy Land seemed likely and relatively painless.[78]

Even before Ahad Ha'am's article, however, there were signs—visible only to the closest observers of the Yishuv—that conditions in Palestine were not yet ripe for a sizable immigration. The fact that Ahad Ha'am was the first to air them publicly was viewed with considerable irony, since he had vigorously preached about the need to attract Jewish settlers able to support themselves, criticizing the Hovevei Zion's reliance on the poor as self-destructive and shortsighted. When for the first time in the society's brief history reasonably large numbers of self-supporting immigrants were arriving, he still managed to find reason for complaint. Even some of his more stalwart admirers were surprised.

What prompted his trip to Palestine were allegations of mismanagement in the Hovevei Zion's Jaffa office. The trip was organized at the last minute and took place in winter, a bad time for overseas travel; the Mediterranean leg of his journey was so bad that his boat nearly shattered near Mt. Carmel. But the mismanagement allegations that prompted this trip were of special concern to Ahad Ha'am since the office was run by Bnei Moshe members who were accused of mishandling land purchases for prospective immigrants and contributing to soaring land prices. There had been a 400 percent increase during the previous year. Some saw the crisis as a by-product of the impossible nature of Tiomkin's job; others credited it to his lack of linguistic knowledge (he knew neither Hebrew nor Arabic) and his inadequate grounding in Palestinian affairs (he had lived in Jaffa only for about a year). There were those who implied, however, that Tiomkin had benefited financially from the ever-spiraling land prices. Even worse, the Jaffa office was facing internal stife between the secularist Tiomkin and his religious staff.

Beset by the rumors of scandal on the part of members of his elite corps, embroiled in a quagmire of land deals in a place that he knew no better than the others in his Odessa-based delegation, and faced with the prospect of mounting tensions between the pious and secular members of the Bnei Moshe, Ahad Ha'am's time in Palestine was unhappy, stressful, and also exceptionally wet. He exonerated Tiomkin, deciding he was clumsy but not dishonest; further, having reached the conclusion that Tiomkin could no longer work with Pines and Ben-Tovim, Ahad Ha'am fired them both and left Tiomkin in command along with Barzilai.[79]

His tour of Palestinian colonies disappointed him. He had some good things to say about Rehovot, though here too he managed to bruise the colonists with badly timed and insensitive remarks. (Other members of his delegation had inspired the colonists with words of encouragement. Ahad Ha'am instead told them only how difficult their task was and that the timid should pack up and return to Russia.) He nonetheless concluded that Rehovot was reasonably viable. The rest of the colonies were supported, he insisted, by a system of financial aid little better than that of the traditional *halukah*, which typically supplied funds for pious Jewish settlers in their twilight years. Like the old halukah system, the Hovevei Zion too had consigned their charges to penury and stagnation.[80]

Point by point, "Emet" delineates common assumptions about Palestine and shows them to be fatuous, beginning in each instance with the words "We are accustomed to believe . . .": not only isn't Palestine empty, as many contend, but arable land is now at a premium and little more of it actually exists; far from being unaware of Jewish designs, local Arabs are shrewd and ready to exploit the settlers; and there isn't any truth to the belief that the Turkish government can be easily manipulated to satisfy Jewish colonial aspirations. The problems then are overwhelming. They could be handled by suitably prepared settlers under the aegis of an exemplary leadership. Instead, what exists is disastrous: leaders who are cynical and patronizing and, aware that few Jews are really very interested in Palestine, they have decided that rather than educate Jewry, they must simply lie about it to encourage Jews to move there. Those who arrive are insufficiently committed and inadequately prepared.[81]

The improbable image projected by the Hovevei Zion, says Ahad Ha'am, is of a "new California," an idyllic place free from the miseries of Europe. The little that had been accomplished is praised shamelessly, for instance, the dubious productivity of its grape industry, which has yet to capture a solid market. Arguably, the capital already invested in viticulture, the most visible of Palestinian Jewry's economic activities, has been wasted because of haphazard planning and bad administration.

In any event, Ahad Ha'am adds, (alluding too, perhaps, to his own family's earnings from liquor distillation in the recent past) it is unseemly—"a bad omen for our people's moral condition"—if Zion is resurrected in this way, if "all of this holy land is transformed into a vast field of intoxication."[82]

In light of the instability of the Palestinian experiment, he contended, only the most idealistic settlers are likely to remain. Others, especially those who choose to come for financial gain, will abandon it when they discover that the Hovevei Zion has wholly misrepresented it. What Jewish nationalists must realize is that neither speculators, self-seeking entrepreneurs, nor even harassed and poverty-stricken Jews in search of some semblance of comfort can constitute the basis for Palestine's rejuvenation. Rather, what is required are

people who, wholeheartedly and with complete honesty, have abandoned their disgraceful and thoughtless lives and who went to the land of their forefathers with the firm decision to relinquish all the attributes and consequences of a commercial existence and to devote themselves with all their hearts to physical labor for the sake of spiritual tranquility.[83]

Those who now set the tone for Palestinian Jewish life are a motley population of former tailors and shoemakers who have abandoned the slums of the Pale of Settlement and conspire in Palestine to drive land prices up while the Arabs watch carefully, ready to take advantage of the anarchic conditions. The Turks will not permit this situation to continue indefinitely and are certain to reimpose serious obstacles to Jewish settlement. The contrast, he said, between the feverish and exploitative activities of the Jews and the dignity that he encountered in the small German colony that he visited on the road from Rosh Pinah to Tiberias was dramatic and depressing. Here land was purchased without fanfare and inexpensively: "Recalling [the Germans], I said to myself, 'Blessed is the gentile who says little and does a great deal and all that he does is performed with wisdom and good order.'"[84]

More troubling was the arrogance of the Jewish settlers and their disregard for the Arabs. The first Jewish nationalist to see the darker side to the relationship between Arabs and Jews in the Holy Land, Ahad Ha'am insisted that what others believed to be merely haphazard skirmishes in fact threatened the integrity of the Jewish enterprise. His brief treatment of the problem is chilling and prescient.

The brutal treatment of Arabs by some Jews was, he felt, a tragic reaction to a history of Jewish subjugation in the diaspora. For them, attacks on Arabs represented a way of celebrating their newfound freedom. Even more serious than such violence, at least in the short run, was the likelihood that Jewry's inexperience would be exploited by savvy, underestimated Arabs: "We are accustomed to believe that the Arabs are all desert savages, asses, who neither perceive nor understand what goes on around them." But, in fact, they are sharp and cunning, and, especially those who live in towns "see and understand what we are doing and what our aspirations in Palestine are, but they keep their silence and pretend not to know, because at present they do not perceive our actions as a threat to their future; they are trying, therefore, to exploit us as well, to derive advantage from the new visitors insofar as they are able. Yet they mock us in their hearts."[85]

How was it that he arrived at these conclusions, so out of kilter with those held in Palestinophile circles? They are consistent, of course, with his overriding pessimism. But he had no conversations, at least so far as he recorded, with local Arabs; his exchanges with Palestinian Jews did not at all dwell on the theme. Confronted though as he was during his trip with reports of clashes between Jews and Arabs, he tended to see them in the context of his understanding of Judeophobia as a resilient, even chronic feature of civilization. Unlike other Jewish nationalists, he did not view antisemitism as a unique feature of modernity; he denied its economic motivations (stressed by Lilienblum) or the prospect that antisemities themselves might usefully cooperate with Jews to solve the Jewish problem (as Herzl would later argue). Closest to him in this respect was Pinsker—and his belief that Judeophobia was something innate, a psychic disorder—but where Pinsker allowed for the possibility that the creation of a Jewish homeland would cure the malady, Ahad Ha'am held out no such hope. Some things, Ahad Ha'am believed, were permanent; antisemitism was one of these and would eventually exist also in the Holy Land. The grossly insensitive behavior of the settlers had only given the issue prominence, thus fueling anti-Jewish prejudice. Perhaps he exaggerated in his essay the coherence of Jewish attacks on Arabs at this time, but the weight he gave to this feature of Jewish colonization put it for the first time on the Zionist agenda.

At the essay's close he speaks of his Passover in Jerusalem without so much as a hint of the lyricism with which he writes of the same experience in his diary. Ahad Ha'am is glum, even hostile, toward the religious Jews whom he encounters at the city's holy sites and particularly beside the Wailing Wall. They are even less likely than the colonists to contribute toward building up a pioneering elite, and he concludes that his hope that the diaspora might contribute to its formation was misplaced. He ends on a note of complete despair:

Filled with melancholy thoughts after what I had seen and heard in Jaffa and in the colonies, I arrived on the eve of Passover in Jerusalem, there to pour forth my sorrow and my rage before the stocks and stones, the remnants of our former glory. I went first, of course, to the Wailing Wall. There I found many of our Jerusalem brethren standing and praying in loud voices. Their haggard faces, their wild, alien gestures, their fantastic clothes—all this merged with the ghastly picture of the Wall itself. Looking at them and at the Wall, one thought filled my heart. These stones testify to the desolation of our land; these men testify to the desolation of our people. Which of these desolations is worse? For which should we shed more tears? When a land is destroyed, there may yet arise a Zerubabel, an Ezra, a Nehemiah who could bring forth their people with them and restore the Land. But when a people is destroyed, who can come to its rescue?[86]

The debate that erupted once "Emet" appeared was intense, highly personal, and something of a family affair. Day after day the front pages of *Ha-Melitz,* which ran it, carried criticisms of it; Ahad Ha'am responded in print only once to the barrage, with a pained but unequivocal reassertion of his original ideas. What was most striking about the debate was that among his chief detractors were members of the Bnei Moshe. Apparently, Ahad Ha'am did nothing to discourage critics of "Emet" within the group to voice their disagreement. He assured the head of Poltava's office, who requested guidance concerning a member who had openly criticized the article, that "the society is one thing, literature another" and that anything he published was fair game for debate.[87] The ferocity of this internal criticism was indicative of the wide diversity of opinions within the group, a factor that would contribute to the Bnei Moshe's disintegration.

Perhaps most surprising were the replies to "Emet" from Elhonan Levinsky and Ussishkin. Not only were both men Bnei Moshe members, but Ussishkin had been part of the delegation that had accompanied Ahad Ha'am on his trip; Levinsky, though not yet a part of the Bnei Moshe's Odessa circle (he would move to the city in 1896), was closely connected to it by bonds of friendship and ideological kinship.

Levinsky's article—cogently entitled, "Love for the Community, Hatred for Its Individual Members"—was, despite his ties to Ahad Ha'am, relentless in its denunciation. "Emet" itself wasn't mentioned; nor was Ahad Ha'am. The implications, though, were unmistakable: there are those, Levinsky explains, for whom love of the Jewish people represents merely an abstract attachment to Jews of the ancient past, "to all those Mordecais, Baruchs, Jacobs, and Josephs." When such people are confronted by the descendants of the patriarchs, they recoil with revulsion. Abstract love for the dead ancients is rather easy—clean, simple, unburdened by the messy complexities of daily life. It is also superficial and rarified. It is in such rarified company that Levinsky obviously consigns Ahad Ha'am.[88]

Ussishkin was more explicit in his denunciation. Blunt, unimaginative, and single-mindedly devoted to Jewish nationalism, Ussishkin even challenged Ahad Ha'am's honesty; he claimed that there was little relationship between the reality of Palestine and the glum reportage found in "Emet," which he simply dismissed as fiction. As a member of Ahad Ha'am's delegation to Palestine, he disputes nearly every point published. He couldn't, of course, deny stories of soaring land prices which were by then commonplace in the Hebrew press, but he insisted that, contrary to Ahad Ha'am, the colonies were thriving, viticulture was in exemplary shape, and the Arabs were happy: "The Arabs have lived in peace until now and have much greater fear of the Christians than the Jews." Needless to say, Ussishkin's sturdy optimism was far more consistent with the tenor of their nationalist movement than Ahad Ha'am's carping, bitter complaints.[89]

For a short while it had seemed that Ahad Ha'am would emerge as the leader for whom Jewish nationalism had searched since its beginnings in the early 1880s: those who had been tested before him and found wanting were the English mystic and philosemite Lawrence Oliphant, the Anglo-Jewish philanthropist Moses Montefiore, Edmond de Rothschild, and Leon Pinsker.[90] Of course, even after the publication of "Emet" he remained in the minds of most Jewish nationalists a distinguished essayist and a perceptive thinker. Earlier, however, it had appeared as if they had found in him the luminary who would unite the movement around his banner. That no longer seemed quite so likely.

Looking back on the eve of the Jewish New Year in the fall of 1891, Ahad Ha'am wrote in a brooding letter to the Jaffa branch of Bnei Moshe: "Yesterday night, the last night of the year, I sat alone in my room and made for myself a reckoning of the past year." The assessment was a glum and depressing one. "We have not now, nor did we ever really have a movement," he writes in another letter soon afterwards. "It was all a delusion." There was good reason for him to despair. The Jaffa office was still in terrible shape (Tiomkin himself, by July 1892, would be replaced), and tensions between religious and irreligious members of the

Bnei Moshe were approaching the boiling point. The Jewish nationalist world had been divided down the middle before the publication of "Emet," according to Shmarya Levin, between supporters of Ahad Ha'am and Lilienblum. Now it appeared to be lined up entirely against the controversial leader of Bnei Moshe. Earlier that year he was the darling of a close-knit but increasingly influential sector of Russian Jewry; suddenly he seemed something of a pariah.[91]

The Bnei Moshe would manage to repair some of the damage wrought by the debate over "Emet" though the group's initial, optimistic élan would be blunted. And though Ahad Ha'am would half-heartedly attempt to extricate himself from the leadership of the Bnei Moshe, he would nonetheless remain in charge of the group until its dissolution in 1898. He came to credit Bnei Moshe's internal problems to the inadequacies of its membership—its political immaturity, wretched impatience, and lack of vision. The wrong people had been recruited (for which he mostly blamed Barzilai), and it had attempted too much too quickly so that it had to pay the inevitable price for its impetuousness. He said that he yearned for the old days when harmony reigned and for the camaraderie of his small Odessa circle.[92]

Yet in the midst of the attacks on him in the summer of 1891, Ahad Ha'am admitted that he didn't altogether mind the adverse attention and that dissent and strife quickened his pulse and excited him. Indeed, he would recall with considerable fondness the debate over "Emet" when in 1910 the Hebrew literary world attacked him in a controversy in which once again many of those otherwise friendly to him deemed his actions ill-conceived and destructive.[93] What seems to have been a tragic turning point in the very early stages of a brilliant political career he clearly did not view as an unmitigated disaster. Surprisingly, he would remember the period following the appearance of "Emet" with some nostalgia.

He obviously enjoyed—he freely admitted as much—being center stage; he also hated the attention, seeking adulation while repelling the worshipful with jaundiced barbs (as he did during his tour of Rehovot). He craved the adoration lavished on him in the first year of the Bnei Moshe's existence; but he also insisted on acting as if he was a writer without institutional ties, a man unbound by constraints of any kind though he stood at the helm of a nationalist group with considerable political ambitions. The publication of "Emet" at this particular juncture of his career, just as the Bnei Moshe was getting underway, has generally been viewed by his biographers as an act of moral courage. It can also be seen in another way: the act of a man who craved the sensations of dissension, and who, although hungry for power, nonetheless sought out ways to undermine the very authority that he had so laboriously worked to attain. Without doubt, the publication of "Emet" demonstrated considerable moral commitment; at the same time it was self-destructive and a predictably unwise political move. This even Ahad Ha'am recognized. That he wrote it anyway—focusing his attention on what he himself characterized as "the ugliest" features of Palestinian Jewish life—testifies to his profound limitations as a politician. These limitations were the products of a traditional, primarily hasidic, political style that he hoped to secularize. But they were also shaped by idiosyncratic influences—by an overwhelming desire both to succeed and fail, to be both celebrated and denounced, to be singled out as the outstanding representive of his generation and yet also to be the object of abuse, rejection, and rebellion. Is it surprising that the biblical Moses so intrigued and inspired him?

The Prophet, he would soon explain in "Kohen ve-navi" ("Priest and Prophet"), was by nature extremist, one-sided, neither capable of compromise nor of directly shaping the sentiments of the masses. Such tasks were left to less original men, so-called priests who lacked the prophet's genius but who played an essential role as the ones who transformed his austere message into something palatable and concrete. What was left for the prophet to do: "When the Prophet saw injustice, either on the part of men or on the part of Providence, he did not inquire closely into its causes, nor bend the knee to necessity, and judge the evil-doers leniently; nor did he give himself up to despair, or doubt the strength of righteousness, or the possibility of its victory. He simply complained, pouring out his soul in words of fire; then went his way again, fighting for his ideal, and full of hope that in time—perhaps even 'at the end of his days'—righteousness would reign over all the earth."[94]

In a world divided between narrowly focused but practically adept priests and rarified prophets who, like Moses himself, might well die before their dreams are realized but whose task it was to dream and admonish, Ahad Ha'am knew well the tasks for which he was best suited. "Priest and Prophet" represented a retreat from politics, an acknowledgment that even the deliberately cautious strategy employed by the Bnei Moshe was itself precipitous, hasty, and self-destructive. In this essay he justified his isolation by insisting that prophets had always been vilified and ultimately proven to be absolutely correct. The essay makes a rather equivocal case for the suitability of someone with a prophetic temperament to fill the role of a temporal leader; Ahad Ha'am would not abandon this quest, but his hunger for political power now slackened somewhat, without ever being completely sated, during the next few years. To a greater extent than ever before, he insisted that Jewry must proceed with caution in its revival in Zion, and now introduced into the Zionist lexicon the concept of a "spiritual center," an idea he refined after his 1891 trip. Jewry's preparation for redemption would, he concluded, be long, laborious, and analogous to their ancient wanderings in the desert under the watchful eye of Moses. And under such circumstances who was better suited to lead them than the prophet, whose commitment to righteousness never waned and whose zealotry, although excessive in normal times, was precisely what was required at moments of cultural transformation and national reconstruction?

3

A Spiritual Center

The cement which bound them together was a common alienation from existing society, and a common belief in the sovereign efficacy of ideas as shapers of life. They lived precariously suspended as in a void, between an uncomprehending autocratic monarchy above and an uncomprehending, unenlightened mass below. Their mission as independent thinkers was to be critics of the world in which they had no place and prophets of a world that had not yet come into being, and might have no place for them either.

Bertram Wolfe, *Three Who Made a Revolution*

I

Dissatisfied as Ahad Ha'am was with nearly all the groups with which he was associated, most of the people with whom he came into contact, and even the places in which he lived—he heaped scorn on Gopchitse, and hated both London and raw, restive Tel Aviv—his feelings about Odessa were surprisingly warm. "My longing for Odessa," he wrote Rawnitsky from Warsaw in 1896, "and all that I love there is— greater than I could ever have imagined . . ."[1]

There was much about the city that he could have criticized (and sometimes did): its municipal government was dominated by antisemites, the once healthy local economy was in shambles, and it had become a major breeding ground for pogroms; he himself would suffer a beating in 1907. But as an intellectual center, he found it extraordinary: not only did many of his most devoted followers live here but so did his most compelling and influential ideological opponents, Dubnow and Lilienblum. Together they helped fashion one of the most fertile intellectual circles in modern Jewry.

On one level, this was an unlikely Jewish intellectual center. Odessa had long been an important center for the institutions of the East European Haskalah, and its modern Jewish schools, synagogues, newspapers, and publishers were among the best in the Pale. But even local maskilim tended to look elsewhere, typically to Vilna, "the Jerusalem of Lithuania"—with its venerable tradition of rabbinic learning—for ideological direction and expertise. They viewed their own city as relatively comfortable, rich, politically benign (until the 1880s), and institutionally vibrant but obsessed by commerce. Jewish life in Odessa was dominated by the grain trade rather than by scholarship or culture. "A city of life," is what Ahad Ha'am's friend, Elhonan Levinsky, called it in an 1896 essay, and he described it as characterized by hedonism, rapaciousness, and indifference to learning. Its cafes and upper-middle-class salons were full, he said, whereas its libraries were almost empty.[2]

Since the 1860s in particular Odessa had been a lodestone for maskilic provincials eager to attend its secondary schools or the New Russia University founded in 1865. Some like Asher Ginzberg had simply been attracted to a larger community of like-minded intelligentsia. That they made up a tiny proportion of the city's Jewish community (numbering 52,000 in 1873) did not particularly concern them: more importantly, they managed to establish, albeit at the margins of this bustling and none-too-reflective port city, a richly variegated maskilic culture. Some were employed by the Jewish community's schools or organizations; several were paid functionaries of the Hovevei Zion, which remained based there even after Pinsker's death. They encountered little opposition from traditional Jewish forces whose influence in the city was muted, but were by no means insulated from the poverty of the Pale (especially at the city's edges there were slums with large numbers of impoverished Jews) or its officially sanctioned indignities.[3]

By the early 1890s, local maskilic nationalists emerged as a particularly vocal group. There were no more than a dozen or so in their inner circle;

when by 1910 five or six of them had moved from the city, Ahad Ha'am observed sadly in a letter that the Odessa he had so loved had disappeared. What singled out the intellectuals with whom he felt closest (not all of whom were either Hebraists or Palestinophiles) was their commitment to a nationalist agenda predicated upon the creation of a thoroughly integrated Jewish identity—one that was natural, unselfconscious, and all-embracing. Theirs was a contentious yet surprisingly congenial and self-important group. Frequently it acted as if its internal disputes—debates conducted between friends over tea which often spilled onto the pages of *Voskhod, Ha-Melitz,* and other Jewish periodicals—represented the most important and emblematic differences among the Jewish people as a whole. Dubnow, for instance, would speak of the Western as opposed to the Eastern camp of Jewish political thinking, when what he was describing was an ideological debate between himself and his friend Ahad Ha'am. Mostly self-taught, intellectually prodigious, and obsessed with the need to salvage as much as could be legitimately saved from the wreckage of traditional East European Jewish life, they confronted contemporary Jewish affairs with a rare degree of erudition, moral earnestness, and urgency.[4]

They felt themselves to be at the cutting edge of Jewish politics, even if they remained rather marginal to the Jewish communal affairs of the city. The central issue for this maskilic circle was the prospect of Jewish renewal whether in Palestine or in Europe as Dubnow would eventually promote in his call for a diaspora-based Jewish nationalism. Without doubt, they were blessed with extraordinary talent. Ahad Ha'am, Dubnow, Mendele Mocher Seforim, and Lilienblum, all figures of distinction and achievement, occupied its core. Bialik—congenial, moody, and expansive—also actively participated, and though not one of its commanding figures (he tended to defer to others, especially Ahad Ha'am), he was recognized quite early as a literary talent. Others, including Zalman Epstein, Rawnitsky, Mordecai Rabinowitch (Ben Ami), and Levinsky, although less influential Hebrew literary figures, were lively intellectuals of a special mold: enlightened yet without any true kinship (and, in the case of Ben Ami, with intense antipathy) toward the larger non-Jewish world; ex-yeshiva students or hasidim whose very cadence in Russian, the language typically used by this circle, was informed by a rich traditional background that they never managed—nor wished—to reject.

Take, for example, Frankfeld: described in Tchernowitz's memoirs as "stub-nosed, with a loose beard and tangled hair that never saw a comb," he spoke incessantly, and still acted much as he had as a hasidic youth, though his conversations were now sprinkled with quotations from his beloved literary critic Dmitri Pisarev and Tolstoy as well as the mystical Kabbalah and rabbinic literature. "He was able," says Tchernowitz, "to speak for hours and he would move from the Bible to the prophets, from the prophets to the Talmud and Zohar . . . and would connect them with Darwin, Buckle, and Spencer, along with the rabbis of the Aggadah and Midrash."[5]

At the margins of the commercial center in which they lived, they constructed a congenial subculture with its own salons (at Dubnow's or Mendele's; the Bnei Moshe continued to hold meetings at Ahad Ha'am's), journals (*Pardes* and later *Ha-Shiloach* were essentially house organs of Odessa's Palestinophile nationalists), and synagogues (Odessa's Yavneh synagogue was, at least for a time, their favorite).[6] They even vacationed together. Dubnow described a summer evening in a cottage outside Odessa spent in

drinking wine, . . . lively conversation, and singing folksongs. Mendele was full of energy. He reminisced and came up with some original ideas. [Simon] Frug sang a hasidic parody beautifully. Ben Ami, who felt peaceful that night, sang a sad hasidic tune and we all sang with him. The Jewish folksongs echoed through the sleepy German colony, and we had the resounding waves of the sea for accompaniment. We all felt so good that night, all of us who are so sad, so worried, and so oppressed by our troubles and by the troubles of our people.[7]

This was the closest that Ahad Ha'am himself would come to the "spiritual center" he espoused in his Palestinophile ideology. Odessa, or at least the small, marginal, culturally fertile corner of it that he came to know best and to dominate, represented for him an inspiration, a lifelong and abiding model. It is ironic, of course, that this spiritual center was formed on foreign soil. He and his friends would later reconstruct what was a vaguely similar community in Tel Aviv in the last years of his life; but it too was modeled, and with considerable self-awareness on the part of its founders, after Odessa, the acknowledged precedent. In 1908, when the original circle had mostly dispersed, Ahad Ha'am remarked in a letter written from his new home in London to Dubnow, who now lived in St. Petersburg where he felt uncomfortable, that all of their old circle were somehow "out of tune" with the present. It was all the more necessary, mused Ahad Ha'am, to find for themselves a "sphere" (sevivah) of some sort that would serve to complement rather than conflict with their work: In other words, for all of them to move once again to an urban center putting an end to their dispersal, "with some of us in the west and others in the east. Sometimes on sleepless nights, I dream of a literary center (naturally in Palestine) in which the remnants will be gathered together which will provide us with that opportunity to live our lives in ways that are natural to us."[8]

The greater irony was not that he would, despite his clearly stated convictions, encounter this sort of community only in the diaspora; it is hardly surprising since he lived the bulk of his life outside Palestine. But, arguably, only in Odessa could this particular symbiosis of Judaism and modernity occur. What served to animate the cultural lives of his Odessa circle was the way in which—and only for the relatively brief period between the late 1880s and the turn of the century—a variety of intellectual, cultural and political factors coalesced there: Jewish and non-Jewish, political and literary, local and more generally Russian. These influences combined to set the stage for what Ahad Ha'am would contend was the quintessence of Jewish modernity. Crucial in this regard was the interplay between this urban culture's long-standing tradition of relative freedom (particularly from Jewish traditionalists) and the increasingly oppressive local government that served to undercut the aspirations of Odessa's Jewish liberals. No less important was the way in which Odessa constituted a haven for someone like Asher Ginzberg— steeped as he was in Jewish tradition and hungry to escape its constraints but without traducing those elusive boundaries that (as he was convinced) separated Judaism from the larger cultural world. Odessa was a natural setting for experimentation and still a place where he knew that he continued to be seen, and to a large extent also continued to be hated, as a Jew. Odessa reinforced the belief that national identity was self-evident: permanent, secure, but also by no means immutable in its essential form. Shtetl culture was sufficiently distant to be rendered unoppressive yet close enough (just across town in the southern reaches of suburban Moldavanka) to serve as a nearly constant reminder of its wretched shortcomings, its vulnerability and needs.

Theirs then was a culture fashioned by the interplay between oppression and freedom, immersion in Jewish culture and the sudden, recent, mostly self-taught discovery of a larger but still suspiciously alien, anti-Jewish world. In Odessa they could live at the fringes of Jewry but still not far from it and its miseries: their haven was, as they sensed, a tenuous one dominated by illiberal local political forces and at the edge of a hateful regime nearing the end of its long, reactionary life. This very tenuousness, however, lent what they wrote, as varied as it was, much of its urgency, its willingness to confront Jewish problems in a manner that was both comprehensive and self-confident and with an overriding conviction in its essential Jewish authenticity.

Ahad Ha'am had his most fertile and important exchanges with Dubnow and Lilienblum, the two men in this circle who most vigorously disagreed with him. Their polemics were conducted in full public view through articles and books produced over the course of some two decades. Both Dubnow's seminal statement of diaspora nationalism, *Pis'ma o starom i novom evreistve* (*Letters on Old and New Judaism*), and the essays republished in the first two volumes of Ahad Ha'am's *Al Parashat Derakhim* (1895 and 1904) were the products of their prolonged dialogue that provided the basis for Jewish nationalist discourse.[9]

Dubnow would come to be one of Ahad Ha'am's closest friends. Their relationship, although always somewhat stiff and correct, was one of the very few that Ahad Ha'am enjoyed with an equal: his lifelong friend Rawnitsky tended to defer to him; Bialik literally worshipped him. Ahad Ha'am's later friendship with the Berlin-based Hebraic scholar Shimon Bernfeld (which eventually soured), even at its most intimate, lacked the polemical edge and intensity of his relationship with Dubnow. It is impossible to understand each of their contributions to Jewish nationalism, particularly in their Odessa years, without reference to this friendship.

Their first meeting in 1891 about a year after Dubnow's move to Odessa, was friendly if inconclusive. They quickly learned that they had much in common. Dubnow, erudite and self-taught, was the scion of a well-pedigreed Belorussian rabbinic family and, like Ahad Ha'am, he had long ago thrown off the yoke of traditional Judaism. By the time they met, Dubnow, then thirty-one years old, was already a regular contributor to the respected St. Petersburg Russian-Jewish monthly, *Voskhod*. His politics were liberal and his attitude toward Jewish nationalism equivocal, though under Ahad Ha'am's influence he would modify his ideas considerably over the next few years. He had heard of the hasidic-like circle surrounding Ahad Ha'am—this is how he refers to it in his autobiography—and distrusted it, but nonetheless found its leader to be impressive. Their conversation was far ranging: they spoke of European classics and about the texts that Dubnow was then examining in preparation for his pioneering social history of hasidism, and Ahad Ha'am astonished him by demonstrating his deep familiarity with this literature.

Their first meeting, however, did not cement their friendship; Dubnow admits that he remained wary of Ahad Ha'am's reputation as a leader of a cadre of worshipful and secretive men and kept his distance.[10]

Perhaps some of this awkwardness, which persisted for several years, had something to do with the fact that their meeting followed in the wake of an exceptionally heated and rather embarrassing literary encounter. When they met Dubnow had recently published a review in *Voskhod* of two publications—the Bnei Moshe's *Kaveret* (the group's connection to it was unascribed, of course) and *La Gerbe,* published by *Archives Israélites.* Dubnow's criticisms of the former were withering. Though designed to showcase the best Russian Jewish nationalist talent—Ahad Ha'am had no fewer than three pieces in it—Dubnow described it as provincial and narrowly conceived and thought it promoted an image of Judaism inferior to that presented in the expansive, universalistic *La Gerbe.* In particular he castigated Lilienblum who inexplicably affirmed in *Kaveret* the archaic strictures of the guide to traditional Jewish practice, the *Shulchan Arukh,* a surprising reversal of his formerly enlightened maskilic commitments. Ahad Ha'am's essays, Dubnow felt, were vague and surprisingly pessimistic for a supporter of Jewish nationalism.[11] Dubnow's contrast between the cultivation of the politically free Western Jew and the civic as well as moral subjugation of those of the East especially enraged and also probably bruised Ahad Ha'am, who was sensitive to the charge that his Hebraist entourage had not transcended their cloistered pasts. Dubnow had no way of knowing that Ahad Ha'am had edited the journal, which listed Lilienblum's home as its editorial address, and paid publication costs.

Ahad Ha'am's reply in "Avdut be-tokh herut" ("Slavery in Freedom,") employed for the first time a technique that would prove to be one of his trademarks: in his defense of what was, in fact, a small, dissident subsection of the Jewish nationalist movement, he acted as if he was defending the good name of the entire Hovevei Zion whose integrity, he claimed, had been challenged by Dubnow:

The opponents of the Hovevei Zion writing in Russian [in the Jewish press] think that they have no more formidable weapons at their disposal than the same ones that they used when they fought the battle for "enlightenment" against the "obscurantists." That is to say, instead of examining and proving us wrong on the basis of arguments drawn from facts and reason, they think that they can discredit us by an array of distinguished names; they think that they can frighten us by pointing out how drastically we differ from our Western brethren and from the Jewish thinkers of Western Europe. They forget that their new opponents include many who are familiar with Western culture and who are aware that even professors sometimes make mistakes and even members of academies have been known to cling to obsolete beliefs.[12]

"Slavery in freedom" is, he said, the most apt way to describe the condition of *La Gerbe*'s contributors, the cream of French Jewry, so unperceptively celebrated by Dubnow but who were, in fact, a sadly disquieted and perplexed lot. Their assertions that the French Revolution was sacrosanct and Jewish peoplehood (as opposed to religion) without real relevance were belied, Ahad Ha'am detected, by their thinly veiled but still resilient Jewish ethnic-cultural attachments. These remained evident despite their hollow protestations. Western Jews were unable to acknowledge such feelings for fear of looking unpatriotic; they were forced to sacrifice their authenticity as Jews for the sake of emancipation. What Dubnow mistakenly identified as "spiritual exaltation" was self-denial—an abiding, raw fear: "We hear cries of defeat, not calls of triumph, . . . an undercurrent of grief and a dark thread of lamentation."[13]

Fear of antisemitism, the need to hide their undeniable Jewishness—indeed, to obscure all that was instinctive and authentic—was the terrible price that they paid for their so-called freedom: "Try as they will to smother [their Jewish feelings], seek as they will for ways to deceive the world and themselves, these live on; resent it as they will, it is a force that is at the very center of their very being."[14]

He concludes with a powerful attack on Jewry's antinationalists and on the legacy of emancipatory haskalah with its belief in diaspora-based rapprochement with the gentile world. The passage is ironic, passionate, and as emphatic as anything he would ever write:

Today . . . I try to give my weary eyes a moment's rest from the sight of ignorance, of degradation, of terrible poverty that confronts me here [in Russia], and I find comfort across the border where one can find Jewish professors, Jewish members of Academies, Jewish officers in the army, Jewish civil servants. And there I see, behind the glory and grandeur, a twofold . . . slavery—moral slavery and intellectual slavery—and ask myself: Do I envy these fellow Jews of mine their emancipation? I answer, in all truth and sincerity, no! a thousand times no! no! . . . I may not be emancipated but at least I have not sold my soul for emancipation. I can at least proclaim from the rooftops that I love my people no matter where they happen to live, without being constrained to find some forced and unsatisfactory excuses for my feelings. I can recall Jerusalem at times other than those of "divine service" . . . without fear of being asked what Zion is to me or me to Zion. I at least have no need to exalt my people to Heaven, to proclaim its superiority above all the other nations in order to find some justification for its existence. I at least know "why I remain a Jew" or, rather, why I find no meaning in such a question, any more than if I were asked why I remain my father's son. I at least can speak my mind regarding the beliefs and opinions that I have inherited from my ancestors without the fear that the bond that unites me to my people will snap. I can even embrace that "scientific heresy which bears the name of Darwin" without any danger to my Judaism. In a word, I am my own person, and my opinions are my own. I have no reason for concealing or denying them, for deceiving others or myself. And this spiritual freedom—scoff who will!—I would not exchange for all the emancipation in the world.[15]

Dubnow had obviously touched a raw nerve and Ahad Ha'am responded in an unusually declamatory manner. Neither man moved in the other's direction at this point and they continued to speak past one another for several years. By the late 1890s, Dubnow would come to express considerably greater sympathy for Jewish nationalism; Ahad Ha'am had by then emerged as the most vocal opponent of Herzlian Zionism within the nationalist camp and isolated himself from his erstwhile supporters who tended to support Herzl at first despite many private misgivings. It was in these years, as we shall see, that each began to exert a decisive influence on the development of their respective nationalist ideologies.

Lilienblum, as Ahad Ha'am said upon hearing of his death in 1910, was "the most formidable and important of my opponents, and nearly all my communal and literary work is connected to him."[16] In contrast to Dubnow, who would eventually emerge as something of an ally, Lilienblum remained an ideological foe, a relentless and subtle critic of Ahad Ha'am to the end. Yet, a strong bond of sorts existed between the two: Ahad Ha'am mused, upon hearing news of his illness a few weeks before Lilienblum's death, that his feelings toward him constituted proof of the attraction of opposites, an attraction that was no less profound—he claimed this on the basis of the recent findings of psychologists—than ties between similar sorts of people. On another occasion, he recalled with amusement the shock of a provincial maskilic nationalist who stopped at the Odessa office of the Hovevei Zion and spotted Lilienblum and Ahad Ha'am chatting quietly beside a corner window. After having followed their disputes in the Hebrew press for so many years he had assumed they were mortal enemies, which in the early 1890s they clearly were.[17]

Many of the issues they raised in their polemics are prefigured in their first published exchange, Lilienblum's reply to "Lo zeh ha-derekh." Lilienblum began by observing that for some time the Jewish press had been inundated by articles about the meager impact of Jewish nationalism on the Yishuv. Despite six years of activity, only nine colonies had been established with a population of a mere three hundred families, most of which were still being supported by Rothschild. In Ahad Ha'am's article he proposes that the Hovevei Zion refocus its attention away from colonization and toward the revival of the nationalist sentiments of the Jewish people which have declined since they were at their height in the first temple period.[18]

Lilienblum contends that not only are these recommendations impracticable but they are also based on an altogether inaccurate reading of Jewish history: the national ties that Ahad Ha'am celebrates for being historically crucial to Jewish existence were never a significant feature; indeed, he argued (betraying his continued debt to Russian nihilist Pisarev) they are not characteristic of any human society. Collective ties are the exception not the rule, and the Jewish past was dominated, as the Bible vividly demonstrates, by tribal jealousies, strife, petty hatreds. During certain fleeting moments such as the reigns of David and Solomon "there emerged even among [the Jews] a national consciousness and they came to see themselves as a single nation." That consciousness ended abruptly, though, with the death of these extraordinary monarchs.[19]

Moreover, inasmuch as general rules can be formulated about Jewish spiritual or ethical conduct based upon the past (the assumption at the heart of "Lo zeh ha-derekh"), the only conclusion that can be drawn is that Jews, or anyone else, are incapable of commitment outside of the context of concrete action. If Jewish spiritual life can be characterized by anything in particular, then ever since Moses received the commandments on Mt. Sinai and his people declared "We shall do and obey," it has been clear that for Jews belief is simply a by-product of concrete activity. To cut off their spiritual reeducation from the actual rebuilding of Zion, as Lilienblum claims Ahad Ha'am wishes to do, is inconsistent with the natural, time-honored inclinations of the Jewish people.[20]

What was it that really prompted Jews to settle in Palestine in recent times? It was not the nationalist sentiments that Ahad Ha'am mentions, but rather untrue rumors of grand schemes like the sort surrounding Lawrence Oliphant, the English mystic and adventurer who was purportedly eager to invest millions of pounds in the resettlement of Jews. Most of those already settled were poor, and the poor would continue to be the chief settlers for the foreseeable future. Lilienblum writes with glum resignation; he paints the real and potential colonists in Palestine in drab, uninspired colors. Sadly dispirited as they may be, no prospect remains for the success of Ahad Ha'am's Palestinian colonization schemes. Lilienblum claims that Ahad Ha'am misreads the Jewish past and shows little understanding of human nature, or, for that matter, of politics or the vagaries of the Jewish character.[21]

It was partly in response to Lilienblum's charge that he had nothing positive to offer as a political solution that Ahad Ha'am proposed the idea of a "spiritual center." The idea was first utilized by him in the wake of "Emet me-eretz yisrael" where he had left little room for meaningful action except for whatever technical or financial contributions Western Jews might make to the Jewish nationalist cause. Russian Jews represented, of course, the bulk of his readership and Jewish nationalism's most receptive constituency but could contribute little as pioneers (land was both scarce in Palestine and prohibitively expensive) and even less as politicians (the Hovevei Zion's government-approved charter of 1890 permitted fundraising, not politics). With his idea of a "spiritual center" Ahad Ha'am sought to show that he was more than a mordant critic and that he could make concrete solutions to Jewry's problems.

He drew from the Spencerian French psychologist Frédéric Paulhan who taught—as Ahad Ha'am would later explain in the 1895 introduction to his collected essays—that for both the individual as well as the collective it is inevitable that "a particular spiritual factor in the depths of the soul [gains] predominance over all other affairs, until it succeeds, even imperceptively, in uniting all those around it, in making them subservient to its own purpose, and in changing the character of all of them in accordance with its needs." Such concentration of spirit was a well-known psychological principle; Paulhan's book *L'Activité mentale* sought to substantiate empirically the principle of the concentration of the spirit by tracing it in the biography of Charles Darwin. Ahad Ha'am applauded Paulhan's achievement:

He succeeded in providing a lucid portrait, based on the process of concentration as employed in the life of this great man. And what is possible for the life of a single individual cannot be said to be impossible for the spiritual life of a nation.[22]

Ahad Ha'am first used the idea of a spiritual center in his essay "Even le-matsevah" ("Tombstone," or "Memorial"), a eulogy for Pinsker which appeared soon after his death in 1891 in which Ahad Ha'am intended to clarify Pinsker's legacy. He gave a sympathetic summary of *Autoemancipation* and spoke of Pinsker's subsequent ideological odyssey. Ahad Ha'am revealed that close to the end of Pinsker's life he lost faith that the legalization of the Hovevei Zion would resolve its fundamental problems: Ahad Ha'am's readers were introduced to a Leon Pinsker who sounded in fact very much like the author of "Emet me-eretz yisrael"— who was obsessed with the insurmountable obstacles facing Palestinian Jewry and with the paramount need to revive Jewish national identity. Ahad Ha'am explains how he arrived at these conclusions:

What was left for him to do when experience taught him that it was extremely difficult to put his ideas into practice in [Palestine] and that members of the Hovevei Zion too were "only Jews," [and not yet prepared for nationalist tasks]?[23]

Pinsker therefore concluded—and told Ahad Ha'am on his death-bed—that Zion could only provide in the short run a "secure haven not for Jews but for Judaism." This he characterizes as Pinsker's *tsava'ah leumit* (nationalist testament), as dictated, significantly, to Ahad Ha'am. Given both the content and the timing of the essay it represented Ahad Ha'am's way of putting himself forward—albeit still tentatively and with the option to retreat if he met with resistance—as Pinsker's heir as the leader of Jewish nationalism. Never before, though, had his intentions been quite so transparent.[24]

For some time Ahad Ha'am had been moving in the general direction of the idea of a spiritual center. Earlier in "Avar ve-atid" ("Past and Future") he had contended that a preoccupation with the future had always been the hallmark of the Jewish people and that this must now serve to guide Jewish nationalists who held their people's destiny in their hands. Indeed, the reason why the Jews had not succumbed to the "verdict of history" and disappeared like other ancient nations was because of the way in which an image of the future had remained at the center of their national consciousness. This was responsible for their survival when other nations, even those with more brilliant pasts, had perished.

By way of example he argued that the observance of rabbinic ritual, while often credited with sustaining Jewry, had done so only in the most limited sense: ironically, it was not the laws that Jews actually obeyed but those that they did not that served to ensure the continued existence of the Jewish people. These were the laws bearing on future life in Palestine and which had no real applicability to Jewish existence in the diaspora, while serving to reinforce faith in the future.

Such precedents, he argued, should help point in the direction of the current political tasks of the Jewish people: consistent with the way in which Jewish existence had always been nurtured by the people's ability to rally their spirit, this trait must be reinvigorated in anticipation of the time when Jews would be prepared and objective conditions (in Palestine and elsewhere) would be suitable for a thoroughgoing return to Zion. This resurgence constituted a renewal of what had been the spiritual politics employed by Jews through the ages: his tactics, he believed, possessed authenticity and proven effectiveness.[25]

How the growth of a "spiritual center" would counteract the assimilatory trends threatening the Jewish people he explained in "Hikkui ve-hitbolelut" ("Imitation and Assimilation"). All social life was the product of imitation; the way in which social forces were molded into coherent units resulted from their attraction to "some center . . . which thus becomes the single or chief object of universal imitation." Imitation of this sort was an inevitable and healthy feature of society. Assimilation was not the same; when imitation degenerated into "self-effacement" and natural inclinations were repressed, assimilation occurred. Drawing on the mechanistic terminology of Herbert Spencer, Ahad Ha'am explained that "it is not imitation as such that leads to assimilation. The real cause is the original self-effacement that results in assimilation through the medium of imitation."

Once applied to nations, he continued, cultural submergence could be avoided by an essential action: to encourage nations to "love themselves." Self-love would reinvigorate innate strengths and Jews would achieve renewed self-confidence and national vitality. True, in recent times the ability to renew themselves had been weakened, but this talent was not yet lost. Even a movement like Reform Judaism, flawed though it was, and despite its public statements, continued to embody in its affirmation of a Jewish "mission" a semblance of national longing. It was apparent, then, that widespread Jewish assimilation was unlikely since even the least nationalistic Jews retained at least some collective commitment. If current trends were left unchecked, however, they could produce a permanent fragmentation of the Jewish people, rendering Western and Eastern Jews into discrete entities—with their distinct rites, aspirations, and character—and comparable in this respect to the lost tribes of ancient Israel.[26]

A spiritual center was therefore crucial. In the past, he argued— attempting to usurp one of Lilienblum's arguments—outstanding kings (David or Solomon) had succeeded in creating around themselves, by virtue of their military prowess or brilliance, an inspirational icon for their nation. In the current absence of comparable leaders, a geographically coherent center was all the more necessary so that Jews could reclaim their fragmented allegiances and redevelop their national individuality:

Today, in [Jewry's] old age, neither strength nor wisdom nor even wealth will succeed in creating a center anew. And so all those who desire to see the nation reunited will be compelled, despite themselves, to bow before historical necessity and to turn toward the east, to the land that was our center and our essential framework in ancient times.[27]

Hence it was assimilation, not antisemitism, that threatened the Jewish people most compellingly; it threatened not only Western Judaism but all Jews, even in the cloistered, seemingly timeless confines of the Russian Pale. The decline of the theological foundations of Judaism (inevitable but as yet unacknowledged by most Jews in the East), the loss of the best minds to gentile culture, and the fragmentation of the Jewish world in the wake of emancipation—all these had already done their part in disfiguring West European Jewish life and their impact would not stop there. Hovevei Zion, as Ahad Ha'am understood it, represented the natural heir to the legacy of the Jewish people—the focal point of Jewish identity in a world where both the refusal to assimilate outside influences and an unchecked readiness to do so would result in precipitous, perhaps permanent national decline. It was essential, then, to create a Palestinian spiritual center that would in turn establish the basis for a rich and variegated modern national Jewish culture.

The relationship between this emergent Jewish culture and religion was one in which the former usurped the outdated role of the latter (although Ahad Ha'am obscured this point because of his political designs). His espousal of the need for a spiritual revival had attracted to his banner some religious nationalists from the Hovevei Zion who preferred to overlook or reinterpret the secular underpinnings of his nationalist ideology; Bialik had managed to do so in Volozhin. Nor did Ahad Ha'am flaunt his irreligion: when he first moved to Odessa, he attended the Yavneh synagogue for a short while; but even afterwards, he remained discreet in his secularism. His many years at Gopchitse had taught him to be circumspect about the expression of radical ideas of any sort, especially religious ones.[28]

He had believed at first that it was possible to attract Jewish nationalists from all sectors of the community, including the traditionalist sector, to the Bnei Moshe. This was not because he shared a vision of a pluralistic Judaism whose future would be determined, more or less equally, by both religious and irreligious forces. Nationalism, not religion, was the original and thus the essential bulwark of Judaism; that this had altered at some time in the Jewish past was a consequence of exile and dispersion—of the inability of post-exilic Judaism to revive its national consciousness after the destruction of the first temple. Now that Judaism had the opportunity to return to its original cultural foundations in Palestine, the dominant role played by religion in Jewry's exilic past was nearing its end. The religious sentiments of the past obviously would have to be treated with respect, particularly since they contributed in one measure or another to the eventual redefinition of Judaism. In the end, however, these traditions were certain to be surpassed by more relevant, authentic, and compelling forms.

His affirmation in "Lo zeh ha-derekh" that the land had become "the goal of our hope, our people, the anchor of our faith" represented, then, a challenge of the first order to traditional Judaism. This challenge went far beyond the Haskalah's attempt to reconcile religion and the demands of contemporary life and envisioned a transcendence of religious Judaism with the revival of the Holy Land as the primary focal point of Jewish aspirations. The Haskalah had historicized religious rituals. What Ahad Ha'am claimed was more radical: that religion's prominence had always been provisional, a notable but by no means abiding detour in Jewry's passage through time.

The union in the Hovevei Zion of secularists and religious had been a marriage of convenience from the outset. The secularists assumed the movement's helm and saw pious Jews mainly as foot soldiers—as supporters and financial contributors, not the ones who would determine the movement's direction. To be sure, religious Jews recognized that the secularists possessed crucial skills—knowledge of European languages, modern sophistication, greater technical expertise—which is why they, however grudgingly, supported Pinsker; the good bourgeois doctor was seen by them as a skilled and devoted messenger to the larger world. The traditional Jewish belief in messianism meanwhile made the bulk of religious Jewry unsympathetic to Jewish nationalism, which they viewed as a usurpation of the role of the divine. This same messianism sharpened the receptivity of a minority of traditional Jews to calls for the rebuilding of Zion whose productivization—as spearheaded by the nationalists— they applauded as strengthening the Holy Land.[29]

Relations in the nationalist camp between religious and irreligious devotees were further reinforced by the belief, shared by most of the movement's maskilic leadership, that if the revival of Zion were feasible it demanded the participation of all sectors of the Jewish people. (One new recruit to the Warsaw branch recalled how he and his brother members, the first Bnei Moshe members in the city, translated their commitments at first into renewed religious observance: "We wished 'to go to the people' and didn't know how. We decided that we had to begin with absolute religious punctiliousness. We went daily to synagogue to pray, we wore ritual undergarments, we did not eat with an uncovered head, we recited the blessings after the meals, etc. . . .") More broadly, though, animated as Jewish nationalism was by populist sentiments, it was encouraged to stress how it epitomized the national urges of the *folk;* and even its least traditionally oriented recognized that if only for the sake of the credibility of the movement they could not ignore the vast number of traditional Russian Jews. The affiliation of a broad cross-section of Jews was deemed crucial by both religious and secular na-tionalists to reinforce their ideological standing as the natural heirs to rabbinic Judaism's legacy and for the sake of Jewish nationalism's fi-nancial viability and political influence.[30]

The terms that the maskilic leadership used to describe the nationalist enterprise drew extensively on Judaism's messianic arsenal. As Eli Le-derhendler has perceptively observed,

their argument represented a post-traditional celebration of tradition, not so much as a way of life for the contemporary Jew but as a national asset that ought not be heedlessly squandered.[31]

Already in the 1870s Peretz Smolenskin spoke of Jewry's "life spirit" as its bulwark of survival. Such concepts, says Lederhendler, served to link nascent nationalism with higher purposes and established a "living tradition" for the movement, at least retrospectively. They substantiated its moral claim to leadership which might otherwise have appeared as sheer hubris, given the movement's actual size, the inexperience of most of its leaders, and their modest standing.[32]

By the time that Ahad Ha'am's "Lo zeh ha-derekh" had appeared, religious Jews were accustomed to maskilic nationalists supporting the Jewish nationalist case by using borrowed religious terms. Such acqui-escence may well have created the impression that they were unaware of how traditional categories were being expropriated and secularized. And when they finally did object, their reaction was particularly surprising since their opponents were convinced by then that they were a neutral-ized, spent political force.

Ahad Ha'am had put great efforts into avoiding conflict with traditionalists—the Bnei Moshe required its members, at first, to declare their commitment to the religious dictates of Judaism, hence affirming the importance of nationalism as a source of unity in Jewish life. (Of course Ahad Ha'am did the same earlier in his celebration of the maskilic nationalistic Fin.) It seems ironic that when the debate over the role of religion in the Hovevei Zion broke out it was directed at him and the activities of his group. But, as we shall see, the Bnei Moshe represented an unsurprising target, though it was not its work in Eastern Europe that made it suspect as much as its nationalistic-oriented Jaffa school.

Since its opening by the Bnei Moshe in 1893, the school had met with the fury of many Palestinian traditionalists, including some of those who otherwise supported Jewish nationalism. They saw the school as a provocation, an attack on what was widely conceded to be the right of religious Jewry to control the educational life of Jewish Palestine. In such circles it was assumed that even if much of European Jewry was or would soon be lost—swept away in the maelstrom of emancipation, Haskalah, and assimilation—the Holy Land would remain a bastion of piety. The incursion of the Bnei Moshe into Palestine, especially into an educational arena that traditional Jews claimed as their own, called for the strongest condemnation. The Bnei Moshe's school, cosponsored by the Alliance, employed, or so its critics claimed, secularist teachers who were certain to infect students and eventually the entire Holy Land with heresy. None of the Bnei Moshe's other projects had ever encountered a comparable reaction. Earlier the Bnei Moshe had opened schools in Russia and Poland, though it had been careful to concentrate on the mostly marginal sphere of female education (shunned by the region's *melamdim* as tertiary). And of course, the Bnei Moshe had published literature that was provocative from a religious standpoint and it had deftly infiltrated into the very center of the Jewish nationalistic movement in the face of continuing resistance. But never had it faced such concerted opposition.[33]

Relations in Palestine between nationalist pioneers and the so-called old yishuv (the product of East European Jewish immigrants dating back mostly to the mid-nineteenth century) were until then rather congenial, with the term "old yishuv" referring (in the minds of those in the "First Aliyah") to a group of people who were old not chronologically but in terms of their values. At the same time few of the Hovevei Zion settlers were sympathetic to social or political radicalism and, outnumbered as the nationalists were by the old yishuv (as late as 1914 by as many as six to one), conservatism was reinforced. An earlier dispute in 1889–1890 over the observance of the *Shemitah* year (the biblical practice of leaving the land of Palestine dormant every seventh year) was fierce, but instead of dividing strictly along religious lines it divided some religious authorities themselves from other important rabbis such as the nationalist Samuel Mohilever who endorsed a liberal compromise.[34]

True, from the beginning there remained much potential for conflict. Even otherwise religiously sympathetic nationalist pioneers viewed the old yishuv and its center, Jerusalem, as anachronistic; Jaffa (and, eventually, its suburb, Tel Aviv) was the place where forward-thinking Jews could still make their mark. And at the heart of this new, raw, self-consciously antireactionary Jaffa-based culture was the Bnei Moshe-run school, with its nationalist curriculum that included some instruction conducted in Hebrew and emphasized the study of the Bible, Jewish history, and an integrated program of Jewish and secular subjects. Once the dispute erupted it concentrated on the hiring of secularist teachers instead of on the program. They were seen as a competing source of authority in a still mostly homogeneous Yishuv and were attacked as a source of divisiveness, even of anti-Turkish sedition.

Seen broadly, the school and its Bnei Moshe sponsors came to serve as lightning rods attracting tensions that conspired to undermine the rather benign relations between traditionalists and nationalists in Jewish Palestine as well as in Eastern Europe. The legalization of the Hovevei Zion in 1890 by the Russian government meant that leaders could only be selected from Odessa, which undermined their religious competitors in the strongholds of Lithuania and Belorussia. Meanwhile, religious Jewish leaders were concerned about the rumors of the Bnei Moshe's aspirations. But the secretive Bnei Moshe evaded attack and the Hovevei Zion's governmental charter was impervious to change so the school proved an excellent target. The campaign against it was spearheaded by Yehiel Pines who had been fired by Ahad Ha'am in 1891 from the Jaffa office of the Hovevei Zion and stripped of his membership in the Bnei Moshe.

Once launched, the campaign inspired a vast body of antinationalist literature, much of it concentrating on Ahad Ha'am whom it depicted as a dangerous, antireligious force. In one lithograph circulated, for example, in Jerusalem he was shown as a plump, self-possessed bourgeois—the picture scarcely resembled him—and he was posed beside the sham portraits of other Hovevei Zion leaders, Samuel Pinchus Rabinowitch and Nahum Sokolow. Beneath Ahad Ha'am's name on the lithograph was the following: "Over and above them all, directing them like a choirmaster, is the high priest of the well-known society which is rotten to its core, the Bnei Moshe. Isn't this man Ahad Ha'am?"[35]

The document claimed that the three depicted were "responsible for shameful deeds at the expense of the community of Israel. How dare they desecrate the holy city [of Jerusalem]? And put at risk the entire Jewish settlement in the Land [of Israel] . . . ?"[36]

In this and similar broadsides Ahad Ha'am and other leaders were accused of terrible transgressions: Rabinowitch, for instance, dressed as a priest in one attack, was thereby linked to missionary activity, a standard charge in religious, antimaskilic literature. Elsewhere leaders of the Bnei Moshe were shown as Dominicans, as men who devour ritually forbidden foods, as Parisian sinners (the Bnei Moshe had hoped to relocate its center to Paris, a den of radicalism in the minds of many religious Jews, which may have been the background for this particular accusation) or, quite simply, as dogs. The more drastic charges accused them of being engaged in political sedition threatening all Palestinian Jews: as one leaflet affirmed, the patriotism of the vast majority of Palestine's Jews was secure but there were those few in the Bnei Moshe who were capable of the most heinous crimes, not excluding anti-Turkish treachery.[37]

It was announced, for instance, in the traditionalist newspaper *Havazzelet* that "the society's goal is to teach the sons of Judah the ways of war and to introduce them gradually to all sorts of secret and cunning actions until such time that their hearts are filled with rebellion and treachery toward God and King that they (it is only the members of the society of Moses who should be included among these heretics) will rise up and attack the entire religious tradition like the followers of Robespierre in their time!"[38]

In this way the campaign passed from vague if troubling innuendo to charges of treason: in December 1893, an article appeared in Eliezer Ben Yehudah's Jerusalem-based nationalist newspaper *Ha-Zevi* which urged more attention to the festival of Hannukah. The article was denounced by the ultraorthodox (whose conservatism made them distrust any hint of political activism) as a call for rebellion against the Turks. The writer, who was Ben Yehudah's father-in-law, wrote that the ancient Judean hero Judah Maccabee should be seen as someone who taught how to "defend lives, gather together strength and march forward." On the initiative of these detractors, guided it seems by Pines, the Turkish authorities threw Ben Yehudah into jail.

Pines no doubt understood that *Ha-Zevi* was not calling upon Palestinian Jewry to rise up and fight in the tradition of the Maccabees. But his annoyance with the nationalist cause, especially the forces of the Bnei Moshe, was intense and it meshed with his attack on the Jaffa school as he recognized that these forces represented a powerful challenge to traditionalist hegemony. Earlier, the mostly agricultural projects of the Hovevei Zion were not viewed as especially threatening: so long as traditionalist authority in the Holy Land was left unchallenged the work of the Jewish nationalist movement—no doubt the subject of glum disapproval by much of the old yishuv—was tolerated without much disruption. Ahad Ha'am was different: his talk of spiritual renewal, which had so beguiled some of them (including Pines), was now seen as undercutting traditional Judaism—how Jews educated their children, celebrated their festivals, charted their destiny.[39]

Earlier projects of the Bnei Moshe—even those that had seemed at first rather innocent—were now reinterpreted in a new light: Pines, for instance, was aware that the first book financed by the Bnei Moshe was a Russian volume entitled *Khanukah,* which retold the festival's story and affirmed its nationalist centrality. Written by Boris Brandt under the close supervision of Ahad Ha'am, the booklet was launched as the first in a series of publications that would highlight the still-relevant Jewish symbols, despite the waning of religion's hold. Hannukah, it proclaimed, was the nationalist festival par excellence:

Hannukah! So many glorious deeds, so many wonderful memories are associated with it. Next to Passover no other Jewish festival has such profound national-historical meaning. . . . We celebrate not only the consecration and renewal of the temple, some two thousand years ago, . . . but also the renewal and revival of this same Jewish nation, reviving its soul once again for a new life and new and glorious historical activity.[40]

The festival was interpreted, then, as an inspirational tale of Jewry's struggle against the seemingly insurmountable assimilatory forces of Hellenism. Its message was of special significance during what the book called the "third epoch" of Jewish history, following on the heels of the Mosaic and rabbinic ones. Hannukah constituted proof of Jewry's particular genius for survival and renewal:

Matthathias, the Hasmonean, and his five sons, especially his third son Judah, heroes of the most elevated and idealist sort, are rarely found in history and then only when produced by the genius of the Jewish nation.[41]

At the time of its publication, Pines and other religious members of the Bnei Moshe had viewed it as anything but provocative: whatever might have been the author's motives its call for Jews to celebrate Hannukah was seen by the traditionalists as consistent with their own desire to win back as many Jews as possible to the fold. Nor were they put off at first that Ahad Ha'am saw Hannukah as one of a cluster of practices that would survive the waning of religion's role as the defining force in Judaism. Ahad Ha'am had always broached such issues with great care, convinced that an open struggle in a fragile, secularizing Jewry could be disastrous. He believed that change best occurred all-but-imperceptibly, barely recognized even by those most profoundly affected by it.

His opponents forced him to confront the radical implications of his arguments and he found himself attacked within the ranks of the Bnei Moshe itself: its Vilna branch, dominated by religious members, rose up in open rebellion and he reacted by lashing out with uncharacteristic fury.[42] In the past, irony and detachment had served him as the key features of his polemical arsenal; they also lent his essays authority and made them subject to widely differing interpretations. In the articles he wrote during the Jaffa school debate, however, he threw caution to the wind.

He quickly retraced his communal tactics vis-à-vis the religious: as of 1893 he had set his sights on attracting russified, irreligious, even previously "assimilated" Jews to the Bnei Moshe and supported a proposal that the Bnei Moshe drop the clause in its bylaws that members respect dictates of religious Judaism even when they conflict with their inclinations. The discarded clause was itself a modified version of an earlier draft that made members affirm their adherence to the laws of the Torah. In justifying the change, Ahad Ha'am explained that it hindered the recruitment of russified Jews. This signaled his abandonment of the hope to attract more than a handful of them to his group.[43]

On an ideological level, his response was even sharper. "Behold the head of that band, a thinker and philosopher, who says that the destiny of Hovevei Zion is to destroy religion,"[44] remarked one religious nationalist leader upon reading "Torah she-balev" ("Law of the Heart"), Ahad Ha'am's reply to the anti-Bnei Moshe campaign. This reaction was typical and by no means altogether unfair. In that essay he argued more clearly than in anything he had written before that the divide between the way Jews lived in the past and how they would need to construct their future was so vast that it left readers puzzled whether Ahad Ha'am saw a connection at all. Not only was the tone of the piece different from his earlier, more moderate statements but its argument appeared to belie his belief in cultural continuity.

The essay's most radical feature was its attack on the hallowed designation, people of the book. The cultural artifacts of a "normal" people, he claimed, are by-products of their everyday life and these, in effect, are seeds that blossom once circumstances demand. A natural connection exists in such circumstances between society and its fundamental needs and culture. The difference between this healthy scenario and the one that characterizes the experience of a people of the book is vast: in the latter case one's "very soul" is sacrificed to the written word:

> The book ceases to be what it should be, a source of new inspiration and moral strength; on the contrary, its function in life is to weaken and finally to crush all spontaneity of action and emotion, until people become wholly dependent upon the written word and incapable of responding to any stimulus in nature or life without its permission and approval. . . . The people stagnate because heart and mind do not react directly and immediately to external events; the book stagnates because, as a result of this absence of direct reaction, heart and mind do not rise in revolt against the written word at such times when it has ceased to be in harmony with current needs.[45]

Tracing how this stagnation had transpired in Jewish history, Ahad Ha'am found that before exile the Jews were able, like other healthy peoples, to mediate between the demands of law and life. By the end of the second temple period this ability began to break down and their culture started to demonstrate the thin line between spontaneity and an inability to negotiate self-reliance, between a receptiveness to change and belief in the integrity of tradition. Eventually the oral law, which was originally the "inner law, the law of the moral sense," was written down and hopelessly fossilized: "[Jewry's] moral sense was left with only one clear and firm conviction—that of its own utter impatience and its eternal subservience to the written word. Conscience no longer had any authority in its own right; not conscience but the book became the arbiter in every human question."[46]

This criticism went much further, he recognized, than standard, well-rehearsed maskilic diatribes against contemporary rabbinic conservatism. Classically, maskilim had faulted the harshness and insensitivity of individual rabbis for Judaism's internal decay. The problem, he now insisted, had much deeper roots in a system that stifled Jewry's natural inclinations. The Haskalah was incapable of understanding this because its formative ideas were imported from the outside—they were alien to the Jewish consciousness. No solution to this malaise would be possible

until such time that a new and compelling urge for normalization arises among us from within as a result of the demands of our Jewish lives and is communicated to the younger generation through education and literature, so that it might fuse with the humanism of the Haskalah and prevent it from overwhelming and destroying our intrinsically Jewish character.[47]

He identified this "urge" with the Hovevei Zion. It encompassed much more than its name implied: solutions to Jewry's fundamental problems. Above all, the organization's stress on Jewish unity and its belief that universal human values can only be expressed in terms authentic to its people singled it out as the foundation for the renaissance of Judaism. The problem at the essay's core, though, was how Jewish values could be expressed outside the framework of religion. Never was he more explicit on the subject: "Hovevei Zion is not merely a part of Judaism, nor is it something added onto Judaism; it is the whole of Judaism, but with a different focal point."[48]

When this essay was read in conjunction with his "Shete reshuyot" ("Two Masters"), written a year earlier and also in response to the Jaffa school controversy (and probably also the 1891 expulsion of Moscow Jews), its analysis of the withering away of rabbinic Judaism under the influence of nationalism is provided with political, even tactical underpinnings. This horrified and delighted his critics for as Pines explained with the publication of "Shete reshuyot" Ahad Ha'am had finally provided a clear description of the Bnei Moshe's far-ranging aspirations, a blueprint for its plans to transform the Jewish people.[49]

Ahad Ha'am explains at the beginning of the essay—echoing almost word for word Herbert Spencer—that social stability results from the ability to hypnotize individual members to act in compliance with societal needs. Obedience is attained by various imperceptible means— mostly all-but-invisible. Of particular importance are those that can be traced back to the very beginnings of time and which are "handed down from generation to generation without any fundamental change." Hence, the heavy hand of the past exerts an extraordinary influence over everyday life and in ways too elusive for any single individual either to control or understand fully. Ahad Ha'am considers this hold as inevitable but also taxing since

the chief hypnotizers, the all-powerful masters of the individual and society alike, are those of the past . . . , their voices are still obeyed, their commandments are still observed with love and respect, and there exists no man or generation who can say precisely where the dividing line is between himself and them, between his and theirs.[50]

Individuals are normally unaware of this legacy and make their way through life circumscribed by boundaries of which they are, at best, dimly aware, "knowing and feeling nothing of the iron chains by which they are bound." At other times this "spirit of the age" is confronted by new forces and old and new forces are compelled to subsist side by side. They coexist until the potency of the older manifestations diminishes and eventually disappears.[51]

Ideally they must be left to coexist until the vitality of the older, outdated one is spent. This is not inevitable, though. Confrontation between the two is sometimes foisted upon history by virtue of the work of radicals, intent on highlighting social anomalies that are best overlooked. Their meddling—unnecessary, awkward, and unwise even by their own standards—also makes change much more cumbersome:

There is a lesson to be learned here by . . . today's priests who wish to challenge the past: they must try as best as they can, in fact, to put off all open conflict until the impact of their doctrine has been felt, by virtue of work done in secret, and old beliefs have so weakened that they are easily done away with. If this course is not followed . . . they will actually prolong the lifetime of the old beliefs . . . by making society more amenable to conflict.[52]

Such radicals can benefit society to the extent to which they manage to wean themselves of its dominant influences and discern what Ahad Ha'am calls "half-truths," radically new ideas that, although never identical to what will actually transpire, serve to dislodge orthodoxies. True, in the end they are always wrong: the past can never be swept away as decisively as they assume. The future can only emerge in an organic fashion, equally oblivious to the demands of those who try to obstruct it as those who press for rapid change.

Radicals must keep in mind that conservatives cannot dominate indefinitely. Armed with this knowledge, advocates of change should work slowly and secretly. With the passage of time, their enemies will be demoralized, radical ideas will be adapted to meet social needs, the larger population will be sensitized to new ways of living, and the slow, patient, laborious work of a small number of dedicated men will be rewarded. Progress, Ahad Ha'am teaches, is essentially undramatic but it is also irreversible.[53] Although not, perhaps, identical in content to the ringing call for change in "Torah she-balev," "Shete reshuyot" did provide a remarkably candid glimpse of the workings of the Bnei Moshe.

II

Ahad Ha'am published much of his work in the first half of the 1890s, including "Past and Future" and "Two Masters," in *Pardes*. Years later, he said that he had hoped initially that his connection with the new journal would help him to retreat from the political battlefield and to look at Jewish affairs at some remove. Alas, the pressures of the moment had not permitted it. Because the larger world gave him no rest, even the essays that he sent to *Pardes,* he explains, were engaged, politically charged, and (as he hints broadly) less reflective than they might otherwise have been.[54]

He failed to acknowledge—even in this letter, written in 1907—that his association with *Pardes* was itself a consequence of his role as a political leader. Not only was it edited by his Bnei Moshe brother Rawnitsky (at first Ahad Ha'am had planned to edit it) but it was secretly sponsored by Ahad Ha'am's group. His articles in the journal were, as much as almost anything else he wrote since 1889, part of an effort to disseminate the ideas of the Bnei Moshe beyond its rather small membership. Even though his pieces in these years mostly polemicized with such now-arcane bodies as the Argentinian-bound Jewish Colonization Association, they still retain much of their freshness, testimony to their considerable intellectual rigor and breadth. But when they were written, the last thing on their author's mind was philosophical distance; these were political documents, albeit nuanced and sophisticated ones.

One example is "Hatsi nehama" ("Some Consolation"), published in *Ha-Melitz* in September/October 1892 and structurally similar to those that appeared in his *Pardes* column. Its subject is the revival of anti-Jewish blood accusations (which charged Jews with the use of Christian blood for ritual purposes); naturally he saw the revival of such charges as abominable and distressing. His real concern is not the accusation itself but Jewish responses to it (as well as other antisemitic attacks) and what it reveals about them.

The persistence into the nineteenth century of antisemitism is unsurprising; the emancipation of Jews was foisted upon communities that were unprepared for attitudinal changes of such magnitude. Despite the periodic resurgence of antisemitism, he writes, its virulence will dissipate with time and with the weakening of the social forces that have sustained it. But apologetic literature that sees antisemitism as an artificial growth, as alien to the newly enlightened Europe, is deluded. It is Jewish emancipation that is artificial, whereas antisemitism is only a natural reaction, consistent with the ethos of a larger society that, despite the public statements of its elites, remains inimical to Jews.[55]

In this way, Ahad Ha'am managed to subvert a seminal body of Jewish apologetics, literature that was not merely useless but deeply troubling: it was, then, the excessive preoccupation that Jews have with contemporary antisemitism that implied that there was something in the charges leveled by antisemites that touched the souls of modern Jews and made them react with indignation and—more importantly—with barely disguised shame. It is ironic, comments Ahad Ha'am, that earlier in Jewish history when comparable accusations would have been immeasurably more threatening to Jewry's well-being than they are now, responses to them were much more sensible and balanced, and in keeping with the actual character of the threat. Ahad Ha'am suggests that this is true because the antisemitic canards of the past did not produce shame in Jews who saw them as the accusations of inferiors whose views did not disturb their own self-image as chosen by God. Jews today feel no comparable distance between themselves and the sentiments of the larger world so its view of them hurts them in ways previously inconceivable. They are incapable of dismissing antisemitic accusations that now fester in their minds; they cannot help but see some of these charges as more than absurd, even persuasive: "There is nothing more dangerous for either a nation or an individual than to plead guilty to imaginary sins."[56]

For this reason the blood accusation can constitute a curious but essential source of consolation. Here is one charge that all Jews must recognize as false. Nonetheless non-Jews continue to consider it credible, which should serve to remind an otherwise insecure Jewry that here, as with much else that the world teaches about it, false and baseless accusations are ranked as true. "'Is it possible that everybody can be wrong and the Jews right?'" he asks. "Yes it is possible; the blood accusation proves it."[57]

This was a remarkable performance. He took on a vast, much-prized literature whose professed intent had been to console Jews threatened by antisemitism. He shows that just under the surface it reveals a fundamental flaw in the very people it seeks to defend: in fact, the real needs that it addresses are not the same as those that superficially preoccupy it. The sweep of the essay is itself extraordinary: in a very brief piece he manages to range across medieval as well as modern responses to catastrophe and to challenge the fundamental underpinnings of Jewish self-perceptions about disaster. It is simultaneously an exercise in subversion and mordant inspiration.

By this time he had perfected a distinct discursive style. His articles, like most of those in *Pardes,* began with a general observation from recent scientific or philosophical literature. He particularly liked using either Thomas Hobbes or Darwin. This approach served, Alan Mintz suggests, to disabuse his maskilic readers of some of their fundamental rationalist assumptions. Once this was done, says Mintz, "we [were] in his hands. It is in a classic sense a coup in which the old order is suddenly overthrown and we are thrust into the hands of the new regime."[58]

In these essays, built as most were around the tension between two concepts (priest and prophet, sacred and profane, imitation and assimilation, positive and negative), he traced the meanings of these dualities in the past and present. He cited scientific literature throughout, mainly to establish his authority but also to provide for a constituency hungry for knowledge of the larger world with information they would likely deem worthy. The presentation of this broader knowledge alone in a style that was both lucid and richly textured served to distinguish him from run-of-the-mill maskilic scribblers. Only at the end of his articles would he relate his larger lessons to Jewish history: "No new structures are presented, elaborated or refined; rather, all that has already been shown to be true about nature and man is now transferred and applied to the Jewish sphere," observes Mintz who suggests this as one of the truly distinctive features of his essays: by the time he turned to specifically Jewish concerns he did so with the full weight of Western knowledge behind him.[59]

In "Le-toledot ha-hiyyuv ve-hashelilah" ("Positive and Negative"), for example, he starts with a social Darwinian portrait of struggle and aggression, one that constitutes, he says, the essential fabric of human society: "Even when the world as a whole is at peace, there is no rest or peace for its inhabitants." Peace is the name given to "continuous, gradual development." Struggles between old and new forces are almost always invisible; only at rare moments are such battles apparent even to the combatants. New systems appear almost always only in the "minds of a select few." They serve to generate new ideas that coalesce into full systems—the lodestones of what he calls "new positive principles." Naturally some opposition to what currently exists occurs, producing its own reaction that intensifies once newer forces grow in power and prestige. It is typical, though, for the opposition to deny that it has any intention of garnering power for itself; indeed it is often unaware that precisely this is taking place.[60]

In describing how new social forces respond (with both shock and genuine disbelief) at the charges leveled against them by the establishment, he recalls accusations made against him and the Bnei Moshe:

At first, the disciples of the new teaching are astonished at the accusations being made against them, namely that they are attempting to overthrow established principles, and they protest bitterly that such thoughts had never entered into their minds. And they are altogether sincere since their aim was neither to add nor take anything away. Intent upon such tasks, they tend to overlook the degree to which negation is a part of their program which they seek to keep hidden from others and even from themselves.[61]

Such battles extend over many years with each side advancing somewhat and then losing momentum. Eventually the shortcomings of the newer forces are subjected to scrutiny, bolstering the confidence of the conservatives, says Ahad Ha'am. But reaction can gain only a limited influence before it is forced into retreat. Out of an excruciating and lengthy process, a social composite drawing both on new and old forces emerges in the end. Radical change is thus instigated, while a return to the ways of the past is inconceivable. Judaism, Ahad Ha'am says, underwent something similar during the last century when the Haskalah challenged the self-sufficiency of traditional Judaism. Enlightened Jewish critics of Judaism insisted upon too drastic a break from the patterns of the past and they proved themselves incapable of nurturing the sort of "positive national conceptions" crucial for a people's national spirit. This left many Jews dissatisfied and prepared to embrace again, albeit temporarily, otherwise discredited traditional ways.[62]

In response, a new force appeared that occupied that crucial middle ground between the radicalism of the Haskalah and the obscurantism of traditional Judaism. It represented a

system capable of restoring both in a single new form. We stand and look at this form, so simple, so natural, so easily intelligible and we wonder why it was so long in coming about? Is it necessary to name this movement? Or is it enough just to point to the east, to the land of our ancestors?[63]

The style of his articles in *Pardes* would come to be the main way in which he aired his political views—through philosophical excursions strengthened by his descriptions of new discoveries, especially in psychology. But at the same time that the first of these pieces appeared in 1893, he also produced a major essay differing drastically both in tone and content that shows a different side of him: his sequel to "Emet me-erets yisrael." The article, which recorded a trip that he then hoped would mean the beginning of his permanent move to Palestine, was something of a bookkeeper's account of the Yishuv—which, excepting a few brief inspirational asides—seemed altogether bloodless in its appraisal of Jewish Palestine's (minor) achievements and (vast) shortcomings. In the end, he decided, not surprisingly, that to move to Palestine now was premature.

His diary once again indicates, as in 1891, that his initial reactions to Palestine were very different from those that found their way into his published account. What characterized his impressions on this occasion, most of which were no more than the terse jottings of a busy traveler, was their almost unrelieved unhappiness. Confronted again with the reality of Palestinian Jewry, he recorded one miserable observation after another, though once he readied these for publication depression gave way to sober and unsentimental, if at times also savagely chilling, reportage.

His arrival in Jaffa, as he indicated in his diary on 15 June, necessitated bribing the authorities, which "grieved [his] soul deeply." The sight of Arabs harvesting crops at Rehovot three days later "depressed me very much." The colony's half-completed buildings "break one's heart." Rishon Le-Zion's settlers are "very miserable." He examined students at the local school and left feeling glum and unimpressed. The maskilim of Jerusalem, he found, "hate and try to degrade one another." At Ekron, harvesting colonists made his "heart expand with happiness at the sight of real Jewish farmers in Palestine"; nonetheless, that visit, too, left him more depressed than inspired when he recalled that the colony received subsidies from Rothschild and could be undermined if those funds stopped. "With the blood of my heart I wrote this article," he said of this installment of "Emet."[64]

He still viewed Rothschild's impact as inimical to the growth of a self-respecting pioneering elite. Here he insisted, as he had in the original "Emet," that Rothschild's system of subsidized agriculture had sapped the colonists' initiative, resulting in a generation of idle, cunning, spiritually depleted settlers. Clearly support for the Palestinian Jewish infrastructure remained a necessity but the elaborate system of handouts now in place must end, in his view, if the Yishuv was to achieve a modicum of dignity and financial stability.[65]

At this moment, he writes only in the realm of education is growth feasible. Ahad Ha'am provides an empirical justification for arguments he had made elsewhere, mostly on moral grounds. Expansion of education is essential, even if this means that instruction cannot be conducted in Hebrew. There are still few Hebrew textbooks, and qualified teachers are almost as rare. Hebrew must remain, of course, a centerpiece of the school curriculum and at the core of the Jewish nationalist educational enterprise, but its use as a classroom staple was still unrealistic.

These, he insists, are the foundations on which Jewish Palestine must be built. To ensure financial stability, Jewish nationalism should transfer its central offices from Eastern Europe to the West, preferably to England or the United States. A movement based in the West would probably exert greater leverage over the Turks in negotiating the relaxation of Jewish immigration restrictions. It is also likely, he says, that Western supervision would translate into a more orderly and efficient Yishuv.[66]

Dry and matter-of-fact as this report was, he ended it on a deeply personal note (like in the first "Emet") with his impressions of Jerusalem and the Wailing Wall. He observes that on this occasion he, quite literally, had to steal into the city "like a thief" because his papers were not in order. He arrived in Jerusalem three days before Tisha B'Av, the fast day commemorating the destruction of the first and second temples in Jerusalem. On the eve of the holy day he went to the Wailing Wall where he found old and young men sobbing, chanting ritual dirges, studying, and debating arcane points of the law. Despite himself, he says he recalled his ruminations of two year's earlier. His ancestors, he knew, had sacrificed their lives on this spot near their besieged temple. He imagined these ancestors inspecting the scene beside the Wall "with great confusion," staring with consternation—and presumably with keen disappointment—at the men with books in their hands who now stood on their graves: these bookish anachronisms were the unlikely heirs to a grand and imperiled legacy.[67]

This Palestinian trip, and nearly everything that he did in the Jewish communal sphere until the creation of the monthly *Ha-Shiloach* in 1896, was part and parcel of his leading role in the Bnei Moshe. Even *Ha-Shiloach,* he would claim in 1896 in a letter of resignation from the Bnei Moshe (which, in the end, he would also rescind) was an offspring of it too: "After all, everyone knows that it is the spirit of the Bnei Moshe that made this a reality as well."[68] True, he said this in a somewhat self-aggrandizing letter in which he sought to extricate himself from the group's leadership with as little difficulty as possible. The comments were probably an accurate gauge of his sentiments, though. His attachment to the Bnei Moshe was abiding; in the end, his disappointment with it was all the more intense.

It was in the wake of the Tiomkin debacle that he first started to question whether the Bnei Moshe had accomplished much in its brief existence: he marveled at its inability to stick to its original goals and at how it had been so easily swept into the maelstrom of Palestinian land fever of the early 1890s. He worried it might not be able to pay back the debts it had incurred by its unwise investments in Palestine; if it didn't, the land acquired at inflated prices would likely fall again into Arab hands. He berated himself for being unable to maintain order in his ranks. This, he complained, in a letter of 1893 to the Warsaw branch, is "my way, my weakness."

Nevertheless he did not disengage himself from the group despite his repeated and rather half-hearted attempts (in 1891, 1893, 1895) to resign as leader: in 1891, for instance, he wrote to the Warsaw branch that he could only effectively rebuke Tiomkin if he resigned as head of the Bnei Moshe and spoke with the Jaffa leader as a fellow member—as just another brother. His notion that once he stepped down Tiomkin would overlook the fact that he was speaking with Ahad Ha'am seems rather fanciful. On this and every other occasion before the group finally dissolved in 1898, he managed to be dissuaded from abandoning his position.[69]

Not only did he formally retain his leadership, but he frequently demonstrated keen political savvy: in attempting in 1891 to chart the Bnei Moshe's course, for instance, he insisted it must maintain all possible distance from the discredited Tiomkin; its chief problem was to recoup its financial standing after its recent losses in land speculation, and this might be achieved through vigorous fundraising in the West, particularly in England. Tellingly, these instructions were written on the morning of Pinsker's funeral in December 1891 in the form of a long letter about the Bnei Moshe's future strategy. Despondent as he was by what he saw in Palestine during his first trip, by no means had he abandoned his intention to pursue his battles, especially now that Pinsker's death seemed to expand his options.[70]

Ahad Ha'am showed great tactical skill even when his group faced a vigorous campaign to discredit it as it did first in 1891 in the wake of

Lilienblum's attack on Ben Avigdor's "Shene hezyonot" and then two years later during the controversy over the Jaffa school. When the Bnei Moshe found it necessary to renounce its secrecy and its name, he proposed *Agudat Moshe*—the society of Moses—free as it was from the messianic connotations of Bnei Moshe. Meanwhile in anticipation of awkward public disclosures about the group, he devised a plan to transfer its more important papers to one trusted member from each branch.[71]

Throughout he presented himself to his constituency as ill-suited for leadership. In a detailed summary of the Tiomkin affair written to the Jaffa branch, he muses that he should have acted more firmly and decisively. But, he adds, knowledge is not the same as action: "I had recognized this though I found myself incapable of acting upon my impulses." On the whole, he insists, the best way to proceed in the midst of crisis—from mid-1891 until the Bnei Moshe's closure seven years later he saw the organization in a state of almost perpetual turmoil—is "to sit with folded hands and a raging heart and attempt to gather together all my spiritual strength, whatever modicum of 'philosophy' that I possess, in order to prepare for the disaster to come, or, at least, to face it with a bit of wisdom and 'stoic' patience."[72]

Though he showed himself capable of charting the Bnei Moshe course with some shrewdness and cunning, to his constituency he insisted that it must play by a higher standard than others and must not participate in the sordid intrigues that otherwise marred Jewish politics: as he wrote to the Warsaw branch in the spring of 1892,

It is time for us to recognize and understand that our way is completely different from that of the "men of action" [anshe ma'ase] and our weapons differ greatly from theirs. As far as those people are concerned who resort to intrigues and act as informers and do other fine things—with people of this sort we can have nothing to do and must not interfere in their affairs.[73]

It would be better in his view to put an end to the Bnei Moshe than compromise its integrity by associating it with activities or individuals who might drag it into the mud.

By the fall of 1894 he had tired of his role. This disenchantment followed in the wake of the turmoil over the Jaffa school. He had hoped the publication of "Torah she-balev" would quiet the controversy, but it only further intensified it. He also suffered a decline in his personal fortunes. When in the summer of 1893 he spent some time in England and France, he still had some hope to recoup his investments; by late 1894 this hope had dissipated and it was patently clear that he would not (in the short run, at least) recoup his fortune. Previously his wealth not only had shielded him from the need to support himself from the meager institutions of the maskilic world, as was necessary for many of his friends, but it also lent his leadership a greater legitimacy in both his eyes and those of his followers. He had carried himself from the beginning of his public career as a maskilic nationalist and as a man of means and substance. His criticisms, particularly those directed at the pettiness and shortcomings of his class, carried more weight since he wrote as an insider. Now, for the first time, he was economically little better off than the rest of the *batlanim melamdim* (idlers and tutors) of his dissident circle. Probably his financial decline played a role in his desire to extricate himself from the leadership of the Bnei Moshe which he no longer felt, now that he was poor, quite as qualified to direct.

In addition, by late 1894 Ahad Ha'am was seriously ill. A nervous disorder that would haunt him, on and off, for the rest of his life had so weakened him that he took to his bed and stopped writing while his doctors ordered complete rest. He feared that he was dying, apparently with good reason, and, as Yosef Goldstein has suggested, his decision to collect his essays in book form was motivated by his belief that they might represent his life's work. The book's title, *Al Parashat Derakhim* (*At the Crossroads*) was intended, then, to signify not only changes in the destiny of the Jewish people but also a dramatic and tragic change in Ahad Ha'am's personal affairs, a convergence here, repeated so often in his writing and politics, between collective and personal prognosis. The volume appeared in the spring of 1895.[74]

Earlier that year Ahad Ha'am's health improved: he resumed his correspondence, apologized for long delays in answering letters, and again took charge of the affairs of the Bnei Moshe. The administrative details had long been delegated to the heads of the Warsaw branch; its official central office had moved to Jaffa.

It was, in fact, a shift in the staffing of the Jaffa office, following the death of the Hovevei Zion's local head, Judah Leib Binstock, in October 1894, which brought on the group's final crisis and its eventual closure. Only two years earlier Binstock was appointed to replace the ill-fated Tiomkin. Efficient, bright, Jewishly literate, Binstock managed during his short tenure to impose some order on the affairs of the new Yishuv. The sudden death at the age of fifty-eight of this popular and well-respected man was a considerable loss.[75]

Immediately, anti-Bnei Moshe forces sought to appoint someone outside the group in anticipation (they were, in fact, correct) that the

Bnei Moshe would seek to appoint one of its own. Lilienblum, the influential Odessa jurist Menashe Margolis, and religious opponents of the society joined forces to block the Bnei Moshe's further advance. Pines still spearheaded the opposing forces in Palestine; he was now assisted in Odessa by David Shlomo Slouchz, Moldavanka's rabbi and Hovevei Zion executive committee member. Margolis, a communal figure of prominence, moderately pious, and stolid, had long distrusted Ahad Ha'am and his mysterious visionaries; this represented his first major public campaign against him.[76]

He aired his misgivings with candor, even fury. He announced his intentions in January when it became clear that the Hovevei Zion's Jaffa representative seemed certain to be chosen from the ranks of the Bnei Moshe. At a meeting of the Odessa executive of the Hovevei Zion on which Ahad Ha'am also sat, Margolis announced that he planned to resign since he had recently received information from Palestine of a secret society within the Hovevei Zion that had for several years manipulated its internal affairs. He named the Bnei Moshe and pointed to Ahad Ha'am as well as the Hovevei Zion's secretary, Zalman Epstein, as leaders of a cabal. Incredibly, he also accused Epstein, a rather pious Jew, of being a Karaite who scoffed at the corpus of rabbinic law because of a misreading of one of Epstein's recent essays; he said it made no sense for him to remain in an organization that was being run by a shadow government. Ahad Ha'am and Epstein both immediately announced their resignations from the executive committee pending an investigation of these charges by a commission of the Hovevei Zion.[77]

The commission did not meet until mid-April (one of its members was ill); all those named to it were men of means—the same sort whose hegemony Ahad Ha'am had criticized since his first appearance on the public scene—including Samuel Barbash, Moshe Fishrovitch, Abraham Greenberg, and Kalman Wissotzsky. True, several of these had close, long-standing relations with Ahad Ha'am, especially Barbash, a man of considerable erudition, and Wissotzsky, who was one of his most loyal financial supporters. In anticipation of the meeting, the Bnei Moshe's ultraorthodox foes launched a smear campaign, circulating copies of one of its documents on whose cover appeared an acronym for what was in reality an innocuous title: it stood for *sakh ha-kol* (summation); they insisted (in a reading that required an inversion of the title's words) that its true meaning was *sod kohanei ha'am,* or secrets of the priests of the nation. In turn, Bnei Moshe firmed up its allies, including Rabbi Samuel Mohilever. Other trusted leaders of the Hovevei Zion, including several secretly connected with the Bnei Moshe, lobbied commission members. If only the Bnei Moshe were powerful enough to fight its enemies openly, Ahad Ha'am mused in a letter written in January 1895, it could forgo these degrading political machinations. He also managed to persuade the Bnei Moshe, and despite some rather stiff resistance, that finally it must abandon its secrecy and tear down the "Wall of China" (as he called it) surrounding it. The group did so a few months later.[78]

On the first day of the commission's deliberations, Margolis not only accused the Bnei Moshe of attempting to take control of the Hovevei Zion but also of spreading religious heresy. Ahad Ha'am in his reply admitted the existence of the group—as he had earlier at the Hovevei Zion meeting where Margolis had first aired his objections—but insisted its goal was simply the promotion of Jewish nationalism. At a second meeting some two weeks later Margolis continued his attack, concentrating this time on the Bnei Moshe's leadership. Ahad Ha'am responded with a four-hour oration that proved so dramatic and effective that at the end of it Margolis took his hand and begged his forgiveness. The commission dissolved; the affair was over. Soon a Bnei Moshe member was selected to head the Jaffa office; of his staff of two, one of those appointed came from the society (Barzilai whom Ahad Ha'am himself chose) and another from outside it.[79]

Even though the episode ended favorably, Ahad Ha'am was not dissuaded from his belief that, irrespective of what was decided, a dark cloud would now hang over his group. He stated flatly in early February 1895, "I cannot imagine under any circumstances that I could return to [lead the group] in peace." He was prevailed upon to remain its head but he henceforth refused to shoulder the leadership that his constituency, newly energized by the dispute, hoped to foist on him. He refused to compose a new set of bylaws; he insisted that he had already written two versions and if they no longer represented the sentiments of the Bnei Moshe the group must find someone else for the task. With mounting venom and self-deprecation, he blamed himself for not bringing greater stability to the society; he was not a good administrator, he declared, and was unable to "command and order with the requisite energy." He reminded his constituency that he had tried on more than one occasion, to remove his "unsuitable crown." Despite these misgivings, he continued to chart its course in this delicate period when it first emerged into the public light. He advised, for instance, that full disclosure of its internal documents was unnecessary and imprudent. The transition required much "aptitude and tact."[80]

Clearly he had lost interest in the Bnei Moshe which, he now came to be convinced, had lost its reason to exist. This occurred, ironically, at a rather successful, upbeat moment in the group's checkered history: it was now running a vigorous publishing house, Ahiasaf, with its own journal, *Luah Ahiasaf*; its Vilna branch had been revived and was purged of its more recalcitrant members; the Bnei Moshe's internal structure was revamped to give its leader, Ahad Ha'am, greater authority in running its branches' affairs. The Jaffa office now played an active and constructive role in the Yishuv.

Nonetheless, Ahad Ha'am circulated a letter in the name of the Odessa branch in late 1895—signed by himself and Rawnitsky—that spoke of the "internal sickness" that had characterized the Bnei Moshe since its beginnings and that never abated. Three times its bylaws were changed; three times its central office was moved; three years ago its base of operations was transferred and recently an attempt was made to make its activities public, but still the stubborn illness persisted.

What this demonstrates, Ahad Ha'am's letter said, is that the group lacked from the outset any "spark of life" of the sort essential for a healthy organization. Members differed too much over its goals and, in the wake of years of disappointment and discord, many came to despair of it achieving anything at all. Most of them had come to ridicule it and its commitments. They warned that this was the beginning of the end, signaling "the entry of the angel of death." Of course, the bonds of fellowship nurtured by the Bnei Moshe would remain intact after the group disappeared; but the need to put an end to it as a distinct group was self-evident. They asked the branches to respond within a month, or their silence would be taken for acquiescence.[81]

Ahad Ha'am probably had anticipated that some members would object; in fact, the branches fought back vigorously. Warsaw's reply insisted that what Ahad Ha'am saw as chronic sickness were merely the "birth pangs" of an organization still in its infancy. He must recognize that it was still in the midst of a slow formation process. At a conference of the Bnei Moshe held in Odessa in the fall of 1896 and on the heels of a Hovevei Zion congress, its members affirmed their commitment to the organization's existence. In its new bylaws they managed to confront with considerable finesse any religious objections to the group by stressing that the society was committed to pluralism and it opposed no faction in the Jewish world. Membership in the Bnei Moshe was open to all Jews who believed in the rebuilding of Jewish Palestine, had a high regard for ethics and Hebrew knowledge, and had an acquaintance with at least one foreign language. This was a considerably reduced version of the austere demands made on the Bnei Moshe's original members; the group was poised for a vigorous membership drive.[82]

And yet by late 1898 it ceased to exist; Ahad Ha'am's leadership of it for the previous two years was, in fact, nominal at best. The dissolution can be traced in part to Herzl's dramatic impact on the Jewish nationalist scene which consigned even the Hovevei Zion to something of a shadowy existence from the time of the Basel Congress in August 1897. At least Ahad Ha'am explained its end thus. In fact, it was his loss of interest in it that concluded this saga, indicating the pivotal role he had played since the society's first days. In a letter written to the Jaffa leadership in December 1896, he insisted that his responsibilities at Ha-Shiloach, which had begun publication two months earlier, would not permit him to continue as Bnei Moshe's leader. He characterized his editorial work as "holy labor" and made it clear that through this activity he was continuing in the footsteps of the Bnei Moshe which had inspired the project. He added that, because of his new financial situation, he had to rely on the earnings of his journal to support his family. "One who is engaged in the performance of a good deed is freed from doing other deeds," he reminded them, echoing the well-known rabbinic maxim. This time he left little room for doubt that he intended to close the door behind him.[83]

The letter betrayed his grand hopes for Ha-Shiloach. He wrote: "If, Heaven forbid, this venture fails it will constitute a major disaster because faith will be lost in the revival of our literature." It also betrayed his lack of faith in the future of Bnei Moshe. Perhaps Margolis's disclosures—admittedly venomous yet partly accurate—left him dispirited, resentful, or despairing that their impressions would ever fade away. Perhaps, despite his advocating that Bnei Moshe redefine itself as a public body, he felt little commitment to it now that it was so drastically different from what he had originally envisioned and now that it seemed on the verge of becoming something of a mass membership organization. He objected to its members' desire for public gatherings (sihot she-be'al peh, he insisted, have no real impact) and probably resented its new, populist bent. He seems, quite literally, to have recoiled from it. In the absence of a credible leadership structure independent of their chief (who remained at its helm, however grudgingly, until the end), the society fell apart.

He later insisted on describing it as "an experiment that failed" and tried to distance himself from it and its uncertain legacy.[84] Indeed, in retrospect it looked exotic, excessively quarrelsome, self-important, and very quickly dated. No important sector of the Zionist movement saw it as its imagined ancestor as, for instance, the Second Aliyah later viewed the Bilu, the pioneers of the 1880s. The fact that the young Chaim Weizmann, Leo Motzkin, or Ussishkin joined it was, or so it seemed in retrospect, of little more than passing biographical interest. There were no Zionist institutions committed to sustaining its memory or relevance and its erstwhile members went on to pursue priorities more pressing than those set down in its strangely lyrical declarations.

Nevertheless, despite his rather deprecating assessments of its achievement, Ahad Ha'am continued to see it as perhaps his most important hour. The single essay he wrote about it, "An Experiment That Failed," he would select as the final item in his four-volume collected works. Throughout his life he planned to write its history, and he spent a good deal of time in his last years in Tel Aviv collecting material on the Bnei Moshe for what he hoped would be the definitive archival collection. He mused frequently about the joy he had felt during its first days and complained that he should never have permitted it to grow beyond its original size.[85]

What the Bnei Moshe represented for him was his most congenial foray into politics. True, Ha-Shiloach, too, was profoundly political in its goals, and never, not even after he resigned from its editorship in 1902, would he retire from the ranks of political activists despite an abiding ambivalence about the value of a public life. But the Bnei Moshe constituted a unique departure for this otherwise cloistered, closed, and reserved man, and, as much as he resented the way in which it imposed on his time and energy, he craved the engagement and fellowship.

Perhaps it was the fellowship that he missed the most. Indeed, this was the feature that he tended to stress in his recollections of these years. As he had insisted in his letter of 1895 calling for the dissolution of the group: "Needless to say, our call for the 'end of the society' is not a call for an end to the authentic ties that have been forged over time between many of its members, especially among the original ones."[86] This solitary man, by the time that he abandoned the Bnei Moshe, embarked on the editing of an ambitious journal without the help of editorial assistants, admitting he simply did not know how to delegate such authority. His role in the Bnei Moshe had demanded a greater participation with people, more human engagement than he had experienced before or, for that matter, ever since. He both hated and craved the intrusion.

Ahad Ha'am in 1877 or 1878.
Photograph reprinted from Pirkei
zikhronot ve-igrot *(Tel-Aviv, 1931).*

Ahad Ha'am in Palestine in 1911.
Photograph reprinted from Pirkei
zikhronot ve-igrot *(Tel-Aviv, 1931).*

Ahad Ha'am's London home at
12 Glenmore Road in Maida Vale.
Photograph by Todd Endelman.

Ahad Haʾam in St. Petersburg in August 1907. On his right: Listerian and Jewish communal activist Alexander Braudo. On his left: historian Iluii Gessen and his wife Adelʾ Iosifovich. Photograph courtesy of Valery Gessen.

S. RASKIN

A Palestinian Gallery

WE REPRODUCE on this page four sketches prepared specially for THE NEW PALESTINE by Mr. SAUL RASKIN, the well-known Jewish artist, who is now in Palestine. These are the first of a series which Mr. RASKIN has undertaken for us and which will be reproduced in forthcoming issues. The comments to the sketches are supplied by Mr. RASKIN.

ACHAD HAAM

Quiet, retired, infinitely modest—this is A c h a d Haam, the father of spiritual Zionism, one of the m o s t distinguished men of this generation. You may see him at every meeting in Tel Aviv, withdrawn somewhere in a corner, smoking his eternal Russian cigarette. He comes to listen, and not to speak. He is watching others develop the dream to which he gave the earliest inspiration, and he does not interfere. But on the rare occasion when he does take part in a debate or discussion, he has the breathless attention of the entire audience, and his words are greeted like manna from heaeven.

CHAIM NACHMAN BIALIK

Bialik is, in one sense, a new-comer to Palestine; but in the real sense of the word, he is one who has never been outside of Palestine. He is a part of Palestine wherever he is, and carries the country with him. But he came to Palestine with a difference — he has removed his sparse Russian moustache. He has something of the American in his appearance, and sometimes, in certain lights, and in profile, he awakes distant memories of Woodrow Wilson. I made the above sketch while he was addressing the assembly of school-children who had turned out to bring him greetings. For a new-comer Bialik speaks good Hebrew.

MAYOR DIEZENGOFF

Mayor Meyer Diezengoff, of Tel Aviv, who became mayor and remains mayor without being a politician—certainly the most popular man in Tel Aviv, and one of the most popular men in Palestine. He built a city and became mayor of it—and he is still adding to it. Always busy—without a chance to recuperate in Palm Beach, eternally concerned with all the details of his administration, following with loving care even the most trifling developments in the city. And withal a charming personality, as American Jewry can now attest.

M. GOLINKIN

M. Golinkin is the Director of the Palestinian Hebrew Opera. Directing Hebrew Opera in Palestine is not merely a matter of music: to a love and understanding of music the pioneer of Hebrew O p e r a must add an iron will and unquenchable faith. Mr. Golinkin has all of these. He has brought opera of the highest standard into Palestine. His conductor's baton is a kind of magic wand, which inspires the young men and women of Palestine to an understanding of music, and, stranger still, to the ability to sing.

Line drawings by Saul Raskin from The New Palistine.

Tel-Aviv in 1921. Photograph by S. Narinsky.

4

The Politics of Culture:
Ha-Shiloach and
Herzlian Zionism

*To the true reformer no institution is sacred, no beliefs
above criticism. Everybody shall conform to equity and
reason. Nothing shall be saved by its prestige.*
        Herbert Spencer, "Manners and Fashions"

*Only by revealing to the people what has taken place and is
taking place, and the real relation between it and the
surrounding world, only then will it be possible for [Jewry]
to find its way and fully reform its life.*
        Ahad Ha'am, in *Ha-Shiloach*'s "Statement of Purpose"

I

The use of journals as a political tool seemed altogether
natural for the cultural nationalists in Ahad Ha'am's circle. *Der Yidisher
Veker* had represented their first excursion into politics; more or less the
same group went on to establish the Bnei Moshe and among their first
tasks was to issue *Kaveret*. Soon they turned their attention to *Pardes*.
They felt that journals affirmed their credentials and political wisdom
and served to counteract the charges of provinciality that were frequently
leveled against them and the Palestinophile enterprise. They saw peri-

odicals as highlighting their movement's breadth, moral vision, intellectual underpinnings, and progressivism.[1]

They also hoped that their publications would, at least, dent the influence of the dominant left-liberal, populist "thick journals" of the 1880s and 1890s, the weighty *Otchestvennye Zapiski* (*Annals of the Fatherland*) or *Russkoe Bogatstvo* (*Russian Wealth*). They obviously knew that they were unlikely to garner equal prestige or influence, even among the budding Jewish intelligentsia that followed the Russian press no less avidly than did others. These publications nevertheless provided models and, no less importantly, suitably formidable foils for attack.

On the Jewish street, the most important intellectual journal of the period was the St. Petersburg-based Russian monthly *Voskhod*—liberal, antinationalist, politically moderate, and committed to rapprochement of Russians and Jews. In challenging the journal's hegemony, which was the intent of all Jewish periodicals in the 1880s with any semblance of intellectual ambition, Jewish nationalists first built upon an already existing network of maskilic weeklies: Hebrew newspapers, like *Ha-Melitz* and *Ha-Maggid*, established in the 1860s, were now remade into their unofficial organs. Most of these newspapers were haphazardly printed weeklies-turned-dailies, with a hodgepodge of essays, poems, and news reports, all of greatly varying quality. It was in such newspapers that Ahad Ha'am's career was launched. The use of Hebrew as their lingua franca (though Yiddish was sometimes favored, as in *Der Yidisher Veker*) was seen as crucial, as representative of one of the few concrete signs of Jewish nationality linking Jews worldwide. It possessed, as Robert Alter puts it, "a unique aesthetic dignity and a unique historical resonance."[2]

Only marginally more demanding on readers were Hebrew monthlies like *Ha-Shahar* or *Ha-Boker Or*, which tended to publish somewhat longer and denser articles but drew on the same stable of writers, albeit a shrinking one. By the 1870s Hebrew literature found itself in competition both with the Russian-Jewish and Yiddish press. The former provided a natural destination for university- or gymnasium-trained Jews; Yiddish, meanwhile flowering in these years under the inspiration of luminaries like Mendele, Sholem Aleichem, and, somewhat later, Isaac Leib Peretz, was in a naturally better position than Hebrew to command a large and enthusiastic audience stretching far beyond Eastern Europe, even to New York or Cape Town. It also better satisfied the ambitions of writers seeking to reach beyond the rather small coterie of like-minded maskilim fluent in the Hebrew tongue.[3]

This sense of desperation in the Hebrew literary world—which itself constituted the backdrop to the fin de siècle cultural politics of Ahad Ha'am—was a consequence of larger changes in late imperial Russia. On the surface, and from the vantage point of Western Jews who saw Eastern Europe mostly as the staging ground for tsarist oppression, the region seemed overwhelmingly traditional in Jewish terms, even culturally dormant. This lack of progress was credited to benighted official policies that, it was claimed, rendered Jews all but oblivious to the modernization that transformed much of the rest of European Jewry. From the vantage point of Ahad Ha'am, it was in the throes of a thoroughgoing change that was certain to render not only the aspirations of the ultraorthodox out of touch but those of the nationalists as well.

The clearest example is education. From the mid-1850s, as a result of the policies of Alexander II (1855–1881), much larger numbers of Jews began to attend Russian secondary schools and universities, and this trend continued after official policy shifted in the 1880s with the imposition of educational quotas on Jews. By the turn of the century, some 1,750 were enrolled in Russian universities with another 2,000 to 2,500 who despaired of being admitted into Russian schools attending universities abroad. In 1912, some 8.5 percent of the students in Russian universities and higher institutes were Jews. Russian literacy among Jews was also on the rise: in a study of literacy conducted in 1899 in a small provincial town in the Kiev province—much like Ahad Ha'am's native Skvire—33.9 percent of the Jews claimed Russian to be their most fluent language. The figure seems inflated but, even if halved, it is telling; indeed, the claim itself suggests a transformed attitude that had to concern Jewish nationalists. From their perspective something of a Jewish brain drain was occurring that, if left unchecked, would deplete the number and quality of those engaged in Jewish communal life and would eat away at its cultural vibrancy.[4] To address this dilemma it was essential to deploy the tool of "literary politics"—to highlight Judaism's cultural treasures with the publication of journals, books, pamphlets, perhaps an encyclopedia with a tendentious bent—scholarship with a polemical edge.

Indeed, by the 1890s, parental resistance to Jews attending Russian schools had so abated, observes Dan Miron, that battles about such practices—once the staples of Yiddish and Hebrew literature—were now viewed as laughably anachronistic. If the literary public should encounter stubborn resistance to the modernist aspirations of a young writer, as in the case of Mordecai Zev Feierberg whose father's opposition to his son's tragically short literary career was fierce and uncompromising, the behavior was seen as grotesque, as belonging to another time and place. Their departure from traditional Judaism, so different from Ahad Ha'am's, was not marked by a comparable misery; tradition's yoke on them had been less pronounced.[5] Ahad Ha'am was certain that it was the young who vanquished their elders and set the tone for the future and found this unsettling: "History has shown that in a war between parents and children it is always the children who win in the end: The future belongs to them."[6]

His new role as editor of a Hebrew monthly was in his eyes no retreat from politics. His experience with the Bnei Moshe—whose failure he chiefly credited to an insufficiently sophisticated Jewry—reinforced his belief in the need to reconstruct Jewry's cultural foundations and to recast the sensibility of a generation of Jews who might otherwise be lost. Whatever was built by Jewish nationalism would be otherwise fragile, probably useless. "Holy labor" is how he termed this work, at least in its first few heady months.[7]

He had frequently complained in the past that he hated business; he had dreamed of working as a man of letters but he took the plunge only when absolutely forced to do so after the loss of his and his father's investments. He had started to explore the possibility of editing a journal in 1893, at the first signs of financial difficulty; the family business finally collapsed two years later. During those two years he worked hard to acquire the necessary funding. He tested several options (including the possibility of paying for it out of his own pocket), wooed several potential backers, writers, censors, and a host of literary go-betweens. He would enter into these discussions with energy and enthusiasm and, though he would find them dispiriting and even humiliating at times, he saw them through to the end with as much determination and confidence as he would ever muster.

As he confidently declared to Rawnitsky in a letter in the winter of 1893, he was intent on becoming "an editor in Israel"—or, in other words, a Jewish editor.[8] He wrote that letter while in London, soon after he had heard of the death of *Ha-Melitz*'s editor Zederbaum. He held out little hope that he could acquire Zederbaum's St. Petersburg-based newspaper (nor did he wish to move there from Odessa) and felt that it was probably more feasible to start a new journal with the help of Ahiasaf, the Bnei Moshe's publishing house. During the nine-month trip (his longest stay abroad that took him to Palestine, England, France, and Germany) he devoted much time to launching a publication. First, he turned for help to a Parisian-based writer for *Ha-Melitz*, Abraham Ludvipul, with whom he struck up a warm friendship; together they looked over Hebrew printing facilities there which they soon realized were inadequate. Ludvipul then proposed that Ahad Ha'am consider Berlin, which had fine Hebrew print shops and, unlike Paris, a sizable number of maskilic writers who could be relied on for copyediting and other chores.[9]

By this time Ahad Ha'am had spent some two months in England; he was feeling increasingly desperate and keenly disappointed with the obstacles that he had encountered in Paris. He resisted at first Ludvipul's conclusion that publication in France was unrealistic, rushing back from London with the hope of proving him wrong. He nonetheless remained adamant about launching a periodical. He acted upon Ludvipul's advice with great deliberation and caution; he even made his friend promise to tell no one of his publishing plans. He intended to win first the confidence of Berlin's Hebraist colony before he unveiled the idea of a journal. First, he would probe to see how receptive they might be. "I beg you to believe," he wrote Ludvipul, "that I can ask my questions in such a way that no one will know why [they are being asked]."[10]

Arriving in Berlin in November 1893, he was not even deterred by the news that the journalist Reuven Brainin had also set about to start a Hebrew journal there. He courted local writers—the most important being the young, energetic Micah Joseph Berdyczewski—and spoke with them at length about literary issues. Not only did he impress them with his knowledge and insight but he also flattered them intentionally by virtue of the attention he lavished on them. By the time he revealed his ideas for the journal they were won over and abandoned Brainin.[11]

For someone as unskilled as he claimed to be in the ways of the world, he handled himself here in these prolonged and often delicate negotiations with tact and considerable evasiveness. Tellingly, the name he chose for the journal, *Mi-mizrah u-mi-ma'arav* (*From the East and the West*), although a logical name for a publication edited in a Western city by East European Jews, was the very same title that Brainin had selected for his. Ahad Ha'am claimed that he had not known this. At the same time, he gave Berdyczewski the impression that he and Berlin's other Hebrew writers would be collaborators in what they had now come to see as a joint venture. Once *Ha-Shiloach* (the name he chose eventually in lieu of *Mi-mizrah u-mi-ma'arav*), based in Berlin, won Wissotzsky's financial support and Ahiasaf took it under its wing, Ahad Ha'am made it clear that he planned to run it alone and required assistance only in the performance of the sort of menial, day-to-day tasks that Ludvipul had said could be better done in Berlin than Paris. Eventually he claimed that he couldn't even rely on Berlin's maskilim for these tasks, which were too important to delegate. This left them perplexed as to why at the outset he had so assiduously sought their support.

Indeed, when he outlined for Berdyczewski in 1893 the raison d'etre of a journal, he carefully avoided touching upon what he already knew to be fundamental differences between them, preferring to overlook them momentarily. The proposed statement of purpose affirmed that Jewish nationalism must ensure that Jews remain, as in the past, a mediating force in world culture rather than a cloistered entity without any impact beyond their limited province. Differences over precisely this issue would later prove to be the most important item in the ideological debate between Ahad Ha'am and Berdyczewski; at this juncture Ahad Ha'am avoided all confrontations and the draft was left intentionally vague. The document continued that to accomplish these goals the currently fragmented forces in Jewish life must join together to attain national revival. In the absence of a coherent political framework and since religion ceased to unify the Jews, this would have to be accomplished by "culture." Cultural projects like the proposed journal must take responsibility for inculcating a "sense of national identity" into the Jewish people, in forging links between it throughout the world.[12]

In the spring of 1894, Ahad Ha'am informed Ahiasaf that he intended to go ahead and launch the journal without the help of a subsidy; it would be funded at first from his own pocket on a trial basis for one year. His heart, as he recorded in his diary, was "filled with literary dreams." His "sun might yet shine," he enthused though this could also be "its last flicker of light."[13]

He soon admitted his plan had been unrealistic. His financial position had so deteriorated that the financing of a journal for even a short period would be too great a burden. Ahiasaf tried instead to make available to him an existing publication, thus hoping to avoid the cumbersome and frequently unsuccessful application to the censorship authorities. These negotiations, too, proved abortive. Ahad Ha'am returned to Odessa with few additional options, dispirited though still not without hope. His stay abroad, he concluded, had been fruitful, if not conclusive.[14]

He stayed abroad for as long as he did for several reasons. Of course, in Palestine he had inspected the conditions in the colonies and the Jaffa office and collected the material for his sequel to "Emet." He had also looked into settling there but decided against it. He explained this in terms of Ottoman immigration restrictions, but it was probably also the crudity of Palestine's cultural life that put him off the idea. Arriving in Europe that summer, he explored the possibility of reestablishing the base of Hovevei Zion's operations in the West, a move that he and other leading Jewish nationalists believed was essential for both political and financial reasons.

He later described the trip in a footnote in his collected correspondence in the following terms: "I went from Palestine to London via Paris with the hope of persuading people there of the urgency of establishing in the West a large organization to support Jewish colonization in Palestine."[15] The reasons for his stay were, as we have seen, more complicated. True, he hoped at the time that it might be possible to set up a viable Jewish nationalist center—preferably in England—where, as he had declared in "Emet me-eretz yisrael," the movement could rely on foreign Jews to play an influential role free from the constraints of tsarist officialdom. At the time he hoped that, as he made clear to his Bnei Moshe brethren, England would become the center of the Hovevei Zion, with Paris as the base of the Bnei Moshe.

He also anticipated that he might secure a firmer market in the West for Palestinian wine exports. He spoke at length during his stay in London with supporters of the Hovevei Zion there about how this market might be developed, and he made the case that this represented an ideal way for them to lend their hand to the construction of an economically self-sufficient Jewish Palestine. He had hoped the idea would make sense to English non-Jews, though as he soon admitted he had overestimated the depth of such sentiments in the land of Daniel Deronda. He sought to firm up his own English business connections, and he remained hopeful on this score even after his return to Odessa. His efforts at launching a journal were conducted, then, against this rather feverish backdrop of negotiations to firm up his own financial affairs as well as the organizational and fiscal standing of both the Bnei Moshe and the larger Jewish nationalist movement.[16]

Perhaps the most enduring feature of his stay in Western Europe was his encounter with England. He left nearly as excited about the country as when he first arrived, which is surprising since the trip was full of the sort of minor annoyances that were known to aggravate him. He arrived in the summer only to discover that nearly everyone he hoped to meet was away on holiday. He soon abandoned London for Paris and returned to London in the early fall. He complained about drafty English rooms (he spent the months of September through November in London) and yearned for family and friends. But he took the time to study carefully a British tour guide, strolled through Hyde Park on Sundays, and found the sturdy political culture around him to be nearly as impressive as he had imagined it. He wrote in his diary about one Hyde Park demonstration:

I was in Hyde Park today and saw the large demonstration conducted by Londoners in support of the coal miners who have not worked for about two months because of disputes with their bosses. Because of this their families are dying of hunger. How pleasant it is to see a great and free people, showing itself openly and in full view of the heavens.[17]

Even the mindless festivities of Lord Mayor's Day he found touching. The fact that a "people as great and busy as the English, occupied as they always are with weighty and important matters" allowed themselves such frivolity revealed something salutary about them and their culture. The celebration was, of course, mere "child's play" but at the same time it was

pleasant to see thousands of people gathering in one place, where a feeling of order and submissiveness in the face of the authorities are the dominant characteristics. And where the waving of one hand by a policeman can impose order upon a mass of people.[18]

Here he saw firsthand the quiet dignity of a culture whose national characteristics were pronounced without being self-conscious and whose everyday life mirrored a healthy and stable political legacy. The essential decency and orderliness of its social life demonstrated a sensibility that he had discovered long before when he read and came to treasure its journals and the writings of English social philosophers. His belief in the impact of thinkers on popular mores, he observed, was reinforced by the experience.

Although the English impressed him, British Jews left him cold. Support for Jewish nationalism appeared far more tepid here than he had imagined. Aside from a few rare and expansive souls, English Jews were simply too mortifying to describe: "I am flushed with embarrassment. I just can't speak about them," he admitted. The Jaffa branch of Bnei Moshe had been led to believe that English Jews could be induced to provide substantial financial support for the Yishuv. He wrote to Bnei Moshe that, at least for the moment, these would remain empty dreams. Here and there, he said, he was meeting supporters of Jewish nationalism who might eventually do something for the cause "but this will require a great deal of time and much exertion (that is, exertion of both an intellectual and moral character, and on top of that financial support)." He added dourly: "In England everything is done in small and deliberate steps."[19] His trip yielded neither solid political achievement nor additional security for his business. But he left England with his admiration for the country essentially intact. Perhaps he had lost some of his

extraordinary predilection for the English. Now I can see that even they have their good and bad qualities, like all other nations. . . . Nonetheless, a great and superlative people they most certainly are.[20]

Back in Odessa, he again announced that his journal—now billed as a Hebrew annual—would soon appear in Berlin. Soon afterwards, probably because of his mounting financial problems, he put that project aside and turned his attention to an altogether different literary venture, a multivolume compendium in Hebrew of Judaic knowledge. By no means were the two projects mutually exclusive; both, indeed, addressed the same basic cultural concerns. The encyclopedia had a clear advantage over the journal because Wissotzsky had already pledged 20,000 roubles to support it. The *Otsar ha-yahadut*, as Ahad Ha'am called it, would, he hoped, contain contributions by leading scholars and he would be its chief editor.

For years he had dreamed, he told Wissotzsky, of finding a patron for this project. The goal of the enterprise would be little less than to reinvigorate the most important strategy in the Jewish cultural arsenal. At every crucial juncture in Jewish history—when faced with catastrophe, dispersal, or vicissitudes of any kind—Jews had managed to seize the moment and renew their commitment to Torah, thereby reaffirming their unity and faith in their continued existence. The best example of this was, of course, Yochanan ben Zakkai to whom Jewish tradition attributed the recentralization of a nascent rabbinic Judaism in Yavneh after the destruction of the second temple in 70 CE. Ahad Ha'am also supported his case, though, with reference to the legal codifications of Judah Ha-Nasi, Maimonides, and Joseph Caro, all of whom he saw as part of the same legacy. The decline in this propensity for cultural renewal was itself, he insisted, a by-product of a larger process of deterioration that threatened the existence of the Jewish people. He believed that the *Otsar* could contribute toward checking this decay and bringing it under control. He told Wissotzsky: "The leaders of the [Jewish] people who wish to ensure its continued existence must first concentrate their attention on the state of Judaic knowledge in our midst and attempt to improve it with the help of methods suitable to our present needs." In the past this had meant the codification of Jewish law; Ahad Ha'am now proposed the additional compilation of all aspects of ritual, folklore, and Jewish history to take full advantage of the diversity of this experience and to make it accessible—as well as, it was hoped, compelling—for a new generation of Jews.[21]

Every Jewish home used to serve, he continued, as a *mikdash me'at* (little tabernacle). Each household was connected to tradition by ties that were all the more profound precisely because they were unconscious. Under such conditions, the dissemination of Jewish knowledge was not so essential as it had now become. This is not to say that Jews were much more knowledgeable in the past; rather, irrespective of what they knew about Judaism, their ties were intense. Thus, it required little more than the publication of dry ritualistic compilations like the *Shulchan Aruch* to sustain their fervor. For them "even without great and detailed knowledge of Judaism, its spirit entered the hearts of its sons, it permeated their limbs as a result of familiar rituals and practices."[22]

In the absence of comparable contemporary bonds, he said, a ritually based Judaism can no longer call upon comparable sentiments. To the extent to which there is any hope of sustaining these ties, this is possible only through the spread of knowledge: "Only in this way will [Jews] appreciate its value and know all the good things hidden" in Judaism. Jewish nationalist sentiments are now in decline since no longer are they nurtured by the performance of religious ritual.

Another reason the project was so important was that in the past Jewish love for learning had propelled the best minds into the *batei midrash*—the traditional Jewish study hall. In Ahad Ha'am's day, the passions of the mind, although no less apparent in Jewish life, fixated no longer on the traditional curriculum and were dominated instead by secular subjects, a body of knowledge vast enough to overwhelm the most intellectually preoccupied Jews. As Ahad Ha'am asked, how can they learn to honor—to the point of self-sacrifice or martyrdom, as they must—a people about whom they have learned so little, whose spirit is alien to them, and whose legacy is virtually inaccessible?[23]

Thus, "a new book is urgently needed once again." It must be written in simple Hebrew and include information on all aspects of Jewish life. If successful, Ahad Ha'am wrote—paraphrasing Maimonides on *Mishna Torah*—one ought to be able to say upon closing its pages that all that there was to learn about Judaism is contained in it. The project would play a role in consolidating the future of the Hebrew language, whose fate in contemporary Jewish life was also wholly dependent on the dissemination of learning. In the past, knowledge of Hebrew was part and parcel of the role exerted by faith—as illustrated by the recitation of daily Hebrew prayers—on the Jewish consciousness. Nationalism is well on its way toward replacing faith; in his view, it was learning of the sort that would be disseminated by the encyclopedia that represented the most potent vehicle for this form of Jewish self-expression.[24]

The *Otsar* would be modeled on Diderot's *Encyclopedie* and made up of twelve or as many as fifteen volumes. Precisely because of its serious intent it had to be designed for casual reading with entries that were brief as well as lucid. Its audience was to be much the same intelligent non-specialists who Ahad Ha'am had long believed would be the backbone of the Jewish revival: literate, maskilic, already committed, basically middle class, and the same sort that he would soon court for *Ha-Shiloach*.

Though initially funded by a sympathetic donor, the project failed to materialize. A small volume in the form of a prospectus eventually surfaced but Ahad Ha'am proved unable to galvanize sufficient financial and scholarly support for the undertaking. Perhaps he capitulated too easily under pressure: rather predictably, the project was criticized by the ultraorthodox camp who rightly suspected that he intended the *Otsar* to supplant the sacred works of Judaism. (This reaction was more fierce than he expected, though.) Others argued that the project could prove valuable only if it encompassed all areas of human knowledge, not only Jewish ones. The distinction made in his proposal between Jewish and non-Jewish topics was too stark, pedantic, and artificial. Others, including several potential contributors, insisted that they couldn't understand how they were expected to write articles with scholarly originality for nonspecialists. Ahiasaf proved an unreliable publisher; Wissotzsky provided funding for only a year and much more was necessary for the project to be feasible. In the end it was scrapped, leaving Ahad Ha'am once again frustrated by what he considered to be the pettiness of those around him. He continued to feel very strongly about the idea and, as late as 1902 (when again he was faced the prospect of unemployment following his resignation from *Ha-Shiloach*), he still hoped that the *Otsar* could be revived with him as editor-in-chief. The project proved still to be impossible, a failure that came to represent in his mind one of his greatest literary disappointments.[25]

By the time these plans had broken down, Ahad Ha'am was in bad health, his business closed, and he had no apparent source of support.

Wissotzsky knew of the loss of his livelihood—Ahad Ha'am had mentioned his financial troubles when he first floated the idea of the *Otsar*—and Wissotzsky undoubtedly came forward with funds for *Ha-Shiloach* because he wanted to provide assistance to a distinguished Jewish nationalist who was suddenly in need. By early 1896, Ahad Ha'am, his health now much improved, took a job as editorial director of Ahiasaf, relocated temporarily to its headquarters in Warsaw, edited the annual *Luah Ahiasaf*, and performed other editorial chores for the publishing house; his employment as a paid functionary at Ahiasaf aggravated him as did his separation from family and friends. It was at this point that Mendele and Dubnow proposed to Wissotzsky that instead of the encyclopedia project which had proven to be too complicated, he fund a journal for Ahad Ha'am. Wissotzsky provided the bulk of the first year's expenses, 4,000 roubles with the Ahad Ha'amist stalwart Barbash putting up the rest. Once again, Ahad Ha'am's Odessa circle had worked to assist him behind the scenes.[26]

Immediately upon its appearance in October 1896, *Ha-Shiloach* established itself as the arbiter of good taste in the Hebrew literary world. To be sure, the competition was rather lax and unimpressive—the same generally sloppy maskilic journals that had so frustrated Ahad Ha'am over the years. From the outset he made it *Ha-Shiloach*'s goal to establish a standard for clear, "European-like" expression in Hebrew; the greatest compliment elicited from the normally taciturn editor was that an article had a European flavor to it. And although Hebrew literature had long devoted itself to the task of "Europeanization," never had one of its journals attempted to perform the task with such consistency, seriousness of purpose, or influence.

In certain respects, Ahad Ha'am courted his writers: he paid them well and, even before the appearance of the first issue, he managed to extract promises from nearly all the prominent Hebrew writers of the day (promises that, much to his chagrin, were frequently broken) to send him pieces and honor deadlines. He had from the very outset a clear notion not only of the publication's goals but also its intended audience: it set out to attract two thousand subscribers (soon the goal would be reduced downward to one thousand) who would be drawn mostly from the stolid maskilic middlebrow. As he wrote in the journal's introductory statement of purpose:

It is not a study hall for scholars that we are establishing, who will then argue with one another and make new discoveries in order to further the cause of pure knowledge. Rather, we plan to reach out to the entire people who will find in this publication a way to nurture their soul.[27]

These would be readers already persuaded of the wisdom of Jewish nationalism but hungry for more solid fare than the current range of Hebrew periodicals. He sensed an "emptiness" afflicting his constituency which could be traced directly to the poverty of Hebraic intellectual life: "The Jewish mind," he warned, "is accustomed to hard labor and cannot remain indefinitely in a state of inactivity." *Ha-Shiloach's* task was to revive this taste—and to reinvigorate it with serious, demanding intellectual fare.[28]

His readership, as he later described it, consisted roughly of two different groups—the first consisted of "enlightened" Jews or maskilim, the second were middle class Jews); he sometimes referred to the latter as "enlightened *balei batim.*" They were, he felt, more or less comparable to those who served as the bulwark of the English journals that he so admired: readers who were cultivated but not foppish, serious without being specialists, committed to their people without falling into the trap of blind partisanship. *Mevinim benonim* is how he had once referred to them; "middlebrow" is probably the closest English equivalent.[29] Hebrew, in contrast, had many rather primitive, unsophisticated readers, as he reminded his prospective writers:

And just as no . . . Frenchman would demand of *Revue des deux Mondes* and no Englishman would ask of *Contemporary Review* that they engage in specialized research into any particular field, it is no more appropriate for Judaica scholars to ask that *Ha-Shiloach* embark on individual investigations into issues bearing on the "science of Judaism." But *Ha-Shiloach* can ask that they speak to their people in an appropriate way. Why is it that men like Stuart Mill, Lecky, Spencer, et al. were not embarrassed to write popular articles in newspapers to teach the people the general principles of knowledge?[30]

Eventually he would come to despair of attracting the Jewish middlebrow and even ceased to believe that more than a handful of such readers existed; true, in 1901, with the subscription list of *Ha-Shiloach* plummeting to just over five hundred, he still contended that although his periodical was not suitable for the "multitude of *balei batim*" it was aimed at the "multitude of modern [Jews] and maskilic readers of Hebrew." Soon he admitted that he was no longer convinced that many of them existed either. Ahad Ha'am had not expected such disinterest: he embarked on the project full of hope in its likely impact, its intended readership, and its compatibility with his own predilections and strengths.

Its statement of purpose identified the following tasks: *Ha-Shiloach* would set out to clarify the essential characteristics of the Jewish nationality for which "we have battled the entire world for thousands of years." It would explain what continued to unify Jews and how such links could be further solidified. Finally it would address how and when Jews would finally reach their ultimate destination as a nation—or, as he put it, "make it to the shore."[31] With this last item, Ahad Ha'am obliquely linked the journal to the Palestinophile cause that represented his primary inspiration.

These goals that he had so cautiously formulated seemed unlikely to ignite much controversy. One feature of the statement proved to be very hotly contested, though: Ahad Ha'am's flat refusal to publish any material without explicit Jewish content. Its priorities, as he outlined them in order of preference, were scholarship, journalism, criticism, and literature; whatever was accepted, including fiction, had to demonstrate that it had direct relevance to the Jewish experience which, in the minds of some readers, narrowed unnecessarily the horizons of a modernizing Jewry. To be acceptable, fiction must consist of "good stories from the past or present of our people that provide a faithful portrait of our conditions in various times and places and illuminate some aspect of our 'inner world.'" Writing devoid of such substantive content—without direct bearing on the journal's pedagogical and political tasks—had no place. No more than one poem, he proposed, would be published in any issue; fiction too would take a back seat to other, more important, influential forms of exposition.[32]

The first issue of Ha-Shiloach was handsomely produced with a light green cover. It ran one hundred pages in length (the standard length during Ahad Ha'am's stewardship). By no means was its nationalist character self-evident, at least to the casual reader. It was staid and dignified, cerebral rather than provocative. Some readers would soon complain that they found it too staid, which Ahad Ha'am attributed to their being accustomed to the vague, woolly "casuistry" (pilpul) of a beit midrash and to writers drawn from the stable of "poor yeshiva students and melamdim": cloistered, predictably maskilic, and often comically pompous. Confronted now with a monthly journal adhering to European cultural standards, such readers looked back with nostalgia at the primitive but familiar publications of the past. Such complaints must be ignored, he warned his patron's apprehensive son-in-law in January 1897; Ha-Shiloach's goal must be to "refine the taste of its Hebrew readers so that they would no longer find pleasure" in vulgar sensationalism.[33]

Despite Ahad Ha'am reservations about fiction the inaugural edition of Ha-Shiloach led off with a section from Mendele's Be-emek ha-bakha

(*In the Vale of Tears*). But it was the sociological not the aesthetic importance of the novel—which depicted the vagaries of shtetl life—that won the editor's admiration. The same issue included scholarly articles on the nationalist thinker Ernst Renan and his view of Judaism, the medieval poet Ibn Gabirol, educational issues in Jewish life, and the modern Hebrew poet Judah Leib Gordon. Except for the article on education (written by Yehudah Leib Dawidowicz, now a devoted follower of Ahad Ha'am) none of the pieces dealt with a contemporary theme, nor did they speak directly to any of the major concerns of Jewish nationalism. The publication's tenor would remain more or less the same during Ahad Ha'am's six-year editorship. The journal's goals were grand but, in terms of their manifestation, the publication was sophisticated and intellectually demanding rather than particularly lively or daring. Ahad Ha'am's chosen course frustrated his financial backers and alienated many of his readers.[34]

He insisted nonetheless throughout his tenure as editor that its character be left entirely unchanged: even when he placed his friend Shimon Bernfeld temporarily in charge during his trip to Palestine in 1900, he did so because he trusted that Bernfeld would make no serious changes. He explained to Bernfeld in great detail how every issue would begin with two or three scholarly or perhaps literary articles. "Some belletristic item," should follow, then something light, perhaps a story, a sketch, or a casual exercise in literary history. Then should come a poem—not more than one, he still insisted. This would be followed by literary criticism or book reviews, items about contemporary Jewish affairs (he proposed "Jews and Judaism in America"), and, finally, some easily digestible endpieces. These final, unessential contributions, which included his own column "Yalkut katan" ("A Small Bundle"), provide a useful respite from hard intellectual labor. At the publication's core, then, was scholarship—elegantly presented, neither extensively footnoted nor rendered arcane in any way, and accessible to the intelligent East European Jewish gentleman. The scholarly articles selected were to be linked however vaguely to *Ha-Shiloach*'s agenda. Abstract scholarship he rejected out-of-hand, or he read into it tendentious goals; such exercises had little value, "bricks" without an edifice.[35]

He was a relentless taskmaster—rigid, even brutal with his writers who were accustomed to the casual methods of the maskilic press. For several years he edited everything himself, often changing articles thoroughly before publication; many thanked him for his efforts, but when they did not he labeled them ingrates and incompetents. Despite his early enthusiasm about the prospect of earning his living as a literary man, he found his new life exasperating. The drudgery exhausted and unnerved him. The constant challenge of deadlines, the need to cajole writers to honor commitments, the task of making their work publishable, all depressed him. At the same time he fell quite comfortably into the role and never found it difficult to impose his editorial will upon others. As a political leader, he appeared reticent and uncertain; as a guiding editor he acted with undisguised confidence and assertiveness. Perhaps he permitted himself this because the role of Hebrew editor lacked precedence in Jewish tradition. He perhaps felt in this context freer to exert his authority without recourse to the Jewish leadership patterns of the past.

Nevertheless, so resilient was this image of him as a man paralyzed by ambivalence that some readers claimed to have found telltale evidence of it in the first sentence of *Ha-Shiloach*'s statement of purpose. It reads: "In now establishing this new journal we are, I think, doing something that our times demand." Its use of the qualification "I think" precipitated something of a literary war. His opponents claimed that here was vintage Ahad Ha'am: uncertain, wary, tentative, indirect, and consequently ineffectual. Admirers took advantage of the controversy to praise his proverbial modesty and good taste and his unwillingness to impose its austere standards on the rest of the Jewish people. Neither side saw the introduction for what it was: a literary device culled from the English publishing arsenal that Ahad Ha'am so admired. This battle raged briefly but in its sudden (and rather comical) intensity it presaged other considerably more prolonged literary fights still to come.[36]

Most of these fights were with writers. He saw *Ha-Shiloach* as "the only place to publish for a [Hebrew] writer who has any respect for either literature or himself," and treated his contributors to a combination of professionalism, intense scrutiny, and scorn. The veteran writer Mordecai Ben Hillel Ha-Cohen was one of these who soon became a close friend and eventually a relative through marriage. He was stunned when Ahad Ha'am, whom he respected but also viewed as a newcomer to Jewish letters, sent him the edited version of Ha-Cohen's first contribution to *Ha-Shiloach* with numerous changes. And rarely would Ahad Ha'am permit writers to forget their errors even once they were corrected. Those who had been late with submissions and who subsequently sent pieces on time had them acknowledged with tart reminders from Ahad Ha'am that they must not revert to their old ways. His rejection letters were pointed, sometimes merciless; almost all his acceptances were terse and unenthusiastic. As he wrote Berdyczewski, who be-seeched Ahad Ha'am to tell him what the editor had liked about his articles: "It is obvious that I liked all your articles that have appeared in *Ha-Shiloach* or else I would not have published them."[37]

His chief adversary, as he understood it, was *batlanut*, the meander-ing, wordy, sloppy prose that filled so much of the contemporary He-brew press. Indeed, Ha-Shiloach's articles were much better than those that appeared elsewhere: they were lean, lucid, and often sardonic. In short, they read much like Ahad Ha'am's own writing.

Ironically, a good example of the sort of writing that he sought to avoid in his journal—and hoped to obliterate in Hebrew letters—can be found in the review of *Al Parashat Derakhim* published in *Ha-Melitz* by friend Joshua Sirkin:

I was pleased to find in the hands of the wise writer Dr. Isaac Kaminer (with whom I am now staying in his country house in order to strengthen myself after a recent illness) a new book *Al Parashat Derakhim*, that contains all that has been published until now by our superb writer "Ahad Ha'am." I immediately set out to reread all the articles which tasted like sweet honey in my mouth even though all of them were already known to me. Though I recall every one of them from the day that they first appeared on the scene and up until now, neither their spirit nor good judgment have paled with time.[38]

Self-indulgent, self-referential, fawning—these were some of the fea-tures that Ahad Ha'am sought to transform during his tenure as *Ha-Shiloach*'s editor. He set out at the same time to turn Hebrew into what was his vision of a modern literary language: taut, efficient, unequivocal, and free from its older, crippling dependency on the terminology bor-rowed from biblical and rabbinic literature.

His effort to impose a standard literary style was controversial, es-pecially among younger intellectuals, most importantly Berdyczewski, who objected to Ahad Ha'am's assertion that Judaism was (and would always be) characterized by certain unchanging spiritual characteristics. It was its spiritual character, as sustained by its "national will for sur-vival," that transcended time and place and that informed Judaism with its fundamental morality. Ahad Ha'am taught that the Jewish "national spirit" dictated a normative behavior (as exemplified, above all, by the aspirations of the Prophets, the Pharisees, or Yochanan ben Zakkai); once revived, secularized, and geographically recentralized in the Holy Land this should translate into a code of behavior no less comprehensive and creative (and, arguably, a good deal more so) than in the rabbinic one of the past.

Berdyczewski, nine years Ahad Ha'am's junior, spent much of his fertile literary career—he was the author of hundreds of essays, stories, novels, and literary anthologies—polemicizing with Ahad Ha'am over these and related issues. The appearance of *Ha-Shiloach*, and especially its assertion that it saw a fundamental division between the functions of Hebrew literature and the literature written in non-Jewish languages, served to place special emphasis on this literary debate.[39]

For Berdyczewski, as shown by Marcus Moseley in his recent dissertation, perhaps the only way that the terrible split in the modern Jew could be healed in wake of modernity's attack on the unself-conscious patterns of the Jewish past was through literature. The trauma to Jewish culture caused by Haskalah was immeasurably more serious than Ahad Ha'am recognized. ("Cursed be the day when the Haskalah took me under her wings and hewed down the forest that grew in me, the forest of generations," an autobiographical narrator says in his *A velt mit veltlakh*.) The solution cannot be (as proposed by Ahad Ha'am) a new, comprehensive Judaism—as dogmatic as the former one but predicated now on dubiously secular foundations. The alternative as Berdyczewski saw it was a Judaism immeasurably more eclectic than either traditional or Ahad Ha'amist categories would allow: a Judaism whose elastic character would be made up of "ancestral-traces" (in Moseley's felicitous words). These traces, argued Berdyczewski, were most apparent in autobiographical literature, and he searched for forgotten autobiographical fragments with great assiduousness. What most interested him in this regard, and what in his view could best serve the needs of contemporary Jews, was literature produced by those in the past who found themselves outside the reigning consensus: marginal Jews whose psychological and spiritual journeys between individual expression and collective attachment were now of special relevance. What he called "historical anguish," he argued, is a feature of the Jewish experience as a whole and its fundamental source of creativity.[40]

Hence Ahad Ha'am's countermyth of an overweening morality dictating normative Judaism was no less oppressive in its own way than the rabbinic hegemony of the past. Nor did it possess historical validity. The Judaic monolith constructed by Ahad Ha'am was undermined by the Bible with its tales of intrigue, bloody relations between Judea and the tribes of the north, by the Hasmoneans, and the martyrs of Masada. In fact, it was the pre-Mosaic age—the "golden age" of Jewish history, according to Berdyczewski, when the people did evil in the eyes of the Lord and before the giving of the law—when Jewish vitality was at its height. Such behavior was suppressed by Moses who imposed upon Jewry the heavy weight of a rigidly homogeneous tradition alien to them, their past, and human nature. Berdyczewski, and the other Nietzschean "youth" (the name they chose for the publishing house they established in opposition to Ahad Ha'am's Ahiasaf was *Tze'irim*, or Youth) who clustered around him in opposition to *Ha-Shiloach*, fired upon the most vulnerable points in Ahad Ha'am's intellectual arsenal. It was his subjectivity that they attacked and not because they reviled subjectivity, which they did not, but because they knew that Ahad Ha'am abhorred it; they saw his solutions, which were, to date, the most comprehensive in the Jewish cultural debates of the period, as misguided, as half-measures, as unwilling to face up to the fundamental tragedy at the core of modern Jewish existence. Berdyczewski took solace in his discovery of a vast, previously obscure "counter-history," a tension-filled creative legacy running parallel to the normative Judaism that Ahad Ha'am sought to secularize and sustain. Later critics of Ahad Ha'am like Brenner would deny Judaism even this semblance of consistency or cultural continuity.[41]

It was precisely Ahad Ha'am's assumption that the "national will for survival" could be substituted for Israel's belief in God, that ethics could replace law, that the history of the Jews (and, more importantly, their eternal role in history) could be understood in secular, not supernatural terms—these underscored the power, and the limitations, of his ideology. These features of his thought were never so visible as during his first years at *Ha-Shiloach* when he was subjected to the furious attacks of the youth. Ahad Ha'am responded like a patient, stern, unruffled father; he said little that was new and usually elaborated on what he had said before. In his replies, and in the other pieces of his published in *Ha-Shiloach*, emerged the journal's editorial line, one set down already in *Al Parashat Derakhim*. What he produced in these years was a sort of running commentary on his definitive statements of the past.

When Ahad Ha'am first secured this editorial post he took for granted that it would allow him the time to write, at least more time than he had before when he made his living as a businessman. He envisioned himself serving as a high priest in the temple of literature. He soon claimed that he had had more free time when he ran his various businesses than now when he made his living from literature. His best hours were spent correcting the prose of others, leaving him exhausted and unable to do much more than respond to correspondence or light reading. In fact, he wrote little during his first year as editor. When Wissotzsky and others prodded him to write they complained that subscriptions to *Ha-Shiloach* would improve if he wrote for it regularly. He answered that he expended his energy improving the work of others: if his critics knew anything about Western journalistic practices, they would realize that editors edit and writers write. He said this with mock annoyance, feigning surprise that the complaint had ever surfaced, even though he was already exasperated by the burdens of his schedule. Within a year of the appearance of *Ha-Shiloach,* the advent of Herzl and his Zionist movement would bring Ahad Ha'am back to his writing desk. Thus, he wrote a fair amount from 1897 until 1902 before he retired as editor. Nearly all these pieces were attacks on the new movement. As a writer he required an object to attack: the Hovevei Zion had in fact served as his foil when he first emerged on the Odessa scene, but by the mid-1890s it no longer could be used quite as effectively, particularly since he had come to play so large a role in shaping its priorities. The Herzlian movement was admirably suited to the adversarial role. With its appearance and the convening of its first congress, Ahad Ha'am gained once again a timely, publicly accessible, and unquestionably important forum for the airing of his views on politics and society.

Although he wrote little for *Ha-Shiloach* in its first year, the journal always served as a vehicle for the promulgation of his ideas. True, he claimed that it was nonpartisan and that it took no definite side in the various disputes in the Jewish nationalist world. But clearly it did take sides, with its direction charted by his own column that appeared at the back of nearly every issue—printed in small type and located in what was the least prestigious spot in the issue. Yet in keeping with his long-standing tactics that were proven effective, placing his pieces here served to heighten their visibility. This column appeared at first as one of a series of random reflections written by several hands; soon he took charge of the section, called it "Yalkut katan" ("Small Bundle"), and made it the monthly's most important regular feature. Here he produced a terse, sporadic but running commentary on the Jewish world, and these brief pieces—sometimes no more than three or four paragraphs long—were pithy and relentless as they focused their attention on the foibles of modern Jewry.

One of the first, entitled "Ha-Yovel" ("Jubilee"), explained the term as having always been intended as an affirmation of the future, a celebration of hope and renewal: "The Jewish Jubilee is a festival of the future, a festival of slaves who emerged from servitude into freedom." How, he asked, is it used today? Oddly, as an exercise in narcissism where those deemed to be luminaries (mostly by other mediocrities) celebrate their respective achievements in ceremonies that only serve to belie their people's historic revulsion for idolatry. Moses himself managed to be commemorated without any sort of monument; we've grown accustomed to hero worship that is really the by-product of cultural sterility. It has no basis in the authentic mores of Jewry: rather it is a foreign and dangerous innovation.[42]

In a similar vein, "Mitzvah ha-bah me-averah" ("Redemption Through Sin") attacked the Hebrew press's practice of announcing the names of Palestinophile donors. They encouraged the giving of money, sometimes a mere pittance, simply for the purpose of admiring one's name in print. When one compares the way in which money is raised in Eastern and Western Europe, he suggests, it is obvious that in the more cultivated parts of Europe (meaning the West), philanthropy is in the hands of committees who do not even list the names of the biggest givers. Even when named, it is not with the gusto that we see among Eastern European Jewry. The article ends on a thoroughly uncompromising note: he recalls a recent debate in the Jewish press between "two famous writers." One argued that donations for Palestine be designated for the support of the Jaffa school since education, he argued, must take precedence over all else. The second defended funding agricultural colonies. Writes Ahad Ha'am: "And I, if I believed that my words would be heard, I would intercede and say, 'money that comes as a result of sinful practices, give it over to the *egel* [literally, *calf*; Hebrew abbreviation for *incest, robbery,* and *slander,* or *the golden calf of the desert*], so that the *mishkon,* the tabernacle, might be relieved and rescued."[43]

The article caused an enormous stir. Various provincial committees of the Hovevei Zion claimed it hurt their fundraising and, whether or not it did, it seems to have dampened the enthusiasm of some *Ha-Shiloach* readers. Not only was *Ha-Shiloach* demanding, stolid, and sometimes a bit dull, it also, they discovered, insulted the sensibilities of the nationalist partisans who subscribed to it as an act of allegiance and good faith.[44]

At other times in "Yalkut katan" Ahad Ha'am published effectively secular sermons: pieces built on biblical passages and designed as inspirational lessons, albeit typically with an ironic, idiosyncratic twist. He argued in "Samaritans," for instance, that had Jews remained hostile to all accommodation with the larger world in the wake of the destruction of the second temple—much as today's obscurantists would now like them to be—they would have made no links with non-Jews and would have found themselves far more vulnerable and friendless. Without these essential connections, the hostile passions of their enemies would, if anything, have been more deadly—perhaps irredeemably so. Hence he acknowledges here that, despite the wretched legacy of gentile antisemitism, some degree of cooperation between Jews and non-Jews is a part of the historical record: it is both feasible and essential in the shaping of the Jewish agenda of the future. Later he would ridicule Herzl's excessive faith in the good will of Gentile allies, but he nonetheless recognized (though he rarely stressed the point quite so explicitly) that such cooperation was an important feature of Jewry's passage through time—and perhaps was especially significant now when Jewry set out to rebuild its own national culture.[45]

Irony was the single most pronounced feature of these essays. Elsewhere, in his diary for instance, he permitted himself to be lyrical; in his published work, though, this lyricism was all but concealed. In one of the more memorable contributions to "Yalkut katan," entitled "Sam hayyim" ("Elixir of Life"), he managed to combine irony and lyricism to reveal as vividly as in anything he would write a certain quirky vision of the world—sardonic, deadpan, and at the same time overwhelmingly hopeful.

Ahad Ha'am celebrates in "Sam hayyim" the coining of a new Hebrew term that indicates an important turning point in Jewish culture: the term is *zevel*, fertilizer. He says that he just read a detailed exposition in the newspaper *Ha-Zevi* on the rich varieties of fertilizers suitable for the Palestinian agrarian economy and

the odor of the fields, the healthy odor of nature fills our nostrils from this fertilizer and makes us realize that, despite the poverty and lassitude of the new Yishuv, there exists embedded within it something of an elixir of life for our nation. Slowly, and without our awareness, this elixir will help transport us from one world to another.[46]

The pungent odor of fertilizer serves here as an inspirational clue to the way even the profoundly flawed Jewish enterprise in Palestine is preparing the basis for the revival of contemporary Jewry. Probably he also intends to satirize here an entire genre of literature inspired by the Hovevei Zion (and which would be perpetuated by the Zionist movement) that spoke in purple language of the reclamation of the land, the achievements of the colonists, and the unsurpassed grandeur of manual labor in Zion. He means here to be both ironic and self-deprecating: as the well-known chief internal critic of Palestinophilism, the one most likely to see the ugliest aspect of the nationalist enterprise, he turns the table on his more sanguine critics and assures them that he is able nonetheless to recognize that the foundations for Zion's rebirth are being established—slowly, imperfectly, but relentlessly. And what is it that reminds him of this? It is the rancid-smelling manure covering the fields whose stench helps reassure him of the eventual transformation of land and people.[47]

A frequent theme of "Yalkut katan" was the misperception of East European Jews by their Western brethren, whose condescension, even whose desire for their social betterment implies an utter incomprehension. In "Go'el hadash" ("A New Savior") he responds to Solomon Reinach, the French archaeologist and leader of the Alliance Israélite Universelle, who wrote a piece about the deplorable social conditions of the Jews in Eastern Europe. These conditions, he claimed, could be traced to archaic Jewish attachments to rituals like the Sabbath (that impeded efficient work habits) or dietary laws (that forbade the eating of inexpensive meats). Reinach judges them obscure and superstitious, thereby highlighting how alien they are to an emancipated age. The argument, says Ahad Ha'am, is rational, sensible, and also devoid of "any true Jewish feeling." Why can't he see that

one can be extremely intelligent and familiar with the theories of the learned world and the origins of the Sabbath and other religious rituals . . . [which evolved] . . . out of the crude beliefs and emotions of the primitives, but can still find the Sabbath a delight, still respect and hold sacred the day which has been sanctified by the blood of our people and has preserved it for thousands of years from spiritual degeneration.[48]

The Jews of the East—the "paupers" now pouring into the West, much to the chagrin of so many emancipated Western Jews—if listened to, can help teach their brothers how to extricate themselves from their "spiritual bondage." It is they who can fill the "spiritual emptiness" of Western Jewish life: "[W]e will bring you Judaism, and not the nice-sounding, meaningless lip service which is your confession of faith, but rather a living Judaism of the heart inspired with the will and power to renew its strength." Like the paupers from the East, whom the Romans also found contemptible before they in turn were vanquished by them, these newcomers, too, will take over the Western Jewish world. Until then—and so that the inevitable dislocation felt by the once-powerful West is kept to a bare minimum—it is essential that they begin to look upon their Russian and Polish brothers as more than mere objects of pity but rather as guides to a more coherent future.[49]

II

By the time this article appeared in 1901, the pretensions of Western Jewish leaders already keenly preoccupied Ahad Ha'am in the wake of the rise of Theodor Herzl. Herzl spanned eight years as a Jewish nationalist leader; he died in 1904 at the age of forty-four. He transformed the loose patchwork of Russian Palestinophilism into an international movement with a respectable if still modest diplomatic standing. The relationship between them—the two outstanding Jewish nationalists of the period—was complex, vituperative, laced with condescension on both sides, and replete with chronic misunderstandings and conscious and unconscious slights.

The movement's center moved westward now from Eastern to Central Europe, though the bulk of its membership—and, alas, most of its still-meager financial resources—were still drawn from the East. Ahad Ha'am could not but recognize that the battle he had fought since the mid-1880s for the hegemony of cultural politics in the Jewish nationalist movement had reached a crucial if not perilous turning point.

Before Herzl's arrival most of Ahad Ha'am's ideological foes were notables of local standing and, with the exception of Lilienblum, without either his intellectual standing or prestige. The often bitter battles he engaged in with Hovevei Zion he conducted as an insider, a member of its executive board, a friend of Leon Pinsker, and as someone who called himself a Hovev Zion. Indeed, as we have seen, he went so far as to claim that Pinsker himself had sworn allegiance before his death to Ahad Ha'am's viewpoint and that this represented Pinsker's true legacy. Hence, Ahad Ha'am managed to tower over all his foes, who may have at times outnumbered him but could never match him.

Herzl in contrast was a famous writer, though perhaps less famous than Zionists preferred to believe. He and his considerably more distinguished colleague, Max Nordau, were the best-known figures ever attracted to Jewish nationalism. Both had published widely and were masters of European literature (at the very least, Herzl must be recognized as an outstanding feuilletonist). For his part, Ahad Ha'am was the editor of a small monthly distributed mostly in the obscure margins of the Russian empire, a member of the executive committee of an equally obscure nationalist society, and a thinker whose rather paltry body of published work (printed in one modest-sized volume in 1895) remained untranslated and inaccessible to all but readers of the biblical tongue. For the first time it seemed as if he would be overshadowed in the Jewish nationalist world.[50]

As if this were not bad enough, from Ahad Ha'am's perspective Herzl's aspirations were incomparably more ambitious and reckless than the staid if somewhat pathetic aims of Hovevei Zion. Not only did he fail to take culture into account, but in his style of politics he represented a sharp, sinister break with Jewish history: his cultivation of the masses (which Ahad Ha'am immediately denounced as demagoguery) coupled with his promise of rapid redemption conjured terrifying comparisons with messianic pretenders of the past. Ahad Ha'am repeatedly likened him (sometimes explicitly, usually not) to the seventeenth-century Sabbatai Sevi whose messianic adventurism and cynical mass manipulation unleashed one of Jewish history's worst episodes. He went so far as to charge Herzl with heresy. On a practical level, Herzl's plans were no less dangerous. His declaration that he intended to extract a Charter from the Turkish Sultan for the establishment of what he brazenly called a *Judenstaat* was not merely a fanciful notion with no chance of success but an act that placed the Palestinian Jewish colonies at risk.[51]

All these charges appeared in 1897, in the wake of the First Zionist Congress. Ahad Ha'am previously had greeted the call for a congress with silence. Though (very critical) mention was made of Herzl and his 1896 pamphlet *Judenstaat* in *Ha-Shiloach,* the congress itself wasn't mentioned until Ahad Ha'am's own condemnation of it several months afterwards. As he wrote a friend in July 1897, a month before the congress, he had decided to publish nothing about it in *Ha-Shiloach* because he couldn't bring himself to extoll it (as he felt did most of his colleagues) and felt that whatever criticisms he had were best aired afterwards: "I'm already viewed by so many as a pessimist who sees and predicts only bad things. So what impact will my words have?" Perhaps he also hoped that once the congress took place his misgivings would gain wider credence.[52]

He admitted to others that he held out some modest hope for the meeting, even though it was likely to have a detrimental impact on Turkish policy. But a show of highly visible support for Jewish nationalism could influence the mostly unsympathetic Jewish rich of the West to embrace (or, at least, to finance) the cause. He remained skeptical of what diplomacy could accomplish and remained convinced that the future of Palestine would only be secured slowly through the building of colonies. But he went to Basel with a degree of optimism. He also urged his devotees to attend and to join him in defending the Hovevei Zion's achievements.

Reactions to Herzl by East European Jewish nationalist leaders were in fact considerably more mixed than they (or Ahad Ha'am) cared to admit. Suspicious, perhaps also envious of the dazzling newcomer, many of them spoke of his galling ignorance of Jewish affairs, including his unawareness until after he wrote *Judenstaat* of the existence of their movement. Moreover, his inability to attract to his banner Baron Rothschild left them unsettled; Palestinian Jewry's primary benefactor made his dislike for Herzl well known. Herzl's lack of sympathy for Palestinian colonization efforts, which he considered fragile and tenuous, insulted them and their accomplishments. What was essential in Herzl's view in the primitive reaches of Eastern Europe was to court rabbis and not the maskilic nationalists of the Hovevei Zion who claimed to speak for the East but who as neither traditionalists nor real modernists lacked (as he saw it) a following and legitimacy.

They also fretted about how they would likely be marginalized at a congress whose proceedings were in German and, still worse, that would take place in Switzerland, notorious as the center for Russian radical emigrés so that the Russian secret police would likely view them as politically suspect. Herzl decided against having the congress at Zurich, the major Russian emigré center, partly out of regard for their apprehensions. Hence, before the congress there was probably little difference between Ahad Ha'am's doubts about Herzl and those of other leading Russian Jewish nationalists.[53]

Public criticism was nevertheless muted. Eventually Herzl would go out of his way to calm most of their fears, and his reputation was salvaged somewhat when Max Nordau, whom many of them (including Ahad Ha'am) read with great respect, announced his support for him. Rumors, soon proved false, that the chief benefactor and founder of the Jewish Colonization Association, Baron Maurice de Hirsch, agreed with Herzl calmed somewhat fears over Rothschild's negative reaction. By the end of the congress, nearly everyone cast their reservations aside, eager to share in the limelight that their movement suddenly enjoyed. For all Herzl's flaws he had given them visibility; indeed; the European press extensively covered the congress. For the first time since the 1884 Kattowitz congress, nationalists saw some prospect for success. Misgivings remained about Herzl but they were mostly silenced, at least in the first few heady years of his leadership, which owed as much to his charm as to the Hovevei Zion's glum recognition that there were few alternatives. It was feared that without Herzl, nationalists would find themselves once again spinning their wheels in the obscure arena of maskilic politics.

No matter what they happened to think of Herzl, he had rapidly made himself into a folk hero in the East European Jewish world. His handsome appearance, his literary importance, his many important connections (frequently exaggerated but not wholly imagined) made Jewish nationalism into an object of great interest: the Hovevei Zion had a mere seventy branches in 1896; within two years some three hundred new ones came into existence. As Hovevei Zion activist (and erstwhile Bnei Moshe brother) Leib Jaffe noted in a letter written soon after the congress:

The topic of conversation everywhere is the Congress in Basel. Now attitudes toward Zionism have changed completely. This is true of the rabbis, the intelligentsia and the community as a whole. Oddly enough, the religious do not seem to feel the need to scrutinize the religious credentials [livdok et ha-tzitzit] of the foreign Zionists, as if they are simply outside of their jurisdiction. The intelligentsia is still thunderstruck by the grand impressions left by the Zionist Congress, which transformed Zionism all at once into a movement with the eyes of the whole world upon it.[54]

His own experience there persuaded Ahad Ha'am that Jewish nationalists like himself, contrary to widespread assumptions, were certain to find themselves more marginalized than ever before. In Herzl's eyes, he warned, an East European secularist like Ahad Ha'am was seen as no less cloistered and culturally irrelevant than the fiercest traditionalist. Quite simply, Herzl wasn't equipped to distinguish between them: to Herzl, both were foreign and backward and must be treated with a combination of caution, studious manipulation, and distance. Ahad Ha'am felt like "a mourner at a wedding."[55]

The fact that Herzl treated him shabbily at the congress rankled him. In the first of two conversations they had in Basel, Ahad Ha'am queried whether it was wise to pursue the creation of a National Fund as Herzl had suggested publicly. Ironically, the idea had been proposed years earlier by the Bnei Moshe, though of course Ahad Ha'am did not mention this. Ahad Ha'am felt that the movement was unlikely to collect much money and the premature exercise would prove ineffective. Herzl responded that if the amount collected was too small it would be kept secret. This failed to satisfy Ahad Ha'am; nor did it convince him of the

Zionist leader's trustworthiness. He found Herzl frivolous and glib rather than thoughtful.[56]

After this conversation—in which Ahad Ha'am no doubt made his disapproval clear—Herzl seems to have avoided him until they chanced upon one another on the street one evening and spoke briefly about Herzl's Turkish negotiations. The Hebraist explained to Herzl that, as a member of the Hovevei Zion executive committee, he was obliged to report on these when he returned home. Based on this exchange, however, Ahad Ha'am concluded that Herzl had achieved nothing serious on the diplomatic front. Ahad Ha'am sensed that he was being treated as a nuisance (which was probably how the Zionist leader saw him) and left the congress feeling personally wounded and deeply disturbed about the future of Jewish nationalism. As he wrote Rawnitsky before leaving Basel, "Yesterday evening the congress ended. My head and bones still ache and I cannot permit myself to express what is in my heart because I would not be able to control my emotions." Basel, he was convinced, had destroyed more than it built.[57]

The fact that his savagely critical essay on the congress echoed recent, muted criticisms of Herzl shared by many of its Russian delegates made it especially provocative. It was the familiarity of the arguments, not their novelty, that made them all the more threatening. It was also his harshest piece to date—the least compromising, constructive, or empathetic—and he acknowledged its severity in a sequel that he claimed was designed to soften its blow but where he failed to disavow any of the points made in it.

Indeed, Herzl's sudden prominence seems to have unsettled him and probably helped cause Ahad Ha'am's strikingly uncivil tone, especially in his first piece on the congress: to see, as he had in Basel, young, impetuous throngs gravitating to the new Zionist leader made Ahad Ha'am frightened, resentful, and perhaps also somewhat jealous. He all but admitted this—or, at the very least, acknowledged how odd it felt to be thrust aside for Herzl when he himself was at the height of his own power—in one of his last articles, written in Palestine in 1923 for a commemorative volume on the congress:

The First Zionist Congress! My heart pounds and I cannot manage to calm myself even as I now recall those good days. Then I was in my prime, with my literary and communal work at its height. Not even a year had passed since the launching of *Ha-Shiloach,* and I was immersed in both mind and soul in making it into a nationalist platform honored by the best of our people. And then comes the first congress that brings about a revolution in our world.[58]

"The salvation of Israel will be achieved by prophets not by diplomats," he warns at the end of his 1897 article. True, it is Nordau to whom he refers in the text as speaking with a prophetic voice at the congress and he contrasts his brilliant address with Herzl's tepid performance. But ever since he first appeared as public figure, Ahad Ha'am had closely aligned himself with prophetic politics. Although the diplomat to whom he refers in his declaration is undoubtedly Herzl, his claim that the pretensions of the diplomat must give way to the prophet seems only a slightly veiled bid for his own primacy or at least for the primacy of his brand of politics.[59] This was especially the case since he sensed at this moment and to a greater degree than ever before that the movement he had claimed was slipping from his hands.

At the article's beginning, where he managed to sound both world-weary and mean-spirited, he says that the tumult surrounding the congress can only be understood as a by-product of the drabness of everyday Jewish life: "The Zionist congress . . . that has filled the emptiness of our little world for some months is now a thing of the past." Had the delegates been clearheaded about what the meeting could, in fact, achieve it would have been at worst innocuous. If they went to Basel with the intention of announcing to the world that the Jews still existed as a nation, the meeting—dignified, large, and highly visible as it was— might have been something of a success. Not only are declarations of this sort important as reminders for the larger, non-Jewish world, but Jews too need them to arouse themselves from their national degradation. Having done this, delegates should have returned home to set about doing the sole thing that they can at this juncture: renew Jewry's moral fiber, strengthen its national unity, and thus contribute to its moral transformation. Indeed, even had Palestine been given over immediately to the enthusiastic crowd at Basel, they would not have been prepared to assume control of it. What they would establish would be politically inept and unworthy of the legacy of the Jewish past: have Jews suffered in exile for thousands of years, he asked rhetorically, to claim control over a culturally marginal strip of land dependent for its existence on the sufferance of other nations? Such a state would be "tossed about like a ball between its powerful neighbors, and would maintain its existence only by virtue of constant diplomatic shifts and jockeying for favors":

An ancient people that was once a beacon to the world cannot possibly accept as an adequate reward for all that it has suffered a thing so trifling that many other peoples without either standing or culture have achieved in a short period of time and without enduring a fraction of our suffering.[60]

Long ago the prophets warned that it was impossible for Jewry to remain at peace in a land buffeted by hostile forces. It was, he says, with this in mind that they formulated their vision of the end of days and "this ideal for humanity has always been, and will always be, an essential part of the national ideal of the Jewish people."[61]

Ignoring this lesson, oblivious both to the Jewish past and the grim limitations of the present, the First Zionist Congress, Ahad Ha'am explained, showed once again the terrible impatience of the Jewish people: their inability to wait until conditions in Palestine (and elsewhere) are suitable. They had squandered an excellent opportunity to make a real, if less flamboyant; contribution. The same impatience for immediate redemption was the cause of much suffering (what he means here is Sabbatian messianism) in the immediate past; now it was the impatient East European Jewish youth—desperate for change and certain, as a result, to meet with disaster—who have found in Herzl a ready ally. During the congress, and immediately following it, Herzl did his best to "kindle their . . . feverish enthusiasm." What could well have been a dignified and momentous event was transformed into a mockery, a showcase for Jewry's worst characteristics.[62]

As much as one wished to ignore these premonitions, continued Ahad Ha'am, there were clear signs that the project was ill-conceived even before the congress began. Its emissaries hinted at imminent redemption, whetting the appetite of the masses and thereby attracting to Basel "a rabble of youth, young in both years and in understanding." Once it concluded, the same enthusiasts felt it their responsibility to bring back the good news that the establishment of a Jewish state was imminent.[63]

To Ahad Ha'am, as he watched the congress unfold before his eyes, it had seemed to resemble rather uncannily the events of 1891 when Palestinian land fever had so unsettled Jewish nationalism. Ahad Ha'am reminded his readers that he alone had issued a stinging warning, alluding to "Emet me-eretz yisrael"; he expected this piece to ignite a similar torrent of criticism as well. The land fever had been a dark and even scandalous episode but he emphasized that the current threat is immeasurably greater since the hopes that it has aroused are all that much keener. Back in 1891, he reminded his readers, he was accused of being a traitor to the cause of Jewish nationalism, but history in the end proved him correct. Certain that his views yet again will be pilloried, he predicted with confidence that now, too, they will stand the test of time.[64]

The article, wrote the veteran Hebrew journalist Abraham Judah Slutsky, made a "uniformly bad impression." In fact, the response was

furious. Ahad Ha'am had frequently claimed that the positions he espoused isolated him from allies and support; in the past he had always
exaggerated. Even in 1891 in the wake of the furor that broke out over
the publication of "Emet" he managed to sustain the support of most
of the Bnei Moshe. Now he had radically but momentarily marginalized
himself. Even his loyal, stalwart Bialik published an ode to the First
Zionist Congress—in, of all places, *Ha-Shiloach*—and his Bnei Moshe
"brother" Leib Jaffe enthused about the Basel meeting on the pages of
Die Welt, Zionism's official newspaper, which Ahad Ha'am derisively
called its Bible. Ben Hillel Ha-Cohen, another Bnei Moshe devotee, later
recalled the period with great pain. Everyone he knew was furious with
Ahad Ha'am, and interpretations of what the article meant differed
widely. Again as in the past the front pages of the Hebrew press was
filled, day after day, with replies. Perhaps bluntest and most facetious was
by one V. Shor:

Ahad Ha'am, that dangerous scoffer, in his despair has said things . . . that can
never be forgiven! Ahad Ha'am hovers over the world in an ethereal state and
can't see the ground beneath his feet; he hovers over the world fixated on what
the prophets have promised will come to pass: "those who have seen in a vision
that justice will reign in the world at the end of days," and he wants the Jews
to wait until then [and when there is peace on earth for all, including the Jews]
before we claim our homes in the land of our fathers. But if we wait that long
we will never go. For by then the lands of our dispersion will be [wonderful]
places where the Gentiles are all good to us.[65]

Slutsky, unlike Shor, thought that Ahad Ha'am's position had become inconsistent with his prior ones: what he had stressed in the past,
said Slutsky, was how to revive the collectivist sentiments of the Jewish
people and, he insisted, isn't this precisely what the congress did? Yet
Ahad Ha'am seems oblivious to its accomplishment. Others who agreed
with Slutsky proposed that the only reasonable explanation for his
reaction must be jealousy of Herzl. Those close to him (like Shmarya
Levin) claimed that Ahad Ha'am was quite simply incapable of appre-
ciating the value of emotional appeals, the sort at which Herzl excelled.
Ahad Ha'am was too cerebral and rational to understand the workings
of mass politics.[66] Levin's explanation proved the most influential; his
mentor did find something fundamentally distasteful in the hurly-burly
of popular politics. As for the role of emotion in political mobilization,
however, Ahad Ha'am had time and again stressed its importance.
Sentiment, he insisted, was the key factor in human behavior. Strangely,
Levin overlooked this in his attempt to make sense of what was widely

seen as an intemperate outburst by the Hebrew world's paragon of self-control and discipline.

It was again Lilienblum who wrote the most significant reply to Ahad Ha'am. His private feelings about Herzl were ambivalent, though probably no more so than those of other Russian Jewish nationalists; he found Ahad Ha'am's complaints, though, to be mere diversions and he was again unsettled by the apparent indifference in Ahad Ha'am's essay to the physical suffering of the Jewish people. He compares Ahad Ha'am's "astonishing" argument to the advice to a battered daughter that she should not marry until she finds her herself an exemplary and scholarly groom even though marriage would allow her to escape the brutality of her parental home. The wretched Jewish people like this unfortunate woman—a reference probably to *Lamentations* where Jewry is likened to a defiled woman—is not in a position to seek a reward, merely a refuge. Contrary to Ahad Ha'am's insistence that a reconstructed Palestine be worthy of the prophets, the Jews, says Lilienblum, "will gladly accept and with great happiness the prospect of living in a small state."[67]

Not only are Ahad Ha'am's goals grandiose, writes Lilienblum, but he seeks to achieve them in a manner that is wholly impracticable. The moral reeducation he promotes as a prerequisite to resettlement is cumbersome, lengthy, and probably unachievable; Herzl, however, whom Ahad Ha'am considers guilty of dangerous fantasies, has meanwhile set out to persuade a small group of powerful men of Zionism's efficacy, an immeasurably more sensible tactic. Ahad Ha'am's only answer to Herzl's stress on diplomacy is to caution us that Zion should not be rebuilt before peace reigns on earth—strange advice for a nationalist, indeed, it is advice that echoes traditionalist criticisms of the Palestinophile enterprise. If such arguments prove decisive, they are certain to derail the movement. Nor is Ahad Ha'am's charge correct that Herzl conceives of a rapid solution to the Jewish problem. Once again Ahad Ha'am's reading of the Jewish past is idiosyncratic and highly selective: on what basis, for instance, does he make his case that Jewish salvation comes from prophets, not diplomats? No prooftext is cited; he seems here merely to be airing his own predilections. Irrespective of how he reads the Jewish past, in the future, according to Lilienblum, it will be "men of action" who bring about this redemption; but exactly how they bring it about cannot be predicted. Ahad Ha'am acts as if Judaism elaborated a set of immutable rules regarding the end of days; but as Ahad Ha'am knows, the stance of Judaism is less fixed and definitive than he admits.[68]

Ahad Ha'am was stunned by the response and seems this time to have found the controversy unpleasant. He complained to friends that his critics read into his essay all sorts of strange things; for instance, they mangled his statement, or so he now claimed, that prophets not diplomats were the key to Jewry's future. He credited this to the excessive casuistry of a rabbinic tradition whose impact on Jewish reading habits was still felt: Jews refused to believe, he complained, that a text could be read to mean exactly what it explicitly stated and no more. His congress article, he continued, had been mistakenly credited with "hints and intimations" of all kinds which he had never intended. Most offensive of all was the charge that he envied Herzl; this presumption keenly disturbed him—no doubt because he was not unaware of its veracity—and he continued to brood over the accusation in the turbulent period following the congress. His insistence in this essay that texts must not be read for their hidden meaning was laden with precisely the sort of laboriously constructed ambiguity that Ahad Ha'am attributed here to the residual impact of rabbinic learning. And, of course, it was this residual rabbinism that he hoped to harness for the reconstruction of contemporary Judaism: its source of knowledge and authority.[69]

A few months after the publication of his first piece on the congress, he wrote a second one ("The Jewish State and the Jewish Problem"), where he admitted that he felt badly about the "harsh expressions" (such as calling Herzl's followers "ignorant youngsters") that he had used. He nonetheless affirmed that although it might well have been written in "anger," the article was not "written in error." Characteristically, he insisted that its excessive brevity could be the cause for such mistaken reaction from some of his readers; the new article was thus intended as a "commentary."[70]

In the second article, then, he responds mainly to Lilienblum and, despite his claims to the contrary, this piece is hardly less sardonic than the first. At present, he argues, every aspect of Jewish nationalism—including fundraising for Jewish colonization in Palestine—is being held up in anticipation of the dramatic announcement that "the messiah is at the gates." Eastern European Jews, the movement's mainstay, are intimidated and cowed by the new organization's Western name, its German newspaper, and its new leader.[71]

Ahad Ha'am found it particularly ironic that at the congress its outstanding orator Nordau affirmed, without having owned up to it, a set of commitments similar to those of Hovevei Zion—precisely those ideas that otherwise received no acclaim at the meeting. Ahad Ha'am, whose admiration for Nordau remained intact, had hoped to turn him into an Ahad Ha'amist, as he had done posthumously to Pinsker, and he observes how Nordau had spoken movingly of the spiritual tragedy facing alienated Western Jews left without any anchor in Jewry. There he claimed that it was the main task of Zionism to alleviate Western Jewry's suffering, thus providing an alternative to Herzl's blindness to the cultural dimension of the suffering. True, Nordau remained incapable of understanding the spiritual plight of East European Jewry whose needs, insisted Ahad Ha'am, were no less pressing. Nonetheless, the thrust of his argument was familiar, persuasive, and wholly unaligned with that of Herzl. In the past, Ahad Ha'am continued, the Hovevei Zion had attempted to pursue doggedly a political agenda, much as the Zionists are doing now. But, as sensitive as the Russian-based movement was to its community's anguish, its members soon recognized that mere "sentiments and fine phrases" couldn't relieve it. No matter what stance the Zionists took it became clear that their actions did nothing to satisfy "the stomach" of the Jewish people; all they could do was to address its "heart." Fortunately, enthusiasm for the nationalist cause was not thus dampened. Instead the constituency of Zionism found itself impelled to continue to act in the name of nationalism—without regard to concrete achievement—sensing, as they did, "instinctively that they should do so."[72]

Such devotion is the product, Ahad Ha'am suggests, of an instinctual commitment to the reconstruction of Palestinian Jewish life. Although "Western Zionism" (a term he used now to contrast with "authentic" Eastern Hovevei Zion) was born of antisemitism, its Russian counterpart would exist even if anti-Jewish sentiment disappeared. Eastern Hovevei Zion appeared because of the recognition that conditions in the diaspora no longer were tolerable and that Jews must return to their historic center "in order to live a life of natural development there, and bring Jewry's power into play in every sector of human culture . . . and thus contribute in the future as in the past to the common stock of humanity. The product will be a great national culture, the fruit of the unhampered activity of a people living comfortably with its own spirit."[73]

This, he claims, sums up all that is legitimate (and attainable) in Jewish nationalism. The mere creation of a state will not accomplish this: Jews would continue to be dispersed and no less impoverished whether they moved to Palestine or not; repressive governments would be no less threatening. Essential in the short run for Jewish nationalism, then, is not the hasty construction of a Jewish state, but the securing of favorable conditions for a "good-sized" and multifaceted community in Palestine that occupied all spheres of economic life from agriculture to handicrafts and from science to literature. Over the course of time, according to Ahad Ha'am, this community will capture its place—slowly, carefully, but also inevitably—as the focal point of Jewish life: here Judaism will find its purest expression, achieving "the highest degree of perfection attainable." Its impact on Jewish communities elsewhere will be felt: it will help preserve their unity, it will inspire their belief in continuity, it will point in new directions of Jewish expression. Once accomplished, "we can feel confident that we are able to produce a state that will be"—in contrast to Herzl's inauthentic model—"a Jewish state and not merely a state of Jews." Indeed he understands why the *medinim* of the West— the political Zionists of the Herzlian mold—find it so difficult to fathom why the Hovevei Zion remains preoccupied with culture, even at a time when economic disaster threatens them. But, similarly, the solution proffered by Yochanan ben Zakkai was in his age no more comprehensible to many of those around him whose agendas soon proved unrealistic, even catastrophic.[74]

For Western Jews—linked as they are to Judaism by vague sentiments that they themselves cannot comprehend—political Zionism represents a sensible way of reentering Jewish life. Denied access to power in the larger, non-Jewish world (access they would much prefer to the influence that they now seek in the smaller Jewish realm) by the forces of antisemitism, the idea of channeling their thwarted ambitions into a nascent Jewish state attracts them; it also serves to reconnect them to their people, and so for them it appears to be a harmless exercise. As far as East European Jews are concerned, their own enthusiasm for the new movement—their "bowing their knees before an ideal that has no roots in their essential beings, simply because it originates in the West"—is, in Ahad Ha'am's view, alarming, depressing, and potentially dangerous.[75]

He continued to subject Herzl to a barrage of criticism: he called Herzl's followers *erev rav,* a mixed multitude, the sort of dubious camp followers who left Egypt with Moses but abandoned him at the first sign of trouble. He continued to accuse Herzl of false messianism: for instance, when assessing the critical responses to him following his first piece on the congress, he writes that anyone refusing to blow the *shofar,* or ram's horn, for the new Zionist messiah was accused of undermining him; this was precisely why he had no plans to attend the Second

Congress, for "what value is there in seeing the whole thing and keeping silent?" Herzl's much-publicized comment before the Second Congress to a Jewish crowd in London's East End that there would soon be a momentous announcement regarding Palestine—one of his many predictions that failed to amount to much—was interpreted by Ahad Ha'am as representative of the same unforgivable messianic bravado: "And what do you think of Herzl's speech in London?" (he asked Jehiel Tchlenow, the Russian Zionist leader). "Doesn't he say quite clearly that today or tomorrow the Messiah will come?"[76]

Though Ahad Ha'am continued to snipe from the sidelines throughout this early Zionist period, his position on participation in the movement was more equivocal than his articles professed: until the last moment he remained rather coy as to whether he would attend the Second Congress, and he did not try to dissuade others from going. (In the end he explained in a polite letter to Herzl that he could not attend because he had not applied in time for a visa.) Quite the contrary, he encouraged erstwhile supporters to join; he advised them on strategy and corresponded at length about tactics with both Jacob Bernstein-Kohan and Yehiel Tchlenow, two of Russia's leading Herzlian Zionists. Both deferred to him, sought his advice, and tried to win him over as an ally. He instead hoped that they would come to recognize how futile Herzl's machinations were. He carefully monitored their frustration with their new leader and needled them on how Herzl acted without the consultation of the supervisory bodies set up at the congress, suggesting that he seemed unwilling or incapable of taking their views into account.[77]

Ahad Ha'am also took very seriously his work on the Zionist Cultural Commission—to which he was appointed in an eleventh-hour decision at the First Zionist Congress—and he remained sorely disappointed when the movement failed to act on the commission's recommendation that it sponsor a Russian Jewish school association. He scoffed at the reaction to the proposal from the Zionist center in Vienna that it was "politically unacceptable." "What connection does a school association have with politics?" he asked his friend (and the Herzlian partisan) Marcus Ehrenpreis. It was a question that doubtless he meant to be taken as sincere but also mirrored some highly debatable assumptions: his whole framework for Jewish nationalist education was politically charged. Though frustrated on this score, he continued to cooperate informally with the movement and hoped that all his Russian Jewish colleagues would tire of the demeaning and senseless role they had been consigned—to wait patiently until Herzl wrought a diplomatic miracle.

These first years of Herzlian hegemony were for him, in fact, the worst and the best of times. His was initially a solitary voice of protest; but slowly this began to change as the anti-Herzl sentiment that was always just beneath the surface began to be aired at the congress and elsewhere. No less important was the fact that now that financial support for the Hovevei Zion was reduced to a mere pittance, its attention had to shift to less expensive ventures—schools, libraries, periodicals, and so forth—the sort of good, solid cultural fare that he had always promoted and that had been the mainstay of the Bnei Moshe. Moreover, his role in the Hovevei Zion was enhanced in this period since so many other Russian Jewish leaders, especially younger ones like Chaim Weizmann and Leo Motzkin, devoted their energy to "Western Zionism." In the Zionist movement's first years, relations in Russia between the new-style, Herzlian Zionists and the Hovevei Zion nationalists were at times uncomfortable—indeed, the Hovevei Zion supporters found themselves forced out of some of their own organizations, even some of Odessa's branches—but a tenuous alliance of forces existed that Ahad Ha'am assumed would with time fall apart.

This maneuvering on his part helps explain Ahad Ha'am's behavior at the Warsaw meeting of Russian Zionists soon before the Second Congress. It was called to air issues likely to surface at the congress. Many of those who came did so apparently because they heard that Ahad Ha'am would attend and they came to debate him over his opposition to the movement.[78] Normally he avoided such encounters: he hated crowds and felt demeaned by the necessity to hide from police interference. (The organizers were forced to move participants from hall to hall in an effort to ensure that the authorities left the illegal meeting alone.) Even when he attended large gatherings he normally said little if anything at all. At Warsaw, though, he proved to be animated, voluble, and even charming. The Saturday afternoon session—its scheduling indicative of the rather secular cast of the movement—was spent mostly debating his take on Jewish nationalism: Ahad Ha'am's long address, which was followed by a spirited debate from the floor, was tactful, conciliatory, and surprisingly persuasive especially in light of the hostility that so many brought to the meeting. Ahad Ha'am left Warsaw justifiably convinced that he had won the participants over to his side. Although this initial assessment was too sanguine, he had managed to plant some serious doubts.

In Warsaw he began his talk by asserting that there was nothing in the Basel platform that a Hovev Zion could not embrace wholeheartedly, except for the final plank that affirmed the congress's commitment to "obtaining government consent, where necessary, to the attainment of the aim of Zionism." This one item was in any event a statement of faith; since nothing concrete had been done to attain government consent there was no good reason why it should block Jewish nationalists from participating. The problem, then, was not the platform but, rather, what activities the movement had chosen to emphasize in its first year.

Its emphasis, he says, has been the creation of a Jewish refuge in the Middle East, a place for Jews either too poor or too culturally backward to assimilate into European society. The ancient vision of Zion as the home for the entire Jewish people is traduced by this narrow, ahistorical interpretation of an age-old longing for a return to Palestine, but it also exaggerates the impact that this return is likely to have on the material conditions of the Jews. At the very most, he predicted, no more than 10 or 20 percent will benefit economically from the creation of a Jewish state; perhaps more than 20 percent will come to Palestine, but in view of the meager finances available for colonization, it is unlikely to improve much the condition of the poor who settle there.[79]

The fact that the masses prefer Herzl's promises to those of the Hovevei Zion should not demoralize Russian Jewish nationalists. They gravitate to Herzl because he promises a grand, materialistic salvation that cannot be accomplished; the Hovevei Zion cannot allow themselves to follow in his footsteps. It must be stated unequivocally that all that Jewish nationalists can accomplish is the cultural revival that the Hovevei Zion has stressed for years. As Yehiel Tchlenow's summary of his remarks records: "He called upon those gathered there to engage in spiritual work, to educate their nation and raise its intellectual and moral level, to prove that Palestine is better for us than anywhere else and not merely because of its historic importance to our people but since our cultural life there will not be confronted with the sort of negative forces [so evident in Europe]." He added that it was fortunate that Turkey had no interest in the cultural lives of its minorities, and although the government is likely to react to Herzl's aggressive diplomatic moves by restricting the growth of the Yishuv, so long as nationalists pursue an exclusively culturalist agenda they will be permitted to go about their work without restriction or interference.

The speech, says Tchlenow, was received with unusual interest. There were some fifty people in the hall, twenty of whom asked to comment. There was time for only a few responses; these probed the reasons for his assessment, which was too pessimistic in the view of most of those who spoke, of the limited potential economic impact of a Jewish state. He had nonetheless clearly impressed the crowd: many of the delegates insisted on shaking his hand once the session was brought to a close; he was justified in counting it a great success.[80]

The impact of the speech was felt immediately in Basel because most of those who had just met in Warsaw went immediately to the Second Congress. There a vigorous case was made for a culturalist agenda which (according to Jehuda Reinharz) could be traced directly to Ahad Ha'am's influence.[81] Russian delegates pressed for a resolution committing the organization to "practical" or agricultural work in Palestine and to cultural activities throughout the Jewish world. Opponents countered that the Basel platform already affirmed the need to strengthen and foster "Jewish national sentiment and consciousness"; more importantly, religious opponents rightly saw culture as a euphemism for secular Judaism and fought it fiercely. Their counterproposal suggested that Zionism should declare itself committed to the Torah.[82] In the end Herzl managed to shunt aside all these suggestions. Soon, by the winter of 1900, Russian nationalists, influenced by Ahad Ha'am's performance at Warsaw and disappointed at their inability to push a culturalist plank in Basel, were considering the establishment of a faction of the movement devoted solely to cultural concerns. Within a year it would crystalize into the Democratic Faction, the first coherent party within the movement, and one that viewed itself as closely aligned with Ahad Ha'am's culturalist viewpoint.

Despite his unexpected influence on the Russian delegates at Warsaw—and their frustration at being unable to give higher priority to culture at the Second Congress—no one, probably not even Ahad Ha'am, would have believed in 1898 that his stance would soon be the central plank for a vocal faction that would pose a serious problem for Herzl. Ahad Ha'am acknowledged soon after the First Zionist Congress that Zionism considered him to be an "enemy." The battle with Herzl (as he described it to Berdyczewski in July 1898) was likely to be a long, lonely one, and he would have to be cautious: "For as you know, this battle of minds with western 'Zionism' is holy in my eyes . . . and since I am essentially alone in my struggle I must protect myself against charges that I am fighting him merely as an individual [be-tor ish perati]. If you have read *Ha-Melitz,* you know that I have already been charged with jealousy."[83] But in light of Herzl's success with the masses and the movement's rapidly increasing visibility and worldwide standing, within two years of the launching of Western Zionism it looked like the only congenial home for Ahad Ha'amism was in his thick journal *Ha-Shiloach,* whose shrinking readership was arguably a sign of its editor's idiosyncratic, unpopular views. Never had Ahad Ha'am seemed less in control, more isolated, and uninfluential.

By 1903, though, the chief battle within the movement was again over culture. That year the German Zionist Max Bodenheimer, in the sort of complaint that many Herzlian partisans would come to air, stated his amazement at the fervor of the "so-called question of culture." Why, he asked, did so many of the younger Zionists believe "the creation of a new Jewish culture to be more important than extracting a charter for the Jewish country?"[84] The question was rhetorical—an expression of combined frustration and bemusement. The "culture debate" would cause the splintering of the movement, still in its first half-decade of existence, into an array of warring factions. It would also contribute to the emergence of an organizationally coherent religious opposition fearful of the growing prominence of their culturalist foes. Not surprisingly, it also signaled the reappearance of Ahad Ha'am as a factor with which to be reckoned in Jewish nationalist politics. And with the expansion of Zionism's influence—as it stretched beyond its original core of East European maskilic nationalists and embraced a larger, more variegated constituency—Ahad Ha'am's reach extended as well.

His impact on the culturalist opposition to Herzl, which he neither led nor controlled, was, as we shall see, neither so direct nor so deep as is sometimes assumed. Ahad Ha'am served as a symbol for the movement's culturalists, their faction's most coherent totem. He was, however, not—certainly not to the extent to which members of this group, especially Chaim Weizmann, would later contend—its chief ideological influence.[85] Their attitude toward him was polite and respectful, but he was not, as he had been for the previous generation, their primary link to a larger intellectual world. They saw him through very different eyes, and, if later some of them would claim him to be their mentor, it was a by-product of his fame as well as their way of "judaizing" cultural politics that were, in fact, shaped primarily by influences outside the

Jewish camp. In retrospect Ahad Ha'am seemed to loom much larger for them than he actually had at the time.

III

The prehistory of the Democratic Faction can be traced to the university towns of Central Europe, particularly of Germany and Switzerland, where Jewish students denied entry to Russian universities came to study and sometimes formed nationalist societies. Several of these societies were launched before Herzl's appearance, and several of their leading members—Leo Motzkin, Joseph Lurie, and Chaim Weizmann—had, in fact, been inducted into the Bnei Moshe. They were very young men and, like all of its members outside the central circles of Warsaw and Odessa, they had not had much immediate contact with the secret society. In certain respects, then, their politics were similar to those of the maskilic nationalists surrounding Ahad Ha'am since the beginning of his career, the product of Jewish attachments too intense to abandon. They found assimilated Jews pathetic, the socialists self-deluded, and the Jewish folk lethargic and superstitious and in need of moral and political transformation. "There is a digressed dull state of mind everywhere," Weizmann writes in 1895. "People expect something, some sort of miracle and look vacantly into the future. After all this it will be clear to you how deadly boring it is here! The monotony is only broken occasionally when one indulges in indignation at the emptiness and nastiness of our leading Jews, their slavishness and cruelty. It seems to me that on no one did the exile have such a noxious influence as on the Jews of Pinsk. What is happening in Berlin?"[86]

Earnest, highly committed, and intellectually charged, the young university students welcomed Herzl at first with enthusiasm; some found him to be facile, even frivolous, but all were impressed with how he expanded Jewish nationalism's horizons.[87] On the surface, then, they seemed little different from the older, Russian-based Hovevei Zion devotees who abandoned Ahad Ha'am with the advent of Herzl—an abandonment he had deeply bemoaned and had hoped to reverse. But appearance was deceptive; differences far outweighed the similarities.

True, they were familiar with Ahad Ha'am's writings and, like other Hebraists, eagerly read whatever he wrote. Several had indeed met him in 1896 when he had come to Berlin to set up the printing of *Ha-Shiloach* and sought to persuade him to speak at a conference they planned to hold that year, one that would be canceled after Herzl's call for a Zionist congress. They were at first, as Weizmann made clear to Ahad Ha'am, willing to move the venue for the conference from Berlin to Odessa to suit his needs. For, as Lurie reiterated to Motzkin, they could not accomplish nearly as much "without the name of Ahad Ha'am" associated with the meeting."[88] Interestingly, they did not initially look to Ahad Ha'am's expertise or wisdom; rather it was his standing as Jewish nationalism's preeminent intellectual that they hoped to capitalize upon since they were mere students with vast aspirations but little else. Avid readers and in some cases Bnei Moshe members though they were, they were not in fact his disciples.

Weizmann first met Ahad Ha'am as part of this "official delegation" (as the self-important young Weizmann put it) seeking to convince him to participate in their planned conference; Lurie, too, made contact with him then. What is most striking about the impressions of both of them at the time is what they do not say. Neither left Ahad Ha'am—as did so many of his maskilic contemporaries—awestruck or overwhelmed either by his personality or wisdom. They found him to be cultivated, bright, and well-informed, yet slightly too cynical for their tastes. Their comments were rather similar. In Weizmann's view he was a man who made "a very pleasant impression as a European. He spoke about the Palestine cause with restraint, not too much, without heat and, or perhaps it only seemed to me, with a little pinch of skepticism."[89] This skepticism— rarely all that assiduously hidden—Lurie also noted and he gives a more nuanced and perceptive description:

I found him to be a man with a great deal of knowledge in philosophy, psychology, sociology, and in both general and Jewish literature. His moral character is entirely pure. He has a vigorous and sober mind, if practical, too practical it seems. His "opportunism" expresses itself only in caution and fear in connection with anything that demands initiative, so that this characterization does not fit him entirely.[90]

What he meant by Ahad Ha'am's "opportunism" isn't clear. But he didn't seem to see the trait as something negative, and he only criticized the Odessa sage in his inability to translate this "opportunism" into concrete achievements because of a paralyzing ambivalence. More interesting, though, is Lurie's perspective on Ahad Ha'am the intellectual: Lurie like Weizmann found him serious and worthy of attention; but, just as clearly, he concluded that this Russian Jew was not an original thinker, and perhaps even lacked a first-class mind. He was "vigorous and sober" but too fixated on everyday affairs to be an outstanding intellectual. The contrast between these impressions and those of the worshipful maskilim of the previous generation cannot be more stark, especially when one bears in mind that it was precisely men like Lurie and Weizmann who would carry his banner in the Zionist movement.

They differed from their maskilic predecessors in their systematic education. Ahad Ha'am's articles did not provide them with a rare opening to the larger world; even as poverty-stricken externs their systematic training was exhilarating, but the absence of much prospect for employment in Russia coupled with ugly encounters with Central European antisemitism engendered in them political inclinations unknown to earlier Russian maskilim. Their experiences in the West expanded their mental horizons whereas their dignity as Jews was bruised. They emerged with a heightened self-awareness of themselves as men of enlightenment and transformative *Bildung* and a strengthened belief in the inescapability of Jewish identity.

They embraced Jewish nationalism with great fervor and intellectual commitment but also with a distinctly Central European slant. This, above all, explains the primacy they placed on *Kultur,* or culture. Norbert Elias argues in *The History of Manners* that *Kultur* represented especially for German intellectuals the designating mark of a society seeking self-definition and trying to distinguish itself from others. Indeed the use of the term *Kultur* is the closest German equivalent to the English term "civilization" and it was infused in the late nineteenth century with a national content unlike the more universalist connotation of "civilization." Above all, Elias says, it refers "to intellectual, artistic, and religious facts and has a tendency to draw a sharp dividing line between facts of this sort on the one side and political, economic and social facts on the other." At the same time,

whereas the concept of civilization has the function of giving expression to the continually expansionist tendency of colonizing groups, the concept of *Kultur* mirrors the self-consciousness of a nation which had constantly to seek out and constitute its boundaries anew, in a political as well as spiritual sense, and again and again had to ask itself: "What is really our identity?" The orientation of the German concept of culture, with its tendency toward demarcation and its emphasis on and detailing of differences between historical groups corresponds to this natural process.[9]

Nationalism, of course, made sense to Weizmann and his circle before their encounter with the West; most had left Russia as secularists who were nevertheless preoccupied with the need to integrate some Jewish cultural forms (such as Hebrew and the ancient homeland) into a transformed Jewish identity. Moreover, their polemics with Russian Jewish intellectuals opposed to nationalism (who vastly outnumbered nationalists in the expatriate student colonies) further attuned them to the need to define Zionism in cultural terms relevant to an intellectually sophisticated clientele that shunned Jewish parochialism and was unlikely to be moved by the diplomatic machinations of Herzl.

A combination, then, of maskilic assumptions of East European and Ahad Ha'amist origin with a renewed appreciation for the importance of *Kultur* (as reflected both in its primacy in German national life and in the feverish discourse of the foreign-student colonies) attuned them to cultural politics. Ahad Ha'am influenced them inasmuch as he provided a Judaic framework and terminology. Yet they felt no compunction about drawing on Nietzsche, whose thinking Ahad Ha'am saw as antithetical to Judaism. (Weizmann to his fiance, in 1902: "I am sending you Nietzsche. . . . This is the best and finest thing that I can send you."[92]) Their anticlericalism was much fiercer than Ahad Ha'am's—less predicated upon a positivist belief in progress than on an overpowering distrust of the mysterious staying power of religious reaction. Much later, as plans for the founding of a Jewish university took shape and as the groundwork for a national library proved feasible, many of the same men sought to locate their long-standing commitment to these projects in the ideology of Ahad Ha'am; but their origins were much more eclectic.

Take, for example, their most sophisticated spokesman, Leo Motzkin, who was their undisputed leader before Weizmann managed to push him aside. In an address entitled "Yahadut leumit" ("Nationalist Judaism") delivered in 1891 to the Russian Jewish Academic Society—this occurred, appropriately, on the festival of Hannukah—Motzkin drew from various influences, only one of which was Ahad Ha'amist, in making his culturalist case:

The cultural mission of the nineteenth century has been the granting of freedom to nations. Our epoch has given the majority of nations the opportunity to open themselves up to their unique characteristics. Why should our fate be different from all of theirs?[93]

Nonetheless our Western brethren, he bemoans, have responded to the mounting misery of East European Jewry with only philanthropic solutions and without the recognition that what is required is to abandon benevolent work for "politics." He defines this political approach as one that affirms the need for Jews to gather themselves together in one place, their ancient homeland, so that they can live "a national-cultural life," with its distinctive heritage (masoret), history, language, and literature.[94]

Of course, Motzkin's vision meshes easily in some respects with Ahad Ha'am's: the belief, as expressed by Motzkin, in the creation of a co-herent Jewish culture in Zion, his despair over shortsighted philan-thropy, and his conception of a Jewish culture that has transcended and incorporated religious forms. All this seems drawn from the legacy of Bnei Moshe. There is much here, though, that is not. Contrary to Ahad Ha'am, Motzkin sees nationalism as a new phenomenon—a product of modernity that Ahad Ha'am roundly rejects. He also explicitly refers to his approach as political rather than philanthropic and would later affirm that he saw himself as a *medini*, a political Zionist in juxtaposition to the purely cultural or Ahad Ha'amist kind. This statement contains a "syn-thetic" view of Jewish nationalism—the term would later be used to describe the Democratic Faction's ideology and Weizmann picked it up as early as 1901. Ahad Ha'am's ideas were one piece of a complex set of motivating influences.

In its stress on culture there was, as David Vital has observed, also at least one important tactical factor at work, especially once the faction constituted itself in opposition to Herzl. They were poorly prepared to dispute him because they lacked any knowledge of the details of his diplomatic activities (he tended to keep them under wraps); nor did they have a coherent alternative to his activity on the international front. They could best attack him where he was the weakest: in his vision of Jewish culture, which they considered ill-informed, superficial, and awkward.[95]

No less tactical was the decision to call themselves, from their first appearance as a party at the Fifth Zionist Congress in 1901, the Dem-ocratic Faction. They were a group of thirty-nine members out of several hundred delegates with no reason to believe that they stood for the sentiments of even a sizable minority. How, then, were they "dem-ocrats"? Primarily in the sense that they sought to unsettle Herzl's absolute hold on the movement, and they objected to his tendency to act on his own and his failure to consult even the movement's standing committees. In short, they favored democracy insofar as it would ensure their own more active participation in its leadership. No doubt, their choice of the term was part of their attempt to attract otherwise Jew-ishly uninvolved intellectuals to their camp, those who would be more inclined to associate themselves with a movement with progressive, liberal underpinnings.[96]

Throughout the short, turbulent career of the faction its leaders sought Ahad Ha'am's advice, listened to it with care, but then usually discarded it as impracticable: he urged them in 1901 to break from the Zionists and set up a new movement for cultural politics. He advised them on how to fight Herzl and he sought to reorient their priorities especially by placing more emphasis on educational reform. One Aaron Gurland captured in a 1901 letter to Weizmann the faction's attitude toward him: "As much as I respect Ahad Ha'am as a writer, insofar as political advice is concerned, I cannot agree with it. I (as well as all the Jewish people) am committed to a real nationalism and not to the transcendentalism promoted by Ahad Ha'am and many of the contributors to *Ha-Shiloach*."[97] Gurland was being harsh, but also honest. There was, in his view, something dated, old-fashioned, and wrongheaded about much of what Ahad Ha'am had to say. Gurland read his writings, respected him, and looked elsewhere for fundamental guidance at least in terms of day-to-day politics.

This was especially apparent when Ahad Ha'am's negative stance toward parliamentary democracy—the cause championed by the Democratic Faction—is taken into account. At the Third Congress the address of Motzkin, the faction's leading ideological figure, later published as "Zionism and Democracy," was itself a celebration of democracy. It emphasized how crucial it was that all constituents of Zionism actively cooperate in what was certain to be the slow process of state building. In stressing gradualism he echoed Ahad Ha'am; in his faith in democracy, they were poles apart. It is ironic that at almost the same moment Ahad Ha'am published a lengthy (and rarely quoted) essay that aired his feelings on democracy, "Yahid ve-rabim" ("The Individual and the Masses"). Its writing was seemingly unconnected with the work of Weizmann and his circle; the piece aired thoughts about mass politics that had plagued Ahad Ha'am for some time and that had found their way into earlier pieces, albeit haphazardly. Never, though, had he faced the issue directly, and the article points to the stark divide separating him from the Zionists most closely associated with him and his culturalist line.

Ahad Ha'am says that he was prompted to write "Yahid ve-rabim" by an encounter at the Warsaw meeting with a "simple Jew of the old school" who told him that what disturbed him most about Ahad Ha'am were his views on parliamentary democracy. Why was it, he asked, that he described Jewry's supreme democratic institution, the Zionist Congress, in such negative terms? Wasn't it, at the very least, "a shadow of a parliament"? Ahad Ha'am admits that he brushed the question aside at the time, but wanted to address it now.[98]

Not that he could avoid patronizing the inquisitive man: he acknowledges, perhaps in an allusion to the Friday-evening talks he overheard as a boy at Skvire's synagogue, that Jews love "to sit beside the stove" and swap views about "politics," talking to their hearts' content about the "defense of kingdoms, and partisan and political battles among the nations of the world." Is it any wonder that the young especially feel a rush of "national pride" now that they too have something of a shadow of a government, now that they can speak about their very own politics?[99]

All this seems no more than a harmless excess, little more than a verbal exercise. But there is, he proposes, also something deeply worrying about it since in our veneration of the congresses we fail to take into account how they are built on political foundations that bring out the worst in government and society. This is because those elected to parliamentary bodies inevitably are *anashim benoni'im min ha-shuk*, men of middling qualities, of unexceptional talent, of little potential for greatness or distinction of any kind. Their election results from a host of factors that do little to test their qualifications, primarily "financial as well as verbal bribery," untruths, demagoguery. The fate of nations rests today, then, in the hands of unworthy men, creatures of a parliamentary system that makes them preoccupied solely with their reelection. Not surprisingly, nepotism, influence peddling, and corruptions small and large, dominate their careers.[100]

Those who defend parliamentary democracy insist, he continues, that these drawbacks do not render the institution itself flawed. Rather, such practices are actually corruptions of democracy and caused only by flawed men; elect the right men, or so it is argued, and democracy will flourish.

Friends of democracy have long argued this but recently some of the more important social theorists have demonstrated, he declares, how parliamentary rule is rotten to the core and conspires against excellence of any kind in its pursuit of mass appeal. Ironically, one of them is Theodor Herzl's close associate and the leading orator of the Zionist Congress, the literary giant Max Nordau. In *Paradoxes* (1885) he shows—and Ahad Ha'am quotes at length—that whenever, say, four hundred people are brought together in a room and even if the majority of them are excellent, all tend to be dragged down to the lowest common denominator and to the most dispiriting of public behavior by the pressures of the mob. General will, Nordau contends, overwhelms even the best individual qualities. The quote, drawn as it was from the repertoire of Herzl's most important supporter, was used by Ahad Ha'am to call attention to the way in which even Nordau had undermined the efficacy of Zionism's Congress as a democratic emblem.[101]

Many recent studies of "mass psychology," the most important of which is S. Sighele's analysis of sects, have further substantiated Nordau's conclusions, Ahad Ha'am continues. (Sighele's reflections drew on his study of the exceptionally corrupt Italian parliament, and Ahad Ha'am failed to consider that its excesses might not prove universally applicable.) According to Sighele no large group can arrive at decisions nearly as intelligent or valid as those "formulated in the mind and heart of one excellent man." The problem with democracy is not merely that it produces less than exemplary laws. Rather, its inevitable product is mob rule. Even an otherwise impressive parliamentarian is transformed by virtue of his participation into (as Sighele puts it, with Ahad Ha'am's concurrence) little more than a "hysterical woman." Decisions are arrived at by chance interventions, inspirations of the moment, or catcalls from the corner of the room. Someone shouts and suddenly there is a decision, one that completely contradicts another formulated a few minutes earlier. Ahad Ha'am writes: "It is neither the intellect nor common sense, neither objective reality nor experience that are the decisive factors in such meetings." All is reduced to a visceral, emotional level, to the passions of the moment.[102]

Jews too, of course, are subject to the same psychological principles—in Ahad Ha'am's phrase, "slaves to the same laws." True, he admits, rare moments do occur when public gatherings are extraordinary; but only because of the presence of a great man who towers over and dominates all, "with the eyes of everyone upon him and with his spirit dominating all aspects of the meeting and its work." Everyone else at such gatherings is there merely for the sake of "decoration"; they function as a "platform" for the leader. Only in these circumstances does parliamentary government work, when its premises are traduced with the great imposing themselves upon it, thereby transcending the wretched constraints of mass psychology.[103]

If the Zionist movement insists on maintaining its "quasi-parliamentary body," limits must be set on its inevitable shortcomings: delegates must be screened with great care and their numbers must be drastically reduced to check some of the evils of democratic rule. Some shortcomings can only be entirely overcome, however, by doing away with the institution.[104] Nothing that Ahad Ha'am wrote at this time would underline quite so vividly the distance between his politics and that of the Democratic Faction: few of his pieces would, in fact, so clearly date him, his politics; and his assumptions about public life.

He does not seem to have sensed this distance. Soon after the First Zionist Congress he began to feel, despite his isolation as one of Herzl's first vocal critics within the nationalist camp, that the tide was beginning to turn in his favor. He explained this to Ehrenpreis, a friend who was now a Herzlian partisan, and who asked him in March 1898 to describe Russian Jewry's attitude toward Zionism:

As far as your question is concerned regarding the attitude of [Russian Jews] to the Second Congress, it is difficult to answer it directly. In our country there are now two camps: The old Hovevei Zion people and the new Zionists. The former were set afire in the days of the [first] congress and began to move over to the Zionist camp. But, if I am not mistaken, slowly their enthusiasm is cooling, and they are beginning to recognize that it is not from Vienna that the messiah will come. And, thus, most of them have their feet both here and there and they themselves have no idea what to do. And the new Zionists, like all neophytes, burn like fire and bend their knees before everything that comes from abroad. Herzl is their messiah, and *Die Welt*—their Torah. In this camp there are mostly "youth"—students and various intellectuals, all of whom knew nothing about the nationalist movement, which was brought to their attention only because of the tumult caused by the congress.[105]

The Russian Zionist movement—disorganized and laughably inefficient—was, he was convinced, in the initial stages of disintegration.

Subsequent events appeared to bear out his predictions: the enthusiasm generated for him in Warsaw, the birth of the Democratic Faction, and the disenchantment with Herzl on the part of several of his key Russian organizers (including Bernstein-Kohan, head of the movement's "correspondence bureau"). Indicative of his new optimism, the article he wrote on the eve of the Second Congress was surprisingly mild and constructive. He suggested that now that the Second Congress was being held in Basel, too, it would be suitable to concentrate on correcting the errors of the past. He urged those who were willing to do this— meaning those committed to the ideals of the Hovevei Zion—to consider that the last Basel meeting failed because it was too preoccupied with the larger world, with how the congress looked to those outside it. What was now essential was a reexamination of Jewry's internal dynamics.[106] Unlike the speeches given last time, directed primarily to

Europe and not to the Jews, the new congress must forget self-advertisement and move toward a new beginning after its disappointing start. Even if the congress did not live up to his expectations as expressed in his article, he felt sufficiently expansive to congratulate Tchlenow on its accomplishments and expressed his pleasure at the successful way in which Russian delegates had promoted Palestinian colonization and culture there. Clearly, he added, this will have little immediate impact but it was a sensible, decent course for them to take. He felt that the worst of the Herzlian storm had passed. He continued to denounce him and his movement (for instance, he was furious about its bank, whose charter did not limit its activities to Palestine). Appalled as he still was by it, he nonetheless stopped speaking with the fervor of his pieces of 1897 and early 1898. He would still attack Herzl, and in his lengthy review of 1902 of Herzl's novel *Altneuland,* would poke fun at him with merciless delight. A preoccupation Herzl remained, but never again would Ahad Ha'am consider Herzl quite so serious a threat.

By the last years of the nineteenth century most Zionists now saw Ahad Ha'am in the same way as Aaron Gurland: highly intelligent, sincere, even exemplary, but wholly impractical. They might not have gone quite so far as Gurland (who accused him of a "transcendental" nationalism), but by opposing Herzl he had placed himself in opposition to what seemed to many to be the only credible prospect for Jewry's national redemption. Even those who came to doubt much of what Herzl said tended to remain in his camp for want of an alternative. What many in the movement had come to see as the excruciatingly gradualist, elitist, vague notions of Ahad Ha'am—and which seemed, in the minds of many Zionists, to belie not only grand Herzlian diplomacy but politics in general—constituted no serious substitute. Is it surprising, then, that even those in the Democratic Faction who sometimes billed themselves as his devotees spoke, as early as 1901, of a Zionist approach that represented a synthesis that drew on both the politics of Herzl and those of Ahad Ha'am? The term synthesis, which came to be closely associated with Weizmann as well as Ahad Ha'am's abiding influence on him, also demonstrated a recognition that to chart a sensible Zionist course it was necessary to part company somewhat with Ahad Ha'am.

No less ironic than the Democratic Faction's reliance on a thinker who decried democracy as fraudulent, inefficient, and inferior to one-man rule was the way in which Ahad Ha'am—that emblem of the ethereal in Zionist politics—came to be identified during Herzl's tenure as the leading partisan of what would be known as "practical work" in Palestine. Of course, such practical work was seen by the Herzlians (at least in their movement's initial stages) as wholly impractical, irrelevant, and premature: this term referred to colonizing efforts of the Hovevei Zion and Baron Rothschild concentrated mostly near the Mediterranean north of Hadera and the Galilee. Despite having to battle Ottoman authorities, malaria, resentful Arab neighbors, an uncongenial, unfamiliar agrarian climate, hostile traditionalist Jews, and impatient, often unyielding colonists, by 1900 some 6,000 acres had been planted with vines, and 5,000 Jews had settled on agricultural settlements. Vital provides a vivid portrait of turn-of-the-century Palestine:

[H]owever defined, it was a poor and univiting place, small in territory and population (some 25,000 square kilometres and between 500,000 and 600,000 inhabitants all told) and virtually devoid of commercially exploitable natural resources, apart (potentially) from the minerals of the Dead Sea. Some 70 percent of the population lived off agriculture, but poorly. Little of the land was cultivable, at any rate above subsistence level; most of it was either rocky terrain or semidesert or swamp. Much of it was owned by absentee landlords, or by the state, or by religious and philanthropic institutions. . . . There was no industry, except of the most elementary kind (soap production in Nablus, for example). The supply of drinking water was inadequate and much of what was supplied was impure, notoriously so in Jerusalem. Roads were extremely poor. . . . The population was plagued by diseases typical of a warm climate and a land where virtually no attention was paid to public health either in the strictly medical context or in that of civil engineering: dysentery, malaria, trachoma, typhoid, and, periodically, cholera (of which there were severe epidemics in the winter of 1902/3 and in 1910).[107]

From Herzl's vantage point, it would be absurd to build on these meager foundations without a Turkish charter and the outpouring of investment capital from the Jewish world that would result from such a diplomatic victory. He gave rather tepid support to colonization efforts, and the Basel platform affirmed the movement's devotion to such work only "along suitable lines," a phrase left intentionally vague. So Ahad Ha'am emerged as the defender of colonization and a relentless advocate of the achievements of the Hovevei Zion: the author of the most searing internal attack on the colonization practices of the Hovevei Zion had become, within less than a decade, its most vigorous booster and not because of an ideological shift either in the group or on his part.

How Ahad Ha'am negotiated his way between cultural and so-called practical approaches to Jewish nationalism he demonstrated in "Shalosh madregot" ("Three Steps"). He sets out to criticize "Zionists" (he would always put the word in quotation marks) who divide the Jewish world between themselves and those they call "assimilationists." He comments that it has lately become clear, though, that there is a broad cross-section of Jewish opinion which, although not necessarily embracing Herzl's approach, has despaired of assimilation in favor of a Judaism with greater authenticity. This development, he says, ought to interest all "true devotees of the Hovevei Zion."[108]

For example he cites what he considers a path-breaking article written by a Central European rabbi on the question of why to maintain a Jewish identity. Ahad Ha'am notes that only seven years ago he himself had attacked *La Gerbe* for rehearsing its tired, obsequious, and at the time wholly typical ruminations on the same issue—statements showing the journal to be almost paralyzed by the fear of how it was viewed by the larger world and prepared to sacrifice Jewish authenticity on the altar of emancipation. How different is this rabbi's statement today; he, in Ahad Ha'am's estimation, has produced "words of fire, an echo of the true sentiments that live in the hearts" of Israel. He declares that the question itself is absurd: "Ask the fire why it burns, ask the sun why it shines, ask the tree why it grows!" Neither philosophy or, for that matter, even Torah are essential for the sustenance of Judaism. What is crucial—as Ahad Ha'am had of course long insisted—is "Jewish sentiment" (regesh yehudi).[109]

This is how "new Jews" are likely to show their commitment. The rabbi, in his article, is concerned about the terrible dilemma that such Jews are certain to encounter, one that perhaps is, as Ahad Ha'am says in an extraordinary statement, the most tragic in Jewish history. Earlier, when Jewish sentiment was natural and unfettered—and was conducted within a mostly insulated Jewish world—it was possible for Jews in the diaspora to express a full range of emotions. Later, with the onset of emancipation, however, modernized Jews came to prefer a bifurcated existence, with the larger society serving as the primary source for cultural inspiration and Judaism consigned to the synagogal realm. Now that Jews are once again turning inward, where can they go to find the full range of what Jewish life can offer? This is all the more troubling now that the self-contained Jewish society of the past has been dismantled (or at least is rapidly disintegrating):

Jewish sentiments, seeking to recapture their former glory, would like to be translated into what was their former predominance in everyday life, to make themselves felt, as in the past, in the actions and behavior of their people. And how can they achieve this in a world that is not theirs, where alien forces dominate and do not permit the outsider to secure a place within it?[110]

Dubnow's solution to this dilemma ("Shalosh madregot" was intended as an attack on his autonomist ideology) was the creation of an autonomous Jewish communal structure within the already-existing European states. This, believed Ahad Ha'am, is honorable but unrealistic. For example, the other smaller, struggling nationalities seeking a place in the sun—he cites the Poles in particular—have made it clear that they expect the Jews to relinquish their own national aspirations and embrace theirs. Unrealistic as it may be, Ahad Ha'am says, Dubnow's approach exemplifies the "second level" of nationalist sentiment among Jews—a new, encouraging development that points to inexorable movement in the direction of national Jewish rights. True, Dubnow's approach is inadequate; it promotes (like the thinking of the Western rabbi quoted above) a diaspora-based nationalism. But once these shortcomings are recognized, as they must be, the Jews

cannot but come to recognize that only national rights can satisfy our national requirements without which we will never achieve our goals. And these are that we too will come to constitute the "majority" in one land under the skies, a land in which our historic rights are not in any doubt . . . and in which in an atmosphere infused with a sense of history our national lives will be permitted to develop according to their own distinctive spirit and not remain reduced to limited and circumscribed corners.[111]

This was the closest he would ever come to outlining clearly the practical underpinnings of his plans for Palestine's future. Later, when responding to charges that he envisioned in Palestine little more than a university campus, he would point to this essay as refutation. The crucial difference on this score between him and others in the Jewish nationalist camp, he would point out, was in the means that he promoted, not in the end result. The claim was somewhat disingenuous, particularly since he stressed how crucial the interconnection between means and ends was in politics; nonetheless, he indicated here that his vision of the Palestinian Jewish future was not quite as different from that of others in the Hovevei Zion as some believed it to be: he supported a Jewish majority in Palestine and clearly believed that population concentration was a crucial feature of cultural rebirth. During the Herzlian years, he felt, objective circumstance had intervened to make his viewpoint—once marginal to Hovevei Zion discourse—into rather standard fare. He seemed confident that he now spoke as its conscience, as representative of a movement albeit reduced to a shadow of its former self.

And this is precisely what he attempted to do in what were effectively his newest sequels to "Emet me-eretz yisrael," published after a stay in Palestine from late November 1899 until mid-March 1900. He explained that he chose not to refer to them as sequels. Conditions in Palestine were too complex to try to encapsulate in a single essay, as he did in the past, all aspects of Yishuv life; instead he intended to write a series of pieces devoted to discrete problems: education, colonization, politics, and economics. He came to Palestine at a particularly stressful moment: the deficit of the previous year in the important viticulture market unsettled conditions there and left colonists fearful about the future, concerned that Rothschild might abandon them, and doubtful that the crops on which the Yishuv had depended for the last two decades would continue to sustain them. That deficit may have influenced Baron Rothschild's decision to place his Palestinian affairs now in the hands of the Jewish Colonization Association. Ahad Ha'am returned home from the trip exhausted and sick. He spent the entire summer and much of the fall of 1900 recuperating and, as a result, did not manage to complete his reports until a year or two later. Even then, he finished only two of the proposed series, both of them very long and copiously detailed. The first was on the Jewish schools of Jaffa, the second assessed agrarian colonization. Together they present as full a portrait of Palestinian Jewish life at the time as is available: Ahad Ha'am's tone here, as in his earlier reports, was rather dry, instructive rather than inspirational or denunciatory. At the same time, both evince the same decorous passion, the same interplay between intensity and empiricism that rendered all of these writings on Palestine into minor masterpieces.

In his essay on education he found achievements in Palestine were minimal and obstacles overwhelming; and, in comparison to what had appeared to exist a few years earlier, prospects were rapidly deteriorating.

He begins with the flagship of Hebraist education in Palestine, the "Jaffa school": he explains, in a rather sanitized version of its origins, that the school "was established in 1893, and like all the other institutions of the new Yishuv, as something of an accident without specific goals, a clear plan, an intelligent program, or a secure source of funding." It was set up to serve the needs of Jaffa's Jewish poor, the children of its artisans and workers; eventually the local Jewish leadership saw that it should take responsibility for the school and found a patron in the Paris-based, non-nationalist Alliance Israélite Universelle. Its most fervent Jaffa-based supporters were drawn, says Ahad Ha'am, from the ranks of maskilic intellectuals and, as he puts it, from various members of the Hovevei Zion. Never does he mention the role the Bnei Moshe played in its formation, despite the essay's call for candor and the fact that the Bnei Moshe had disbanded by the time it was written. As Ahad Ha'am knew well, the Bnei Moshe had infiltrated the local branch of the Alliance to influence it to support the school, which had long attracted its interest and which was run almost from its first days by a Bnei Moshe member.[112]

Ahad Ha'am further explains that to understand the school and its subsequent development it must be kept in mind that it was supported for much of its existence by sectors of the Jewish community with very different agendas. Its maskilic nationalist supporters saw it as an attempt "to establish in the Land of Israel a Hebrew school, Hebrew not only in incidental and external ways, but in its very soul." For them it served to showcase the potential power of Jewish nationalism. That they believed it possible to do this in conjunction with the Alliance—and in an institution that drew the bulk of its students from an impoverished sector of Jewry—was surprising and shortsighted.[113]

The chief problem for both the boys' school (established first) as well as its affiliated girls' school, was not, as was often charged by nationalists, that the stubborn attachment to French culture of the Alliance made the arrangement unworkable. Some of the local Alliance administrators had attempted to foist vigorously French culture onto the students but this, Ahad Ha'am contends, had less to do with organizational policy than the excessive zeal of badly selected employees. The Alliance itself had no overarching goal in this respect. Its agenda was much more reasonable than was widely assumed.

In fact, what went wrong from a Jewish nationalist viewpoint— particularly for the boys' school—was due to its lack of attentiveness to preparing its students for work. The most fortunate were those accepted to the agricultural training school Mikvah Israel, but its Hebrew and Jewish studies curriculum was poor and it did little to reinforce what the Jaffa school taught them. The rest were even worse off: they left to compete in the labor force as artisans without having the benefit of training that others received while they were being drilled in Hebrew. Under these grueling circumstances they naturally forgot the language; other Jewish subjects proved even less useful. In the end, the school accomplished nothing at all toward consolidating a Hebraic culture in the Yishuv.[114]

Ahad Ha'am supported his arguments with a wealth of documenta-
tion: lengthy footnotes gave detailed statistics on the occupations of the
parents of the student body, past and present, and the number of hours
students spent on the various parts of the curriculum, including Hebrew. The true level of Hebrew instruction in the school, widely celebrated by Jewish nationalists, is, he claimed, worse than that of a modernized *heder* in the Pale: of all the students he tested in Palestine, only
one managed to speak what he called an unself-conscious Hebrew. The
schools' teachers, alas, were little better, and their command of the
language was tortured and their sentences excessively complicated. Recommendations to resolve these problems by transforming the school
into a teachers' seminary, and in this way to prepare its graduates for
work, are absurd in light of the paucity of teaching posts available in the
Yishuv, in Ahad Ha'am's view. Teaching credentials would only force
them to take their skills abroad. And if the Hovevei Zion assumed full
responsibility for the school—as those who blamed the Alliance for the
school's shortcomings have pressed it to do—this too would be disastrous, because if properly funded it would demand as much as ten times
its current operating budget. To run a proper school, decently paid
teachers must be induced to come from abroad and students have to be
provided with subsidies, housing, and food. The cost of this would
break the movement; how could it justify such expenditures at the
expense of its agricultural colonies?[115]

But, then, there was the girls' school: it came about, Ahad Ha'am says,
as an afterthought and has never enjoyed the recognition or attention
lavished on the boys' school. Nor did it seek it: a place with few pretensions, a modest curriculum, and with the manageable goal of producing Hebraically literate, marriageable women for Jaffa's Jewish artisans. In fact, its shortcomings are also its considerable strengths: in
contrast to the position that the male graduates faced upon completing
the school, the females (who tend to live at home, do not have the same
financial concerns as boys, and have no need to prepare for occupations)
have the opportunity to devote their school years exclusively to study.
Currently their curriculum is a rather undemanding one; the Alliance
had insisted that this be so in order to ensure that they would not
produce overly educated girls who had so outdistanced their husbands
as to make them unsuitable as marriage partners. Their curriculum was
therefore weak in Hebrew instruction (according to the Alliance only
potential scholars needed this knowledge) with an emphasis on home
economics. He remained convinced, though, that the Alliance could be

persuaded to improve the school and that this would have a major impact on the cultural life of the Yishuv.[116]

This brought Ahad Ha'am to a recommendation that he admitted was very radical and probably would be rejected out of hand: the boys' school should be closed. The Hovevei Zion should redirect its attention to the girls' branch since it represented a much surer route to shaping a Palestinian-Jewish nationalist culture. With the time to read, female students will more likely emerge fluent in Hebrew and comfortable with Jewish cultural forms; they will become crucial to the shaping of, what he calls here, a true "Hebrew atmosphere" (atmosferah ivrit). When they graduate and marry, if properly trained they can be certain to establish homes where the Hebrew language reigns supreme and the reading of Hebrew literature is seen as a natural and unquestionably important task. It is precisely the girls' school's lack of distinction that lends itself to the task; the position of its students outside the workshop and marketplace puts them in a prime position for the promulgation of culture.[117]

Ahad Ha'am shows here, once again, that he was anything but indifferent to the gnawing impact of economic difficulty; at the same time he affirms his belief that it was not those who were the most economically vulnerable who were most likely to be receptive to his message. Culture was no luxury but those best equipped to promote it had to be free from pressing economic burdens. The article also managed masterfully to subvert its readers expectations: its recommendation that priority be given the girls' school was made in the context of an article devoted almost entirely to the much better-known, prestigious male academy. He gave readers no clue that he was leading them in this wholly unexpected direction. Perhaps the most interesting feature of all was the vivid portrait he provided of the prerequisites of a national culture and how cultural politics must be implemented on the ground. The "Hebrew atmosphere" he envisioned would have to, he felt, make its impact on the living rooms and kitchens of the Yishuv (and, eventually, also the diaspora) and only in this way would it transform its values, reshape its dreams, and prepare its men, women, and children for their revival.

His ashen appearance upon his return to Odessa so frightened his friends that they were especially pleased that he spent the summer away from the city in the country house of Ha-Cohen near Gomel. In letters, Ahad Ha'am described it as a "Garden of Eden" (it would become his regular summertime home), and he boasted about how much he rested and the vast quantities of food that his generous hosts fed him. His younger daughter Rachel accompanied him on the trip and Dubnow also spent the summer there. The Ginzbergs were housed in a separate dwelling near the main house where he strengthened himself before his return to Odessa and his responsibilities at *Ha-Shiloach*.[118] Even once the summer ended and he returned home, though, his strength continued to fail him, so *Ha-Shiloach* suspended publication until late 1900.

Illness would plague him for the rest of his life. He described it in June 1899, several months before his departure for Palestine, in a letter to the scholar David Neumark, as the sort of "sickness that generally inflicts women and intellectuals (talmidei hakhamim)—a nervous disorder." The doctor prescribed complete rest, and Ahad Ha'am hoped (as he told Kaplan a few days later) to extricate himself from *Ha-Shiloach* for some two months abroad.[119]

His mood swings in this period were sharp and troubled his friends. Only a few days after he informed Kaplan of his expectation that *Ha-Shiloach* could operate without him for awhile, he wrote Bernfeld that he had no idea "where my salvation will come from," that he was inundated by sorrows the most recent of which was his bad health. Soon his health took a turn for the worse: "The last few weeks have been very bad for me," he wrote Kaplan in mid July. "My nervous disorder is now so bad that I haven't been able to write a simple letter, and it has been about three weeks since I have abandoned my work entirely and I have done nothing at all."[120] In an especially revealing and despairing letter written on 12 August, he says:

And what can I write you about my personal affairs? Unfortunately, I have nothing good to say. As far as my financial situation is concerned, there is nothing to tell but the real disaster is that the source of my greatest strength—my peace of mind—has on the whole recently disappeared. I don't know how this happened but I feel that there is something awful inside of me that is sick: a constant emotional drain, nervous irritation, and a loss of any inclination to work.[121]

Ha-Shiloach did not reappear until November 1900. Even after Ahad Ha'am resumed work he complained of a "dark melancholy" that refused to leave him in peace. As late as August, he could work for no more than two or three hours a day. He remained obsessed with his health, even once it improved; he told his friends that although he was now healthier, he had not yet managed to regain his former peace of mind. Soon he resumed many of his old, unhealthy habits—he started drinking tea again, which he had had to abandon when he was sick—but, as he would complain to Ha-Cohen in March 1902, his "soul knew no peace."

Indeed, that summer, upon returning from the nationalist congress in Minsk where he had given a major address on Jewish culture, he found his daughter Leah ill and complained that he himself was constantly exhausted in body and soul, listless, directionless, unhappy. "God only knows how all this will end," he added.[122]

He had, of course, been very sick before in 1895, and had managed to regain his health and throw himself into the running of a new journal and battling the forces of the Zionist movement. Now, though, his ailment attacked—as he complained repeatedly—both body and soul and robbed him of his peace of mind which, he feared, he might never regain.

No doubt Herzl's appearance and his sudden prominence in Ahad Ha'am's own political backyard had unsettled him, but by 1900 Herzl's star had started to dim, or so Ahad Ha'am convinced himself. Still another source of tension for him in this period—one especially difficult for him to comprehend in view of his lifelong commitment to sublimating unruly emotions—was his romantic interest in Tsina Dizengoff, wife of Meir Dizengoff who was later the founding mayor of Tel Aviv. The attractive, literate, russified woman settled in Odessa with her husband in 1897, and Ahad Ha'am and she pursued a passionate (and, apparently, platonic) relationship for several years.

"I don't know how this happened," he stated in one letter written in 1899, where he also explained that his illness made him feel that there was something profoundly wrong with him although he couldn't point to anything precise. Clearly, he feared, that this was more serious even than a nervous disorder. But what had brought it on at this moment, he said, was a mystery.[123]

Mysterious though he claimed it was, it coincided almost exactly with the death of his father. By January 1899 Isaiah Ginzberg had been ill for some time. Responding then to an invitation from the Hovevei Zion to visit Palestine and report his findings to the committee, Ahad Ha'am wrote that although he would very much like to do this, "one of the ten plagues has now come to hinder me. My father has been ill for several months and he will not permit me to travel such a far distance until he is well. And since I am an only son, the decision is his (ha-din imo)."[124] His tone is petulant: Ahad Ha'am writes as someone hemmed in by filial obligation; he seems acquiescent rather than sympathetic and betrays little concern for his ailing father. Indeed the use of the biblical allusion to the ten plagues serves to distance himself from the news and to belittle its importance or its potential impact on him. It is the same tone he had always used when writing about his father.

Those close to Ahad Ha'am saw his father rather frequently when the meetings of Bnei Moshe took place in a house that the two shared; they described Isaiah as a hasid who carried himself with some self-importance, a rich man (as indeed he was until a few years before his death) who wasted few words and spoke with a pleasant voice. He was tall, learned (profoundly so according to Joseph Klausner), handsome even in his old age, and a generous philanthropist—one of Odessa's outstanding hasidim.[125]

That he died within four years of the loss of his fortune is perhaps unsurprising. His health had always been tenuous and without his fortune he lost his local standing and the power that he had exerted in Odessa's leading ultraorthodox synagogue where he was an officer and a guiding presence.[126] Dating back to their last days at Gopchitse his son played a significant, at times even decisive, role in charting their mutual business concerns with mixed success. For a while in Odessa they made money, but a downward business cycle, bad luck, and perhaps young Ginzberg's inattentiveness contributed to their reversals. That Asher may have held himself responsible, as a result, for his father's physical decline, or even in some respects for his death, is possible.

At no time before his father's illness had Ahad Ha'am written about him with tenderness. Years later when Ahad Ha'am himself was dying and relating to Rawnitsky and Bialik the story of his life, all that he managed to recall about his father was his cruelty, his wretched impact on the young Asher which left him flawed, uncertain, and unhappy. Nonetheless, upon first realizing that his father might be deathly ill, the cool, distant way with which he had before described his sickness gave way to deep despair. In a letter written only a few days after he spoke of his father's condition as "one of the ten plagues" he told a friend: "My father's condition is progressively worsening. And the condition of my soul—God help it!"[127] For the first time he had linked his father's decline—perhaps, his imminent death—with his own mounting sense of desperation.

Within weeks, by 7 February, he was more explicit in a letter to Rawnitsky: "My father's condition is very bad. And if I am not mistaken only God himself can help him. Since I have come to this point, I cannot continue to speak about other matters because my heart is full of sorrow."[128] His father died some months later. "In the past week," he writes Neumark in late April,

a very terrible tragedy occurred in my family: My father, whom I loved very much, died and left me with a set of family problems that are complex and terrible.[129]

Never before had he so much as hinted at this love for his father or how his loss served to "burden him," as he would now repeatedly put it. In letters written after his father's death he speaks, rather ambiguously, about his financial and emotional burdens (he had now to take on the support of his mother) without saying which was worse. He writes a great deal about his financial problems, describing them in the same terms time and again as "complex and terrible." Other tensions, he implied, were still worse. He wrote Bernfeld in early May: "It is possible that the pressures of life will drag me down into the great sea and I will perish in its depths. At the moment I am bewildered and confused and my head is spinning." Within a month he was diagnosed as suffering from a nervous disorder. From this point on, his letters stopped mentioning his father or his death even though they were replete with details of his physical and emotional suffering. He tried to make major changes in his life: he would soon attempt unsuccessfully to remove himself from communal activities; when he managed to resign briefly in June 1901 from the Hovevei Zion executive committee, the reason he gave was "to devote his time to moral stocktaking." This, too, failed to cure him of the deep malaise that he claimed dominated much of what he did: his health had by now been restored; his emotional life remained deadened and unchanged.[130]

He would never say what it was that haunted him about his father's death. His mother's death had no comparable impact. But from the time he realized that his father was likely to die the prospect of this loss and subsequent reality terrified, and even temporarily debilitated, him.

He and his father had, of course, worked together and even lived in close proximity throughout their adult lives, but their relationship seemed at best correct rather than intimate. Probably Asher felt some responsibility for their financial ruination; more importantly, the origin of his ambivalent feelings toward his father date back much earlier and feelings of anger seem to have been linked for him with those of remorse and guilt, which literally overwhelmed him for a time. Within weeks of Isaiah's death, he ceased to speak of him, except on rare occasions; when he did it was with much the same disapproval and apparent dislike with which he had described him before his dying days.

Ahad Ha'am wrote a poem a month after his father's death, which he composed on his father's gravesite according to his sister Esther who includes it in the Russian typescript version of her memoirs. The poem is strikingly impersonal in its tone. Rather than speak personally to his own sense of loss or for that matter about his father it talks—and in rather positivist terms—about the significance of the passing of Isaiah's generation. Curiously, Ahad Ha'am built the poem around his own name—or, rather, his pen name—with the two lines of the brief poem beginning with the words "Ahad" and "Ha'am." Presumably he intended this as a signature of sorts; in this literary device, he also adhered to a medieval Jewish form of poetic and liturgical exposition. But its use also implied a form of usurpation, his attempt to impose himself onto his father and his memory. There was something altogether odd about the performance: his choice of his pen name for use at this intimate moment, his need to impose his own name onto a poem written in honor of his deceased father, the apparent impersonality of the poem which was especially striking in light of the impact that his death had had. He did not mention the poem in his memoirs; it was deleted from the privately printed Hebrew edition of his sister's memoirs:

אֶחָד   אֶחָד   הֵם   הוֹלְכִים   לִמְנוּחָתָם
שְׂרִידֵי   דּוֹר   יָשָׁן   הַתּוֹרָה   נִשְׁמָתָם.

הָעָם   זֶה   יָצְרָם   עוֹד   יוֹלִיד   כְּמוֹתָם
אַךְ   זִכְרוֹנָם   לוֹ   קָדוֹשׁ,   קְדוּשָׁה   אַדְמָתָם.

[AHAD] One by one they go to their resting places
The remnants of the old generation with souls of Torah

[HA'AM] The nation they created will never again
give birth to those like them
But their memory will retain its holiness in their
sanctified ground.[131]

Though he returned to the editorship of *Ha-Shiloach* in the fall of 1900, he left it permanently two years later at the end of 1902. (By 1898, in fact, he flirted already with the idea of returning to business.) Except for some moments of pride in the excellent journal, his last two years as editor were deeply frustrating: the constant search for writers who could produce credible work and respect deadlines, the tedious task of editing (he took on Rawnitsky as an assistant only in December 1901), and his dissatisfaction with the publishing house, Ahiasaf. Of course, Ahad Ha'am was himself the director of Ahiasaf (itself originally a creature of the Bnei Moshe), but he complained, and with mounting bitterness, of the way in which its staff disregarded him and how it made decisions that he would never have endorsed. "I am a king without a people," he wrote already in August 1896 about his relationship with it. He grew increasingly dissatisfied.[132]

His misgivings about Ahiasaf and *Ha-Shiloach* intersected: Ahiasaf, responsible for the funding of the journal, pressed him for ways to expand its subscription list. It estimated that it needed at least 1,000 subscribers to remain afloat. In 1897, following Ahad Ha'am's first attacks on Herzl, the subscription fell to 500, a drop from some 1,115 subscribers the year before. During Ahad Ha'am's tenure it would peak at a mere 700. Ahad Ha'am was urged to write for it more frequently, to send wealthy Jews complimentary copies (he characterized this suggestion as beneath contempt), or to include additional pieces of fiction. His vigorous campaign against Herzl did little to improve its circulation among Russia's middle-class Hebraists; in its first year they were the mainstay of its subscription list and the ones who could best afford its rather steep rates. Ahad Ha'am agreed to have his salary cut but absolutely refused to budge in any other way. From the vantage point of Ahiasaf, he was a stiff and uncompromising pedant but also their great genius who deserved deference; he viewed them (though he looked kindly on their office manager Eliezer Kaplan) as weak-willed, inefficient, lacking in vision and as the wrong men to implement his dreams.

He treated them, particularly in his capacity as Ahiasaf's director, to a brisk diet of contempt and abuse. Their choice of projects he found in bad taste (the decision to translate Herzl's play "The New Ghetto," the prudish Ahad Ha'am referred to as "literary prostitution"). He repeatedly scolded them for their unprofessionalism and their excessive preoccupation with costs and profit, and he claimed that ever since he had agreed to direct the company he had not enjoyed "a single day of peace of mind." Judging from the venomous letters he sent to Ahiasaf, they probably felt rather similarly.[133]

Of course, he did raise some very serious and unanswered questions about their publishing house and its larger goals, precisely the sort of probing, mostly unanswerable queries, in which he excelled. In May 1898 he wrote:

Perhaps it is true . . . as you say, and it might very well be, that our community does not demand important books and has no need of them. But nonetheless you still haven't responded to my major question: If so, why "Ahiasaf"? Occasional publications and the like can be produced by the private presses . . . at the expense of individuals. For the purpose you had outlined there was no reason to establish an entire company in which five lovers of literature work. . . . I cannot tell you how much this all pains my heart.[134]

In the end, though, it was sheer economics that put an end to Ahad Ha'am's reign at *Ha-Shiloach*. In the spring of 1902 Ahiasaf made it clear that unless the magazine erased 1,000 roubles from its deficit it could well close. Similar threats had been leveled before since its budget had to be approved annually, but this time the crisis seemed ominous. Ahad Ha'am found it humiliating (especially since, as he complained, the amount of money was really quite small), and he mumbled about how he hoped to resign but held his peace. That fall, *Ha-Shiloach*'s fiscal crisis remained unchanged with few new prospective subscribers and with its editor unwilling to do much to improve the situation. Whether Ahiasaf engineered his final departure—or whether Ahad Ha'am summarily stepped down when informed that he would have to take still another salary cut—is unclear. Ahiasaf then hired a recent Russian-born graduate of a Central European university, unmarried, otherwise unencumbered, and willing to work for a pittance—a protégé of Ahad Ha'am, Joseph Klausner. Clearly he was more amenable to pressure from Ahiasaf. More poems and fiction now appeared in *Ha-Shiloach* and at the front of the journal; among these were included such contributions as those by the "Hellenist" Saul Tchernichovsky whose Judaic credentials Ahad Ha'am found dubious; the journal was also opened up to articles of general interest without specific Jewish content that never would have appeared under Ahad Ha'am's tutelage. Some of Ahad Ha'am's friends were justifiably convinced that he had been treated shabbily. When his retirement was announced in October 1902, he had no idea how he would earn his living. He had incurred debts in 1900 during his long convalescence and he despaired of his dependence upon the Jewish nationalist movement which he excoriated mercilessly.[135]

When his old friend Lubarsky found him a job as a southern Russian representative of Wissotzsky's tea company (in fact, several maskilic nationalists were employed there, and Ahad Ha'am, with his extensive administrative experience, was better qualified than most of them), he rejoiced at being saved from the brink of starvation. Perhaps he exaggerated, but clearly he found his position as a supplicant untenable, and he was relieved that he had not needed to contact Wissotzsky directly. The whole matter, he announced with satisfaction, was set up by others and without their even having spoken with him about the plans. He was pleased that he was no longer forced to draw his salary from Jewish nationalist sources. He also used his predicament as a way of trying to embarrass Ahiasaf: in his last letter to them as the editor of *Ha-Shiloach* he questioned with a rhetorical flourish whether it would be believed in the future that

in a generation such as this one with all of its talk about [Jewish] revival, that one of the most important of the nationalist writers, who occupied for six years the position of editor at the only journal worthy of the designation "literature" had to abandon the task and was pushed out, to become a clerk in a commercial house?[136]

Although he did not embark on his new career with similar dreams to those he had when he had become "an editor in Israel," he nonetheless took for granted that the new work would give him more time for study and writing. It did not: he found himself confronted with a grueling schedule that demanded frequent travel throughout New Russia and the Crimea and which strained his health and robbed him of time and stamina. He proved to be a very conscientious employee, therefore leaving him little energy to do the work that mattered most to him. More importantly, larger events intervened—the Kishinev pogrom, the Revolution of 1905, the bloody wave of pogroms in 1906—that wouldn't permit him to retreat into the privacy of his study, even in those moments when the job left him in peace.

He also remained active in the Zionist movement as the chief critic of its leader who was beginning to look more and more frayed as time went on and whose diplomatic initiatives failed to produce much. Herzl's mounting vulnerability seemed to inspire Ahad Ha'am who, in his final year as editor of *Ha-Shiloach,* produced several of his most important essays: "Moses", "Spiritual Revival," and his controversial review of Herzl's novel *Altneuland.* None of this work—not even what purported to be a scholarly excursion into the medieval Jewish philosophy of Maimonides, "The Supremacy of Reason"—was written with any real detachment. All of it, as we shall see, was profoundly engaged and the turbulence of the nationalist movement would clearly reverberate through it. In his last year as editor, as he was in the process of easing himself out (or being eased out) of his role as the chief arbiter of Jewish cultural politics—and even during the early period of his employment at Wissotzsky's—Ahad Ha'am wrote with greater power than at any point in his career. His final years in Russia, before he left to settle permanently in London in 1908, were spent in the midst of great political upheaval. He encountered, first in a Russia torn apart by the convulsions of pogroms and revolution, and later in liberal, benign England, very different versions of the curses of diaspora life, and these served only to confirm and deepen his commitment to Jewish rebirth in Palestine.

5

The Curses of Exile

*The three curses of exile are . . . lack of courage . . . lack of
honor . . . and lack of government.*
Isaac Abarbanel, fifteenth-century Jewish philosopher

Rather late in his life, once he had turned fifty and began
to speak of himself as someone on the threshold of old age, Ahad Ha'am
recalled how in his youth he had managed to shut out the larger world
and spend days, even months, within the confines of his study. He looked
back with considerable nostalgia and bemusement at his self-discipline,
rectitude, and reticence during these years and dreamed, if often only
half-seriously, of recapturing some of their sense of purpose and scholastic direction. In 1902, his retirement from *Ha-Shiloach* seemed to him
to signal an opportunity to extricate himself from the excessive demands
of Jewish communal life and to retreat into scholarly activity of immeasurably more meaning and influence. Later, on the eve of his 1908 move
to London, he felt much the same way, and convinced himself that he
would retreat to the British Museum at the end of each business day to
write finally his major theoretical work.[1]

To retreat into scholarship, even the sort of profoundly engaged
scholarship that Ahad Ha'am had in mind, proved impossible for him.
This was not merely because Herzl distracted his attention or because
of the murderous turbulence of the Kishinev pogrom or because of the
1905 Revolution. Dubnow, no less politically involved in these years

than Ahad Ha'am, managed to "live with Yochanan ben Zakkai" (as Ahad Ha'am put it) and labor on the historical reconstruction of the second temple period at the same time that he occupied center stage in Russian Jewry's political transformation. For Ahad Ha'am, the task of balancing conflicting commitments proved impossible and often crippling. Scholarship, he told himself, was what he wanted to do but too many years in communal politics had sapped him of the necessary self-discipline, stamina, and the ability to concentrate on anything but issues of the moment. "Both a sense of obligation as well as the demands of my inner nature" stood in the way, he admitted in 1906. He would never be at peace with how his best writing always demanded some item in the news to which to react and to summon up the decorous disdain or the barely contained fury that set his prose apart. He would always remain an essayist, though to the end he aspired to be something he considered more serious.[2]

While still *Ha-Shiloach*'s editor, he wrote Lubarsky in September 1900 that barely a night passed without the need to attend a meeting of one sort or another. He mentioned in the same letter that his wife had been ill recently with a nervous disorder that was now waning but that might recur, but "who can pay attention to such things in our times?"[3] Of frustrating yet seductive community politics he wrote Dubnow in January 1904:

I, too, have endeavored with all my strength to remove myself from the community and to retire to a better world, one that for some time I have seen from afar. But a "sinner" like myself, who has spent most of his years in meetings and gatherings—is beyond redemption. Consider this, for all my efforts to extricate myself from gatherings, I have attended three of them this week.[4]

That particular week included meetings of the Hovevei Zion executive committee (from which he had repeatedly, though half-heartedly resigned), the executive committee of the Odessa branch of the Society for the Promotion of Enlightenment among the Jews of Russia (OPE), and the "national"—or cultural—committee of the Zionist movement. None of these left him terribly satisfied. As a leader he was typically an obstinate and unyielding purist. This was not always the case, though. Sometimes, and for reasons that are difficult to explain, he could be a model of pragmatism who espoused virtues of compromise without a semblance of irony. What drove him from his writing desk was an abiding sense of responsibility, an albeit vacillating but firm belief in his own ability, a lack of faith in those around him, and a restlessness that somehow never abated. These served to propel him into a surprisingly wide range of tasks.

His involvement in communal politics was especially active in the first years of the century, until he and his family moved to London because he was offered a different job with Wissotzsky. Before the move, particularly between 1901 and 1906, he attempted to translate his agenda into reality to a greater extent than he ever would outside the secretive, oligarchical framework of the Bnei Moshe. These attempts were sporadic and often explosive and resulted periodically in spells of disappointment and recrimination. By the end of this period he emerged more skeptical than ever of what could be achieved in exile, more disdainful of the designs of those (whether Zionists, socialists, liberals, or Dubnovian autonomists) who believed redemption of one sort or another was possible in diaspora. Russian Jewish life, he had long before concluded, was thoroughly humiliating; life in England, or so he came to learn, was empty, without Jewish vitality or, perhaps, even meaning. "In the torments surrounding Palestine," he wrote in April 1906, "there is at least something of the torment of love. But as far as the torments of exile are concerned—how vulgar they all are!"[5]

I

In his last years in Russia he would be immersed in the torments of homeland and exile both. Despite his self-willed isolation from Herzl's movement (he served from time to time on an odd committee but avoided most official ties) and his unwillingness to attach himself formally to the Democratic Faction, he retained a highly visible role in Zionist affairs as a leader of the Odessa-based Hovevei Zion, which had become much more amenable to his designs. During these years he also emerged as an important force outside the Zionist sphere: together with Dubnow he led the fight for the introduction of a "national" plank in Russia's leading Jewish organization—the Society for the Promotion of Enlightenment among the Jews of Russia (OPE); with the advent of the Revolution of 1905, his standing as a spokesman for a liberal, nationally oriented Jewish agenda increased immeasurably. This period was also characterized by increasingly fierce attacks on him from both within the Zionist camp and its culturalists as well as outside

by anti-Zionists on the left who objected to his uncompromising nationalism; and these must be understood against the backdrop of his
extraordinary intellectual and political prominence.

Within the Hovevei Zion his standing throughout this period was
essentially uncontested. He did not run it; in its much declined state it
was chaired by Abraham Greenberg and, after 1906, by Ussishkin; the
still-influential Lilienblum continued to distrust what he considered to
be Ahad Ha'am's rarified politics. Generally, though, it was agreed in the
movement that his line should dominate, conceding as much to practical
reality as ideology. The plutocrats of the past had all but vanished, most
of them having abandoned the cause or having thrown their weight
behind Herzl. Some wealthy Jewish leaders were still on the Hovevei
Zion executive committee, but those who remained, like Samuel Barbash, were men of maskilic inclinations who tended to be under the spell
of Ahad Ha'am. The Hovevei Zion, however, had little money available
for Palestine and the diplomatic scene was now dominated however
imperfectly by the Herzlians so there was little left to do except support
cultural institutions—especially schools and libraries. Small donations
were still provided for agricultural settlement. The Hovevei Zion continued to be generous in its advice to the Yishuv; it still saw itself as the
natural address for the grievances of Palestine's farmers and its growing
army of poorly paid Jewish laborers, especially those grievances directed
at Rothschild who still dominated colonial affairs and the bulk of its
agrarian subsidization work. Except for an occasional boost to a strapped
colony and modest support for a handful of schools and periodicals, the
Hovevei Zion nonetheless had come to function primarily as the movement's conscience, its moral center—in other words, as the institutional
arm of Ahad Ha'amism. What Ahad Ha'am had set down as a principle
was now translated into policy mainly because of pressures of the purse.[6]

It was in this capacity that the Hovevei Zion played a central role in
one of the most contentious Palestinian conflicts of the period. Oddly,
the dispute had little to do with Herzl or the apparatus of the Zionist
movement; it pitted the Hovevei Zion and the Palestinian Jewish colonists and laborers against the Jewish Colonization Association (JCA)
in Paris and its patron, Rothschild. In a confrontation, with clear theatrical overtones that set the great French-Jewish banker against both
Odessa- and Palestinian-based East European Jews, the battle brought
to the surface a host of issues. Should Jewish Palestine be shaped in the
mold of either its Western or its Eastern benefactors? Had the current
system of subsidized agriculture championed by Rothschild stunted the

self-reliance and economic health of the settlers? How could Palestine be best prepared to take a leading role in its own affairs and, eventually, in Jewish life as a whole? In view of its already established client relationship with its Western benefactors, would such a role ever be possible? Ahad Ha'am's answers to these questions would prove seminal.

They surfaced now because jurisdiction over the colonies that Rothschild funded was transferred officially in 1901 from his direct control to the JCA. He in turn provided the organization with large sums to finance them. This administrative reorganization prompted a vigorous attempt by the Palestinian farmers and laborers to redefine their relationship with their foreign benefactors. Rothschild's decision was viewed (in Palestine as well as Odessa) as an admission of failure; when the JCA soon began to evict indebted tenants and expel laborers, the settlers sent a delegation to confer with Rothschild and the JCA. The Hovevei Zion was persuaded to send its own delegation to work in tandem with the Palestinian one. Meanwhile the Ottomans tightened restrictions on Palestinian Jewish settlement and the colonies faced mounting agricultural deficits, some 1.6 million francs in 1900 at Zikhron Ya'akov alone. Rumors were rife that the JCA planned mass expulsions from colonies and the selling of unprofitable farms.[7]

From the beginning both sides understood the dispute to be over the efficacy of paternalism. Those in agreement with Rothschild and the JCA argued that continued technical training and supervision for Palestinian colonists were essential. Their opponents made the case that self-government instead was the key and that the current system required thorough revamping. The price paid for the present system, argued this side, was too heavy: it rendered Palestinian Jews into economic, political, and spiritual dependents, and it consigned the community to a state of permanent marginality in Jewish affairs outside Palestine.[8]

In view of Ahad Ha'am's long-standing vocal objections to the Rothschild system in Palestine, the way in which he had now become closely associated with the so-called practical strain of Zionist thought, and his visibility as editor of *Ha-Shiloach*, he emerged as a key figure in this debate. Not that he had always been an unconditional supporter of the positions taken by Palestinian labor. He had often been faulted by Palestinian Jews for what some felt to be his unrealistic, insensitive criticisms of them and of their harsh lives. Frequently they found themselves talking past him. During his visits to Palestinian colonies they found that he tended to harangue them with sermons on self-sufficiency and often refused to listen to local residents themselves once he had made up his mind. Ahad Ha'am frequently defended stands that were very unpopular in the Yishuv. For instance, in a conflict in 1891 over payment for the laborers at Rehovot, Ahad Ha'am contended—much to their fury—that their salaries were adequate and if workers could not support themselves they should leave to make way for those who could. He opposed the building of subsidized housing to stem the tide of emigration to Europe. The only sustained financial support he promoted was the establishment with Jewish nationalist funds of model colonies drawing on the best of Palestine's workers. These would in the future become self-sufficient economic units providing for all basic necessities of life, including their own eggs, chickens, milk, and vegetables. They would constitute the foundations of a healthy Palestinian Jewish economy, one much superior to what presently existed with its emphasis on exports foisted onto Palestinians by Parisian overseers.[9]

Moreover, in a 1900 report to the Hovevei Zion on the Palestinian Jewish colonies—a meticulously detailed investigation (coauthored with the agronomist A. Zussman) that recommended changes in the plows, irrigation, threshing devices, and fertilizer—Ahad Ha'am insisted upon self-reliance and called for the elimination of subsidies for individual farmers. In his view, the future of Palestine couldn't be built upon the tenuous foundations of subsidized labor—whether this help originated in Odessa or Paris. It was, he argued, self-supporting agriculturists like the farmers of Rehovot who represented the kernel of a local agrarian bourgeoisie and the sturdy, self-reliant bulwark of the new Jewish political culture.[10]

As angry as some colonists may have been at times with Ahad Ha'am, their accumulated antagonism toward Rothschild was of an altogether different character: it was quickly channeled into a new organization, the Union of Hebrew Workers of the Agricultural Colonies of Palestine, established in 1900, which advocated self-government and some economic self-sufficiency, albeit limited. Ahad Ha'am eagerly supported both planks. The formation of the union, its anger over JCA charting a new, dangerous course, and what looked at the time like Rothschild's abdication persuaded Ahad Ha'am that this was a propitious moment for radical changes in Palestine's economic organization. According to Shulamit Laskov, of all the leading Jewish nationalists Ahad Ha'am was the only one willing to unsettle the current system of support for Palestine's agrarian sector. He liked the idea of a Parisian delegation, which was first suggested to him during his last Palestinian trip, and he carried the idea back with him to Odessa. He calculated that it could serve to marginalize Rothschild as well as Herzl in the Palestinian arena. Whatever confidence he felt on this score was undoubtedly reinforced by the JCA's offer, proposed during his trip to Palestine, that he run its office. He turned it down—"I cannot be bound to the will of others in issues pertaining to our people's needs," he later explained; but the offer strengthened his sense of his own standing beyond the parochial circles of Jewish nationalism.[11]

He made his agenda abundantly clear in a speech—delivered with *hitragshut penimit* (great inner emotion) at the February 1901 Hovevei Zion congress in Vilna which representatives of the new Union of Hebrew Workers attended. He argued that the Hovevei Zion must abandon its unwillingness to challenge Rothschild and face up to the fact that whatever might be lost by a confrontation was outweighed by the harm currently being done by the system. It was crucial to put the Palestinians on a self-sufficient footing even if this meant that some would have to abandon the country: a terrible price perhaps, but it was better than the alternative. He admitted that he suggested this with "deep feeling and a broken heart." But what value would there be for the Jewish people if a few hundred more poor Jews—even if they called themselves by the lofty term *po'alim* (workers)—were added to the impoverished 60,000 already there?[12]

The Hovevei Zion must therefore persuade the JCA that the Rothschild system had always been destructive and must be removed from Palestinian life—a radical recommendation that made even the Palestinians cringe. (Despite their severe misgivings about the system they hoped to draw from Parisian sources but without committing past errors.) In place of philanthropy, argued Ahad Ha'am, loans must be made available that would encourage settlers to be industrious, frugal, and self-sufficient within a reasonable amount of time. It would only be possible to determine how such funds should be distributed when the land was freed from foreign paternalism; until then, no money should be forthcoming from the JCA.[13]

Despite his radicalism and the apprehension it caused many of the delegates, he won considerable support here, though, as was so often the case, the specific details he championed were modified substantially. What he proposed was, at the same time, the only coherently articulated alternative to the current system. He insisted that a very large, intimidating delegation be sent to Paris: "At least twenty people" must go despite his firm commitment to fiscal austerity and his well-known hatred of pretence. In this instance, he suggested, pretence, even theater, was called for. There could be no compromise, and if the demand that the current bureaucracy be dismantled was rejected; a huge meeting should be convened in Paris where all the sordid details would be publicly rehearsed. This would, as Ahad Ha'am described it rather improbably, look like a "large congress"—in fact, he compared it to the Zionist Congress; like the Herzlian institution it would awaken public attention. (The official Zionist press, though it found the substance of his recommendations too radical, and also pointed out that he refused to take its own interests into account, took pleasure in his use of the Zionist Congress as a model to emulate.)[14] The confidence Ahad Ha'am showed in this campaign, at least in its early stages, was remarkable: it contrasted markedly with the glum resignation with which most of the rest of the Hovevei Zion greeted this endeavor. Few of its leaders pursued the matter with much hope of success. But as far as Ahad Ha'am was concerned, not since the early days of Bnei Moshe had he been so consumed by a political project. He argued that its success or failure would determine the future course of Palestinian colonization, and perhaps much more.

He primarily orchestrated the Paris meeting and helped supervise the selection of the Palestinians through his chief Palestinian emissary Barzilai, who also played an important role in drawing up a manifesto calling for Palestinian-Jewish self-rule; the document also stressed the centrality of cultural and educational institutions in the Yishuv.[15]

In the end, the encounters with Rothschild—two meetings between him and the Russian delegation, then separate ones for the colonists as well as the Palestinian laborers—were awkward, useless, and humiliating. The failure had much to do with the political miscalculation of his allies; they had assumed, like Ahad Ha'am, that Rothschild had abandoned his role as the patron of the colonies and that he could be turned against the new masters at the JCA. In fact, despite the new supervisory capacity of the JCA, Rothschild made it clear to the delegates that he remained very much in control. In the meetings he patronized the laborers and rejected out-of-hand nearly all the demands of the various delegations; he admitted that more land must be acquired but, with the exception of this point, he made it clear that nothing else they said would be taken seriously.

Ahad Ha'am attended only one of the meetings; he refused to be their spokesman once it became clear that the delegates wouldn't get their way. To the extent to which he said anything at all at the meeting, his comments were carping, disjointed, and confrontational. In reply, for instance, to Rothschild's repeated complaints about the financial irre-sponsibility—he even spoke of the love for luxury—of Palestine's Jewish colonists, Ahad Ha'am shot back that if there was any truth to the charge it was because the farmers were aping the behavior of Rothschild's handpicked bureaucrats. Deflated once the meeting ended, he insisted that a full report of it be widely distributed. He admitted that he could not but marvel at Rothschild's "caprice," at how his philanthropy had reduced the entire Jewish enterprise in the Holy Land to little more than the possession of a single man. "This movement belongs neither to the people nor the nation, just to the Baron alone," Ahad Ha'am now bitterly complained. Palestine's development could well be retarded for another fifty years. Once and for all, he declared, he was convinced that it was time to retire from communal life.[16]

The accounts of others of the meetings with Rothschild were not nearly as damning as his, though of course few had expected initially as much from them. In contrast to his insistence that the rest of the Hovevei Zion delegates sat in Rothschild's presence "like submissive sinners and beggars," both Tchlenow and Abraham Greenberg, the Hovevei Zion chairman, apparently voiced frank disagreement with his policies.[17] Be that as it may, what should have been a decisive victory over the sluggish and destructive forces in power in the Yishuv was, as he saw it, a disaster, and he placed much of the blame on the shoulders of an inadequate Russian Jewish leadership. For a brief moment Palestine's agenda had appeared to be consistent with Ahad Ha'amism, the Hovevei Zion had upstaged the Zionists for control over Palestinian affairs, and Rothschild looked weakened, marginalized, and perhaps even ready to acknowledge the leadership of the authentic Jewish nationalists in Russia and Pales-tine. When optimism proved excessive he turned on his colleagues with venom; he called them cowards, likening them to the generation Moses led from Egypt who were incapable of conquering the promised land themselves: "The meeting," he insisted in a letter to Weizmann, was "a shameful, disgraceful, cowardly" episode. It would haunt him, he claimed, for years to come.[18]

Once again, and as he did previously when the Bnei Moshe proved less amenable to his designs than he hoped, he turned rapidly to morbid recrimination. Both venom and morbidity seemed to those around him out of character for Jewish nationalism's self-declared advocate of mod-eration and caution. Virtue, he still believed, would eventually win out in Jewish politics, once it was freed from populist hubbub. He wanted his political victories (which he continued to desire very much) to be won with apparent unanimity—at least on the part of those sectors of the Jewish people whose opinion he believed mattered the most. He continued to assume that the victories of a true leader should be won without compromise or backroom deals. In short, he wanted to win by his own rules, on the basis of those same political precedents that he still saw as timeless and authentically Jewish. And now as he had earlier he retreated, furious at the world around him and at himself for the elusive victory that had slipped through his fingers.

His brooding was obvious in an essay published in December 1901 on the tenth anniversary of Leon Pinsker's death. Compared to his first article on Pinsker, this one was even more self-referential. The piece was written at a terrible moment and not only because of what had transpired in Paris: he had spent much of the intervening year struggling with an untenable workload at *Ha-Shiloach,* and the financial problems facing Ahiasaf now seemed to threaten the future of his monthly and his sole source of income. Moreover, he now claimed to despair of making any real contribution to Jewish literature or scholarship and shunned even the Democratic Faction despite the success that it scored for its culturalist politics at the Fifth Zionist Congress in August 1901. He seemed especially bitter and reclusive and doubtful of achieving any real success in any of the arenas that really mattered to him. This despair is the essay's starkest feature; curiously, the piece also reveals his still active political appetite.

The article shows him to be aware of the way in which Herzlian politics had somewhat marginalized him; at the same time he remains intent on asserting control over a significant sector of Jewish nationalism. He admits in the essay that Pinsker (and, by implication, himself) would not have been likely to compete successfully for power with masters of popular manipulation like Herzl; the masses are simply too fickle, the tricks used by populist demagogues too variegated, and the charms of men like Pinsker too subtle to exert much direct impact beyond a small circle. The authority that Ahad Ha'am seeks to affirm, however, is over the canon of Jewish nationalism: its theory and its collective memory. Here he feels that Pinsker—and, no doubt, his spiritual heirs—have a good chance to succeed.

In his sketch Pinsker is an all-but-forgotten master, a man recalled as a "precursor" of practical Zionism which itself is viewed as rather unimportant in the Zionist pantheon. This is unfortunate and historically inaccurate, says Ahad Ha'am, since it was Pinsker who "fifteen years before Herzl, worked out the whole theory of political Zionism from beginning to end, with a logical thoroughness and an elevation of style unequaled by any subsequent work." True, Pinsker's arguments were somewhat "scattered," his pamphlet read like a "loud, bitter, heart-felt cry fraught with indignation and grief." But his theory of politics was superior to Herzl's since it showed how national dignity and consciousness were the essential prerequisites of state-building. Pinsker demonstrated, despite his "political bias," how the building of a state was impossible without the national reconstruction of its people. Practical work, education, cultural activity were all essential to any credible political agenda.[19]

In its deprecation of Herzl and praise for the Russian Pinsker, the essay was both predictable and unremarkable. But where it charted new ground was in its analysis of the fundamental failings of Pinsker's leadership style. It is this admission of failure, albeit somewhat devious, and Ahad Ha'am's attempt to describe the fundamental contribution that such men make, that sets the essay apart:

Pinsker was a pure theorist . . . but like all theorists he was of little use when it came to practical work. Men of his type, simple souls and pure minded, know nothing except the naked truth, and such men cannot find their way into popular favor. Their words are too sincere, their actions are too straightforward.[20]

Written some three years before his essay "Moses" (though shortly before he presented a draft of it at Odessa's *Beseda* literary club), Ahad Ha'am's portrait of Pinsker resembles the uncompromising, fiercely truthful biblical exemplar.

Very different from those who pander successfully to the masses, who "bend [them] to their will, who descend to their level," Ahad Ha'am suggests that if Pinsker had remained at the head of the Zionist movement through the 1890s, because of his honesty he probably would not have carried off what Herzl did: he would have made it clear to those around him the movement's finances were in a wretched state which, in turn, might have jeopardized negotiations with the Turks. As doubtful as Herzl's success was in the diplomatic arena, Pinsker's fate would have been still worse. He would not have excited the mob, could not have whetted the appetite of the press, and he would have conducted Jewish nationalist affairs with none of the deftness, let alone the theater, of his successor.[21]

What Ahad Ha'am therefore proposed was a division of labor, an acknowledgment by the Zionist movement that tactical élan like Herzl's and theoretical originality like Pinsker's are rarely contained in the same leader and that this movement had produced two in its brief lifetime. Pinsker formulated its ideology (one that closely resembles Ahad Ha'amism); Herzl has served as its "apostle." In other national movements, apostles seek to promote the reputations of their mentors; in the Zionist movement the apostle has claimed rather improbable originality for himself in a pamphlet that is a dim reflection of Pinsker's masterpiece. It is not Pinsker's reputation that Ahad Ha'am wishes to resurrect—the modest, self-effacing Pinsker would have little interest in sustaining his name. Rather, it is Pinsker's message of national selflessness and devotion that must be promoted as a counterweight to the current crop of nationalist youth and the vapid teachings of official Zionism.[22]

Herzl, then, is a popularizer (and a somewhat dishonest one) of the ideas of another man whose memory he has failed to sustain and whose nationalist tract was immeasurably superior. By pitting Pinsker against Herzl, Ahad Ha'am was juxtaposing, once again, the traditions of the Hovevei Zion as he wished them to be remembered against those of the Zionists. But the essay was much more than an exercise in historical reconstruction. It represented an act of aggression directed against Herzl whose pretensions, vacuity, and posturing threatened what little had been built by Jewish nationalism over the past twenty years. At the same time, it was an acknowledgment by Ahad Ha'am that leaders like Pinsker (and presumably himself) were not adept at the workings of practical politics, although he remained unwilling to confront why this was so. For him this was a product of myopia and the fickleness of the crowd, a sad state of affairs that would persist until the politics he promoted were adopted.

There were many Jewish nationalists who took his declaration at face value following the Rothschild debacle that he had abandoned politics for the foreseeable future. Ahad Ha'am wrote to Weizmann explaining that he would not involve himself in the Democratic Faction because he had decided "to retire from the world to devote himself to self-analysis." Weizmann writes: "I am ashamed to write this, but tears came to my eyes when I was reading [Ahad Ha'am's] words and saw how the vulgarity of contemporary Zionism and the nonentities who are in it have managed to break the spirit of such a man."[23] But, as in the past, Ahad Ha'am proved unable to separate himself from politics and its promise of influence, responsibility, and human engagement. What he did manage to avoid, for at least the next couple of years, was any direct involvement in the affairs of Palestine. To be immersed in Palestine, he claimed, reminded him of the futility of his encounter with Rothschild. It was mostly exilic politics that now commanded his attention, first because it served as a way of extricating himself from his fierce, painful attachments to Zion, and soon, in the wake of the Kishinev pogrom of April 1903, because its demands proved too overwhelming to be overlooked.

Indeed, at almost precisely the moment that he declared himself to be disgusted with communal affairs and unwilling to put any further effort into them once again, he threw himself into yet another communal battle that, as he later put it, "cost me not a little time and strength."[24] This particular battle was conducted outside the Zionist movement or Hovevei Zion but it was fought hand-in-hand with Dubnow. The controversy, which lasted several years, revolved around the curriculum of Odessa Jewish schools that received funding from the Jewish enlightenment society, the OPE. At issue, as Ahad Ha'am argued, was far more than the institutional politics of one local Jewish group but the future of Russian Jewish education.

Since the early 1890s Ahad Ha'am had been active in the "historical-ethnographic commission" of Odessa OPE, which served as a salon for local intellectuals and debated pedagogical reform. It was a distinguished group that included Mendele, Menashe Margolis, and Dubnow as well as the local educationalist Maria Saker, one of the few women who played a prominent role in the overwhelmingly male intellectual world of fin de siècle Jewish Odessa. There were, as one participant described somewhat tepidly, "lively differences of opinion" at these meetings which were aired in a series of reports, the first in 1900, in which the committee split more or less down the middle with the nationalists led by Ahad Ha'am and Dubnow pitted against Margolis and Saker. The items raised in the proposals were debated at a general membership meeting in 1901; the Jewish nationalists, apparently in the minority at the meeting, continued to press their demands before the branch executive committee in March 1902 and again to the membership that May.[25]

On the surface, OPE might have appeared to be far from the ideal setting for debating issues at the cutting edge of Russian Jewish life. It was established in the early 1860s under the watchful paternalism of Moscow's Baron Ginzburg family, among Russia's richest Jews, whose conservative maskilic bent made them favor discreet, moderate Jewish integrationism and the promotion of Russian education for Jews as part of their eventual transformation into a cultivated, "Europeanized," but still reasonably pious community. From the outset, the Odessa branch of the movement was more liberal in its social and political commitments and in the composition of its leadership. As I have written elsewhere about the group in the 1860s and 1870s:

Odessa's men [of OPE] . . . were political liberals, westernizers in the standard Russian meaning of the term. [Baron]Ginzburg . . . also looked to the West for political inspiration but, while [he] saw figures like England's stolid and conservative leader Moses Montefiore as exemplifying the best of western Jewish values, the Odessa OPE looked to a radical-liberal like Gabriel Riesser, whose biography was recounted in their newspapers and whose democratic principles more closely meshed with those extolled by university-trained Russian liberals.[26]

Eventually Jewish nationalists too found the local OPE a sensible focal point for activism: it funded many of the city's best schools, it operated a superb Jewish library (whose Hebrew and Yiddish collections were, in fact, catalogued under the supervision of Ahad Ha'am and Dubnow), and represented a natural clearinghouse for Jewish intellectual talent. Jewish nationalists attempted to infiltrate it, with limited success.

They were thwarted by others with quite different cultural agendas: liberals within the group who found Jewish nationalism retrogressive and insufficiently Western; others still more radical who favored thoroughgoing assimilation and found the nationalists' agenda especially offensive, even tribal. From still another vantage point, Mendele, now one of Ahad Ha'am's dear friends, faulted Ahad Ha'am for antireligiousness; he declared that Ahad Ha'am's remarks on Moses, summarized in a speech at the local *Beseda* club and before the publication of his famous essay, were outright heresy. Margolis as well as Mendele concurred that he had no regard for the sanctity of Israel's supreme prophet.[27]

During this dispute over the curriculum in Odessa's Jewish schools, and in his capacity both as a member of the historical-ethnographic commission and the Odessa OPE's executive committee, Ahad Ha'am made his case on numerous occasions: he cajoled members behind the scenes and delivered two major addresses on curriculum reform in 1902, the first at an executive meeting and a second before the membership. The OPE rejected his proposal at first, even issuing a report criticizing it; eventually it was adopted. But in reaction to the initial decision Ahad Ha'am published and disseminated a pamphlet of his own.[28]

In an introductory note to the pamphlet in which his speech as well as Dubnow's along with the official OPE position paper on educational reform in Odessa were published, he explained that he was reacting to the "dreary situation that exists in the city's Jewish educational scene." Here, he said, "our national language, the language of the Torah and the prophets has been completely banished" and can find no place in the Jewish curriculum. The subjects that should be at the heart of the curriculum were either ignored or poorly taught. It is altogether appropriate, he insisted, that education has now achieved the status of the most "burning issue" on the Jewish agenda since the "national spirit" naturally tends to gravitate first toward those items crucial to the people's existence. If OPE, however, proved unable to face the issue with adequate seriousness, it ran the risk of being rendered irrelevant.[29]

The need for change is clear: in Odessa's schools Hebrew was taught in a "mechanistic" fashion and the Bible itself was almost completely ignored. Otherwise Jewish studies was limited to (what he described as) dry appraisals of Jewish ritual practices and the reading of prayers. On average, Hebrew and Bible in boys' schools occupied no more than one to one and a half hours weekly; the curriculum at girls' schools devoted still less time.[30]

He proposed that a national education would represent an ideal way to remedy this problem. The function of a national education is to ensure that students absorb, preferably "unconsciously," an attachment to their people. Some, like the French, he suggested (probably in an allusion to the national hysteria surrounding the Dreyfus affair), promote a nationalism that is bombastic and xenophobic. But for healthy nations (was he thinking of the English?) "education of this sort comes, as it were, all by itself without any mechanistic prodding from any quarter." Even subjects that might be assumed to be immune to the intrusion of national content, such as mathematics or the sciences, must also draw from this wellspring. Which means that in the teaching of animal or plant life one's immediate surroundings—and for good reason—receive the bulk of classroom attention.[31]

But to a much greater extent than is possible in the case of the sciences, and indeed more than even the study of geography or history, it is language that "provides a full national form to the inner life of the child." It constitutes the most important link between the individual and the collective. In Ahad Ha'am's view, to the extent to which there is a natural connection between Jewish children and their culture this can be achieved primarily through language and literature. This is particularly true for Jews of the diaspora since as a minority people they can never dominate their immediate surroundings: "The only way in which an organic connection can be formed between the individual and his ancestral culture, one in which . . . the 'individual' and the 'Jew' are effectively unified and for whom the inner tension between these two forces are put to an end" is through an emphasis on Hebrew. Inasmuch as Jews are keen on linking themselves to the larger body of the Jewish people—OPE, he reminds them, has declared itself committed to inculcating a "love for one's people"—a Hebraic content to the curriculum is the only way to achieve this. Consequently the OPE's opposition to the improvement of Hebrew instruction is all the more puzzling.[32]

In the past, he continued, OPE had felt that its duty was to promote what it called a general education which would, in turn, prepare children to be a part of both the "human family" and their "specific social and historical entity." Hence it made the case that Jewish studies must not dominate the curriculum over other subjects; the students it produced would otherwise be left with a skewed sense of their place in the larger world.

What, really, asks Ahad Ha'am, is the meaning of a term like "human family"? To the extent to which OPE champions the need for a program that trains students to live as human beings and Jews, it is saying little that is controversial. Beyond doubt, a harmonious relationship must be achieved between the Jewish (or, for that matter, any particular) identity and the other influences in one's life. This is the goal of any sensible education, nationalist or not. But OPE implies in its response that nationalists do not agree, that they seek to extricate Jews from the larger community, to separate them by means of a cloistered, particularist education. There is no merit to this argument. Which are the books that connect us to "the human family"? In any healthy culture these books are precisely those produced within their own society; every nation turns first to its own culture to inculcate a coherent sense of values and commitments. In fact the Jews are the only ones who put themselves in the awkward, unnatural position of picking up these values from external sources: from alien languages, from the cultural artifacts of other nations. Jews thus come to be more closely attuned to alien cultures than to their own. And, Ahad Ha'am continued, when called upon to correct this condition, all OPE feels capable of doing is bemoaning the prospect that Jewishly self-conscious reform could alienate Jews further from the human family. Could there be any greater insult than this to Jewish national identity? Could one not make a comparable case that teaching the Bible might also create obstacles between Jews and gentiles and that it too should not be taught? Even if our national culture was inferior to others, it would still be essential first to acquaint our children with it before they are taught about others. This is what happens in Russian education where children study Pushkin before Shakespeare. And could there be a Russian chauvinist who would contend that Pushkin or Gogol are superior to the English master?[33]

Never had he, or the other nationalists close to him, made the case that Jewish studies should take precedence over others. Such distinctions are objectionable. True, the primary source for the development of a Jewish child's understanding of the larger world should be Jewish texts. But properly studied, this is precisely what should tear down the insipid "spiritual ghetto" dividing the world between the "enemy's domain" and ours; it is this bogus distinction that has served to distinguish Jewish studies from general knowledge in such a way that they seem altogether distinct, even contradictory: "In sum, the goal of the national education that we recommend is to raise full human beings, whose fulfillment of themselves as people and as Jews is viewed as one single and unified goal, not as mutually exclusive."[34]

The position taken by OPE merely serves to reaffirm an awkward, counterproductive demarcation that defines Jewish cultural life to be radically different from other national identities. No other culture views itself in such distinctive or insular terms, in such stark contrast to the "world." And why is not what Jews produce also seen as part of this same world, to no less a degree than Pushkin, Heine, Gogol, or Shakespeare? All these are stamped with their national character—whether it is Russian, German, or English, while being a common possession of humanity. Why cannot Jewish achievements be similarly viewed? Shouldn't they be accepted both by Jews and non-Jews alike and judged as lesser or greater works depending upon their relative quality?[35]

Ahad Ha'am's published speech was unique in its concreteness and its commitment to move beyond what was now the rather familiar medley of Ahad Ha'amist themes onto a practical plane of cultural politics: how was the next generation to be educated? How could this be accomplished in the diaspora where, as Ahad Ha'am assumed, the majority of Jews would continue to live for the foreseeable future? Would an intensified Jewish education close Jewish students to the larger world? Would it impede the relationship that the graduates of these schools had with non-Jews? How, in short, could children be taught to remain Jews and feel free to embrace—in Ahad Ha'am's now famous words from "Slavery in Freedom"—"'that scientific heresy that bears the name of Darwin' without any danger to their Judaism"?

Here he attempted, and with unusual specificity, to define the fundamental underpinnings of Jewish culture and free it from the religious associations of the past. There had once been something fundamentally cloistered and suspicious in the Jewish attitude toward the world and this served to define the parameters of its intellectual horizons in terms unique to itself and its situation. It was essential now to abandon this feeling of embattlement without sacrificing either cultural distinctiveness or the wellspring of Jewry's national genius. At the same time, the Jews must overcome the defensive, modernist stance that defines true culture as the possession of the gentiles and sees what Jews have produced as significant only for its familial associations, not because of its intrinsic worth.

Exhausted, complaining through the summer of the excessive demands the OPE controversy made on his time, Ahad Ha'am nonetheless agreed to attend and serve as the main speaker at the conference of Russian Zionists to be held in Minsk in early September 1902. His talk, which would be turned into one of his best-known essays, expanded on the themes that he had aired in his OPE debates, but the stakes at the congress would be even higher: what he planned was no less than to split the Zionist movement, to establish an avowedly nationalist Jewish culturalist organization built on the remains of Russian Zionism. Its immediate goals would be domestic, not strictly speaking Palestinophile. The recent success of the Democratic Faction at the Fifth Zionist Congress in 1901, where a small, disciplined group exacted concessions from Herzl, no doubt persuaded him that the moment was right to press his case. Indeed, the "cultural question" was put at the top of Minsk's agenda. Herzl's standing among Russian Zionists now appeared to be in a state of steady decline, as he failed to secure any meaningful diplomatic advance. Not since Ahad Ha'am's successful encounter in Warsaw in 1898 had he pushed his position at a political meeting quite so openly.

Ahad Ha'am laid down strict conditions for his participation which the congress organizers—headed by the Ahad Ha'amist partisan Bernstein-Kohan—readily accepted. He was to speak on the last day, he defined the topic in very specific terms, and he made it clear that he did not plan to arrive much before his talk as he planned to spend the summer at the home of Ben Hillel Ha-Cohen.[36]

The conference, with its hundreds of delegates and observers, was the first of its kind since the 1898 Warsaw meeting. Unlike that earlier meeting, it was held with government permission; consequently it was a legal and open affair, the first and last such meeting of Russian Zionism before the Revolution of 1905. The streets of the city of Minsk, half of whose population of 100,000 was Jewish, were filled with Zionist flags. On the eve of the gathering they were filled with thousands of locals who jostled with delegates for admission to the conference hall. The mood was festive. All the leading figures of Russian Zionism attended, but the greatest attention of all, as many participants recalled, was on Ahad Ha'am.[37]

He received so much attention in part because this time he had played his cards with enormous care and wisdom. Slated though he was as the leading speaker in a conference devoted primarily to cultural affairs, he made sure to arrive at the eleventh hour, and he positioned himself in a corner of the room in the section for journalists. These were actions that served to heighten, not diminish, his visibility. Since differences over culture most vividly served to distinguish the position of a highly visible sector of Russian Zionists from those who unequivocally supported Herzl, the Minsk organizers chose to highlight precisely the most divisive issue in Zionism's internal arsenal and the one most closely associated with Ahad Ha'am.

There were, of course, other reasons for Ahad Ha'am's prominence. One young delegate, Moshe Cohen, recalled that although he and his friends talked a good deal about the movement's leading figures—their private lives as well as their ideologies—barely anything was known about Ahad Ha'am, which only served to heighten the mystique; on the eve of his appearance at Minsk his real name remained unknown to Cohen and all the people he knew. He added that, contrary to what others might believe, Ahad Ha'am's celebrity was not so much a product of the prominence of the cultural issue in Zionist circles—this prominence was felt only by those few Russian Zionists associated with the Democratic Faction. Rather, "the name Ahad Ha'am was perpetually on the lips of the huge assembly" at Minsk because of what he stood for in a more symbolic sense: "What Ahad Ha'am represented for us was a nationalist genius, the realization of a pure and successful redemption, revival and renewal. What we saw in Ahad Ha'am was not what might really have existed but rather what we wanted to see. The real Ahad Ha'am was not of any interest to us. In our imaginations, however, there existed an Ahad Ha'am that we ourselves had created. . . . He was shaped by us into a product of the people's dreams, the fruit of its will."[38]

Cohen wrote this account several years after the Minsk conference, and it was published in a journal with a particularly jaundiced view of

Ahad Ha'am, which must be kept in mind when reading his comments.[39] Whether or not the cultural politics of Ahad Ha'am were then quite as marginal as Cohen suggests, the tumult surrounding his arrival in Minsk remained one of the most vivid recollections of many who attended the meeting. Rarely had he been seen at Zionist gatherings; not since the Warsaw meeting had he spoken at one. This helped transform what must have been a most taxing experience for those present—his two-hour talk at Minsk was exceptionally long and Ahad Ha'am delivered it in a deadpan, low, almost inaudible fashion and in Russian (though many there couldn't understand the language)—into an event widely remembered as extraordinary.[40]

At Minsk there was none of the illegality and subterfuge he so despised; the proceedings were conducted openly with representatives of the police taking notes at the first session. Moreover, Ahad Ha'am's agenda, broadly speaking, had already been accepted by the conference leadership as an ideological touchstone. There was no need to work behind the scenes to win the support of a mass of delegates. No preliminary political work was necessary; afterwards, there were no additional meetings required to hammer out compromises. Arguably, he might have devoted greater energy to consolidating his gains since he left the congress after what was a triumphal speech as the unofficial philosopher king of Jewish nationalism. He continued to expect others to spread his message and function as his dutiful priests. But this would never happen mainly because the Democratic Faction—despite its high regard for him—refused to fall in step behind his specific recommendations. The theoretical underpinnings of his remarks had won over an already receptive audience; his practical recommendations—namely the call for the creation of a new organization devoted to Jewish culture—was rejected and Ahad Ha'am did little to further the idea.[41]

Not only was his Minsk speech—which later appeared under the title "Tehiyat ha-ruah" ("Spiritual Revival")—unusually long for an audience accustomed to pithy Ahad Ha'amist statements but it was uncharacteristic in other respects as well. For all its anti-Herzlian content, it was strikingly diplomatic in its acknowledgment of the legitimate if subordinate tasks of the Herzlian movement. To be sure he made this point in an argument calling for a split in the Zionist camp. Nonetheless as he had in his performance at Warsaw, he unsettled many of his critics with moderate rhetoric and his rather disarming praise for those considered his most bitter foes. Although he showed less political savvy than might have been called for in the immediate wake of the congress when he chose to overlook the nitty-gritty work of political organization, beforehand he demonstrated his rhetorical skill as a practiced, effective diplomat.

To be sure, he employed both irony and more than a hint of cruelty in his argument that proof of Jewry's genius was to be found in the achievements of precisely those Jews who had in recent times earned their fame outside the Jewish community. Those who instead gained prominence within the Jewish world were now by and large mediocre by comparison. It was those Jews who obviously neither figured among his listeners at Minsk nor his readers of *Ha-Shiloach* who "embody in their work the natural spirit" of Jewry, and, despite themselves, "the spirit of Judaism comes to the surface in all that they attempt and gives their work a special and distinctive character, which is not found in the work of non-Jews working in the same fields."[42]

In line with this argument, the speech was replete with biological and organic allusions. Jewish exile was compared to a fruit tree sustained by artificial means in alien soil; one's native language, said Ahad Ha'am, was the most natural of all and he reported that in cases where the afflicted forget how to speak and can only remember words in one language, it is invariably their native tongue that they remember and not the language in which they were most fluent at the time at their illness. This represented proof of "the natural, organic link between a human being, his own language" and his "natural" community.[43]

It was the attraction of Jewry's best minds to alien cultures that was, or at least should be, the chief item on the communal agenda. Geniuses sustained culture and they constituted the hallmark of national cultural achievement; the mere existence of widespread literacy could not in itself ensure the vitality of a nation. Take the Swiss, for example, who maintained an otherwise exemplary cultural life but had not produced any extraordinary minds and therefore were justifiably criticized for a lackluster and rather tepid intellectual scene. Jews could well suffer the same fate. A good example of the sort of outstanding figure who was drawn away, perhaps even inexplicably, from the Jewish to the larger cultural sphere was the eminent sculptor Mark Antokolsky. When Antokolsky conjured up images of monastic purity, he thought of medieval Christian saints rather than men "with much broader human appeal who were much closer" to his own experience such as Elijah the Gaon of Vilna, the eighteenth-century sage from Antokolsky's native city. Indeed, Ahad Ha'am argued, "it is beyond dispute . . . that if these scattered forces had been combined in earlier times, [Jewish] culture would be today one of the richest and most original in the world."[44]

In the absence, though, of such a recentralization program—or, for that matter, any coherent campaign to revitalize and refocus Jewry's cultural energies—those who remained most visibly Jewish were unimpressive, derivative, and, in effect, those incapable of embracing a larger and more impressive spiritual world. If this decline were not checked, rot would eventually set in and things would degenerate irreparably. This would constitute a tragic loss for Jews and also for the larger society since assimilation extracted a huge price in terms of the quality and viability of cultural achievement:

For is there no difference between the person who works among his own people, in the environment that gave birth to him, that gave him his special aptitude, that first prompted the growth of his faculties and implanted in him the rudiments of his human consciousness, his fundamental ideas and feelings, and in this way helping to determine in his childhood what would be the character of his mind throughout his lifetime, and the person who works amidst an alien people, in a world that is not his own, and in which he cannot be at home unless he changes artificially his own nature and the basic cast of his mind, unless he tears himself apart so that his work, and his very character, are without either harmony or wholeness?[45]

The many thousands of Jews crisscrossing the Western world in search of bread and safety—the main focal point of Zionist politics—will eventually find homes, Ahad Ha'am argued. But unless Zionism come to be seen as something more than a "romance of diplomatic embassies [and] interviews with prominent personages," it would not be able to inspire the much smaller numbers of Jews upon whom the future really depends. Issues of rather peripheral importance—migration, Palestinian land acquisition, the futile search for a charter—these are the issues that preoccupy Jewish nationalists to the detriment of the much more pressing concerns that, if left unchecked, would leave the destitute Jewish *folk* without leadership, moral direction, or a firm national foundation for their continued existence. Although other nations might, with some legitimacy, first concentrate their attention on diplomacy before busying themselves with cultural politics, the Jews are different. The Jewish nation could be compared in this respect to a grown man who, having long since emerged from childhood, is now being asked to return to the curious regimen of his infant years:

Jews climbed from the lower rungs of the ladder thousands of years ago, and then, once they had achieved a high stage of culture, their natural progress was forcibly arrested, the ground was cut from under their feet and they were left hanging in mid-air, burdened with a heavy pack of valuable spiritual goods but robbed of any basis for a healthy existence and free development.[46]

Pre-modern Jewish exilic life did not require nor did it permit such conditions to be corrected; contemporary Jewish life, however, would be wholly untenable unless these conditions were addressed; the reconstruction of Jewish life in its original Palestinian home was an essential component.

This speech, like the one delivered at the OPE meeting a few months earlier, was surprisingly concrete in its recommendations, though, as it turned out, wholly unrealistic. The Zionist movement, he suggested with uncharacteristic equanimity, was too preoccupied with other concerns to tackle these issues with the seriousness that they deserved—hence the need for a new organization headed by those for whom cultural work was a priority. Naturally the recommendation brought him to loggerheads with the large contingent of orthodox Jews in attendance, but even here too he managed to work out a widely accepted compromise applauded even by his opponents whereby the conference affirmed the need for two separate cultural commissions to make recommendations, one orthodox and one not. The conference found him in a conciliatory mood; the fact that he engineered a compromise with the orthodox forces over the contentious cultural question served only to increase his standing. He scored a considerable victory in Minsk, bringing Russian Zionism's traditionalists effectively to the verge of recognizing the legitimacy of a secular nationalist approach to Jewish culture.[47]

In the end, neither of the commissions met. And Ahad Ha'am's erstwhile culturalist allies—the most important being the Democratic Faction headed by Weizmann and Motzkin—refused to consider seriously any suggestion that would divide them from the Herzlian movement, especially so soon after their heady performance at the last congress. Despite their criticism of what they regarded as Herzl's rather one-sided, limited political approach to Jewish affairs, they saw no one on the horizon who equaled him as a political leader; Ahad Ha'am for them was an intellectual inspiration, a grand Jewish counterpart to their movement's deracinated Viennese leadership but also someone excessively purist, dogmatic, reclusive, and abstract. Philosophically and otherwise, they were eclectic; politically they were pragmatic and, especially under Weizmann's tutelage, well attuned to the wages of power. As sympathetic as some of them may have been to the high ideals of the Bnei Moshe, they were unwilling to help Ahad Ha'am resurrect it, no matter how modernized its garb—which is exactly what he attempted at Minsk.

Once again, he returned to his writing desk where he spent much of the rest of the year editing his last few issues of *Ha-Shiloach* and brooding about the shape of Zionist politics. He came back from Minsk dispirited, nervous, and unhappy. The pressures of family illness (especially Leah's which seemed to have degenerated into a long-standing depression) and the accumulated exertions of the previous year that continued to weigh heavily on him left him drained of energy and initiative. The steady deterioration of *Ha-Shiloach*'s fortunes was also deeply distressing. Curiously, the Russian government, which had watched the Minsk conference very closely, had now formed the impression that it was Ahad Ha'am and not Herzl who controlled the movement's Russian wing. By no means did Ahad Ha'am behave as if this were true. By the end of the year, he had accepted a post as traveling agent for Wisstozsky's firm, he was bitter over his treatment at *Ha-Shiloach*, and unhappy with what Klausner, his supposed disciple, was doing at the journal. He still maintained a friendly if rather distant relationship with the Democratic Faction, which had not managed to sustain the momentum it achieved earlier. Aside from how he earned his living, little in his life seemed to have changed. That he was a figure of great importance in Jewish nationalism he took for granted and had, of course, for some time. But the fact that his movement and much of the world around him insisted upon functioning according to rules that he remained convinced were both unreasonable and unvirtuous—this continued to weigh him down, to alienate him even from those who admired him and who begged him for guidance and leadership. He remained strangely distant, even at moments of real political consequence, and except for his old Odessa friends who revered him to the end, he tended to disappoint followers, to alienate affection, and to dissipate rather than nurture most of his options.[48]

Herzl remained a preoccupation, despite the rather mild things that Ahad Ha'am had said about him at Minsk. There it had not behooved him to attack the Zionist leader with the fierceness that Ahad Ha'am felt he justly deserved, since what he hoped to do was to split his organization in half and remove its most Jewishly literate and committed Russian activists. Ahad Ha'am must have understood that his failure to do so was due in part to Herzl's adroit treatment of Russian Jewry whom he had managed to court and flatter while doing little to satisfy its political demands. At times, he capitulated to its wishes, usually under duress, but with great charm and apparent sympathy, as he had done at the Fifth Zionist Congress, for instance. Herzl knew how to simulate compromise without giving up very much. He was a difficult foe to pin down and very hard to vanquish.[49]

The publication of Herzl's novel *Altneuland* thus seemed to provide Ahad Ha'am with an exceptional opportunity. *Altneuland*, appearing in October 1902, was in his view godsent. Herzl published it at a particularly vulnerable moment in his tenure as leader of the Zionist movement; indeed, Herzl turned to the novel, as he admitted in his diary, because he sensed that his diplomatic initiatives were not as successful as he had expected. In Ahad Ha'am's reading of the novel the flat, characterless, and Jewishly illiterate vision of Herzl's prospective state was apparent for all to see. The fact that it was praised soon after its publication by Western Jews was unfortunate but, he felt, sadly inevitable; the friendly reception that it first received from East European Jews was, quite simply, tragic. Their unconsidered reaction was as important as the failings of the novel itself. In the wake of his attack, Ahad Ha'am managed with greater success than at Minsk to split Herzl's movement into warring factions and to put its leader on the defensive. Herzl would remain on the defensive in his dealings with Russian Jews until his death the next year.[50]

Later, Ahad Ha'am claimed that he was shocked by the reaction to his review, surprised by the ferocity, by the anger of Herzl and Nordau, and by the deep enmities that it engendered. The assertion is difficult to believe. He must have anticipated that this devastating review would deeply wound Herzl and his supporters. This was precisely the sort of battle that Ahad Ha'am preferred: a literary one in which his allies fought much of the battle for him and in his name. At the same time though, he could never have anticipated Herzl's heavy-handed treatment of the controversy which transformed it from a mere literary dispute into an "affair." The *Altneuland* episode may be seen as the first of a series of bitter, divisive debates in Herzlian ranks which extended through the debate over the so-called Uganda plan of 1903 and which served to undermine his authority severely.

II

The assumption that what distinguished Ahad Ha'am from Herzl was that the former was concerned about cultural transformation whereas the latter, indifferent to such transformation, was attuned only to politics was understandable but misleading. It represents an example of how successfully Ahad Ha'am placed his signature on the terms of debate of opponents and supporters alike. The future contour of Jewish culture was, in fact, at the very heart of Herzl's novel, and the cultural theme dominates much of his earlier work as well. Particularly in *Altneuland,* the prerequisite of cultural change is a central theme as the novel's characters make themselves over from the meandering, sadly vague, and rarified souls of the diaspora into the virtuous, solid, and imaginative men and women of Palestine. The battle between Ahad Ha'am and Herzl was over conflicting cultural visions. Ahad Ha'am's review of his book challenged Herzl both in its substance and its tone, which was contemptuous, sardonic, and informed more by ridicule than rage. Herzl saw Ahad Ha'am undermining his dream of a reconstructed Jewry—one that was proud, free from parochialism, moderate in its habits, courageous, and modest: an emblem of liberality and decency.[51]

Herzl's novel tells of Palestine in the near future—some twenty years after the turn of the century—where a New Society, as he calls it, has been established with the help of a Turkish charter. There Jews live, despite some occasional unpleasantness caused by narrow-minded and fanatical coreligionists (the worst of whom in the novel is modeled on the Russian Zionist leader Ussishkin), in overall peace and harmony. Herzl's utopia is fairly conventional in this respect and it depicts a rational, hardworking, technocratic near-paradise. Hence Ahad Ha'am treated it as a social blueprint, not a novel, which was not altogether unreasonable. In his work Herzl had clarified that what he hoped to create was a pluralistic, anticlerical, Western state where everything but the deracinated remnants of Central European Judaism (such as a reform-style temple atop or near the Temple Mount) were eliminated. Its chief influences would be English, French, and German but not Jewish. As Ahad Ha'am wrote in his review:

And since everything that can be found there in the Land of Israel was actually created not there but rather in England, America, France, and Germany, consequently all that happens to be there belongs not to Jewry alone but to all the nations of the world. The fundamental principle of the new society is, as a result, "Without any distinction for reasons of religion or nationality."[52]

Herzl's Jewish world was one in which the hotly contested "language question" that pitted Yiddish against Hebrew in one of the most contentious debates of the period had no resonance at all. In Herzl's Palestine, Jews studied French and German in schools and spoke most probably German on the street although the question held so little interest for Herzl that he did not even feel it necessary to specify the preferred tongue. Hebrew wasn't taught or, if it was, Herzl didn't bother to mention it. To the extent to which a national culture existed, it was an unambiguously Western import—English games, German or French theater, and continental conviviality.[53]

The Arabs in Herzl's literary universe were effortlessly integrated into the fabric of society without displacing them from the land or inviting their enmity. As Ahad Ha'am ruefully observes, "Peace and brotherly love reign between them and the Jews, who took nothing from them and gave them so much. A delightful idyll, indeed. Only, it is not quite clear how the New Society managed to obtain sufficient land for the millions of Jews from all over the world if the arable land that rested previously in Arab hands, i.e., most of the arable land in Palestine altogether, continues to remain in their hands as before." Again, he called attention to this, the underbelly of the Zionist dream, an issue he long believed could represent a significant obstacle. At the same time, his reference here to Arabs, as in his essay "Emet," was a cursory one, linked to his desire to ridicule the omission in Herzl's novel rather than probe the matter with any depth.

The only truly discordant voice in the novel was that of the fanatic Geiger—formerly an ultra-orthodox anti-Zionist, later a fervently religious nationalist, but always self-seeking, pompous, and repulsive. He vied for leadership of the New Society and managed to win some popular support but in the end the rabbis helped win the masses to the side of moderation and good sense. The disreputable Geiger, then, was the only evidence in the novel of a self-consciously Jewish voice and his was provincial and even hatefully narrow.

How inferior, said Ahad Ha'am, was Herzl's utopian novel to that of a much lesser-known work written ten years earlier by a member of his own Hebraist entourage, Elhonan Levinsky, whose fictional account of Jewish life in a futuristic Palestine had the stamp of true Jewish authenticity. Ahad Ha'am managed to contrast two distinctively different views on Jewish life—Herzl's, which perceived things from the outside and lacked a sureness of touch and intimacy with its subject, and Levinsky's view from within:

How much greater is the Zionist ideal of the Hebrew writer than that of the German leader. In the former, there is authentic national freedom and life based on general human principles; in the latter an apelike mimicry devoid of any specifically national character; replete with a spirit of "slavery of freedom," a daughter of exile . . .[54]

Under any circumstance this review would have caused a stir. It became the centerpiece of the *Altneuland* affair when the normally circumspect Herzl received a draft of it from the newspaper *Ost und West* and orchestrated a reply to it through Nordau before the review was published in German translation. Moreover, through the offices of the Zionist movement, Herzl worked behind the scenes to place Nordau's reply in Russia's Jewish press.

Nordau maligned Ahad Ha'am in his article in deeply personal terms: Ahad Ha'am wrote in passable Hebrew, he admitted, but his essays were filled with "insipid prattle whose presumptuous vapidity simply cannot be conveyed in words." Ahad Ha'am, that "enemy of culture," as Nordau described him, presumed to attack Herzl with arguments that were "partly foolish, partly limited, and malicious." Still worse, his vision of Palestine was hatefully byzantine, intolerant, anti-Western, even literally sickening: "Ahad Ha'am does not want tolerance. Aliens should be slaughtered, or at best chased out as they once were in Sodom and Gomorrah. The idea of tolerance disgusts him. Well, what disgusts us is to have a crippled, hunchbacked victim of intolerance, the despised slave of intolerant, knout-wielding pogromchiks, speak of tolerance in this manner."[55]

Nordau's counterattack was, even for a man well-known for his furious treatment of literary opponents, seen as excessive in Russian Zionist circles: they felt it unlikely that he would have treated a Western Jew with such contempt. From the vantage point of those who sided with Ahad Ha'am in this dispute, though, the real culprit was Herzl, not Nordau, who by his inappropriate, partisan behavior had acted in this affair more like a sectarian leader than the titular head of Zionism. Denunciations and counter-denunciations were printed in the Jewish press with signatures by the leading lights of Zionism. The young men of the Democratic Faction who had revolted against Herzl a year earlier at the Fifth Congress, reacted with great vehemence and horror opposing Nordau's attack and Herzl's obvious connivance. Herzl's actions showed them his contempt for Russian Jews. Not all agreed with an anti-Herzlian line, however, and, for instance, the longtime Ahad Ha'amist devotee Shmarya Levin broke with them on this issue. But for most of them Herzl's vision as embodied in *Altneuland* disturbed them, reinforcing their sense of the inadequacy of his Jewish moorings.

"There is no need to defend [Ahad Ha'am], the man who helped to create spiritual Zionism," said a letter circulated to the Jewish press and signed by Weizmann, Martin Buber, and others in the Democratic Faction. "This fearless man of truth in thought and deed; this man of ethical excellence who is regarded by the best East European Jews with honor, respect, and truth. This genuine and perfect Jew who, long before the advent of political Zionism, appeared as the most radical combatant on behalf of the national movement. . . . It is superfluous to defend Ahad Ha'am against the defamations and degradations contained in Nordau's article. But we consider ourselves honor-bound to protest most vigorously . . ."[56]

For several weeks the Jewish press was filled with articles about the affair before the debate quieted down without abating, even with the outbreak of the Kishinev pogrom on 6 April. Most reactions were predictable: Herzlian partisans referred to Ahad Ha'am's review as "olympian" and "destructive" and asked whether Ahad Ha'am, given his lack of literary training and experience, was competent to judge a work of literature by a writer of distinction. Irrespective of their position on the dispute, nearly all Zionists would have agreed with *Voskhod*'s characterization of it as an "inglorious campaign." The rare observer managed to find some semblance of humor in the sordid business: one ironic feature, said a writer for the Russian-language Jewish newspaper *Budushchnost'*, was that although the debate centered on a German-language book that few in Russia had read or for that matter were competent to read, everyone had their opinion of it![57]

A measure of this public clamor was the willingness of the normally reclusive Ahad Ha'am to grant an interview to *Voskhod*, published under the title "The Angry Enemy of Zionism," where he was asked a series of very pointed questions about the political implications of his attack on *Altneuland*. M. Levin, the interviewer, pressed him on whether his decision to criticize Herzl at this particular juncture, and with such severity, was part of his attempt to promote a breakaway nationalist movement, the sort he had proposed a few months earlier at Minsk. Ahad Ha'am admitted that he had on several occasions—first at the Warsaw meeting in 1898, most recently at Minsk—made this recommendation, but to say that his comments were politically inflammatory was to misinterpret his role at the recent Russian congress. He had participated merely as "a member of the press" and had even sat in the section of the hall reserved for journalists. The assumption, aired in certain circles, that he was one of its organizers, he said, was nothing but a "shameful lie."[58]

Why the charge was "shameful" he did not say. No doubt, consistent with his long-standing denial that he had an interest in garnering political influence for himself, he found any implication that his literary politics might have ulterior motives to be contemptible. Yet, as anyone who had attended the Minsk conference could attest, wherever Ahad Ha'am might have sat in the hall the role he played there was profoundly political. He misrepresented this to Levin who failed to press him. Ahad Ha'am, now taking control of the interview, went on to say that he found the fuss over his notorious review to be startling since his criticisms of Herzl elsewhere were far more serious and had elicited less response. Throughout he handled himself with deftness and not a little evasiveness.[59]

In light of the comparison in Ahad Ha'am's review between the utopias of Levinsky and Herzl—and his unambiguous preference for the former—a look at Levinsky's *Masa le-eretz yisrael bi-shnat tat elef ha-shishi* (*A Journey to the Land of Israel in the Year 5800 [2040]*) should reveal something of his own vision of the Palestinian Jewish future, a theme he rarely addressed even in his attack on *Altneuland*. Since Levinsky's piece was first published in *Pardes* in 1892, its links with the Bnei Moshe lent it, even if only indirectly, something of Ahad Ha'am's imprimatur.

The novel's narrator is a Hebrew teacher recently married to a woman who is a keen devotee of Hebrew literature; they spend their honeymoon in Palestine. They live abroad, as do apparently most other Jews, and in cities where Hebrew is among the widely used local tongues; knowledge of Hebrew is one of many ways in which the impact of Israel is felt well outside its borders. The couple discover a technologically advanced, largely agrarian society where peace reigns supreme and where a new Hebrew culture has been resurrected slowly and deliberately yet with overwhelming success. The sort of class or national antagonism that, as the narrator explains, still tears apart much of the Western world, especially Europe and the United States, does not exist in Palestine. The holding of private property is allowed but rigorously regulated. One check is the biblically prescribed Jubilee year, which ensures that all property is returned periodically to its original owners. (This, interestingly, figures into Herzl's utopia, as well.) Complete civic equality between Jews and "strangers" guarantees harmony and prosperity. Sloth, as in much of the utopian literature of this period, is nonexistent; the residents of Israel are obliged to learn a trade, with most choosing to be farmers in small, self-contained economic units that provide their own milk, meat, and other provisions. Some farmers are men of learning with impressive libraries whose tables are the sites of sophisticated, unpretentious talk. Religion is an important but unobtrusive presence;

the temple in Jerusalem has been rebuilt, though this does not seem to impinge on interethnic relations in this land where parks, squares, and buildings are dedicated to the theme of peace. Jews make up a majority of cities like Shechem (Nablus). Although Jerusalem had been largely ignored, as the narrator himself attests, by early Zionist pioneers who saw it as an inhospitable center of Jewish fundamentalism, in his utopia it is the very heart of the reconstructed land. There are a small number of military fortresses that house a tiny army; it is rarely used and is largely symbolic and defensive in character.[60]

It is obvious why Ahad Ha'am preferred this portrait to Herzl's. Levinsky emphasizes the role of a renewed Hebraic culture—one, significantly, that was built with meticulous care and exerts its influence over diasporic Jewry. The reigning culture is Jewish but thoroughly tolerant; indeed, the text is full of humane Ahad Ha'amist maxims. The government ensures basic sustenance and a decent livelihood without imposing equality, and the narrator makes clear his distaste for a socialist vision like Edward Bellamy's and any attempt to do away with private property at the cost of social disruption. It is because radical social experiments of this sort imposed themselves onto the Western world that it is overwhelmed by chaos and despair. Government in Levinsky's work is mostly in the hands of local officials and a rather loose central administration runs the affairs of Israel. The dominant mood is tolerant, moderate, liberal, unrestrictive.[61]

But, aside from the vaguely sketched contour of the central government, unremarkable since Russian Jews like Levinsky and Ahad Ha'am had a distrust of centralized administration, one striking feature of the novel was the absence of explicit mention of Arabs. "Strangers" or "goyim" live there, a satisfied minority in a land that is also described as having been all but desolate before Jews returned to it in modern times: how was it that Jews, even by the year 2040, had become a majority in Nablus without displacing Arabs? Universal brotherhood reigns supreme in this utopia, but the dominant culture is a Jewish one. How the minority feels about this is never addressed.

As it happens, Levinsky himself was by all accounts an exceptionally pleasant, even-tempered man whose sanguine vision of the future may well have been more reflective of his own mild temperament than of the larger nationalist milieu in which he was reared. Clearly, Ahad Ha'am was more attuned to the threat posed by Palestine's Arabs than Levinsky seemed to be. In several of his essays he had referred to Arabs, he had criticized Herzl's handling of the issue in his *Altneuland* review, and he was the first Jewish nationalist to call attention to the problem in his "Emet me-eretz yisrael." But it would be a mistake to exaggerate his preoccupation with the issue. It did not surface with any frequency in his writings on Palestine, nor did it represent for him one of the chief obstacles to Jewish colonization of the land. Essentially the presence of Arabs meant that gentiles lived in Palestine, which implied the likelihood, even the inevitability, of antisemitism. Far more important as an obstacle to the designs of the Jewish people there, in his view, was the unavailability of arable land, the region's poverty, the unlikelihood that Jews would ever remake themselves into farmers, and the lack of money to support those who wanted to try. Inasmuch as Ahad Ha'am remained hopeful, even if guardedly so, about the prospect of transforming Palestine into a thriving home for Jews, there is reason to believe that Levinsky's portrait of its future roughly resembled his own—with its strange lapses, ambiguities, and even its vaguely colonialist assumptions. Ahad Ha'am was, at best, only marginally concerned with the threat posed by the Arabs of the Holy Land until his Palestinian trip of 1911. It was only then, after the 1908 Turkish revolution promised democratization in the Middle East and the rise of Arab nationalism, that the preoccupation with this issue became widespread in Zionist circles and he began to speak of it with something approaching real alarm.[62]

Even by June 1903 Weizmann would write that for Vienna's leadership "everything is judged there from the point of view of the 'Ahad Ha'am-Nordau business.'"[63] Echoes of the *Altneuland* affair reverberated until the very eve of the Sixth Congress that summer and beyond. The Kishinev pogrom that spring cast the literary battle into the shadows. Kishinev soon became the most potent metaphor for East European Jewish misery, and it remained such until the devastating pogroms in the Ukraine in 1919–1920. Quickly the word Kishinev came to represent far more than a provincial Bessarabian capital or even a fierce local riot. It emerged as a metaphor for the vulnerability of East European Jewry and for the inadequacy of standard Jewish responses to oppression. Almost immediately Kishinev assumed a seminal importance in Jewish political and literary discourse. Both within and outside the Zionist movement it captured this symbolic importance; Ahad Ha'am and his circle came to exert the greatest influence in charting a course that left its mark not only on Jewry's memory of this particular tragedy but on modern Jewish assumptions about catastrophe in general. "Since Kishinev everything has changed," said a Bundist newspaper in what was neither an excessively sectarian nor idiosyncratic claim. Most other sectors of Russian Jewry would come to feel the same way.[64]

Over four days in Easter, following in the wake of a vicious local anti-Jewish press campaign in which blood accusations were leveled in an atmosphere of mounting hostility fueled by a singularly unsympathic local administration, mobs attacked Kishinev's 60,000 Jews killing 44, beating hundreds of others, and leaving many of its Jewish neighborhoods in ruins. The number of homeless reached 2,000 with at least 1 million roubles in damage. In this first major anti-Jewish outbreak since the wave of attacks that convulsed the southern provinces in the early 1880s, the local authorities did not act for two days and, even once the pogrom was quashed, continued to behave toward the victims with undiminished hostility. Their disregard in responding to the attacks was due to various factors: a generous measure of animosity and indifference to Jewish suffering, the sort of timidity characteristic of the empire's local authorities who tended to defer taking initiative on any matter of importance, and a jurisdictional confusion over whether military or civilian authorities were responsible for the control of urban riots. It was widely believed at the time, moreover, that the authorities had planned the massacre with orders from the Minister of the Interior, Vyacheslav Pleve. (Soon after the pogrom a letter reputedly from Pleve—much later shown to be a forgery—setting down guidelines for the riot was published by the *Times* of London.) The response of Kishinev Jews to the sudden attack was on the whole unsurprising; they reacted with numbness and shock, though sporadic defense occurred. Indeed, one reason why the pogromists redoubled their efforts at the end of the first day of riots was in direct reaction to Jewry's fierce defense. Such defensive efforts proved inadequate, unsurprising in light of the lassitude or complicity of local authorities.[65]

In his memoirs, Dubnow recorded how news of the pogrom reached Odessa from Kishinev which still remained a cultural and economic satellite, with frequent contact between the two southern cities. For several days, Dubnow recalled, rumors had reached Odessa of anti-Jewish violence in Kishinev but these were vague and they contained no clear information about its size or character. Finally, refugees reached Odessa a few days later with news. In fact several appeared at a meeting of the *Beseda* Club, the local Jewish literary society, which nationalists close to Ahad Ha'am controlled. It was here that Ahad Ha'am had first aired his rumination on Moses, and this night the *wunderkind* (as Dub-

now calls him) Vladimir Jabotinsky—then a precocious Russian journalist, later founder of the ultranationalist Jewish Revisionist movement—was delivering a talk on Pinsker's *Autoemancipation*. Into the hall
came refugees from Kishinev and during the recess some of the writers
there including Dubnow and Ahad Ha'am spoke with the Kishinev Jews.
Shocked by what they heard, they set the date for a meeting to formulate
their response to the tragedy.[66]

Rarely are historical encounters quite so pregnant with symbolism.
Dubnow was an unusually sober memoirist and, in light of his principled
commitment to recording the truth, his rendition of these events can
probably be believed. Ahad Ha'am does not mention the encounter but
no doubt it served to reinforce his belief that his circle was at the very
heart of Jewish cultural and political life. The fact that news of the
Kishinev pogrom reached these intellectuals as it did is itself extraordinary: Jabotinsky, a brilliant speaker, was busy on the podium reasserting
the prescience of Pinsker's *Autoemancipation* whose own unsettling images of an exilic ghost-like Jewry was among the most important proof-
texts to emerge from the last great wave of pogromist violence; the lecture
hall was dotted with several of the leading nationalist mentors of the
moment. They found themselves confronted there as they ruminated on
Pinsker with victimized Jews, fresh from the battlefield, abused and
seeking help, perhaps vengeance. It is surprising that the encounter failed
to enter into the nationalist canon. So much about this circle's response
to Kishinev would.

"The killing in Kishinev has completely filled my heart and I cannot
think of anything else,"[67] Ahad Ha'am said in a letter to Klausner soon
after learning of it. Its impact was international in scope and the first clear
political manifestation of what was by now a sizable East European
Jewish diaspora in the West and outside of Russia, Romania, and Aus-
tria. The increased Western response should help account for the difference between the impact of the Kishinev pogrom and the ones of the
1880s. Changes in the social and cultural complexion of Russian Jewry
between 1881 and 1903 meant that when this new explosion occurred
it met with a highly politicized and organized East European Jewry (in
the region and elsewhere) that had grown deeply distrustful of the state
and mindful of what it believed to be the government's willingness to
unleash the passions of the mob against its Jews.

Already one-half million East European Jews lived in New York alone
by the turn of the century with their own institutions, newspapers, and
leaders; they were galvanized by news of the Kishinev pogrom and

waged an unprecedented and vigorous campaign in American Jewish communal life. For the first time, for instance, they entered into a working relationship with the more acculturated German-born Jews uptown in order to organize their community's response with rallies addressed by the New York City mayor and many of its leading dignitaries. Even Theodore Roosevelt was prodded to speak out: "Never in my experience in this country have I known of a more immediate or deeper expression of sympathy." Within two years of Kishinev and following the pogroms of 1905, the forces that helped generate this communal response gave birth to the American Jewish Committee (for the acculturated, mostly German-born elite), and it also propelled the Yiddish Daily *Forverts* into the front rank of American politics. Kishinev, then, helped impose some semblance of coherence onto an otherwise fiercely contentious turn-of-the-century Russian Jewish scene in America, and elsewhere.[68]

Ahad Ha'am reacted with uncharacteristic speed. In the past he had been described, even satirized, as paralyzed by doubt whenever he was confronted with any decision; at the same time, he was clearly capable of being definitive, even categorical about his interpretation of events. In this case, his reaction was swift and definitive: immediately upon hearing of the massacre, he imposed an interpretation on it that, despite evidence to the contrary, he would maintain. In the process, he introduced his gloss on Kishinev into the historical canon of the Zionist movement.

In Ahad Ha'am's view what was most significant about Kishinev was the way in which it showed the corruption of its victims: "A people that is five millions strong must acknowledge that they are men and not beasts ready for slaughter." Finally it was time to cast off the yoke of slavery that had bound Jews for so long and to declare that they no longer were helpless or dependent upon the goodwill of their neighbors. Self-defense was essential; he was convinced it would not only ward off future attacks by making it clear that aggressors would pay a heavy price but, more importantly, it would persuade Jews themselves that passivity was detrimental to their well-being. Above all, he saw self-defense as an elaborate pedagogical device; potential victimizers would, no doubt, continue to threaten Jews but their actions were bound to be restrained by a militant, self-reliant Jewry. The organization of self-defense units in the diaspora represented part of the ongoing preparation for a reconstructed national existence.[69]

He was bitterly critical of the Russian Jewish delegations seeking to make Jewry's case before the government in the wake of the pogrom. Similar to most Russian Jews, he believed the government to be responsible for the attack, and for Jews to seek out officials (in some cases the same ones who stood accused for fomenting the murders) made them little more than "beggars." When adversity challenges people of real distinction, he claimed in a letter written soon after Kishinev, they manage to rise to the occasion; slaves, however, are dragged still further down, defiled by persecution that reinforces their self-contempt. If, he continued, there are still "men among us," they must "come together and raise a new flag, the flag of inner freedom, the flag of personal honor."[70]

These reactions helped inspire him and his colleagues to launch an attempt to collect information about the massacre that would be distributed abroad. Its dissemination would be used to put pressure on the Russian regime to check its oppressive treatment of Jews, and it would also be used for fundraising purposes in the West. The compilation of data about the pogrom was put in the hands of the most junior of the distinguished circle, Bialik, who spent several weeks in Kishinev gathering numerous testimonies. It was this that inspired the writing of "City of Slaughter" in which Bialik—speaking, despite his apparent reluctance, in a prophetic voice and as spokesman of a Divine narrator—excoriated Kishinev's Jews for their passivity and their cynical reliance on a legacy of martyrology as an excuse for their timidity. Still worse than the beatings of children or the rape of daughters and wives was the way in which survivors exploited misery for their own benefit, manipulating the dead, using their faith, stretching the sympathies of their people and others for their own end. Bialik wrote it in a state of fury and—as Alan Mintz has written—the result was "astonishing, austere, and pathbreaking":

> Come, now, and I will bring thee to their lairs.
> The privies, jakes, and pigpens where the heirs of Hasmoneans lay,
>   with trembling knees,
> Concealed and cowering—the sons of the Maccabees!
> The seed of saints, the scions of the lions . . .
> Who crammed by scores in all the sanctuaries of their shame,
> So sanctified My name![71]

The information collected by Bialik in Kishinev was never during his lifetime organized, printed, or distributed. These were, to be sure, confusing and extraordinarily busy times. The Kishinev massacre, which had followed closely on the *Altneuland* affair, was soon overshadowed in Jewish nationalist circles by the explosion over Herzl's Uganda Plan and the 1905 revolution. Moreover, Bialik's task was an illegal one, and such clandestine activity was essentially alien to bourgeois intellectuals like him and his friends. But a no less important reason why the text was left unpublished was that Bialik felt that he knew what had occurred in Kishinev and that the facts themselves, some of which were at variance with his assumptions, would divert attention from his interpretation of the event. Such, for instance, was his belief in the absence of Jewish self-defense that he overlooked details of fighting by Jews in Kishinev for the sake of other truths, higher truths.[72]

The other task promoted by Ahad Ha'am's circle prompted another response after Kishinev that preceded Bialik's visit to the pogrom-ravished city and was considerably more radical in character: they issued a call for self-defense. A decision to produce a Hebrew-language declaration written by Ahad Ha'am was taken at a meeting in Odessa soon after the incident at the *Beseda* Club and when word spread that the local branch of the Jewish Socialist Labor Bund, the major socialist organization in East European Jewry, planned to call for armed resistance.[73]

The fact that he proved willing to write this document with its call for the use of arms in self-defense might appear incongruent in light of his almost obsessive concern with the roadblocks to provocative action of any kind. This is especially apparent in his writings about political prospects in Palestine. In this instance he saw that militaristic actions that might be unsuitable for Palestine—with its sparse, highly vulnerable Jewish population threatened at any moment with eviction by the Turks—were considerably more feasible in the Pale of Settlement with cities like Kishinev and with their large, compact, and well-organized Jewish communities. Here not only was self-defense reasonable as a response to repression but essential as a tool for the reassertion of Jewish self-respect.

The killings at Kishinev, wrote Ahad Ha'am, must compel Jews to look again at the conditions of their lives in Russia "so that we can better make our choices and stop satisfying ourselves with empty consolations and false hopes." This particular attack must not be viewed as isolated, as the work of random hoodlums, but as a by-product of the sort of treatment meted out to Jews from the government "on high"; he did not name the government directly as the culprit in this, the final draft, though some pressed him. But the implications were clear: it was because of the government's shameful treatment of Jews that the masses saw them as fair game. Neither official investigations following in the wake of the massacre nor punishment could erase the fact that its causes go very deep. And local authorities, who have expended such energy to oppress Jews before the pogrom, could not with any semblance of sincerity now transform themselves into the defenders of the Jewish people.[74]

Ahad Ha'am continued, the supplications by Jews who hope to win over the sympathy of outsiders are, as must now be clear, hackneyed and pathetic tactics that have long been proven useless, even embarrassing: "Our salvation will not come and cannot come from the outside." Indeed, it is useful to see Kishinev as a brutal if inevitable reminder of the inadequacy of such pleas. The lesson is an awful one: "It is a disgrace," declared the document in bold letters, "for five million people to throw themselves on the mercy of others," to continue to cry out for others to protect them without bothering to "protect themselves, their possessions, their honor, their lives." Perhaps, he continued, it is our lack of self-respect that has fueled such attacks on us; perhaps this has served to persuade our enemies that they can beat us with no cost to themselves. Who else in this land of numerous nations would permit themselves to be treated so shabbily without so much as token self-defense? "Only those who know how to protect their own honor are themselves honored in the eyes of others," he says. Jews must show that a few hundred drunks cannot terrorize a community of tens of thousands: "Brothers! The blood of our brethren in Kishinev cries out to us! Shake off your dust and become men! Stop your tears and supplications, stop praying for others to come and save you and, instead, save yourselves."[75]

He recommended that a permanent organization be formed with branches throughout the Pale to coordinate armed resistance whenever there seemed to be the need for it. Since he saw westward migration of Russian Jewry as a by-product of these attacks he also proposed that the same organization hold a conference to coordinate what was hitherto mostly a haphazardly organized mass exodus. The document was to be signed by Ahad Ha'am, Dubnow, Ben Ami, and Mendele. But when hundreds of copies were distributed throughout Jewish Russia, it was issued anonymously under the auspices of the Association of Jewish Writers, a nonexistent group. Ahad Ha'am, who was not privy to this decision—it was made while he was on a trip for Wissotzksy—was furious and insisted that it was an inexcusable act of timidity and undermined whatever credibility the document might have had. Here, too, his argument was categorical, uncompromising, far more so than that of those around him. Kishinev had unsettled him, and deeply distrustful as he was of the prospect for building coalitions with even well-meaning gentiles, he saw Jewish self-reliance as the only credible course. In this way, at least, Jews could minimize attacks against themselves or learn to act honorably in the midst of the untenable, inescapably tragic reality of exile.[76]

The Kishinev massacre was widely interpreted as signaling a new, violent turn in the Russian government's treatment of Jews. Therefore they emphasized in their statement the need for a more coordinated emigration policy that focused on the United States: over 126,000 Russian Jews arrived in America in 1906, compared with some 37,000 in 1900. All sectors of Jewry, irrespective of politics, agreed on the need for better means of escape. For their part, though, the Zionists appeared to offer the least credible of all alternatives. The Turkish charter that Herzl had expected he would deliver with little delay remained elusive, and Herzl's movement—for all its activities since the first Zionist Congress of 1897—was widely viewed as incapable of a meaningful contribution to Jewish safety. The trip that Herzl took to Russia in May 1903 (as he admitted in his diary) was a direct response to this misery in the wake of Kishinev: "I hear from reliable sources," he wrote Pleve, whom he hoped to visit, "that despair is beginning to take hold of the Jews in Russia." He was aware that for his movement such despair took on a distinct character: not only were the Jews at risk but the Zionists in particular seemed to offer no credible alternative for their safety since Palestine remained poor and in the hands of still-hostile powers without much prospect of change in the near future.[77]

It is necessary to keep the declining Zionist influence in mind to understand Herzl's strategies in the period before his death in July 1904. Faced with the prospect of a rapid decline in Zionist sentiment in Russia—his emissaries repeatedly warned of the success of the Bund, now the darlings of the Jewish street, whose advance was unchecked by the Zionists partly because the government had started to interfere with their activities—the Zionist leader was in a state of progressive physical decline which encouraged him to put considerable effort into winning a quick, significant diplomatic victory. A master of public impression, Herzl began to seek some alternative to the elusive Turkish charter. His 1903 trip to Russia must be viewed in this light; so must his handling the next year of England's Uganda or East Africa project.

This trip represented a response to Kishinev and the mounting restrictions that confronted Zionism since the 1902 Minsk conference. Branches of the movement were now being forcibly closed, emissaries arrested, and Zionism treated by Russian authorities as an internal threat after a benign period during which it functioned in a semilegal capacity. Herzl hoped that Pleve could be persuaded that Zionism's goals were consonant with those of the regime in its commitment to checking radicalism's advance and its support of emigration. Pleve informed Herzl at their August meeting that the conference at Minsk had left the impression that Russian Zionists were interested in the promotion of nationalist sentiment (a task he deemed counterproductive, even dangerous), not migration. It was this new slant that was deemed unacceptable. Herzl assured him that his impressions of the movement's priorities (which, of course, were all too true) were misplaced and he added that in order to guarantee their mutual goals, Russia must persuade the Turks to grant them a Palestinian charter. He left Pleve confident that he would do his part, and although Herzl's meeting with Minister of Finance S. Iu. Witte, one of Russia's philosemites, was less pleasant, he remained pleased with his achievement. To be sure, he was bitterly criticized by Russian Jewish leaders for his audience with Pleve—the man held responsible for the Kishinev pogrom—but at the same time Herzl was shown a tumultuous welcome with hundreds lining the streets of Vilna as his carriage passed in the middle of the night bound for the train station. A huge crowd met him there; a Bundist toasted him as the next king of Israel. The ecstatic, nocturnal statement, he said, was of course absurd but "it produced a striking effect in the dark Russian night." As theater alone—and Herzl was one never to decry the dramatic—his trip to Russia was something of a triumph.[78]

Pleve did nothing to promote the Zionist charter; Turkey was unlikely to listen closely to Russia, a rather hostile neighbor in the best of times and one with its own designs on the Holy Land. In the end, Herzl's Russian negotiations yielded no concrete achievement. Herzl was faced with the prospect of arriving at the Sixth Zionist Congress empty-handed, without any visible progress in Russia, the scene of Jewry's most visible misery, or Turkey, where the key to Palestine was still hidden from view. The writing of *Altneuland* had been a welcome escape from the increasingly intractable vicissitudes of Jewish politics. Now he was compelled to face its sordid realities.

Herzl was then persuaded to support a plan, floated first by the English, for the settlement of Jews in East Africa. The proposal represented the first admission by a major power that the Zionists were the legitimate brokers for a territorial solution. Whether he truly thought the plan viable or felt unable to turn the English down flat, he knew that it was likely to be controversial and kept it a secret until the eve of the congress.[79]

Known in Zionist circles as the Uganda Congress, Herzl brought forward the proposal that the movement agree to look into the option. Nordau proposed it in his major address as no retreat from Palestine, simply a concession to the need for a waystation for the Jewish oppressed. The idea met with furious opposition, far more than had ever been unleashed against Herzl: for many it substantiated their long-standing suspicion that his were tepid Palestinophile commitments, precisely what Ahad Ha'am had always insisted. For others it renewed misgivings about his backdoor political machinations. The Russian delegation to the Sixth Congress (a majority of the 596 delegates) split over Uganda: most of its orthodox contingent was won over to it by a combination of tactical considerations; Herzl promised to thwart culturalist proposals if they threw their support behind him. Other members of the delegation believed that a foothold in East Africa could relieve Jewish suffering. This last consideration served, for example, also to persuade the brilliant socialist Zionist Nahman Syrkin. Opponents, some of whom like Weizmann were at first mildly sympathetic, came to fight it as a betrayal of Zion and the ideals that separated them from other, less ambitious emigrationist schemes; they also considered East Africa unrealistic and predicted few would take advantage of it. When the congress finally voted, and by a rather small margin, in favor of Herzl's recommendation, many of the dissenters walked out of the hall, signaling an alarming split that had only been superficially mended by the time of Herzl's death that summer.[80]

Ahad Ha'am stayed away from the congress. His reactions to the Uganda proposal were biting and angry and directed not at Herzl but at the proposal's timid opponents. He reminded them that long before—when Herzl refused to limit the scope of the National Bank to land acquisition in Palestine—he had warned that something like this could occur. These same men, his would-be devotees, had then refused to fight Herzl for the sake of a new bank charter and were now paying the price for their lack of foresight and initiative.

Even in letters to those Russian Jewish leaders who had spearheaded the resistance to Herzl at the congress he refused to acknowledge their achievements or, for that matter, their agony at having to wage battle against the Zionist chief. It was this agony, in fact, that he ridiculed as a sign of how much they had unwittingly sacrificed of their own integrity on the altar of Herzlian expediency. To Tchlenow, the mild, self-effacing, and efficient leader who headed this fight against Herzl, Ahad Ha'am declared that any pain dissidents like him felt at breaking with Herzl implied failings more serious than a lack of prescience or vigor. The decision of the Zionist movement to explore settlement in East Africa was, he insisted, comparable to a "public conversion." Its erstwhile devotees will only briefly press for Jewish emigration to Africa; once this proves impossible they will disappear from the Jewish scene. All that can be hoped is that a new generation will quickly appear to replace them.[81]

The main problem was not these misguided, lost souls or, for that matter, Herzl—"a clever man who knows how to capture the right moment"—but the Russians. They were still unable to recognize that over the last several years Herzl had managed—slowly, with great effectiveness, and contrary to their convictions—to wean them away from the designs of the Hovevei Zion that had originally inspired their Zionism. Herzl had made "a revolution in their own hearts" and reduced their Zionism to something that was pale and merely political. Little by little whatever spiritual component it had contained disappeared.[82]

This insidious transformation was not recognized until the Uganda Congress. His opponents, including some who counted among Ahad Ha'am's followers, cried with pain when forced to fight Herzl; their tears, though, Ahad Ha'am said in his article "Ha-Bohim" ("Those Who Cried"), were shed out of a belated recognition of how they had compromised themselves over the years. Ahad Ha'am predicted that once they stopped their sobbing and faced the fact that their Palestinophilism had been expunged from their hearts, they too would follow Herzl into the African wilderness. Herzl, who had never embraced the true ideals of Zionism, could easily make his way to Africa; for the Russians it was more difficult, so they had to confront their lost illusions. The upshot was clear: "Why waste words? The Zionist movement is no longer in existence."[83]

What should the Russians have said to Herzl? Long before the Uganda plan was ever aired they should have made clear to him that they did not expect Palestine to satisfy the material needs of the Jews: "What we seek in Zion cannot be found in any other place, and there is no absolute certainty that we can even find it there." All that was left to say was that the confusions of the last few years must cease: Herzl must be told, "'Go to Africa, with your bombastic claims for the economic transformation of the Jewish people,' while we, with humility and modesty, with neither noise nor declamations" go off and work quietly to revive our nation.[84]

Having denounced his errant disciples with a ferocity intense even for him, he ended the article on a conciliatory note, making it clear that he would again accept them back to the fold—once, that is, they fully repented. Upon learning of Herzl's death, Ahad Ha'am was gracious, agreeing to deliver a eulogy in his honor but, with more frankness than delicacy, he summed up his life, thusly: "He was fortunate in life, and fortunate in death." Herzl died at the right moment, just before Uganda diminished his standing, which it certainly would have done. The legend was secure and by no means was Ahad Ha'am sanguine about it.[85]

Ahad Ha'am's desire to establish his own posterity, to secure a legacy that would outlive his flawed, temporal achievements—remained very much on his mind as he traveled through Russia during the next few months for Wissotzsky; as he learned of "part two of the Kishinev pogrom," the anti-Jewish riots in Gomel in September 1903 in which Jewish armed resistance was much in evidence; as he witnessed the rapid deterioration of Jewish political and cultural life in his beloved Odessa. That October he reported to Dubnow—who had left Odessa to settle in smaller, more provincial Vilna where he believed he could write with fewer distractions—that Jewish Odessa was now an "empty desert": the *Beseda* Club had not met for some time; Bialik, as well as the writer Simhah Alter Guttman (Ben-Zion), and Ben Ami were all considering moving, Bialik to Warsaw, Guttman to Palestine. Ahad Ha'am admitted, as he did so often (especially in letters to the prodigious Dubnow) that he should settle down and write but he still felt pulled in so many different directions: "A sinner like myself who has been going to meetings for so long cannot any longer redeem himself."[86]

Indeed, he would soon find himself enmeshed in still another communal controversy over the election of an unqualified candidate as "official rabbi" in Odessa—the man, in fact, was Tiomkin whom Ahad Ha'am had first supported in the Palestinian disputes of 1891; now, despite his limited knowledge of Judaica, he was selected by the Zionist movement as its choice because of his nationalist loyalties. Unable though he was to remove himself from politics, he lectured Dubnow not to allow such activity to wean him from his books. He wrote in September 1903:

And you, what are you doing my friend? Have you already gotten back to work? Certainly it is very difficult now to work with peace of mind. But it is necessary for us to remember that our forefathers had their lives threatened constantly and nonetheless they kept their spirits alive and did not cease to produce their scholarship.[87]

Perhaps it was this that he had in mind when he turned to completing his piece on Moses he had started some two years before. He called it, in a letter to his friend Rabbi Jacob Mazeh of Moscow, an exercise in homiletics. More accurately, it represented his most coherent attempt to sketch out the meaning of authentic leadership in Jewish culture; he used as his central motif the image of Moses, around which he had built his still much-treasured Bnei Moshe. The essay was an exercise in scholarship and polemics but the two were for him much intertwined. In the case of "Moses," the link between homiletics and the affairs of the larger world were, albeit just beneath the surface, quite clear. Perhaps it was Herzl's decline, as signaled by the Uganda debacle, that finally moved Ahad Ha'am to turn his attention to finishing this examination of the prerequisites of leadership—it was written for the sake of a Jewry that was soon to be left bereft. But it also purported to say something much more serious and lasting than his other more ephemeral writings.[88]

That the piece took so long to complete is significant; slow and exasperatingly meticulous though he was as a writer, normally when he turned his attention to an essay he finished it rapidly. This particular one was first conceived soon after he was forced to retire from *Ha-Shiloach* and brought to completion two years later after Herzl's embarrassment at the Sixth Congress. It seemed to demand an unusual degree of exertion and anguish. That he turned to it almost at the very moment that he lost his coveted standing as "an editor in Israel" is understandable in light of his attempt to define with greater clarity than he had ever before the prerequisites of Jewish leadership. Consistent with the essay's intent he found himself able to finish it only when Herzl seemed discredited as a Zionist leader and a prospective Ahad Ha'amist coup d'état—harmonious, peaceful, deceptively nonpolitical—seemed feasible. Much more than any other essay of his, the piece is infused with autobiographical content: it transparently represents an exploration of Ahad Ha'am himself while successfully striving to be much more.

On this occasion, as so often before, the writing of a successful piece stood or fell for him on whether he managed to negotiate between ferocious, sometimes almost paralyzing, emotions. As he described this process in connection with the writing of another essay, when he started to organize his thinking and sat down with pen in hand to write, the "fires of hell" begin to churn inside of him and did not allow him to speak, at least not in the quiet, lucid way to which he was accustomed to appear in print. Instead, his inclination was to "shout," to rail in a manner that was uncivil and disorganized—much like, he says, Berdyczewski. Such rhetorical flourishes were unsuitable for him though, obviously, on some level they certainly were not. At such moments he simply stopped himself and waited until the restless spirit passed. Obviously he wrote his essays with inordinate care. The sublimation that he describes—his depiction of what he understood as the willful, ferociously difficult control of what he sometimes feared were uncontrollable passions—reveals how vigorously he worked not only to produce his essays but also to create a distinct image of their author. To be sure, it was substantially different from what he really was; it excised the terrible pain and uncertainty that preceded the detached, decorously passionate declamations that the public witnessed. But, as he would explain in "Moses," what ultimately mattered was not necessarily what was historically accurate but what entered the historical consciousness: its historical veracity was of secondary importance. What was crucial was that it represented the people's best instincts, that it guided them to higher ideals, that it shaped their values, and defined their essential character.[89]

Rarely had he written quite so lyrically as he did at the essay's opening:

When I read the *Haggadah* on Passover eve, and the spirit of Moses the son of Amram, the greatest of heroes, who stands like a pillar of light on the threshold of our history hovers over me and lifts me out of this mundane world, I am quite oblivious to all the doubts and questions propounded by non-Jewish critics. I do not care whether or not this man really existed. . . . We have a Moses of our own, whose image has been enshrined for generations in the hearts of the Jewish people, and whose influence on our national life has never ceased.[90]

Moses's greatness, Ahad Ha'am insisted, was as a prophet, and here he sought to enumerate the prophet's chief attributes. First, he is a man of truth "unwarped by subjective feeling" and for whom "the telling of the truth is a special feature of his genius—a feature from which he cannot rid himself as much as he might wish to." Second, he is an extremist committed to the supremacy of righteousness. As Ahad Ha'am understands, this means that he is not at peace with an inevitably imperfect reality. Since he cannot bend the world to meet his exacting specifications, he tries to influence it. His influence, Ahad Ha'am cautions, is considerable and also subtle: it flows "through various channels in which it is adapted and modified until it becomes conditioned for life."[91]

The Moses to whom he introduces his readers was in his youth surprisingly much like the Jewish radicals or liberals who so exasperated (and impressed him, though he was loath to admit it). He had spent his early years outside the Jewish fold where he "faithfully served the God of the universe" and fought a "hero's battle for universal justice." In Midian and elsewhere he worked to alleviate the conditions of the oppressed but discovered that despite his efforts he was seen as a foreigner, while those around him "took no account of him and paid no attention to his teaching." So he was motivated to return to his people to whom he devoted the remainder of his life. In this, the essay's first section, Ahad Ha'am shows Moses as an instructional example for universalists who could, if only they wished, be redeemed like the Lawgiver himself and rededicate themselves to their nation. Thereafter the essay adheres more closely to his own biography.[92]

Once reunited with his people, Moses set out with considerable optimism and bolstered by the knowledge that the Jews had already declared their willingness to embrace the word of God. He was therefore all the more shocked upon discovering how truly fickle their attachments were. With little compunction they reverted to old ways and old gods. No less surprising was his discovery of how readily the priest Aaron accommodated himself to their needs. Aaron was "a man of the hour" whose main talent was his ability to discern with great astuteness where the wind was blowing and move adroitly in its direction: the similarities between this biblical reconstruction and the history of the Bnei Moshe, especially in the inability of its "priests" to withstand the pressures of the moment and resist the attractions of quick political gain is its none-too-opaque subtext.[93]

The prophet is "seized by grief that knows no bounds," seized by what Ahad Ha'am calls an "impotent despair." Only at this point does he start to confront how difficult it will be to transform a "warped people," to begin to understand with greater clarity that this particular revolution will be a very slow one and will demand the greatest exertion.

By no means, though, is this his last, or greatest, shock. This comes in the wake of Jewry's terror—Ahad Ha'am characterizes it as its "degradation"—at hearing the spies' report on the difficulty of conquering Palestine, which undermined the confidence of the Jews to the point that they immediately abandoned all hope of a "glorious future" and suddenly were willing to embrace other solutions, pathetic half-measures. We are meant to infer that this was the biblical Uganda and the event that persuaded Moses that not even a thorough reeducation could redeem his generation. The only solution, as he bitterly recognized, was for them to die in the wilderness. Upon reaching that conclusion, and despite enormous pressure to change his mind, he remained adamant as was consistent with the stern, overpowering will of the prophetic personality. Posterity would benefit from what he lost in his lifetime; his decision meant that he too would be denied the opportunity of entering the Promised Land:

He brought his people to the border, equipped them for their future, and provided them with a noble ideal to sustain them in times of trouble and to provide them with both comfort and salvation.[94]

Denying Moses entry was a reflection on the limitations of his personality and his talent as a leader; those same traits that made him into the prophetic emblem of the Jewish people would have undermined his continued effectiveness once the Jews had settled down and their heroic period was at an end. After arriving in the Promised Land leaders were needed who were skilled, like priests, at compromise and equipped to live with the pettiness and the harsh limitations of everyday life. Since the prophet's goals were incapable of ever being fully realized—and since he was temperamentally incapable of tolerating anything less—he would have to disappear for his people to embark upon a normal existence.[95]

Nevertheless Moses remained to this day his people's ideal; indeed, the Kabbalah teaches (as Ahad Ha'am reminded his readers) that in every generation he is reincarnated to serve them. His presence has reassured them in their darkest moments. His ideals have helped them to transcend their daily lives and to acknowledge that the future, not the present, is most important. Indeed, "the present, with its evil and its wickedness, has always filled us with anguish, indignation, and bitterness. But just as surely we have been inspired by brilliant hope for the future." This is the task that Moses has performed, his unending achievement. Ahad Ha'am, doubtful that his ideals would ever see the light of day during his lifetime, took solace in the abiding, ultimately victorious legacy of Israel's supreme prophet.

III

By the time "Moses" appeared in 1904, the sort of timeless, midrashic tone that Ahad Ha'am had so effectively captured here seemed nonetheless out of step with contemporary affairs. The essay would remain among his most popular; those who most celebrated its achievement, the same masklilic Hebraists for whom Ahad Ha'am remained the touchstone of Jewish modernity, were more so than ever before marginalized by the events around them.

For a brief, but extraordinary period in 1905 and to a lesser extent in the first few months of 1906, the political conditions that had oppressed Russian Jewry for so long—the seemingly unbridgeable distance separating Jew from non-Jew in the multinational empire, and the generally numbing reality of daily life that had appeared so impervious to change—now promised to alter dramatically. Perhaps most startling from the vantage point of Jews was how in demonstrations in many of the cities of the Pale Jews and non-Jews marched side by side, with some gentiles participating in the defense of Jews in urban skirmishes. The dour message embodied in "Moses"—namely, that "the present . . . has always filled us with anguish, bitterness and indignation"—seemed so outdated against these new events: the present now appeared to promise little less than a revolution and not only in political but also in social terms. Redemption from the bondage, isolation, and indignities of the Pale seemed possible. Ahad Ha'am's dark suspicions of gentiles, of the prospect for political reform in the diaspora, of the political capabilities of the Jews could not have been more anachronistic.

In early January 1905 some one thousand workers were shot in what was intended to be a peaceful demonstration to persuade the tsar to grant political reform. The day became known as Bloody Sunday. Strikes that broke out throughout Russia brought Jews and non-Jews into particularly close cooperation: in some sixty cities in the Pale and Poland Russians, Lithuanians, Poles, and Jews worked together and virtually closed towns down. Such cooperation was not universal; it occurred mainly where Jews were the majority of the population and their political support essential. The reactions of one *Iskra* correspondent in June 1905 were rather typical of the period:

I cannot but emphasize the great respect in which—over the past year and especially the recent months—Christian Lodz holds the Jews. The heroic conduct of the Jews in the clashes with the police and the army units arouses admiration everywhere. . . . Legends are circulating about yesterday's battle between the Jews and the Cossacks on the Wschodnaja—legends which describe the Jewish workers as some kind of Samsons.[96]

As Jonathan Frankel sums up these changes:

Nothing succeeds like success, and as long as the socialists could juggle effectively keeping all the balls—self-defense, interethnic cooperation, economic action, the right for political democracy—up in the air, they had an inspirational effect on those around them. The urge to stand up to the authorities, to insist on one's rights, proved infectious.[97]

Nor was it only socialists who now found themselves propelled into politics: all sectors of society—peasants, professionals, students, workers—seemed to concur with the slogan first proposed by the otherwise ultraconservative newspaper *Novoe Vremia:* "It is no longer possible to live in this way." Unions of all sorts emerged composed of clerks, bookkeepers, and professions; in March 1905 a Jewish union, the "League for the Attainment of Full Rights for the Jews of Russia," grew out of a coalition of Zionists, liberals, and some moderate radicals. A month earlier the rather staid and once staunchly apolitical OPE issued a call for Jewish emancipation: the barriers, social as well as political, that had so circumscribed imperial Russian life appeared now to be extraordinarily fragile and outdated as worker, peasant, and professional, Jew and gentile, socialist, Zionist, and liberal marched shoulder to shoulder to challenge the foundering basis of autocratic rule.[98]

This political turbulence confronted Zionists, and not only someone like Ahad Ha'am, with a host of new problems: How far could they move in support of demands for political liberalization without abandoning their Palestinophilism or, for that matter, their status in the eyes of the authorities as a reasonably dependable form of Jewish politics? What connection was there, if any, between liberalism in Russia and the goals of Zionism, be they diplomatic along Herzl's lines or practical (as promoted by the Odessa-based Hovevei Zion)? How closely could Zionists work with non-Jewish allies and to what degree could they really trust them, especially in view of the belief, embedded in Pinsker's brand of Russian Palestinophilism as well as that of his ideological heirs, that there was something fundamental, even irreversible about Judeophobia? How sturdy was the current philosemitism of Russian progressive opinion and to what extent could its long-standing indifference toward Jewish concerns, especially toward the national agenda at the very heart of Zionism, be considered a thing of the past? Moreover, could Zionism turn a blind eye to these events, thereby marginalizing itself not only from the more progressive members of Russian society but also from the Jewish youth? Well before 1905 Russian Zionists had complained that their movement's fixation on abstractions like grand diplomacy served to alienate the bulk of the young: "The larger part of the contemporary younger generation is anti-Zionist," wrote Weizmann to Herzl in May 1903 shortly after Kishinev, "not from a desire to assimilate as in Western

Europe, but through revolutionary conviction." For Zionists to shun what was happening on Russia's streets would, it was widely believed, turn them into something of a joke, or into a political backwater. With Herzl's death in 1904, Zionism's stress on diplomacy had, in any event, lost much of its momentum, and in the absence of a great man at the movement's center its divisive constituents had more maneuverability. By 1905, there was hardly a sector of Russian Zionist opinion that thought ignoring domestic issues was possible.[99]

Nor, for that matter, did Ahad Ha'am. Later, once prospects for political change had dimmed considerably, he was scathing in his denunciations of those Jews willing to sacrifice Jewish concerns for other, more general ones. But in 1905 he was aware of how the revolutionary turbulence had opened up a window of opportunity for Russian Jews: he encouraged his more skeptical colleagues of Odessa Hovevei Zion to cooperate with the nascent League for the Attainment of Full Rights for the Jews of Russia, and, in particular, to work with Dubnow whom they distrusted as a political foe but whose nationalist platform won the approval of the league at its founding conference in March 1905. For the sake of the league's liberals, the character of these rights was left vague, but the group's stand nonetheless represented a substantial advance for the nationalist camp.[100]

Though Ahad Ha'am was willing to cooperate on one level, he refused to attend most of the league's meetings, shunned a leadership role (or, more accurately, refused to admit to whatever interest he might have had), and showed obvious discomfort with the many ways in which the revolution had shifted the balance of Jewish politics. Mass politics always unnerved him; the prospect of political allies outside his immediate maskilic coterie left him cold, unyielding, and uncommunicative. Both he, and to a much greater extent Dubnow, attempted to adapt themselves to the demands of the hour. Try as they might, their responses were often too hesitant, too staid, and ultimately too distrustful. Once the revolutionary euphoria that marked the early months of 1905 was checked with chilling, murderous suddenness by a wave of pogroms that erupted in October and continued, on and off, for much of the next year, Ahad Ha'am registered little surprise, only a glum, sad resignation. Through the early months of 1905, in those odd moments between his travels for Wissotzsky and the many uninspiring, ineffective political meetings that he continued to attend, he labored on an essay on the medieval philosopher Moses Maimonides, "in whose work I have been immersed since childhood." He completed it in April, and entitled it "Shilton ha-sekhel"

("The Supremacy of Reason"). Although widely viewed as one of his few important excursions into pure scholarship, many of the ideological tensions he felt at the time were, as we shall see, vividly reflected, just as they had appeared in more explicitly political essays.[101]

His reactions to the revolution and the October Manifesto that signaled the creation of a quasi-parliamentary form of government were fairly consistent even after events took an ugly turn with the outbreak of pogroms. On the one hand, his reactions, as he admitted to Ben Ami on the day that the new parliamentary duma had its first meeting in October 1906, were far from despondent. Even if the elected body did not contribute directly toward improving things, "a negative force too has power." He and Dubnow both bemoaned the fact that so many Jews, caught up as they were in the heady revolutionary atmosphere, were eager to abandon calls for Jewish national rights, or to subordinate them momentarily to seemingly larger, more important issues. He envied Dubnow, as he told him in April 1905, for being in Vilna "in the midst of the [Jewish] nation." There, he said, Jewish politics were still taken seriously; in Odessa the Jewish intelligentsia had completely lost itself in the larger struggle:

Here nearly everyone is enveloped by the general currents, and there is no one to promote our national concerns. And if a few remain who are true to our cause, even they express themselves in voices that are faint and barely audible as if they were embarrassed that in a moment of "great" events they were preoccupied with such small things.[102]

He predicted already in the early spring of 1905 that this great moment was on the verge of deteriorating into little more than a "simple comedy." Once peace was reestablished abroad (the war with Japan was then nearing its end), renewed reaction, he was convinced, would come to the Russian streets.[103]

He could not help but be caught up in the events. He writes, for instance, in a letter to Dubnow from Perm in July 1906 about his impatience to receive news of a recent meeting of the league. It is full of genuine pain over his sense of isolation from the important events transpiring elsewhere: "After lengthy travel across land and water, I arrived here about two weeks ago where I live as if I was on the other side of the mountains of darkness." Newspapers arrive a week late; there are a few local Jewish intellectuals and these are mostly ignorant souls whose knowledge of Judaism is made up of rather vague childhood memories. He admits to Dubnow that he fears that the league's meeting might have been disrupted by the police and asks him, rather touchingly, whether the "child" is still alive.[104]

The fierce, obsessive political divisiveness in the Jewish camp produced by this revolutionary turmoil both amused and depressed him. The Bund, for instance, insisted on identifying parties to its right as class enemies and scoundrels. Especially sad in his view was how the Jewish community shamelessly courted "progressive" opinion; this, he claimed, was a new form of moral slavery. Dubnow, too, had argued in a series of highly controversial articles in *Voskhod* that the willingness to defer the needs of one's own people until such time as the progressive agenda might be satisfied was itself a form of "Slavery in the Midst of Revolution," the title being of course a friendly nod toward Ahad Ha'am. Dubnow, with whom Ahad Ha'am had never worked so closely, commented there on the irony that at a moment when Poles, Armenians, and the other nationalities were actively pursuing their revolutionary agenda under their own banners, the Jews (or at least most of them) preferred Russian or Polish ones. The insistence of so many of them to explain away the recent pogroms as "counterrevolutionary," thus deflating them of their specificity and anti-Jewish content, demonstrated this slavery, a subordination comparable to what had existed earlier in relations, say, between Polish nobles and Jewish subjects. In what otherwise could have been a moment of Jewish self-assertion, Jews have reverted to old, discredited political responses despite their revolutionary rhetoric.[105]

Not only did Dubnow by virtue of his article's title refer approvingly to Ahad Ha'am's well-known gloss on assimilation, but the next issue of the journal appeared with a letter from Ahad Ha'am—one of his very rare excursions into the Russian-language press—where he voiced his support for Dubnow. He argues that not even the much-lauded courage of the Jewish revolutionaries contradicts Dubnow's assertion that such Jews remain slaves, willing pawns in the control of others for whom they behave courageously in exchange for respect and goodwill: "Only the masters have changed—the slave remains a slave, as in the past."[106]

He was still blunter in his address to the third conference of the league, held in St. Petersburg in April 1906. Only equal rights for Jews should preoccupy the organization, he insisted. Those who have other agendas should go elsewhere. Parting company with Dubnow, he wrote that to achieve this objective Jews should therefore feel free to form tactical coalitions with any sector of Russian politics that supports their demands for civic and national emancipation:

I can't understand why it is that a monarchist cannot be a philosemite and, on the other hand, is it not true that delegates from the parties on the extreme left have in the past been antisemites, the proof of which were the pamphlets produced by the men of "People's Will" in the 1880s which called for anti-Jewish pogroms.[107]

Reactions to his comments were furious, and not only because he had indelicately (and intentionally) reopened a terrible wound by referring to how some populists in the 1880s saw pogroms as a healthy, politically useful attack on the oppressive status quo; angrier were the responses to his call for a tactical alliance between Jews and antiliberal political forces. Ahad Ha'am's criticisms, claimed the literary historian Israel Zinberg, were shortsighted and also emblematic of what he called "slavery in the midst of nationalism." The Jews who proclaimed sympathy for Russia's progressive forces did so out of an awareness that this was the way Jewish life could be improved. Ahad Ha'am's retrogressive call could well cut him off from "all thinking people in the Jewish community."[108]

Such denunciations did not particularly fluster Ahad Ha'am. His reply to Zinberg was rather perfunctory. True, he found himself deeply preoccupied with the duma elections; to one friend he said that they made him feel like the bridegroom who, according to Jewish law, is absolved from reciting his bedtime prayers because he has too much on his mind. But he was still depressed by the way politicized Jews had reacted to the crisis without a semblance of national self-awareness. The revolution's underside was revealed with vivid clarity by the Odessa pogrom of October 1905—the worst mass anti-Jewish violence of the period—which left five hundred dead and more than three thousand injured; many of the city's Jews were forced to seek shelter on boats in the Odessa harbor. He compared the massacre to the seventeenth-century Khmelnitzsky pogroms (his own small and obscure street, he told Ben Hillel Ha-Cohen, was passed over), but what especially pleased him was the self-evident vigorous self-defense by local Jews; more pogromists were killed this time than Jews, he announced proudly.[109]

Drawn into the revolutionary politics of 1905, nothing better illustrated the distance he maintained from progressive politics in this period than his attitude toward Yiddish. His feelings on Yiddish were aired in an essay "The Language Dispute" written in 1910 and after the Yiddishist Czernowitz conference called for the recognition of Yiddish "as a national language of the Jewish people." Hebraists felt themselves on the defensive in these years: the Revolution of 1905 lifted long-standing censorship regulations on Yiddish, and newspapers in the language quickly achieved a much larger circulation than the older, Hebrew ones. In the revolutionary turmoil Yiddish appeared to be immeasurably better

THE CURSES OF EXILE   223

attuned to the masses than Hebrew. Hebraists would later stage con-
ferences of their own, modeled (despite their vigorous disavowals) on
Czernowitz but without its visibility. With the masses of Jews speaking
Yiddish, with newspapers, books, even theater in the language suddenly
legal and widespread, it was now argued that Yiddish was certain to be
one of the crucial bulwarks of a budding Jewish national identity.[110]

Ahad Ha'am found this ludicrous. In moments of adversity Judaism
had in the past managed to provide itself methods to survive, proof that
its "national will to survive" remained vibrant, he writes. Even before the
destruction of the second temple in Jerusalem three such bulwarks—
religion (in the rabbinic mold), literature (which would later blossom
into the Talmud), and language (always Hebrew)—had surfaced and all
played a crucial role in sustaining the Jewish people through the ages.
Today's debates, he asserts, are similar in kind to those that confronted
first century CE Judaism: how can Judaism be best reconstructed with
full use of the past?[111]

Incredibly, he continues, there are some who contend that with the
waning importance of faith and rabbinic literature Jews should also
abandon their third and last historic bulwark, the Hebrew language.
They argue that Yiddish can take its place since unlike religion the
speaking of Yiddish makes no demands except that one speak a language
that is already well known; it requires of its adherents neither the political
nor cultural demands of Zionism; nor does it entail the intellectual
commitment that had in the past gone into the mastery of rabbinic texts.
It is a form of Jewish identity that is altogether accessible and fresh,
without Hebrew's hoary associations. It links Jews to other Eastern
European nationalities that have come to see their budding identities
centered around folk customs and languages.[112]

However, Ahad Ha'am continues, even if Hebrew had disappeared
it would still be impossible to build Judaism on the tenuous foundations
of this "borrowed language"—created for the sake of utility and never
with more in mind. But rather than disappear, everything treasured in
Jewish history through the ages, all that Judaism wished to be enshrined
in its collective memory, was recorded in Hebrew and this remains true
to the present day. Languages come and go in any cultural community;
but there can be only one national language, and the belief that its role
has been supplanted by Yiddish is an illusion. Precisely because Yiddish
is beginning to feel itself in decline—confronted as it is by the recognition that it will be cast aside by most Jews within the next generation
or two—it has attempted to enshrine itself as a national tongue. Rather

than a sign of confidence as some have thought, it is quite the opposite: it reeks of desperation. Who would ever claim that once Yiddish ceases to serve its immediate purpose in East European Jewish life that the Jewish people will expend any energy to keep it alive as was done so successfully for Hebrew? Only an original language is treated in this way, one that is an authentic reflection of the nation's "mind and heart, its holiest feelings, its joys and sorrows, its tears and lament." Yiddish, he writes to Dubnow,

is simply in my eyes what it has been always for our ancestors: The language used for the daily needs of life, and also for the spiritual needs of the common people, but it is an alien language to us.[113]

Even more bluntly, he declared to Rawnitsky that the idea that the Jews would ever see Yiddish as a key to their national identity ignores that "our entire existence in the diaspora is possible only so long as we feel ourselves to be a 'historical aristocracy'; at the moment this ceases, and we view ourselves just as another small nation of no special cultural or historic worth, with only a new language and a new nationalism, and a 'democratic' one, we shall then become the least important nation on earth."[114] True, he wasn't quite as explicit in his published remarks; but even there his comments on Yiddish reveal not only his unswerving rejection of piecemeal reform of Jewish life but also his deafness to populism and its attraction to the folkways (linguistic or otherwise) of the masses.

Here as well as in other respects he differed with Dubnow. They worked together very closely, especially between 1897–1905, even after Dubnow moved to Vilna in 1903, where he hoped his historical research would proceed more quickly without the distractions of Odessa. These distractions, though, were at the core of his prodigious historical labor (which culminated in the 1920s in a ten-volume history of the Jews, still a standard work) where he affirmed that a key task for the Jewish historian was to explain the various ways in which Jews dealt with adversity: "In times of extreme adversity," as Jonathan Frankel writes of his method, "the Jewish people had in the past found new ways to maintain its sense of purpose, its hold on life, its faith. It was for the historian to understand and explain, not to condemn, these collective reactions to mass suffering, however repellent they might appear to the modern mind."[115] Hasidism and Kabbalah, the Pharisees and Maimonides all represented methods of national self-preservation; at moments when Jews managed to transcend the limitations of their own culture and link their particularistic inclinations with universal ones, the products reached special spiritual heights: the Prophets emerged at a moment when Jews were able to see the interconnection between their preoccupations and those of humankind. But even manifestations of lesser universal importance were expressions of Jewry's desire to maintain its dignity, freedom, and integrity.

No less committed to an evolutionist ideology than Ahad Ha'am— the two of them were nurtured in their youth on much the same self-taught intellectual repertoire (Buckle, Spencer, Mill)—Dubnow asserted that to survive today Jews would need to adapt the various means that had been used to preserve their nation. One particular method, communal self-government, stood out in Dubnow's mind both because of its apparent resemblance to the Russian peasant commune (much celebrated by populists, partly because of their distrust of centralized authority), and since it permitted him to utilize a Rankean statecraft-oriented model for the reconstruction of Jewish history. It represented a compromise between national independence and submergence in an assimilatory *Rechtsstaat:* a compromise of this sort—a solution short of a reemployment of the accumulated treasures of Judaism so that it could once again achieve the heights of its prophetic past—was unacceptable to Ahad Ha'am, with whom Dubnow conducted a lively and fruitful polemic beginning in the 1890s. Dubnow was much more yielding than his friend, less distrustful of the larger world, more willing to accept partial solutions (he refused to reject Palestine or emigration to the United States, or reject Yiddish for Hebrew), less willing to believe that problems were amenable to thoroughgoing solutions.[116]

But like Ahad Ha'am he moved easily (if also at times rather grudgingly) from politics to scholarship, and in line with his populist inclinations proved much more adaptable than his friend to working within the larger political arena: as he saw it, his primary goal was the redefinition of the terms of emancipation to embrace a national dimension to the Jewish future. Less fixated on crisis than Ahad Ha'am, he envisioned a medley of solutions of varying importance: population transfer to the New World, cultural regeneration of a small but significant community in Palestine, national autonomy in a politically reconstructed Europe.[117]

Committed, as both of them were, to gradual progress, to a transformation of Judaism that would build upon what existed in the past, Dubnow and Ahad Ha'am were drawn back to the period of the Pharisees. This seemed to them—they discovered this mutual fascination at their first meeting—something of a paradigm for their time: then the

Judaism of an old world collapsed, and along with it disappeared its now-discredited cultic elite, its militant zealots, its isolationist sectarians, its assimilationists. The emergent Pharisees drew upon a pre-exilic synagogal-based ritualistic life in Palestine, but theirs was a revolution nonetheless. The scope of their transformation, its comprehensiveness (as embodied, above all, in the rabbinic literature), their ability to design a structure that sustained Judaism for two thousand years—these drew Dubnow and Ahad Ha'am back to this period that fed their considerable aspirations and ambitions.[118]

Eventually the pogroms came to an end, though for many months after the murderous outbursts of 1906 there were rumors of the imminent outbreak of new ones; on one occasion, in May 1907, Ahad Ha'am himself was beaten by a policeman, though not seriously, on an Odessa street after a Jew in a nearby city was reported having shot at the police.[119] Soon after the antisemitic turbulence ended so did the political liberalization that inspired it. Tsarist authorities, intimidated by the uncompromising constitutionalism of the duma majority, abruptly changed their policy. That majority was summarily done away with in 1907 by a governmental coup d'état in which new elections (the third in less than two years) were secured under new, considerably more restrictive laws. They resulted in a conservative majority more amenable to the Romanov regime.

Even before these changes in the political map that relegated most Jewish political currents back to the illegal margins of Russian life, Ahad Ha'am began to look again in the direction of Palestine as a source of inspiration and comfort. To be sure, he also considered seriously at the time moving to the United States as head of Philadelphia's new Dropsie College, an idea floated by the Jewish Theological Seminary chancellor Solomon Schechter upon the suggestion of Lubarsky, who now lived in New York. But about Palestine especially he began to feel differently: as he explained in the fall of 1906, he had the growing sense that he could identify some point in the not-too-distant future when a Jewish culture could secure a true foothold in Palestine; by 1908, the Turkish revolution further deepened his attention to Palestinian affairs and made the prospect more likely that the Jewish hold on the land could be strengthened. But it was not only these changes in the larger world that can be credited with his change of heart. Much of this reassessment proved astute; he was never as immune to geopolitical considerations as his critics charged. No less important were personal concerns, especially his ill health, that made his current job with Wissotzsky and the required traveling taxing. It sapped his energy and robbed him of the peace of mind essential for his literary work.[120]

He admitted in the spring of 1906 to a friend who had moved to Palestine that he had quite consciously in the last few years separated himself from Palestinian affairs mostly out of a desire to spend his time producing something enduring that did not reek of the "marketplace." He found himself frustrated that he had devoted so much time to Palestinian affairs and apparently without concrete accomplishment, as the Rothschild debacle in 1901 had persuaded him. The pressure of diasporic or *"galut*-related events" forced him back into communal politics and into battles with everyone around him, "as if this were all decreed for me forty days before my birth." Now tiring of these, he found Palestine at the forefront of his concerns: hence, he demands news from Palestine, and—in an emotional flourish that he quickly asks to be excused (he is old, tired, and it is now the middle of the night, he says)—declares: "Oh, my dear friend, who will give me a forgotten corner of Mt. Carmel, far from the tempestuous masses, so that I may dream great dreams like in the good times of the past?"[121]

Whether or not he was thinking seriously at this point of settling in Palestine, as he indicated to close friends, he pinned his hopes for Zion's cultural transformation on rather slim foundations. He highlighted as a prime reason for optimism the appearance of a journal in Palestine edited by one of his most devoted followers, Guttman, better-known by his pen name Ben Zion, who moved from Odessa in late 1905. Soon after his arrival, he pressed for the creation of a union of Hebrew writers which he hoped would galvanize the literary forces necessary for such a journal. Obviously, it would depend, literarily as well as financially, on contributions from abroad, but to succeed, Ben Zion recognized, it had to create something that was specifically Palestinian-Jewish, which only local writers could provide. Although a clearheaded, talented, and efficient man, by no means was Ben Zion one of the outstanding figures in the Hebrew literary world. In Odessa, where he came to be a part of Ahad Ha'am's orbit (he ran a modernized heder), he felt dwarfed by the luminaries surrounding him. One of his motivations for going to Palestine had been to establish his literary reputation in a place where there were as yet no figures of real stature. A competent though very dry and uninspiring organizer and a good though by no means particularly distinguished literary stylist, he immediately called attention to himself in this sparse literary terrain. What he had come to inherit still represented, it would seem, an unsturdy base for Jewish cultural renewal.[122]

At first, though, Ahad Ha'am seems to have felt otherwise. He suggested that the impact of his new journal *Ha-Omer,* whose first issue was yet to appear, could put *Ha-Shiloach* in the shade. Indeed, the journal was much more significant, as he urged Ben Zion to understand, than the Hebrew weekly newspaper that he was also considering publishing at the time. *Ha-Omer* could firm up the Palestinian literary center (merkaz sifruti) which was, Ahad Ha'am reminded him, the goal of the Jewish nationalist enterprise. He added with characteristic caution that he had no hope that a reestablished center would transpire immediately; if, however, the opportunity was lost it could be "a tragedy greater than any that has yet occurred to us in Palestine up to this time." Perhaps, he warned Klausner, it was premature for *Ha-Shiloach* to relocate to Palestine but it was certain that Palestine would be the venue for literary ventures of this kind in the near future.[123]

He made this same point in the introductory essay written in the form of a letter to the editor for *Ha-Omer*'s first issue and fittingly titled "The Time Has Come." He complained repeatedly to Ben Zion that he had a very difficult time writing the piece. Perhaps this was so because, unlike most of his writings, it was celebratory and could be little else since it was intended to launch the journal of one of his devotees. The role didn't suit him and the piece was flatter, more obviously derivative (of his earlier articles, that is), and had less panache than was typical for him.

He begins by explaining why it is that the launching of *Ha-Omer* has so excited Jewish writers outside of Palestine, who feel it essential to "take an active role" as its contributors. This rhetorical question was more indicative of Ahad Ha'am's own very deep commitment to its success than anything else. He answered by asserting that the moment was ripe, perhaps more so than even its editors realize. "If nonetheless I feel—and I am certain that other writers feel the same way—that it is my duty to take part in your undertaking, this can only be explained by virtue of the fact that it is not merely the condition of Palestinian Jewry but the condition of our people as a whole that has now persuaded us of the need to reunite our land with our language."[124]

Until very recently, he writes, it has hardly seemed possible that Hebrew culture could be nurtured there but recent events (probably a reference to the Russian pogroms) have revealed how truly vulnerable all literary ventures are outside Palestine and without the anchor of a "free center on its native soil." Without the benefit of such a center "the flint of an alien environment can produce a spark that can destroy in one moment all that we have spent many years . . . building."

Some Jewish nationalists—meaning, of course, himself—recognized this very early, even though such leaders did not have a final say on what transpired in a movement whose trajectory was confused, misdirected, chaotic, and wasteful. It was Pinsker who had transformed the love of Zion from a "bookish memory" into something considerably more vivid; he also saw to it, Ahad Ha'am still insists, that this took the form of the revival of the Jewish national spirit. Some went further than Pinsker, arguing that the ultimate goal of Jewish nationalism was spiritual revival: true, this dissident sector of the movement saw that the diaspora was "a very evil thing" but as they declaimed against exile they appreciated that they were unable to free themselves easily from its bonds; exile was terrible, they recognized, but the ingathering of Jews to Palestine on a massive scale remained unrealistic.[125]

What then does the rebuilding of Palestine mean? If the message of this dissident current had proven decisive it could well have meant that the spiritual rather than the material shortcomings of the diaspora would have been forthrightly addressed: it is the way in which the diaspora enslaved the human spirit that will be transformed by a center that would represent a "refuge . . . for the spirit" even if only a fraction ("one-tenth" is what he says here) of the Jews move there. But even if it be small, it will represent proof of what it means to live without external constraints as a Jew, with the freedom to exercise one's prerogatives: "Who could possibly estimate in advance the impact that such a national center could exert?"[126]

Of course, Jewish nationalists have squandered numerous opportunities over the years: eighteen years ago the movement was prodded to move in this direction (by "Lo zeh ha-derekh") but rejected it resoundingly. He adds in much the same vein as in his comments on leadership in his last Pinsker essay: "Not that this instinct was wholly mistaken. It was then only just beginning to make its impact on the masses and here was an attempt to give it a form that would inevitably alienate it from the very masses whose only real interest was an escape from their material troubles!" It is not that Jewish nationalism feared losing whatever following it had managed to muster up, albeit with promises it could never deliver; more importantly, from its early beginnings the movement felt itself irresistably drawn to the masses by a desire to link itself to the democratic aspirations of the age. This predated the 1905 revolution, which served only to reinforce this tendency: ". . . we live in the age of democracy, and everybody believes that not only are the masses the source of light and progress but that any ideas that they cannot grasp are mere nonsense."[127]

The irony is that Jewish nationalism would never manage for long to secure itself as a mass organization and it forsook the chance to move in other realistic directions. It tried, inevitably failing, to satisfy all takers; to secure the favor of the masses seeking refuge from distress, and the intelligentsia seeking a radical forum for the expression of their ideas: "Political work in the diaspora? Of course, it is an essential feature of Zionism. Revolution? Why, who are quite as revolutionary as the Zionists? Socialism? The very basis of Zionism!" What should have been done is to identify a "core constituency" much he says, like the Marxist proletariat. For Jews, this might be best described as a "spiritual proletariat." By Marxist standards, Jews have no true working class, but only an imperiled artisanry, he asserts. This spiritual vanguard could galvanize the Jews, no matter its size. Hence, in this somewhat novel reassertion of his old idea that the Jewish future ultimately rested on the shoulders of its numerically small elite, he went on to argue that despite the corrosive impact of Western assimilation and Eastern radicalism, a vanguard, albeit very small, retains it ability to sustain the Jewish people:

I assert, therefore, that if the majority of our people are unconsciously becoming more and more estranged from the national spirit, and if its children born in exile have made for themselves new gods like the gods of all the peoples around them, and only a few of our people remain faithful to our national idea in its historic form . . . then these few will be the heirs to our national treasures at the present time; it is they who hold onto the thread of our history and do not permit it to be broken. As long as there is a single Jew who holds this thread, we cannot predict what its final outcome will be.[128]

Throughout the piece he mocks the desire of Zionists to court the masses who have a realistic sense of what can, and cannot, help them and who have quickly come to realize that Zionism can't; he also asserts, this time in a vaguely populist mode, that one of Jewish nationalism's more salient features is its ability to speak to still-powerful Jewish yearnings for Zion; hence, it is not entirely alien to the Jewish masses, even if it cannot address their most immediate demands. Above all, the essay serves to spotlight the contribution that a venture like *Ha-Omer* can make to the formation of a "spiritual proletariat" that ultimately would redeem the Jewish people.

Obviously, he picked the term spiritual proletariat to disarm young Marxists of the sort with whom he had come into contact during the recent revolutionary turmoil. No less important, he used it to identify the likely readers of *Ha-Omer* itself—a Palestinian-based readership of laborers who would read (and hopefully also write for) it after a day full of arduous manual work and who thus differed from the bourgeois, yeshiva-trained Hebrew readers of the journals of Odessa or Warsaw. With his use of this term, Ahad Ha'am signaled a recognition that the compass arrow was beginning to move in the Jewish nationalist world toward Palestine and away from the centers of Russian life, whose cities, as Dubnow felt as he wandered through the streets of Odessa in 1910, remained "shrouded in deep mourning ever since the bloody days of October."[129] In Ahad Ha'am's call for an increased emphasis on romanticism instead of Marxist materialism and in its unmistakable optimism, he summarized his views in an uncharacteristically upbeat tone. With the establishment of *Ha-Omer* it appeared to him (at least in the journal's very early stages) that his viewpoint had a secure base in Palestine which it could still fashion in its image.

It soon became apparent that his ideological approach, which he preferred to call in this essay a dissident current in the nationalist camp, had achieved the standing of a reigning orthodoxy that spawned its own rebels. To an extent this had been true ever since criticisms were leveled against Ahad Ha'am's *Ha-Shiloach* by Berdyczewski and his Jewish nationalist "Nietzschean" network of the 1890s. These early critics were initially, at least, Ahad Ha'amists, animated by his vision of a Judaism where concepts such as "that scientific heresy that bears the name of Darwin" (as Ahad Ha'am described it in "Slavery in Freedom") were integrated into a transformed Jewish identity. Ahad Ha'am's subsequent timidity disappointed them—especially his unwillingness, as they saw it, to take his own assumptions to their logical conclusion, and his insistence on denouncing heresies and arbitrating between what could be absorbed into the spiritual domain of a reconstructed, nationally coherent Jewry and what could not (including Nietzsche, militarism, personality cults, materialism, Marxism).[130]

Although Berdyczewski and his circle found themselves scandalized by Ahad Ha'am's apparent faintness of heart, he remained for them an authority of great standing—albeit tarnished and old-fashioned—one of integrity and some philosophical importance who pointed in the general direction of the future. Their continued regard was a product of what he had represented in their youths: many like Berdyczewski himself had faced furious opposition in their early struggle for personal autonomy; Ahad Ha'am's essays lent their quest a Judaic legitimacy and placed it comfortably within the context of earlier, sanctified transformative events in Jewish life (in the pharisaic, maimonidean, or mendelssohnian epochs). Later, their university training, their life outside the confines of imperial Russia, and Herzl's ascendancy opened them to different, antithetical influences. But Ahad Ha'am retained an undiminished charisma, despite his diminished relevance.[131]

Intellectual influences on the new generation of the so-called Second Aliyah were different; it came of age in the wake of the Kishinev pogrom and the revolution of 1905, and already by 1910 it was transforming the face of Jewish Palestine. These men and women came with their political parties (Ha-Poel Ha-Tsair and Poalei Zion were both founded in 1905), and once in Palestine they launched a series of hugely influential institutions: Ha-Shomer for the defense of Jewish settlements; Sejera, Palestine's first socialist commune, set up in 1908; an array of communal experiments, workers' associations, and cooperative villages. Perhaps there were no more than a few hundred young people in the Yishuv at any given time in this period who could be considered part of this ideologically preoccupied if still undisciplined cadre. They came here with their own writers (Joseph Hayyim Brenner, Samuel Joseph Agnon), their own emergent political leaders (Yitzhak Ben Zvi, Israel Shohat, David Ben Gurion), their distinctive reading of Judaism, the Kishinev pogrom, the failed Russian revolution, the gentile world. They were embarrassed by much of the recent Palestinian past and for reasons not entirely different from those of Ahad Ha'am: the JCA-Rothschild patronage system, the original agricultural bourgeoisie with their dependence on Arab labor, the frailty of Palestine's Jewish laborers. For them the maskilic battles of the past, though, were old-fashioned, the youthful "sins" that haunted Ahad Ha'am's generation (and, to only a slightly lesser extent, also Berdyczewski's) were tame in comparison to those they traduced with comparative ease. Ahad Ha'am's meticulously balanced compromises were thus unnecessary to them, even slightly ridiculous; Berdyczewski better understood their rationale even when he disagreed with their specific formulation.[132]

The conditions of Jewish cultural life had very quickly changed here over the last few years. When in late 1905, Ben Zion settled in Palestine he, together with the loyal Ahad Ha'amists Smilansky and Barzilai, were at the forefront of literary affairs and his *Ha-Omer* was supported by all sectors of the still tiny community of writers. Their journal was indebted to Ahad Ha'am and his legacy. ("Rebbe," explained Ben Zion in his first letter to Ahad Ha'am from Palestine, he had not written sooner because, as he was certain Ahad Ha'am understood, he did not want to air merely a series of superficial impressions but only ones that were based on solid foundations. The letter was far more than merely respectful: it was infused with such profound worshipfulness that one can well understand why Ben Zion felt the need to abandon Odessa for freer, less encumbered terrain.) By 1910, though, *Ha-Omer* had disappeared after a mere three issues and it was replaced by journals somewhat thinner in scope and girth, with fewer intellectual pretensions, but with considerably more solid prospects if only because they were bolstered by the same political parties that had so recently been introduced onto the Palestinian scene. Perhaps the most lively was *Ha-Po'el ha-tsair* a party organ, which like its political namesake was labor-oriented but non-Marxist, by 1910 communitarian, and eclectic in its intellectual debts. The political map had changed dramatically: a few years earlier, in 1901, Ahad Ha'am's loyal Palestinian aide Barzilai could orchestrate without undue opposition or resentment the composition of a set of demands from what was then the most politicized sector of Jewish labor; by 1910 this would be unthinkable and Barzilai—along with his eminent mentor—were relegated to the sidelines in an increasingly youthful, volatile, and politically radical atmosphere. The Jewish population doubled between 1904 and 1914 to twelve thousand; a total of twenty thousand emigrated in this period to Palestine. Berl Katznelson, later a leading cultural figure in the Yishuv, when he arrived here in 1909 at the age of twenty-two, was in this milieu seen as rather old.[133]

Ahad Ha'am was aware of the radicalization of Jewish politics in Russia and Palestine since 1905; he often commented on how the Jews, who had once looked to the heavens for redemption, were now convinced that their sole source of hope were *rashei tevot,* the abbreviations for the various political parties. On the whole, he viewed such trends as peripheral, of only passing interest especially in terms of the Zionist movement. He had not toured Palestine since 1900. Though this pained him, his reliance on a regular source of income from Wissotzsky, the revolutionary turmoil in Russia, and his bad health made the trip particularly cumbersome. When he managed to spend a few weeks in Haifa in the fall of 1907 it was to recuperate from a prolonged illness and he did not travel beyond his seaside haven. Visitors streamed to see him. He complained incessantly of the intrusiveness of these visits while begging Ben Zion, Moshe Smilansky, and others to come. His visitors were naturally Ahad Ha'amist devotees, the heads of local literary and political enterprises with whom he had special rapport. When in 1908 he finally abandoned Russia for a position at Wissotzsky's London office—prompted, in the end, by a police investigation of his activities—he spent much of his time settling his family, purchasing a suitable house, and acclimating himself to a new, never altogether comfortable environment.[134]

His move to London wrenched him from familiar, if also increasingly hostile, Russian waters, from his dearest friends, and from the vortex of Jewish nationalist activity. Meanwhile the impact of the Second Aliyah was beginning to be felt widely on the institutional life of Jewish Palestine. Consequently, Ahad Ha'am was somewhat less attuned to events than he might have been had he continued to follow the Yishuv from the more intimate and more central vantage point of Odessa. Once controversy reared its head in 1910 it brought to the surface a host of issues not the least of which was the old, vexing dilemma of the appropriate relationship between an increasingly independently minded Palestinian Jewry and its diaspora patrons. The role that Ahad Ha'am played was highly visible, and according to many in the Yishuv, heavy-handed and intrusive.

As the father of Jewish cultural nationalism, he found himself savaged by restless, radical heirs. Naturally the attacks grated on him; he also found them bracing. He rushed into battle admittedly eager to recreate some of the urgency he had experienced, and enjoyed, as the besieged leader of Bnei Moshe. What came to be known in Jewish nationalist circles as the Brenner Affair revolved around the reaction of Ahad Ha'am to an article by Brenner that appeared in a 1910 issue of *Ha-Po'el ha-tsair*. In his response Ahad Ha'am attempted for the last time to impose his cultural agenda onto Palestinian Jewry. His eventual failure, coupled with his seclusion in Jewishly remote England, where he now chose to have as little as possible to do with organized Jewish life, was for him a crucial turning point. He remained unrepentant about his highly unpopular role in this affair, but he recognized how it had rendered him more politically marginal than ever before—particularly since he was now far from his old diminished Odessa base, shorn of much of his former Palestinian support, without a journal to edit, a movement to run, or a circle in England in a position to promote his designs.[135]

It had not occurred to him when he moved to London that he had cut himself off from the Jewish nationalist world: many of his closest friends had already abandoned or planned to abandon Odessa, with the unsettling interplay between revolution and reaction in Russian life over the last few years persuading them that their work was best done elsewhere, in Europe, Palestine, even America. Still, after his move his advice was widely sought and many of his articles appeared in translation in German, English, and Yiddish for the first time in these years. He complained that he was inundated with requests to write and noted with bemusement the great controversy that erupted in Russia when the rumor spread that he had abandoned Hebrew for Russian. True, Barzilai warned him in late 1908, his circle was losing its hold over Palestine. Not terribly alarmed, though, Ahad Ha'am waited for some three months to reply, only to ask sardonically "how many of 'us' were left in Palestine, anyway?" Clearly no more than a thousand, he suggested. Barzilai's earnestness he found amusing and out of place: a cultural war of any significance was unlikely, and he remained convinced that the forces lined up against Ahad Ha'amism couldn't be as formidable as Barzilai said. Perhaps it was, in part, the physical distance now separating him from the worlds of Russian and Palestinian Jewry; whatever the reason, his reading during the Brenner Affair and his later interpretation of the contemporary Jewish scene in the Yishuv was off the mark: less prescient, less discerning of new trends, and less pioneering in its insights.[136]

The Brenner Affair was sparked by an article Ahad Ha'am wrote on English Jewry, a subject of little import in Palestine. It appeared in Hebrew in July 1910 under the title "Al shete se'ifim"; in English it was published as "Judaism and the Gospels." It was the only piece he would write on English Jewry during his fourteen years there. In reply Brenner wrote a thoroughgoing repudiation of it which also implicitly accused its author of being a cultural anachronism. He had become wedded to a notion of Judaism that conflicted not only with common sense but with Ahad Ha'am's own, earlier perspective on the immeasurably expansive boundaries of Judaism.

Ahad Ha'am identifies in "Judaism and the Gospels" the difference between the spirit of Judaism and Christianity—abstract divinity as opposed to a personified godhead, collective as opposed to individual salvation, and the call for absolute justice rather than altruism (which, in his mind, is akin to egoism). The essay was built around an attack on the Anglo-Jewish liberal theologian C. G. Montefiore whose recent commentary on the Synoptic Gospels saw as its task the reclaiming of Jesus as an outstanding prophet of Judaism. "If Judaism does not, as it were, come to terms with the Gospels," argues Montefiore as quoted in

Ahad Ha'am's essay, "it must always be a creed in the corner, of little influence or expansive power."[137]

Such views reflected a loss of understanding in the tragedy of exile and a sorrow over the isolation of Jews from the larger world which it seeks to alleviate by any means. True, English Jews are "at ease" and they live in a society where few obstacles remain to block their social mobility, where antisemitism has never had in modern times the potency it enjoys elsewhere, and where social relations with non-Jews are fairly unencumbered. For large sectors of the community not only are traditional Jewish rituals consequently discarded but "the fundamental ideas by which [Judaism] is distinguished from Christianity have lost their hold." Nevertheless, no one sensitive to the spirit of Judaism could support Montefiore's position. From the outset, Ahad Ha'am argues, the abstract nature of Judaism's belief in the divinity and in personal redemption probably made it less attractive than Christianity to outsiders; it was comparable to his somewhat more rarified but also more authentic form of Jewish nationalism. In any event, he continues, this does not mean that Judaism is superior to Christianity. Quite simply, its essential spirit is altogether different:

> [E]very true Jew; whether "orthodox" or "liberal," feels deep down that there is something in the spirit of our people—though we know not what it is—that kept it from the high road taken by other nations, and impelled it to build up Judaism on those foundations for the sake of which the people remains to this day confined "to a corner" with its religion, being incapable of renouncing it. Let those who still have this feeling remain within the fold; let those who have lost it go elsewhere. There is no room for compromise.[138]

In his view, Montefiore and others like him were on the verge of apostasy; the prospect of taking a step they found so embarrassing drove them to hope instead to transform Judaism into something that was fundamentally Christian to avoid confronting the awkward implications of their own beliefs. Ahad Ha'am's concern about this case of near-apostasy, as he understood it, was fueled by the appearance in the East European Jewish press that same year of a spate of articles on the subject. They resulted from a rise in apostasy in Russia involving few but nonetheless visible Jews. Apostasy occurred particularly among the secularly educated Russian Jewish young, which was widely interpreted as a product of the political reaction and disappointment with recent revolutionary expectations: the persistence of stubborn and demeaning obstacles was simply too painful and senseless for some to continue to bear.[139]

Such pain, though, had little to do with theology, insisted Brenner in his sweeping, extraordinarily blunt article that appeared in *Ha-Po'el ha-tsair* in November 1910. It was cast with a touch of sardonic understatement as a review of the recent Jewish press which, as Brenner noted, was greatly preoccupied with apostasy. Its perils, as so many have been led to believe, ravaged Western Jewry since the days that the children of the venerable Moses Mendelssohn abandoned Judaism and converted; now, as is widely feared, Russian Jewry faces the starkest choices. Here he takes his first swipe at Ahad Ha'am by using in this context the term *al shete se'ifim,* "at the very brink," the Hebrew title of Ahad Ha'am's recent Montefiore article. With mock despair and reverence he calls upon the grand figures of Judaism to come forward to save their people: "Resolve this problem, great ones of Israel, resolve it quickly because it is your answers and yours alone that we seek."[140]

In fact, continues Brenner, this is a bogus problem: "not an issue, not even a joke," because Ahad Ha'am's assumptions to the contrary, religious matters simply are now of little consequence, whether for those who remain Jewish or others who embrace the trappings of another faith. At one time there were those Jews, those run-of-the-mill *balei batim* for whom religious belief was truly informed by deep devotion and mystery; today a cursory visit to the synagogue will find them devoid of a comparable fervor. This is even more true for the young. What interests them clearly is not religion, but worldly matters: relations between classes, between sexes, between nations. Not one of them would ever think of entering into a conversation about what faith is superior, or whether the messiah has already come. The youth are not self-satisfied; by no means are they pleased about living in a godless world, a world without a national language, a culture, or land. But they are unconvinced that such problems can be solved and this realization, far from providing them with a sense of superiority or confidence, weighs very heavily on them. It represents a painful, terrible truth that they realize they must nonetheless face. To do otherwise would invite hopeless compromise and render oneself ungenuine and insincere.[141]

The much-debated threat of apostasy is then no issue at all. What threat could be posed to a "freethinking Jew" by the assertion that Christianity has a higher claim to truth than Judaism? In the most provocative statement in the article he asserts that, given the overall irrelevance of religion, it remains possible "to be a good Jew and at the same time to be thrilled by the Christian legend of the son of God who was sent to mankind and who atoned with his life for the sins of all the ages." True, an atheist like himself could no more readily adopt Christianity than Confucianism. This was all the more reason why there is no problem in integrating the New Testament into our national literature as Montefiore intended; nor was it a problem that some Jews today feel inspired by the tale of Jesus or moved by the Gospels. Its spirit is no more akin to that of modern Jews than the Old Testament and, indeed, his own reading of the Gospels have convinced him that its "spirit" (once again, a swipe at Ahad Ha'am) is comparable, perhaps even identical. Religions of any kind can exert no seductive power for those who do not share their belief in God, Messiah, or spiritual mysteries of one sort or another. Consequently, Jews who convert—and do so merely for material gain (why else would anyone even bother themselves with religious ritual?)— should not concern us much: clearly Jewish affairs were of little interest for such people before their conversions and hence their apostasy is little more than a reflection of this indifference.

For others, who continue to see themselves as Jews the "future of Judaism" is one that must be studied at its very roots. There was a time when Ahad Ha'am did just this—and then repented: "But for us, his friends and Jewish freethinkers, we retain no connection to Judaism but we are no less a part of it than those who wear *tefilin* and *tzitzit* [phylacteries and ritual undergarments]."[142]

The break with tradition, he argues, is tragic but irrevocable; it signals a break with spiritual matters in general. Berdyczewski's solution had been to broaden immeasurably the limits that determined the boundaries of Jewish spiritual life to encompass even pre-Sinaitic manifestations. Brenner felt this response inadequate because it only managed to account for the cultural dimension of Jewish life; but material factors move people (the Jewish nationalist whom Brenner admired most was Lilienblum, not surprisingly). To the extent to which Jewish life needed to be transformed, its needs were no different from those of the rest of humanity.[143]

Brenner, already a cultural totem of the Second Aliyah in Palestine's tiny literary world, was a precocious, acutely self-conscious man: an agnostic painfully aware of the awful gap left by the death of God; a nationalist who remained unsure that Jews could, or perhaps even should, survive as a people; a man of the left who cringed at any form of dogmatism; a Palestinian pioneer who shunned self-aggrandizement. He was, as Menachem Brinker has observed, no less alienated from his erstwhile mentor Berdyczewski than from Ahad Ha'am since in his view Berdyczewski's ultimately facile analysis of the "problem of Judaism" must be viewed as a simple inversion of Ahad Ha'am's doctrine. The latter saw the root of the problem in the disintegration and fragmentation of Jewish culture, whereas Berdyczewski identified it with the precise opposite—the inordinate lack of differentiation in that culture. Berdyczewski could not conceive of any Jewish problem that was unrelated to cultural issues.[144]

In Brenner's view such perspectives on Judaism fell short of the exacting self-appraisal that he demanded. In particular he ridiculed Ahad Ha'am's belief in his ability to speak the "truth from the Land of Israel"; Brenner questioned whether it was possible for anyone to claim that they possess such truth. Ahad Ha'am's particular assertions are based on wholly unsupportable assumptions regarding the nature of Judaism, the Jewish people, and human nature.

In the traditionalist press in the Yishuv, Brenner's piece was denounced as an outright call for conversion. Deeply suspicious of what they saw (and not incorrectly) as the radical secularism of the men—and still more disturbingly of the women—of the Second Aliyah, the article provided useful ammunition. Indeed, the Christological implications of Brenner's argument justified attacking the new generation with the time-honored accusation of apostasy. Brenner, it was claimed, had become a Christian missionary in England (the Hovevei Zion, although deeply critical of the piece, quickly dispensed with such accusations). Ahad Ha'am's first knowledge of the article came, in fact, from a traditionalist attack on it.[145]

Ahad Ha'am later claimed that at the time of his initial denunciation he did not know that Brenner was its author as it had appeared under the name Yosef Haver. His criticisms of it, he repeated time and again, could not be interpreted as personally motivated. Brenner had met him once in London in what turned out to be a disastrous encounter at Ahad Ha'am's house: Brenner came late, brought a friend, was intermittently nasty and glum while Ahad Ha'am who met them at the door with a watch in his hand immediately indicated that his next visitor was expected soon. The next visitor's arrival happily brought the Brenner meeting to an end. On Brenner's part the encounter was particularly awkward; it seems he was still smarting from Ahad Ha'am's rejection of a piece he had sent years earlier to *Ha-Shiloach*. On his part Ahad Ha'am probably found the young visitor ridiculously rude: Brenner interpreted his queries about his London-based journal, *Ha-Me'orer*, as criticisms; his comments to Ahad Ha'am were defensive, brooding, and terse. Whether or not Ahad Ha'am guessed the article's authorship, he could not help but recognize that it was an attack on him. He thought at first of just writing a reply but soon decided that this would be inadequate, and he contacted the Hovevei Zion executive committee, which provided the journal with a small subsidy (about 10 percent of its costs), and insisted that these funds be terminated.[146]

Throughout the affair he bullied the rather hesitant Hovevei Zion leadership into supporting him, insisting that their ambivalence was merely the product of a desire to court the young. He corresponded with the angry Palestinian Jewish literary establishment nearly all of whom, including Ben Zion himself, lined up in support of Brenner on the grounds of freedom of expression. Ahad Ha'am made the same case over and again: *Ha-Po'el ha-tsair* was free to publish what it wished but if it promoted views contradicting those of the Hovevei Zion, there was no alternative but to deny it funding. Its tone he found deeply offensive, as he explained to one member of the Hovevei Zion executive committee in December 1910, not because of its treatment of him but because of the offhanded way in which it spoke about the Jewish belief "in some father in the heavens." To talk with such indifference about a conviction for which Jews had suffered for thousands of years, and in a periodical subsidized with Jewish communal funds, was intolerable. Some Hovevei Zion leaders had at first suggested a moderate proposal, essentially a symbolic gesture, that would deny *Ha-Po'el ha-tsair* the funds required for the one issue in which the offending article had appeared. In Ahad Ha'am's eyes this mild chastisement was unforgivably timid. Spearheaded by Bialik and Ussishkin, Ahad Ha'am's closest devotees on the Odessa executive committee, the more drastic proposal won out. The Hovevei Zion subsidy was cut; the newspaper was informed that if their editorial line changed, the funds could be reinstated. Ahad Ha'am claimed that he had not recommended this. The action, particularly the effort to sway the publication into changing its line with the use of financial intimidation, shifted the debate away from the content of Brenner's piece to the issue of freedom of expression. Few in Palestine who spoke out in Brenner's defense did so because they agreed with him; in fact, many of them openly stated their opposition to his ideas. But because this was seen as an attempt by the dominant figures of the Odessa nationalist world to muzzle an authentic, if audacious, Palestinian voice, many rose up in defense of their community's integrity, freedom, and autonomy. The fact that it was Ahad Ha'am who had fought Rothschild's paternalism for so long who was at the forefront of this new variant of cultural paternalism did not escape Palestinian Jewish pundits.[147]

The Hovevei Zion's action was almost immediately rendered meaningless by new sources of funding for *Ha-Po'el ha-tsair* that placed it on more solid footing than before. Ahad Ha'am's role in the affair was widely seen as particularly sinister. First, because his participation was unofficial, since he no longer held a position on the Hovevei Zion executive committee, it seemed as if the organization was being manipulated by outside forces unamenable to the normal channels of influence. Second, most of Ahad Ha'am's opponents, even those of Brenner's ilk, remained at least vaguely indebted to him, as was admitted frequently in the debate, ironically for having first taught them the very terms with which they attacked him. Their plaint was thus fueled by a sense of disappointment, by the feeling that someone who had once been respected by them had let them down—someone who was perhaps dated but who had played some role at one time in their intellectual growth.

These concerns were expressed at a special meeting of the association of Palestine's Hebrew writers—called at short order, held during one of the coldest months of the year, and that drew nonetheless participants from all parts of the land. Its transcript is literally filled with direct and oblique references to Ahad Ha'am. The group itself was first launched by Ben Zion to support his explicitly Ahad Ha'amist venture, *Ha-Omer;* its origins served to fuel already existing misgivings about Ahad Ha'am. The long-time *Ha-Shiloach* contributor (and the meeting's chair) A. Z. Rabinowitch said in his opening statement that although he disagreed with Brenner, the piece was written by someone who had devoted his life to his people and who is animated only by his love for them and his pain at their present conditions: he referred to people like Brenner as *ne'emanim pesa'eh ohev,* as people devoted to, at least, the partial consolation of their people in an effort to link him with Ahad Ha'am's brilliant, idiosyncratic exercise in consolation. In explaining why the Hovevei Zion responded as it did to Brenner's piece, a participant alluded to Ahad Ha'am by saying this was the doing of the "original thinker, the leading figure, the seer." Another suggested, in an attempt to highlight the difference between the intellectually expansive Ahad Ha'am of the past and the censorious one of the present—that his "Torah she-balev" was a more devastating indictment of fundamentalist Judaism than Brenner's article. Throughout the meeting comments were made (some with a sardonic dismissiveness, others with genuine pain) on how the great writer (sofer gadol), the indisputable sage had opposed them on this issue.[148]

For the more conservative, older writers at the meeting, the main issue was the Hovevei Zion's meddling, its senseless attempt to censor a serious, intellectually impressive publication. For some younger writers the battle was rather different: in their minds it was symbolically important because it pitted Ahad Ha'am against Brenner—the young, precocious symbol of the Yishuv intelligentsia. Lax, almost ascetic in his personal habits, intellectually voracious, deeply confrontational—Brenner came to personify the ideals of the Second Aliyah, a youthful, eager, easily disappointed cadre hungry for achievement, for mentors and community. His role in this milieu—one that preferred to see itself at the cutting edge of Jewish nationalist discourse—was comparable to Ahad Ha'am's in the stuffy, plutocratic confines of the Hovevei Zion of the mid-1880s.

No one who was on Brenner's side of the debate set out the terms more clearly than A. D. Gordon. Gordon was a figure of considerable charisma in Jewish nationalism—a middle-aged, once economically secure and bourgeois Russian Jew who abandoned job and family for a life as a near-penniless Palestinian laborer. He emerged an ideologist of Jewish agrarianism, a somewhat eclectic socialist whose lyrical nationalist arsenal became part of the reigning ideology of the Second Aliyah. His own Zionism was embedded in a secularized religiosity of the sort that Brenner found vacuous and unpersuasive. He challenged Ahad Ha'am therefore not because he agreed with Brenner but because he saw Brenner representing an authentic Palestinian voice; to silence him would do irreparable harm to the culture of the Yishuv, especially the labor sector that was its bulwark.

Gordon wrote Ahad Ha'am in the wake of his visit to Palestine from mid-September until the end of November 1911, and while the controversy was still raging. The trip was filled, not surprisingly, with bitter, inconclusive encounters with his critics, which Ahad Ha'am seemingly anticipated and their prospect may even have motivated him to come. He admitted he enjoyed the furious contentiousness of this period; he liked feeling once again that he was at the center of the Jewish literary hubbub. With this trip he placed himself where the intelligentsia was furious but also hugely preoccupied with him. For purely practical reasons, it was a difficult trip: he arrived in Haifa in the midst of a cholera epidemic and his plans to tour the Galilee on his way to Hadera and Petach Tikvah were stymied by the threat of quarantines and cumbersome Turkish regulations that he nonetheless managed to circumvent in some quarters when it was announced that Ahad Ha'am was in the entourage. In his numerous exchanges with Palestinian Jews, he found himself unable to persuade sometimes furious groups of the correctness of his position in the dispute with Brenner: they responded angrily when he denied that he had ever suggested that there was a sector of the Palestinian Jewish youth who found themselves attracted to various heterodox influences, including Christianity. (He had, in fact, suggested this in "Torah mi-Zion," an essay on the Brenner Affair that he published just before his trip.) When the socialist agitator Berl Katznelson challenged him on this score, Ahad Ha'am insisted that he had been misunderstood. At a meeting at the colony Ein Ganim, in Gordon's presence, Ahad Ha'am challenged his listeners to show him where it was that he had ever implied in his article, as they contended, that apostasy was rife in Palestine. It was this challenge that prompted Gordon to write his letter.[149]

Gordon begins by insisting the affair has concentrated so heavily on Ahad Ha'am because he is still seen by Palestinian Jews as personifying truthfulness in the Jewish nationalist world. It is all the more frustrating that Ahad Ha'am is unable to appreciate the role played by Brenner in speaking for the Yishuv's new and tenuous agrarian sector: labor's stability must be the top priority of all Jewish nationalists; since Palestinian Jewry has created a highly variegated society, it is only labor that can effectively embody all its interest groups. Hence for economic and political reasons labor's standing, self-confidence, and sense of its own newfound place in the larger Jewish world must be reinforced. Ahad Ha'am used to be in the past sensitive to the need to nurture the ability of Palestine's core constituency so that it could chart a sensible, self-confident course for itself. In his attack on Brenner he instead sets for himself a new, destructive course that renders the forces with which he is linked in the Yishuv vulnerable. Brenner is distinguished by his unwillingness to embrace easy answers or sanctities of any kind. In Palestine there is less need to be preoccupied with an abstract nationalism, and the reactions of Jews can be healthier, less self-absorbed, and more natural than elsewhere. There may be reason for preoccupation with apostasy outside Palestine but here, where Jewishness is both so pervasive and so unobtrusive, it remains a distant, rarified concern. Hence the lighthearted tone of Brenner's piece: its unconcern with an issue that Ahad Ha'am and others in the diaspora took deadly seriously testified not to Brenner's indifference to Judaism but, in Gordon's formulation, to the naturalness with which he lived his new Palestinian Jewish life.[150]

244   THE CURSES OF EXILE

In reply, Ahad Ha'am asked Gordon whether he would have defended Brenner's freedom of expression quite so vigorously if, instead of challenging the religious underpinnings of Judaism, he had questioned the ideal of Hebrew labor in Palestine and called for the use of Arab workers. This retort—which reminded Ahad Ha'am's Palestinian critics that they too espoused orthodoxies of their own—was his most astute contribution to his generally lackluster performance in the Brenner debate. Even here, though, his response was unfair in its unwillingness to recognize that Brenner too had expressed misgivings on this score with the more radical quarters of the Second Aliyah: Brenner, like Ahad Ha'am, in his emphasis on self-reliance and honesty had criticized the emphasis on Hebrew labor and had much more in common with him than either cared to admit. In the willingness of both of them to challenge what they saw as the Yishuv's fixation on Hebrew labor, the subject of Ahad Ha'am's last major essay published in 1912, they insisted on confronting perhaps the most fundamental problem in the socialist or labor Zionist arsenal.[151]

This article of Ahad Ha'am was essentially the culmination of his series on Palestine stretching back to the inaugural "Emet me-eretz Yisrael." In contrast to the earlier pieces, it was written in good humor and with some optimism. He called it "Sakh ha-kol" ("Summation"), which promised to provide the final chapter to a nicely annotated career: in this, his version, his career was launched by "Lo zeh ha-derekh," was consolidated by the recommendations of "Emet," and it culminated with a handy summary of his oeuvre with all the important events signposted—quite literally from beginning to end.

That "Sakh-ha-kol" too proved to be bitterly controversial was probably predictable. By now, as Ahad Ha'am observed around the time of its appearance, and with only a semblance of exaggeration, the very term "Ahad Ha'amist" had become something of an obscenity even in circles otherwise congenial to his teachings. The publication of "Sakh ha-kol" made him especially vulnerable: with this piece he seemed to come full circle from the chief diasporic spokesman for "practical Zionism" to one of its more relentless foes. Specifically his criticisms of "Hebrew labor"—which called for the use of a Jewish labor force in Palestine—as well as his antagonistic and resented role in the Brenner affair alienated him from much of the Second Aliyah. Nonetheless, he seemed in high spirits during his Palestinian trip in late 1911 and returned home energized, happy, and curiously upbeat. He returned to London convinced that

Palestinian Jewry had finally made its breakthrough for there was evidence of a beachhead on ancient soil that could not be dislodged. He felt no remorse about his role in the Brenner affair; he barely noted his deteriorating relationship with the more vibrant, politicized, and self-consciously progressive forces of the Yishuv.[152]

The Palestinian trip followed on the heels of his first foray to a Zionist congress since his dispiriting experience of 1897. The Tenth Zionist Congress in 1911 was a rather dull affair—filled with predictably long speeches, pomposity, and "foolishness and emptiness." But in its halls he found "new sounds, new songs" that convinced him of Jewish nationalism's vitality and impact: "Anyone able to see the new delegates, most of whom are from the West, and who sees how well they understand the national ideal and how it relates to our spiritual heritage— anyone who has experienced this will come away as comforted as I did." He left its antechambers confident of the future; also he claimed that for the first time he felt gratitude toward the Zionist movement for having brought about such salutary changes in Jewish life. Irenic he was not, but somewhat mellowed, and in this reasonably happy frame of mind he set out soon after the congress for his voyage to Palestine.[153]

His main reason for the trip, as he explained in "Sakh ha-kol," was to test whether his life's work was worthwhile now that he was "on the threshold of old age." He seemed obsessed with "Hebrew labor," a credo whose immediate benefits he saw but whose sagacity in the long run he believed was potentially dangerous. The issue came up repeatedly at the congress, he noted in his diary. Following the Turkish revolution of 1908 he aired his misgivings about pushing it too far, especially now that Palestine was "no longer a dark corner in which we can do as we wish once we have paid the requisite baksheesh." In a letter to Ussishkin, he warned: "It will no longer be possible to uproot trees planted by Arab laborers and demand highhandedly that all the work be given to Jews only." Renewed competition from all quarters of the Palestinian economy was certain to intensify; the most feasible course for Jews to take was to assume with renewed commitment "simple, useful work in the fields, in factories, and in schools and other institutions." Efforts to dominate the Palestinian economy were unrealistic, even self-destructive.[154]

His feeling that the call for exclusively Hebrew labor was misguided was the result of his mounting concern over the Arab question. Smilansky met him at the Jaffa port, and he warned him of the "pogrom-like atmosphere" dominating the town: Arabs felt that their own national goals—with which they were considerably more preoccupied in the wake of the Turkish revolution—were being impeded by the incursion of Jews. The Turkish officials, said Ahad Ha'am, who seemed at least vaguely sympathetic to Jews, gave the unfortunate impression of being unable to maintain order in the event that riots erupted. Everywhere, Ahad Ha'am said, in Jaffa as well as in the agricultural colonies, "the Jews were now in fear of Arabs." "It's just like in Russia," Smilansky insisted. In this context the call for Hebrew labor promoted by "radical" though "idealistic" forces was potentially inflammatory. Even more disturbing were attempts to dislodge Arabs from work when no experienced Jews were available: such actions only served to retard the Yishuv's economic growth and fanned discontent.[155]

Traveling primarily in Judea and briefly in the Galilee, he surveyed the use of Arab labor in the colonies and he noted where relations seemed amicable. Economically speaking, the healthiest colonies were those that adopted the cultivation of domestic animals, chickens, and vegetables. Ahad Ha'am had long urged colonists to do exactly this to wean them away from luxury goods like wine production. He admitted that some of the colonies most devoted to Hebrew labor pleased him for national spirit was high, Hebrew was spoken, and economic self-reliance was seen as a priority. In a long exchange with the colonists of Ein Ganim he asked why they had so few Jewish laborers and was told that Jews avoided the harsher tasks and their wages were higher than the wages of the Arabs. He noted, happily, that some of the earlier enmity between the pious farmers and irreligious, younger laborers was waning, in no small measure because of the declining religiosity of the farmers themselves; the size of the Jewish labor force had simultaneously increased at a respectable rate.[156] Curiously, he wrote nothing of his heated exchange over the Brenner controversy at Ein Ganim; in his description of Ein Ganim, too, his main interest was Arab-Jewish relations.

It was only now that the Arab threat to Jewish interests in Palestine emerged as a major concern of his. As he admitted, in 1910, to Ben Hillel Ha-Cohen: "True, I had always thought that in the end this conflict would break out and I said so explicitly [in "Emet"] twenty years ago. . . . but I never thought that it would occur so soon when our power in our country is still so limited and hardly felt." He feared that the attitude of many of the settlers toward Arabs was haughty; he mourned when he heard of incidents when Jews abused them. This could well lead to tragedy, he remarked to Smilansky in November 1913, "even if we manage to achieve control over the land. If Palestinian Jewry is unable to exercise restraint and decency now that it holds little power, how much worse will it be when we control the land and its Arab inhabitants?" The Zionists, he would complain to Smilansky in February 1914, still insist on looking at this problem through the naive prism of Herzl's *Altneuland*. They have proven unwilling to face what it means for them to claim a land on which another people lives and has no intention of leaving. In the future, once this is finally understood, the Zionists will look back with utter amazement at this willful ignorance.[157]

His apprehensions did not completely overshadow his recognition of the Yishuv's achievements in "Sakh ha-kol." There he noted with approval the improvement in the schools of the Yishuv. (Jerusalem's gymnasium, for instance, made a "good impression" on him.) The site selected for the proposed Haifa Technicum impressed him as suitable. Yet, when capturing his impressions of the trip he concentrated mostly on the Jews' desire to conquer labor which was fueled, he admitted, by a commendable rise in nationalist spirit among the Palestinian Jewish youth, but the campaign was inherently unrealistic and not only because of the small size and lack of distinction of the Jewish labor force. More importantly, he argued, Jews cannot be farmers—at least not the sort who throw themselves into a lifelong, intimate, soul-numbing dependency on the land. No doubt, he continued, the shoring up of small colonies in the Yishuv which are frequently very distant from one another but where the Jewish spirit has reached heights impossible elsewhere represents the greatest achievement of Jewish nationalism. And to the extent to which these colonies exert a decisive impact over the cultural life of the area, the Arab question itself will be resolved: "Once the cultural atmosphere of the land is shaped in the Jewish spirit, it is possible that the Arabs too can be absorbed. For haven't they been here since ancient times, and quite possibly some of them are members of our own people?" he jotted down in his diary.[158]

Despite his mounting sense of the tragic implications in the relations between Arabs and Jews in Palestine, he resorted to a vague romanticism typical of his circle: the hope that peace will reign once Jewish nationalism is secure in the hearts of Jews, and Arab enmity will be worn down by a recognition of vague, apocryphal blood ties between the European Jewish settlers and their new, suspicious Arab neighbors. What most enraged his readers, however, were his ruminations about the Jewish character: too urban and Western for a life of soul-numbing rural hardship.

The suspicions about him on the part of the younger, radical set in the Yishuv were already acute in 1911: Abraham Kustitski, a veteran of the Second Aliyah, tells in his memoirs of Ahad Ha'am's tour of Metulah and Yavniel. At Metulah he addressed the farmers and laborers from a podium in the synagogue where he presented "platitudes of the sort that I had already heard a hundred and one times from all of our great ones. In short, that we should work hard, be satisfied with little, suffer, etc." These were leveled with such a pejorative tone, with criticisms aimed not only at the workers of Metulah but at all those of Palestine, that the laborers there were stunned and demoralized. By the time the talk ended, according to Kustinski, and despite the speaker's distinction, the hall had all but emptied. The next day they asked to talk with him to set the record straight—the majority of the colony's laborers had objected even to proposing a meeting; they felt it would be a waste of time but their leaders insisted because of Ahad Ha'am's esteemed reputation. He then told them he hadn't any time. When they criticized his unwillingness to listen to another viewpoint, he replied, "I came here to see and understand, and I now already know it all." The answer sounds somewhat improbable, closer to what the laborers' might have imagined the haughty Ahad Ha'am would say than what he actually said, but, on the whole, Kustinski's reconstruction of a self-righteous, self-confident, patronizing Ahad Ha'am is probably an accurate account. Similarly, an exasperated Berl Katznelson wrote in a letter soon after Ahad Ha'am's appearance at Ein Ganim, "Here today was the 'Guide to the Perplexed of Our Time.' The master of reason. This man, who complains constantly that he is not understood by others—how far is he from understanding us." Katznelson's nemesis, the leader of the rival Ha-Po'el Ha-Tsair Joseph Aharonovich, would later credit the failings of "Sakh ha-kol" to Ahad Ha'am's misguided attempt to transcend his proverbial negativism and make a positive recommendation: the resultant stance was so devoid of pragmatism and ambition as to rob the Yishuv of all chance of success.[159]

At the heart of "Sakh ha-kol" and at the core of what his critics would now call his "national theology," was still his belief in "the instinct of national self-preservation." It was this force that inspired people to shape history for the benefit of their nation irrespective of their stated ideological commitments or their assumptions as to what objective reality would permit:

What does it matter if work is devoted to objects that are unattainable? . . . History does not trouble with programs; it creates what it chooses to create as prompted by our "instinct of self-preservation." Whether we ourselves understand the true importance and purpose of our work, or whether we prefer not to understand it—in either case history works through us, and reaches its goal by virtue of what we do. Only the task will be all the more difficult and will take all the longer if true understanding does not come to our aid.[160]

What he witnessed at Basel and in Palestine reconfirmed his belief that this instinct of Jewish self-preservation was still at work, and that the consolidation of the cultural center he had long predicted essential for their survival was being established.

Extravagant talk of politics and diplomacy notwithstanding, the real work policies of the Zionist movement was in the hands of the practical camp ("for whom a national Judaism is at the very core of their being"). While not officially repudiating Herzl's Basel Declaration, they have come to overlook it. They spend their time launching schools, buying small plots of land for agrarian cultivation—in short pursuing those activities that the more politically minded Zionists have always found petty diversions from the larger task as they understood it. But this work dominates the movement, despite its token loyalty to Herzl. In Palestine itself, the pretensions of the National Fund—whose original goal as Herzl envisioned it was the purchase of all the ancient homeland—has been proven fatuous: land has now become particularly expensive and any purchasing of it by foreigners in the wake of the Turkish revolution is very difficult. But what is being done is exactly what Ahad Ha'am had advocated for decades: with great agrarian flexibility, little interference from outsiders, be they the JCA, Rothschild, or the Hovevei Zion, farmers were happier, the once-hated stratum of administrators encouraged self-sufficiency, and the mood was positive and hopeful: "Any visitor to Palestine who brings with him, as I did, painful and humiliating recollections of years ago, must rejoice beyond measure at all this."[161]

The only feature, then, of this colonization drive that was unrealistic was the emphasis on Hebrew labor. Clearly from the ranks of Jewry can emerge figures like the biblical Boaz, gentleman farmers who "go out every morning to their field or vineyard, who look after their workmen as they plough or sow their land . . . and who do not mind giving them a hand when necessary." But, on the whole, the land is not capable of attracting and holding the urbanized soul, as demonstrated by the large number of children raised by Palestinian Jewish farmers who abandoned Palestine to move abroad. They find it impossible to tie themselves to the yoke of a lifetime of drudgery despite a frequently intense longing for the land. For the true farmer this choice would be unthinkable; such profound ties to the land are only conceivable if civilization exerts little impact.[162]

Most manual labor in Palestine was being performed by Arabs and any attempt by Jews to change the situation was doomed to fail. Even the hope that Jewish laborers from abroad—fired up with enthusiasm and a belief in rural socialism—could prove decisive in settling this issue was groundless. True, it was in the colonies' self-interest to increase the number of Jewish laborers. This pool would certainly remain small, though, and the argument that they were capable of dominating Palestinian labor is simply belied by the desire of the best of them to escape and become self-supporting farmers themselves as soon as they can. The newly created *kvutvot*—the core of what would soon emerge as the kibbutz movement—Ahad Ha'am airily dismissed. (It "cannot be expected to develop to such an extent that it is able to bring about a radical change in the labor problem.") He concluded that any attempt to redeem the Holy Land in a thoroughgoing fashion was bound to fail: in Palestine "it is possible to buy bits of land here and there, but it is not possible to redeem the land as a whole, or even most of it. It might be feasible to establish beautiful colonies on the 'redeemed' land but it is impossible to settle on them more than a handful of poor colonists." Nonetheless what would certainly emerge here—now that its foundations had been secured—was a society where one could begin to point with pride where the very best of Jewish life was at least "in the process of creation." What had been created, and no doubt would be further improved upon, is a place where the collective Jewish soul had been cleansed, comforted, and healed. He did not preclude the possibility of doing still more, but

in our present state of spiritual disorganization we can have little idea of the capabilities of our national strength, nor of what can be achieved once all of its forces are united around a single center and quickened by a single, strong, and healthy spirit. The generations to come will know the full measure of their power. . . . For us, we cannot be concerned with the hidden mysteries of the distant future. It is enough for us to know the things that have been already revealed, the things done by us, and those that will be done by our children soon.[163]

His effort in "Sakh ha-kol" to size up his and his generation's achievements was far more positive than anything he had previously written on Palestine. He still had critical things to say about the pretensions of some of the colonists, the unstable relations between Arabs and Jews that would result from a policy stressing Hebrew labor, and the narrowness of those who still remained convinced of the wisdom of a Herzlian approach to the revival of Palestine. But his stance was less strident; even when critical of certain aspects of the movement, he was more bemused than alarmed. There was every sign, he seemed to be saying, that his side of the Jewish nationalist debate had won.

This, perhaps, is what made his choice for the last essay in the fourth and final volume of his collected essays, *Al Parashat Derakhim,* particularly surprising. "An Experiment that Failed," which appeared for the first time in 1912 in the collection, summed up the achievements, or lack thereof, of the Bnei Moshe. The title, or so it would seem, told it all: here was the only article he ever wrote on the organization that was most closely associated with him and he minimized its legacy, referring to it as an outright failure. (Not surprisingly, he enraged some of his closest friends: Barzilai, devoted to Ahad Ha'am until the end, endeavored to emphasize the group's achievements in the New York-based periodical *Ha-Toren,* and he admitted to Ahad Ha'am that he felt pained by his treatment of their work together.) Ahad Ha'am's article consisted of a brief introduction and a selection of documents, mostly letters he had written. The piece was seemingly constructed to show that the Bnei Moshe's membership was inadequate to the task, its leadership ill equipped, its goals vague. At the time he said that he had planned to write a sustained study of the group, but he eventually found that this was impossible for him to do, perhaps because he was too close to it. For years he had given the impression that his feelings about the Bnei Moshe were lukewarm, that he had been its leader for only a short time, that his attachments to it had been severed years before it had been closed down. Now, in his introduction to the article, he was more candid:

I feel in the depths of my soul that I cannot complete the last portion of my collected essays without putting before my readers a reckoning of my relationship to the Bnei Moshe, my involvement in its work and its influence on the course of my life. . . . The group was established at the same time as the appearance of my first article. . . . and for several years thereafter my literary work was connected and tied to the work of this society, this written work both influencing the group and being shaped by it, as I have hinted on several occasions in my essays, though those outside the group might not always have been able to understand the hidden meaning of such allusions.[164]

Indeed, never before had Ahad Ha'am, who had always insisted that from the outset he had opposed the Bnei Moshe's secrecy, owned up to the extent to which he himself had participated in it, to the point of making the real meaning of some of his more important essays inaccessible to those outside the group. More striking was his admission that it seemed to him wrong, and because of the abiding influence that the group would continue to exert on him throughout his lifetime, to complete his collected essays without this assessment of the Bnei Moshe. Otherwise, he said, it was impossible to understand his life's work. Indeed, he implied, even some fifteen years after the group had disbanded it retained its role in his life as one of the few concrete manifestations of his teaching.

A good many former devotees objected to the essay's title and to its inclusion of material accusing them of a wide range of sins: indolence, incompetence, even betrayal. Some felt that he had mocked them and belittled their legacy, or that the piece was akin to an exercise in sadomasochism—an odd way to cap off a distinguished career.

Odd as it might have appeared, if taken on its own terms it was quite understandable. In fact, he intended the piece as an ode to Bnei Moshe, the centerpiece of his career as he admitted here. His public life began with it, his first article was inspired by it, and he remained, long after its official demise, committed to its values. But he always felt most comfortable speaking, even about things that he loved, in negative terms. Celebration grated on him; even when examining a project like the Bnei Moshe that remained very close to his heart—as the introduction to the piece most clearly attested—he felt easiest airing his misgivings.

When this essay is placed side by side with the contemporaneous "Sakh ha-kol," which was precisely what Ahad Ha'am intended his readers to do since in his collected essays they appeared in sequence, he made it clear that he felt that despite the group's dissolution its values had eventually managed to impose themselves on Zionism. The very term "Sakh ha-kol" was meant to refer readers back to the Bnei Moshe: this was the title of one of its major internal publications. The ultimate success of Bnei Moshe is underlined in "Sakh ha-kol" by his assertion that, quite irrespective of what Zionists might say, they were in the process of creating "a fixed center for our national spirit and culture, which will create a new spiritual bond between the scattered sectors of the people and by virtue of its spiritual influence will move them to a new national life." True, the more ambitious goals of the Bnei Moshe remain unrealized; but time was on their side. His life's work, or so he concluded by the time he brought the last volume of *Al Parashat Derakhim* to press, had been well spent: Bnei Moshe had made its impact (although it was not widely recognized, another reason for publishing this essay); his teachings had their abiding impact, even on circles that at first openly mocked them or perhaps still did. True, the bulk of his time was spent now as a middle-level company employee in London with a decent salary and comfortable home. But, more importantly, he was the preeminent intellectual of Jewish nationalism. This was his other reason for writing "An Experiment that Failed" for, acutely aware as he still was of the politics of reputation, he knew that rumors remained about the Bnei Moshe and his association with it that needed to be cleared up. Perhaps the piece wasn't history, he told Zalman Epstein, but it was essential for the sake of his good name.[165]

Nowhere would he show how deeply he had reflected on what it meant to build and sustain a reputation as in his essay on Maimonides, first published in 1904; he included it as the lead piece in volume four of *Al Parashat Derakhim*. The title of the essay, "The Supremacy of Reason," soon became a euphemism for Ahad Ha'am, shorthand for his relentlessly cerebral approach to life and its problems. In the Yishuv, in particular, that title was widely used to describe him, ironically and deprecatingly. To his loyalists, though, the designation confirmed their belief that his own achievement was comparable to that of Maimonides in medieval Jewry.

Ahad Ha'am began the essay, written to coincide with the seven hundredth anniversary of Maimonides's death, by chastising the cultural-national laxities of his generation. Previously this anniversary went unnoticed but then there was much less need to make a special effort to recall Maimonides whose writings played a role in the daily lives of Jews. His "Thirteen Principles" figured even into the Jewish liturgy; for the elite his philosophical work was deemed truly indispensable. It is precisely the indifference toward Maimonides—"nowadays one may spend a great deal of time reading Hebrew articles and books without coming across a single reference to Maimonides," he writes—that makes it necessary to highlight his life and death and to call special attention to his achievements that no longer are recognized as part and parcel of our routine. With the excessive materialism of our age, spiritual issues no longer dominate "progressive thought" which is inundated by "politics, by hard and concrete facts." To call attention to Maimonides is one way of making certain that issues other than "those of bread and *Nachtasyl*" are addressed—the latter referring to the support for the 1903 Uganda proposal as a temporary haven for the Jews. Here Ahad Ha'am's makes it clear once again that his cultural and political priorities are altogether compatible, even identical with the most definitive of Jewish proof-texts.[166]

There are striking similarities, he shows, between his life and that of Maimonides. As he describes it, the route taken by Maimonides in the direction of rationalism was a singularly heroic one in a medieval Jewish context. He emerged from a milieu that bore an uncanny resemblance to Skvire or for that matter the Sadagora rebbe's court, and which similarly was fiercely opposed to reason; it was narrow, closed and stifling:

The supremacy of reason! Can we today, after the eighteenth and nineteenth centuries, conceive of the revolutionary importance of this phrase in Maimonides' time? . . . Then reason was almost hated, despised as a dangerous tempter and seducer. . . . The simpler and more reasonable the answer, the more suspect and less satisfactory it was; the stranger the answer, the more violently opposed to balanced reason, the more readily it was welcomed and accepted.[167]

It was this extreme antirationalism that Maimonides confronted in his early years in the more militant and oppressive side of Islam, that gave him his "intense antagonism toward blind faith that produces in its wake religious fanaticism." Such blind faith as this caused the greatest distrust for rationalism. He thus emerged as an extreme rationalist, as someone who could not abide with half-measures. It was, explains Ahad Ha'am, Maimonides's earliest impressions of the "ugly side" of antirationalism that never left his side and influenced much of what he would subsequently do. In this description, historical distinctions between the prophets of ancient times, the seminal philosopher of medieval Judaism, and the moral philosopher of contemporary Zionism conflated as Ahad Ha'am showed his identification with Maimonides to be as intense as any in his life.[168]

He made this analogy clear in the way he constructed his argument in the essay to demonstrate how the central components of his concept of a "spiritual center" were prefigured in Maimonides' *Moreh Nevukhim*, his *Guide to the Perplexed*. In this, no doubt the most scholarly of his essays, he also provides his most vivid exposition on the character of this center—and makes clear what sort of relationship would exist between this center and the average Jew. Shielded in "The Supremacy of Reason" by its stated scholarly agenda, Ahad Ha'am made his case more starkly than he would anywhere else.

In defining what was according to Maimonides the purpose of material existence, he explains it as the creation of the perfect human being in possession of "acquired intellect," which itself is the perfect human attribute. What, then, is the purpose for the existence of the human race since the vast majority are incapable of achieving these austere intellectual or moral heights? There are, as he explains, two categories of human beings; "potential" ones and "real" ones. Only the latter, a small and rarified minority, can potentially (though typically it is rare even for them) achieve a state of "acquired intellect." No more than one such person might emerge out of any given generation. It is this small, crucial elite that is engaged directly in the arduous process, and they are therefore dependent on others to fulfill their material needs. Consequently, the function performed by the majority of humanity, incapable as they are of "picturing the idea in their souls," is to provide for the fundamental needs of the few:

> The existence of the majority has a purpose of its own different from that of the existence of the chosen minority. This minority is an end in itself—it is the embodiment of the most perfect form of the inferior world. Whereas the purpose of the majority lies not in its own existence but in that it creates the conditions necessary to the existence of the minority. It creates human society with all its cultural possessions (in the material sense of the term) without which wisdom cannot spread.[169]

It is in society that all people interlink—and irrespective of their capability to "picture the ideal in their soul," it is here that they confront their mutual interdependence. For the potential man society represents the purpose of his being; for the real man, social organisms serve as a means toward an end and one which, unlike transitory human society, is eternal.

As Ahad Ha'am explained elsewhere, and with considerable exasperation, in a 1907 essay in which he said that he hoped finally to put to rest misconceptions about the meaning of the "spiritual center," the essential material needs of people will have to be filled: ". . . although the center would exert a spiritual influence on its circumference," he writes there, "in itself it would be a place like other places, where people were made of body and soul and where they required food and clothing and for these reasons it would have to concern itself with material issues like how to best design an economic system. It could not exist without farmers, laborers, craftsmen and merchants." These, as his critics sensed, would represent no more than instrumental functions for Ahad Ha'am's ideal society where the masses provided the necessary infrastructure for a spiritual elite whose sustenance was their raison d'être. Similar to Maimonides' actual men, a small cadre of rarified Palestinian Jewish pioneers would constitute the core of the Jewish spiritual revival; they would assume responsibility for the future of their people; their own future, on its most prosaic level, would be secured by the work of Palestine's "farmers, laborers, craftsmen and merchants"—Ahad Ha'am's present-day manifestation of what Maimonides intended by term "potential people." Their participation in the rebuilding of their people would be indirect at best. Their role, though, would be indispensable, as he reiterated in every statement he made on the role of those remote from cultural production in the life of the Yishuv.[170]

In his reflections on Maimonides, Ahad Ha'am speculated, that had Maimonides launched his career with *The Guide to the Perplexed*—his attempt to provide religious skeptics with a rationale for a philosophically embedded belief—no doubt he would have been branded as heterodox and ignored thereafter. Rather, and as his sketch of his career makes clear, he remained in his first works on the immeasurably less provocative terrain of rabbinic literature. Then he produced his commentary on the Mishna aimed at providing a clearer designation of doctrine and practice; his *Mishna Torah,* more novel in organization and intent, set out to reform popular practice. Only then did he turn his attention to *The Guide* which, once it appeared, could not be repudiated as decisively as some fundamentalist circles would have liked because of the eminence its author had achieved in rabbinic studies: his rabbinic works were already classics; his philosophy had to be treated with guarded respect (at least during Maimonides' lifetime) even by those who distrusted the philosophical enterprise.[171]

Ahad Ha'am made clear in his appraisal of Maimonides that he found his rationalism excessive and insufficiently attuned to the multiplicity of the human personality; hence, his designation of the philosopher as personifying the "supremacy of reason" was meant, at least in this respect, to be ironic, a way of distancing himself and his own approach from that of the greatest thinker in the Jewish pantheon. At the same time, he appropriated Maimonides for himself, claiming him, however indirectly, as the inspiration for his repertoire's most original concept, the notion of a "spiritual center," and as the personification of reasoned rebellion against the tyranny of obscurantism which mirrored Ahad Ha'am's own education and his rebellion against it. Finally, he made it clear that he saw Maimonides as a guide to the politics of reputation—as someone skilled in the building of careers, in the charting of a sensible course by which ideas that otherwise would have been deemed out of bounds were integrated over time into the corpus of traditional Judaism.

Countervailing forces would at some time be responsible for dislodging his teachings, as when an anti-Maimonidean reaction convulsed much of the European Jewish world in the century after the medieval philosopher's death. Such setbacks, however troubling and demoralizing they seemed, were temporary. Far more important was the fact that the forces were in place to ensure the success of one's ideals, as long as they were truly representative of Judaism's authentic urges. His own quest for supremacy, he assured others, was not personal; nor did he measure success in terms of personal achievement. As his disciple Leon Simon would declaim on Ahad Ha'am's sixtieth birthday, in 1917: "Strictly speaking, Ahad Ha'am is not sixty years of age, or any age at all. Ahad Ha'am is an abstraction, a sort of collective name for a body of ideas about Judaism and the Jewish people."[172] Simon had learned his lesson well: it was specifically this message of impersonality as a prerequisite in Judaism for celebrity that would remain until the end of Ahad Ha'am's life at the core of his thought, the centerpiece of an ideology that saw self-abnegation as a prerequisite of national revival.

6

An Elusive Supremacy

In their days there was no king in Israel and every man did as he pleased.

Judges 21, 25

I

That Ahad Ha'am still remained outside the Zionist movement was by now little more than a curious gesture; it had become an act of public defiance toward an organization that had come to see him as one of its sources of orthodoxy. For the majority of its leading figures, in Russia and abroad, he was a respected teacher who, precisely because he was considered too severe, too principled, and too exasperated with the petty compromises of normal political life, endowed their enterprise with vision and moral underpinning. This did not mean that they looked to him for day-to-day tactical guidance (though during the negotiations over the Balfour Declaration Weizmann would and with considerable benefit). By the turn of the century to be accused of Ahad Ha'amism meant that one was rarified, apolitical, impractical, and culturally behind the times: deaf to the turn-of-the-century modernism that so reshaped Hebraism along with much of the rest of the European scene. Still, the importance of a cultural revival through Hebrew instruction in schools, and a Jewish university, and a solid Palestinian Jewish agrarian base were by now part and parcel of Zionism's agenda.[1]

Ahad Ha'am did not fail to notice this. As he observed wryly at the Tenth Zionist Congress, in 1911, his first appearance since 1897, his ideas were widely embraced even by those who attacked him and praised his enemies. The passionate disavowal of Ahad Ha'am by so many of the delegates appeared to him little more than a ritual of sorts, a reflex born of residual loyalties to Herzl who the movement found unable to disavow formally, though it had otherwise done so. A good example was the fact that the current members of the Smaller Actions Committee, elected at the congress, were, broadly speaking all from Ahad Ha'am's own camp: Otto Warburg, Nahum Sokolow, Victor Jacobson, Shmarya Levin, and Arthur Hantke.[2]

Even his fiercest critics could not avoid his reach, as was clear from the most comprehensive attack on him of the period, the fifty-odd page article "Ahad Ha'am u-venei Bnei Moshe" by Ben Avigdor, published in 1913 in *Netivot*. Ben Avigdor savaged nearly everything about him: his public activity was declared vacuous, his ideology derivative, even his character weak, vacillating, and destructive to all who had dealings with him. For Ben Avigdor the movement's true heroes were Lilienblum and Herzl, its men of action. They, unlike Ahad Ha'am, understood what it meant to play the game of politics. The fact that Ben Avigdor, one of Hebrew literature's most prominent bookmen, felt the need to unburden himself publicly and at such length in an attack on a Hebrew writer without an editorial office, without a formal political position, and who had published barely a word in the last several years, testified vividly to the shadow that Ahad Ha'am continued to cast.[3]

True, Ahad Ha'am may have touched Ben Avigdor's life more than most: Ben Avigdor's first essay appeared in print at more or less the same time when "Lo zeh ha-derekh" was published which overshadowed his own, less celebrated debut. Nonetheless, Ahad Ha'am's essay so inspired Ben Avigdor that he agreed to be dispatched to Warsaw to serve as secretary of its Bnei Moshe and, later, as editor of Ahiasaf, the publishing house under the aegis of the semisecret order. In 1891, as one of Ahad Ha'am's most devoted disciples, he wrote *Shene hezyonot*, the adoring portrait of Ahad Ha'am where he compared him, none-too-obliquely, to Moses. Within a few years, having grown disenchanted with Ahad Ha'am after working with him, he started his own publishing house that broke with the master's standards, placing an emphasis on fiction over nonfiction. Ben Avigdor could not escape, though, what seemed to him the pervasive, intrusive influence of the man. Typical was the way in which, even in a commemorative volume published in 1916, celebrating Ben Avigdor's literary achievements, the cultural historian Fishel Lachower—and in what he may have thought a gesture of considerable generosity—referred to Ben Avigdor as the "Ahad Ha'am of Hebrew belletristics." That here, too, Ben Avigdor was described by Lachower as a worthy, if scrappy and recalcitrant heir to Ahad Ha'am's legacy, bitterly frustrated him.

His essay's shrillness—its raw, staccato, undisguised venom—testifies as little else could to Ahad Ha'am's supremacy. By now he was the emblem of Hebraic orthodoxy; his heirs, dubious, grateful, vengeful, full of awe and frustration albeit deeply ambivalent, attacked him with everything at their disposal.[4]

Not at its very beginning, but some four pages into the article, Ben Avigdor acknowledges that it is for him a very personal exercise: the first thing he ever wrote, his first foray into politics, his first encounter with hero worship, were all, he admits, connected with Ahad Ha'am. Like many others he was stunned and transformed by his reading of "Lo zeh ha-derekh"; but close, day-to-day contact with Ahad Ha'am, with his carping, his lack of confidence, his unending criticisms, all eventually alienated him. As he expressed it in what was one of the few examples of understatement in the essay, Ahad Ha'am's behavior "did little to inspire one's soul." With the appearance of an authentic hero, Theodor Herzl, who exuded both confidence and vitality, finally Ben Avigdor escaped from Ahad Ha'am's dull, infertile corner. He says that he was not surprised when, as soon as Herzl appeared on the scene, he too was subjected to Ahad Ha'am's petty, pilpulistic barbs that served to convince so many in the nationalist camp that they had followed the wrong leader all along.[5]

As a thinker, according to Ben Avigdor, Ahad Ha'am had little to recommend him. Seen widely as a prophet (a theme that dominates much of Ben Avigdor's essay), as the "rabbi of the diaspora," as the father of Hebrew thought in our time, and as our generation's guide for the perplexed, it is clear upon close scrutiny his philosophy is unimpressive ("his Torah is no Torah"), his prophecies clearly false. He offers no coherent guide for the perplexed; how can he since he is so hopelessly perplexed himself?[6]

Ben Avigdor concerns himself particularly with Ahad Ha'am's inadequacies as a man of action. What inspired him to write the essay, he says, was the fourth volume of *Al Parashat Derakhim* with its "An Experiment that Failed," an appropriate epitaph for all Ahad Ha'am's public work. The Bnei Moshe itself can barely be said to have existed: it was not-permitted to experience the normal cycles of birth, maturity, and death. It was instead born sick, already a victim in its infancy thanks to Ahad Ha'am's timidity, lack of foresight or practicality. So his movement left barely a trace, and all that is remembered are a few of its publications, the most memorable of which, he claims, were written by Ben Avigdor himself. Otherwise nothing is left since little existed in the first place. Now, he says, the time has come to examine why it is that whatever Ahad Ha'am attempts is unsuccessful, worse off than before he turns his attention to it:

I think the time has now arrived, with the spectacle of *Al Parashat Derakhim* having been brought to its culmination, and with the passing of twenty-five years since the establishment of the Bnei Moshe, to examine the foundations of this "experiment that failed"—to recite the "truth about Ahad Ha'am" even if this truth is bitter and difficult for him to take, and as part and parcel of this corpus there will also be included the "truth about the Bnei Moshe."[7]

The truth is that Ahad Ha'am is a "European from head to toe," an aristocrat of the spirit, a great writer and "deep thinker" (something that Ben Avigdor alternately admits and rejects) and also "a complete idler [batlan] in regard to practical affairs."[8] Bookish, pessimistic, and lacking faith in himself or those around him, he should have avoided all com-munal activity, which for someone like him is strange, incomprehensible terrain. Though he complains frequently that he is misunderstood, the fact is that it is he who cannot manage to understand the world as he is so alien to its rhythms and demands. Perhaps this is traceable to his "pampered" and "delicate" childhood, which produced an excessively capricious man. No matter how he came to be this way, he remains ill prepared for worldly endeavors of any kind, particularly the revival of the Jewish people.[9]

The sturdy, politically savvy counterweights to Ahad Ha'am in the nationalist camp are Lilienblum and Herzl. When compared with them it becomes all the more clear that Ahad Ha'am has no real agenda and no notion of what he or anyone else should do. Whereas Herzl devoted "all his energy, his life, his soul" to Jewish nationalism, Ahad Ha'am's activities in comparison are "sheer childishness." Carefully scrutinized, all that remains of them is their hubris, as exemplified by his insistence that it is he who possesses the "truth from Palestine": Who has deter-mined that this is the truth? Why does he insist that it comes from Palestine? He continues: "Why not the truth from Odessa, or Berdichev, or the Pale of Settlement?" This would have been more accurate; it also would have then been easier to spot it for what it was—merely off-the-mark speculations of a diaspora pundit.[10]

This was the most extreme example of a trend in prewar Hebraist circles where an antipathy for Ahad Ha'am became something of a trademark, a code for emerging assumptions about Jewry's national culture. His opponents, as Dan Miron argues in his seminal work on the cultural history of the period, sought to overturn his entire lexicon, the "Odessa dictionary" as he calls it, with its emphasis on "Judaism," "culture," "nation," "history," "science," and "development." In its place they substituted a new terminology featuring words like "beliefs," "creation," "individual," "mystery," and "revolution." Ahad Ha'am's decline, says Miron, was probably the outstanding marker of this new epoch in Hebrew literary life.[11]

The change coincided with a profound crisis in which, as signaled at the Hebraic conference of 1909, literary Hebrew appeared to lose much of its readership. What had been for several decades a maskilic readership, dependent upon Hebrew for their sense of the larger world, was now making way for a more Europeanized cultural consumer considerably less dependent upon Hebrew as a linguisitic mediator. Those who sought a Jewish language typically preferred Yiddish to Hebrew, especially when under the inspired leadership of Mendele, Shalom Aleichem, and Peretz it produced some of its greatest masterpieces in these years. Until the turn of the century the writers and consumers of Hebrew came mostly from the *batei midrash,* the traditional study houses, and their backgrounds led them to venerate tradition, or at least to fear a radical break from the traditions of their fathers, thus defining the boundaries of their modernity. For them the delicate compromises of Ahad Ha'am, his belief that change was slow but irrevocable, his preference for the more resonant voices of tradition, even his definitiveness—all these were persuasive. For their children, though, raised in homes where Hebrew newspapers were the norm, and whose Russian schooling was mostly uncontested by parents, the intellectual scene of the previous generation looked timid, bourgeois, and stuffy. The towering intellectual of that earlier generation, Ahad Ha'am, personified its failings. Their prooftexts were different (they preferred Tolstoy, Schopenhauer, and Nietzsche to Buckle, Spencer, Mill, and Renan). The maskilic, middle-class drawing rooms that had featured *Ha-Shiloach* in the late 1890s had given way, as we have seen, to crowded student flats, the collective living spaces of the current arbiters of Hebrew taste. Differences of class, politics, background, and temperament produced a generational gulf to which Ahad Ha'am claimed he was altogether indifferent.[12]

He was the only significant Hebraist of his generation, according to Miron, not to court the youth to some extent. Instead he treated them with cool, distant condescension. Nonetheless, as much as he chose to minimize the younger generation's importance, those around him could neither ignore them nor their influence.[13]

Hence even in the issue of *Ha-Shiloach* published in March 1914 to mark the twenty-fifth anniversary of Ahad Ha'am's literary debut with "Lo zeh ha-derekh," the articles were full of references to his "opponents" who were themselves rather well represented in the issue. Some of the more blatantly critical pieces were rejected by the journal's editor, Klausner, who nonetheless justified the volume's ambiguous assessment of Ahad Ha'am's contribution, saying that this was done out of consideration for Ahad Ha'am himself who was known to shun literary celebrations but could better tolerate a dispassionate evaluation of his work and influence. Klausner therefore called it a "celebration and appraisal," which, he said, better represented Ahad Ha'am's critical attentiveness and uncompromising scrutiny. Klausner's argument seems rather forced: in fact, as was clear from nearly every article, there was no other way to write about Ahad Ha'am now that his aging, self-consciously beleaguered camp tended to define itself in contradistinction to its opponents. No more vivid proof exists of the waning of his power, and at the same time his abiding cultural influence, than this curious 1914 tribute to his achievement.[14]

Among his critics who were allotted space (several of whom numbered among his good friends) were Dubnow, Yehoshua Thon, and also Armand Kaminka, who starts his essay with the admission of how awkward he feels writing for the volume since "from beginning to end" he disagrees with everything Ahad Ha'am stands for. Even others less distant from the strictures of Ahad Ha'amism proved to be remarkably defensive in their praise of him: Shimon Bernfeld, for instance, insisted that he sensed that the tide was changing and—just as the reputations of the philosopher Moses Hayyim Luzzato and the poet Judah Leib Gordon had waned and waxed in recent decades—Ahad Ha'am's diminished reputation was on the verge of an upswing. Both Aaron Abraham Kabak and Thon attempt to answer without attribution Ben

Avigdor's charges: "Heaven forbid," insists Thon, that one should say that all that Ahad Ha'am does is "tear things down." For Abraham Zarvozsky, who identifies himself as a hidebound critic of the cultural Zionist, it is nonetheless clear that Ahad Ha'am, no less than the other great Jewish thinkers of the past (Maimonides is one he cites), tends to be defined in the public imagination by his opponents whose inordinate attention is a sign of his greatness: it suggests, says Zarzovsky, that long after the influence of his opponents has dissipated, his will remain.[15]

Even those who were otherwise comfortable with Ahad Ha'am's formulations admitted in their articles that they could not easily explain the reason for his unparalleled standing. This was a major theme of the volume, and not surprisingly in view of its intent to celebrate and chart his career. What nonetheless stands out is their uncertainty, repeated in essay after essay, and the degree to which his achievement perplexed them, particularly since he produced no pupils, no movement, no party. "Countless times," begins Bernfeld in the lead article, "have I searched my heart for an answer to the question: What is the source of the literary power of Ahad Ha'am and why is it that he exerted such great influence over the Hebraic nationalists of his generation?" This is much the same problem posed by friends (Kleinman, Kabak, Zalman Epstein) and foes (Kaminka, Bar Tuviah); the lines separating the two remain somewhat blurred here, as "supporters" and "detractors" themselves acknowledge repeatedly in the periodical.[16]

For Bernfeld it was the fundamental comprehensiveness of Ahad Ha'am's system that distinguished it; in contrast to Ben Avigdor's view, Bernfeld saw Ahad Ha'am as intolerant of equivocation: he allowed for neither "maybe" nor "perhaps"; all was decided, definitive, complete. Tellingly Ahad Ha'am burst onto the public stage with this system fully intact. (This is not altogether accurate, of course, but it was widely accepted.) He was never known as an uncertain, tentative "seeker" of the truth, like so many others in the maskilic world. From the outset he seemed to know the answers, and with little equivocation.[17]

Nor was it merely his literary style that set him apart. Style, as Thon argues, is idiosyncratic. It cannot be taught and cannot be seen as the source of his extraordinary influence even if he contributed toward Europeanizing Hebrew prose. Not even his ideas were original. In Ahad Ha'am's own testimony in his first essay on Pinsker, he claims the latter as the source of the idea of a "spiritual center," one that was, at any rate, "in the air" at the time. The Nietzschean Hebraist Thon did not make this argument alone. Zalman Epstein, one of Ahad Ha'am's original Odessa devotees, explains that

in our generation there have been those Jews who have reached the highest rungs of knowledge and went on to influence the world of learning and culture. Ahad Ha'am cannot be said to belong with these great figures. In the realm of pure learning, Ahad Ha'am does not occupy a position of the first rank. Nonetheless I feel confident that for Jews in this period of revival the importance of Ahad Ha'am is extraordinary and much greater than that of those luminaries who have to shine in the general world of scholarship. The latter contribute to our glory, the former represents for us the very essence of our source of life.[18]

This remains true, agrees Zarvozsky, though Ahad Ha'am today represents something very different from what he once did. In what he calls a "series of reminiscences," he describes how twenty years ago in his Vitebsk province beit midrash he and his friends did much more than merely read Ahad Ha'am's first essays; they studied them with the care of sacred texts, including in these avid discussions self-conscious modernists (Zarvozsky calls them heretics) as well as traditionalists. This they did because "what Rousseau was for the French and Tolstoy for the Russians, Ahad Ha'am was for us."[19]

By the time Ha-Shiloach appeared and because of its uncompromising anti-Herzlian stance, Ahad Ha'am was deemed too radical for Zarvozsky, too fiercely critical of everything, including even traditional Judaism: he tells that when its first issue was published, with its unvocalized title on the cover (printed without the vowels that appear below Hebrew words) some read it to mean Shelakh (javelin) which they assumed was meant to describe how Ahad Ha'am planned to storm the foundations of Judaism with it. Within a few years the tide had turned: everyone Zarvozsky knew had radicalized their cultural politics under the influence of Berdyczewski and now opposed Ahad Ha'am for being retrogressive. He implies that this opposition nonetheless tended to be soft: so often the same intellectual would spend his nights writing long, complex refutations of Ahad Ha'am's work, attacking him on paper, as Zarvozsky puts it, until the first hint of dawn. Then, having reviewed what they wrote, they would tear it up into little pieces. These writers, Ahad Ha'am's fiercest critics, would find themselves in such moments forced to face the fact that they, too, were still among those who "ran before him"—who retained the abiding devotion of true disciples.[20]

He tended to make devotion extremely difficult, though, even for his most avid followers. His criticisms were frequently about style, not ideology, as he watched others attempt to translate, as they saw it, his ideals into reality; it was this sort of behavior that was so excoriated by Ben Avigdor. In fact, Ben Avigdor wrote his condemnation of Ahad Ha'am soon after witnessing a particularly disspiriting performance by him at the conference of Hebraists in Berlin in December 1909.[21]

Ahad Ha'am had lent his name to the conference, the event inspired as it was by his 1902 Minsk speech where he called for the creation of a separate Jewish nationalist organization to promote culture. The meeting was intended to set the foundations for a full-fledged congress to coordinate and support financially Hebraist activity worldwide. The goals may seem rather rarified and benign; at the time they appeared to be at the cutting edge of nationalist politics. Not only were Hebrew book sales in decline, publishing houses were failing and potential readers as well as writers were being drawn away by Yiddish, Russian, and other European languages. The recent Yiddishist Czernowitz manifesto had affirmed the national aspirations of Yiddish and placed Hebraists on the defensive. Such was the unacknowledged impetus for the event, its "invisible . . . specter," as Stanley Nash writes. Ahad Ha'am's attitude at the meeting—sarcastic, carping, at times even obtrusive (at several points he interrupted speakers with catcalls)—was under the circumstances especially depressing.[22]

When he first spoke, after having sat through much of the preliminary discussion in silence, transcripts of the meeting indicate that he was greeted with "excited and prolonged shouts of goodwill." His first sarcastic barbs were also met with laughter: he proceeded, though, to question whether plans for a proposed congress were feasible: the calling of a congress assumed that there was sufficient interest. Did such interest exist? Would not the premature convening of a congress further alienate Jewish youth from Hebrew? This Berlin meeting, he insinuated, coinciding as it did with the Hamburg-based Zionist congress soon to follow, was itself more motivated by diplomatic than ideological concerns—by a desire to counteract Czernowitz and to reassert the role of the movement's culturalists. His arguments, pointed and also amusing, seemed to many almost ridiculously predictable: to say that plans to launch a culturalist movement were premature was fantastic, claimed Ben Avigdor in a reply that made the case that one should have been launched at least twenty years earlier as Ahad Ha'am himself had argued in "Lo zeh ha-derekh." His opposition to the calling of a congress was viewed by most as a sign of petulance not wisdom and went unsupported when brought to the floor. It is leadership that we seek, cried Yaakov

Kahan, but those who have been our true leaders, Moses, or Herzl, did not stop to ask whether their followers were ready to follow them toward redemption. Our movement today requires a true leader and it may fail without such inspiration: "Ahad Ha'am could have been this if only—he [acted like] Ahad Ha'am."[23]

Ahad Ha'am did not stop his efforts to derail the Berlin meeting even after his proposal to shelve the proposed congress was defeated overwhelmingly. He interrupted Sokolow's comments, calling out twice that he must not refer to a future Hebraist congress since it had been decided (and because of Ahad Ha'am's urging) to call it a *kenesiah* or assembly. This new name, in his view, deflated somewhat the potentially populist connotations of the future meeting and distinguished it from the Zionist congresses that he so abhorred. To a limited extent, then, his arguments in Berlin grew out of his distaste for raucous, populist politics. More importantly, his attitude seemed fueled by sheer obstructionism. He would even argue that it was only Hebrew speakers who should be permitted to participate in the future *kenesiah*. He had vigorously fought similar proposals in the past which, as he knew, would mean that some of the most talented figures in the Jewish nationalist camp (Buber, or the literary critic David Frischman, for instance) would be denied participation. Now he seemed intent on simply derailing the proceedings— premature, potentially populist, unfocused, frivolous as he claimed them to be. No doubt Frischman spoke for the majority there when he described Ahad Ha'am's behavior at the conference as that of a prissy, prudish spoiler. In a striking passage he accused him of besting Saturn by devouring his children *before* they were born: "He runs away from taking action or anything resembling action. Upon seeing something that might demand activity, he is seized by a kind of anxiety. He frets and trembles."[24]

Ironically, at the moment when the "crisis of Ahad Ha'amism" (as this attack on him has been called) was at its height his impact was first beginning to be felt beyond the world of Hebrew letters. A German translation of essays drawn from the first volume of *Al Parashat Derakhim* made the work more widely accessible. When the young Judah Magnes, an Oakland, California-born reform rabbi, arrived in Berlin in 1900 to study at the university and the Lehranstalt für Wissenschaft des Judentums and fell in with Berlin's Zionists, Ahad Ha'am's essays were among the first books he was encouraged to read.[25]

They provided the impetuous, bright man with his "Lebensprogramm" as he wrote his parents: "I no longer picture myself a liberal preacher whose chief duty is to preach goodness and to minister tenderly to a congregation of wealthy Jews. My Zionism makes me more than a preacher or community leader. It makes me a worker for the preservation of the Jewish people as a whole and for their greater glory and better life in their own land. It makes me a politician." His reading of Ahad Ha'am and especially Ahad Ha'am's description in "Moses" of the prerequisites of prophetic politics inculcated in Magnes an ideal of public behavior, a lifelong emblem.[26]

In a sermon titled "The Harmonious Jew" given in January 1907, Judah Magnes proclaimed that Ahad Ha'am's teachings and life constituted the outstanding model for a modernizing Jewry. That old "symphony of goodness and truth-telling" that had characterized Judaism in the past was shattered in modern times, creating a profound cleavage in the lives of Jews torn between a larger world and a small, increasingly unattractive Jewish one. Speaking now as associate rabbi at reform Judaism's premier synagogue, New York's Temple Emanu-El, he acknowledged that reform's efforts in solving this problem had been unsuccessful. Reform Judaism had helped introduce the ideals of the larger world to Judaism but "it has not been able to make the Jewish soul harmonious with its life; it has not helped to bridge over the chasm of the past and the present; it has not given the young men and women an ideal around which they could rally."[27]

It is precisely such an ideal that Ahad Ha'am has produced. In Magnes's description he uses terms similar to those that had in the past been utilized to speak of the young Dessau-born sage Moses Mendelssohn, as emblematic of his generation's enlightenment: Ahad Ha'am was born in an obscure corner of Russia, he studied "quite independently and on his own initiative" Talmud as well as secular subjects. In his role as the leading Zionist intellectual opposed to Herzl's political approach, he "creates souls; the young and the old are rallying around him." His nonritualistic Judaism is sympathetic to the historic importance of observance in Jewish life; though Ahad Ha'am's secularism clearly made Magnes uneasy, nonetheless Ahad Ha'am's emphasis on the role played by the Jewish national spirit in reestablishing harmony between Judaism and the larger world was seen by Magnes as the most significant Jewish teaching of the age: "He is the first of the modern Jews who has seen the great light in the distance. He is the first harmonious modern Jew."[28]

With the writing of "Sakh ha-kol" and with the completion and appearance of the fourth and last volume of *Al Parashat Derakhim*, Ahad

Ha'am proclaimed that his career as a literary publicist was at an end. For someone who claimed to be quite indifferent to public celebration, it is striking that he announced the "summation" of his views on the eve of the twenty-fifth anniversary of the launching of his literary career; he made certain that *Al Parashat Derakhim* appeared just at this moment. The 1914 *Ha-Shiloach* festschrift took him at his word: it assumed that he had retired from literary life and he was described as a thinker of the past—though one whose return to literature, as Klausner said in his introduction, would be greeted with enthusiasm. "What was it that Ahad Ha'am meant to us?" asked Moshe Kleinman in one highly complimentary piece in the volume; he, as nearly everyone else who posed such questions there, did so in the past tense.[29]

Indeed, after his move to England and with the exception of his essay on C. G. Montefiore and a handful of other pieces, he published little. This could probably be traced, as we shall see, to the absence of a conducive maskilic literary community there, a surprisingly taxing job at Wissotzsky's firm, his bad health, and family problems (Leah's increasingly serious illness and Rachel's marriage to a non-Jew). He hoped to devote his free time to scholarship but couldn't seem to manage it. Instead he spent the bulk of his free time on Palestinian-related affairs. He served on a committee charged with establishing a higher institute for technical studies in Haifa. During World War I he was Weizmann's confidant in the negotiations with the British government leading up to the Balfour Declaration. Especially in the discussions over a technical school cosponsored by a German Jewish philanthropy, he showed himself to be a yielding, skilled negotiator—one willing to keep his eye on the larger picture without losing perspective in the midst of contentious, sometimes trivial battles. His participation in the debate bears some scrutiny, especially as it shows him able to balance principle against pragmatism with much greater flexibility than many of his critics believed him capable.[30]

The establishment of Haifa's Technicum—which promised to be Palestinian Jewry's most advanced academic institution—was Ahad Ha'am's chief communal concern in the four or five years before the Great War. The proposal to establish this school primarily with funds from outside the Zionist movement surfaced at a time when talk of a national library or, on a more ambitious scale, of a national university were the subjects of great interest in the movement. The self-evidently practical Technicum, all the more so since its success did not hinge on the Zionists, was greeted with excitement.[31]

Nonetheless, the discussion over the opening of the Technicum, along with a secondary school to train suitable students for the technical institute, were prolonged, at times vituperative, and bore no fruit in the short run. By the time the war ended the discussion, the Kuratorium charged with setting its course on which Ahad Ha'am sat was severely split over whether Hebrew should be the language of instruction, at least in the secondary school affiliated with the technical university. Its German Jewish sponsors, the financial mainstay of the project, opted for German instead and refused to budge on the issue and saw Ahad Ha'am and his colleagues as trying to impose an ideological agenda onto a school whose function was technical education, not nation building.[32]

The nationalists viewed their non-Zionist collaborators as insensitive to what it meant to build a major educational institution at this juncture in Palestine: to use any language but Hebrew, particularly at the lower levels of the school where instruction in the revived tongue was feasible (or so they argued), would demoralize the pedagogical enterprise of the Yishuv. It would send a dismal message to teachers, students, and the Jewish world as a whole. While Wolffsohn was ending his lackluster tenure at the head of the Zionist movement and Warburg was beginning his own tepid regime, the debate over this school's curriculum sent shockwaves throughout Zionism, testimony to the rather grey, directionless tenor of Zionist politics in these years. It was also a period of relative diplomatic stagnation despite the changes wrought in the Palestinian orbit by the Turkish revolution of 1908. Jewish Palestine was witnessing few real advances; acquisition of new land was cumbersome and innovations like the *kvutzah,* or collective farm, still seemed too tenuous to elicit much attention. The prospect of a well-funded educational institute training Jewish technicians and scientists was heady stuff in such times. Even Ahad Ha'am, as Weizmann reported in March 1909, was convinced that the Technicum "will develop into something rather big."[33]

The coalition hobbled together to launch the school was from the beginning an unsteady one. The idea came from Paul Nathan, the vigorous secretary of the Berlin-based Hilfsverein der deutschen Juden, a widely ramified Jewish philanthropy that already ran several schools in Palestine. Nathan thought the Technicum a sensible way of addressing the needs of a growing Middle Eastern Jewish community and, as he envisioned it, its graduates would contribute to communities throughout the Ottoman world. The likelihood of a Haifa-Jerusalem railway, the advantages of Haifa's superb natural port (over Jaffa's, for instance), its potential as a manufacturing center (which Jerusalem could never match given its remoteness), were all factors that helped persuade Nathan that a technical school in Haifa would be an excellent idea. Given the magnitude of the project he sought cosponsors, and he turned, along with Shmarya Levin, to David Wissotzsky. Since 1904 Wissotzsky had been charged with the distribution of a large fund left by his deceased father which was intended to endow new Jewish institutions. The son, a non-Zionist, had resisted the idea of committing the money (100,000 roubles every five years, the first sum to be available in 1909) for a Palestinian project; it was Nathan, also a non-Zionist, who convinced him. The bulk of the funding, as originally envisioned, was to come from the Hilfsverein, which was integrationist and non-nationalist, with additional money from the Wissotzskys and the Zionists. Leading American Jewish philanthropists like Jacob Schiff and the Jewish Theological Seminary's Chancellor Solomon Schechter were also drawn into its Kuratorium, together with a stable of distinguished cultural nationalists like Shmarya Levin and Ahad Ha'am.[34]

After extensive negotiations a draft of its guidelines was drawn up; particularly difficult was the question of the role of religious instruction in the curriculum. Here Ahad Ha'am played the role of mediator between the more secular Zionists and others like Schechter who were attentive to religious concerns. Compromise on this score was rather painless, he insisted to his nationalist colleagues, since it was the teachers who would, irrespective of what the guidelines happened to say, set the tone at the Technicum, as they had at the recently established Tel Aviv Gymnasium; Ahad Ha'am fully expected a faculty sympathetic to Jewish nationalism. Once plans for the building started to be drawn up, he made certain that the contractors selected were Jews and that all efforts be made to locate Jewish laborers when construction began. When the prospect of hiring a non-Jewish director was floated, he quickly quashed it. By and large, his stance during the preliminary negotiations was moderate and yielding.[35]

Even on what proved to be the intractable language question, Ahad Ha'am showed himself at first as one of the less strident of the nationalist members of the Kuratorium. During much of the negotiations the Germans managed to skirt the issue. While Ahad Ha'am tried gently to press them to clarify their intentions, he warded off other nationalists, led by the Yishuv's increasingly vocal Hebrew Teachers' Federation, who argued that Hebrew should be declared the lingua franca of the Technicum. Ahad Ha'am replied that it was not yet proven, except perhaps on the secondary level in courses in mathematics and physics, that Hebrew was feasible for advanced instruction in the sciences. He preferred to leave this question open; with the support of Tchlenow and Levin, the other nationalists on the board, he only pressed the Kuratorium to declare Hebrew the secondary school's language. This seemed to him a fair compromise, a reasonable way to navigate the conflicting apprehensions of the various constituents. Nathan proved unwilling to commit himself even to this idea and during the negotiations developed a distrust (and an intense personal dislike) for Levin, his initial contact in the nationalist camp. He began turning more frequently to Ahad Ha'am, hoping that by winning him over he could persuade the nationalists to put aside for the moment their linguistic concerns. Between the various Kuratorium meetings in Berlin, Ahad Ha'am now exchanged numerous letters with the determined, earnest German Jewish leader.[36]

Finally in the fall of 1913 Nathan sent Ahad Ha'am a lengthy letter—"essentially a booklet," is how Ahad Ha'am described it—arguing that it was pedagogically impossible to teach sciences in Hebrew even on the secondary level. If any other decision was reached by the Kuratorium, Nathan insisted that the Hilfsverein would pull out of the project. In his reply, Ahad Ha'am argued, after apologizing for his own letter's lack of coherence—it was written quickly, he explained, and under terribly hectic conditions at Wissotzsky's—that it appeared to be possible to teach at least some science courses in Hebrew based on what had already been attempted in several other Palestinian Jewish high schools. He told Nathan that he had assumed that they had long ago resolved the language issue. He could hardly believe that it remained an issue of disagreement. Nathan must be aware that sentiments in Palestine in favor of conducting instruction in Hebrew were very strong for nationalistic reasons as well as fear that the Ottoman authorities might view a German-language school as a beachhead for German regional designs.[37]

The two sides were finally aired at a disastrous meeting in Berlin in late October 1913. Nathan made it clear that nothing he had heard persuaded him to support the idea of using Hebrew. The language would be taught and classes in Jewish studies might be conducted in it, but its status would be comparable in all other respects to that of Turkish, French, and English, which would also be on the school curriculum. There would be no official language, clearly not Hebrew, promoted as it was primarily for reasons that had little to do with its educational merit. German would be the standard language of instruction. Once it became clear that Nathan commanded a majority, Ahad Ha'am, Levin, and Tchlenow quit the meeting. With news of their walkout, the Palestinian Hebrew Teachers' Federation announced a boycott against all Hilfsverein schools (an action Ahad Ha'am abhorred). Guards had to be posted at the Technicum site to protect it from vandalism, and the gulf between the two sides quickly widened to the point where many despaired that the school would ever open.[38]

By early December the issue had galvanized the entire politicized sector of Jewish Palestine. At a meeting called by the Hebrew Teachers' Federation representatives came from the executive council of Tel Aviv, the local chapter of the Hovevei Zion, the Zionist movement, various professional associations and guilds, Ha-Poel Ha-Tsair, Poalei Zion, and an array of other bodies. The meeting was followed in four days by a mass rally of thousands in Tel Aviv (according to a report in the Zionist newspaper *Ha-Olam*); it was decided to establish a cultural commission to oversee educational affairs in the Yishuv, to establish a Hebrew gymnasium in Jaffa, and to affirm generally the nationalists' control over this sphere of Palestinian life. The Zionist movement allocated 10,000 francs for a secondary school in Haifa, additional sums for teacher training programs in Jerusalem, and funds for a Jaffa boys' school.

Throughout the controversy, even after the Kuratorium meeting in October, Ahad Ha'am maintained the stance of a mediator. He had serious doubts as to whether he should have walked out of the meeting or remained and fought Nathan. (He was quite concerned about how his colleagues in the nationalist camp might see his action as uncharacteristically theatrical: how, he pensively asked one colleague, was it seen in Odessa?) He denounced the boycott in Palestine aimed at Hilfsverein schools as an excommunication (herem); he despised such behavior no matter what its reason or its source.[39]

He still refused to turn his back on the Technicum which, he said, would be premature and irresponsible. He preferred to press his case before Schechter and Schiff in the United States (his plan was to shift the locus of power away from the Hilfsverein toward a more amenable body in the States), or to moderate Nathan's stance which, as time passed, seemed less and less likely. Once news surfaced of the involvement of the German Foreign Office with the Hilfsverein—before the Kuratorium meeting the government had contacted Nathan and asked that he stand firm on German as the school's primary language, in line with Germany's regional, cultural, and political interests—the prospect of turning the Hilfsverein around seemed very slim. At the same time, Ahad Ha'am continued to fight rumors, spread after the October debacle in Berlin, that he had badly served the nationalist cause in his earlier negotiations with Nathan. Though increasingly doubtful about whether it was still possible to negotiate with Nathan, he remained optimistic that, once the school was launched, and even if the Hilfsverein maintained a role in running it, its character would be determined by its educational staff. By late 1913 the secondary school's principal and much of the faculty had already been chosen and all were drawn from the nationalist camp. Moreover, out of its annual budget large sums would still need to be raised from Zionist sources; this also constituted a way for Jewish nationalists to make certain that they had some say in its operation. The subsequent boycott by the Hebrew Teachers' Federation of the Hilfsverein schools quickly dampened this enthusiasm. And by late December, in a letter to Alter Druyanow, he claimed that the Technicum controversy had reached a very "dangerous" point with both sides further apart than ever and no resolution in sight.[40]

All this took place at the same time as the Beilis trial—a hapless Kiev Jew was accused of blood libel and after nearly two years of incarceration was eventually found not guilty. The trial ended with enormous tumult from points all along the Russian political spectrum, and once it was brought to trial it became a central preoccupation of Russian Jewry. Ahad Ha'am too was captivated and horrified by the spectacle; "it has filled my heart," he wrote Barzilai in December 1913, soon after Beilis's acquittal. But he remained sufficiently taxed by the Technicum controversy to publish, just when the Beilis affair was nearing its conclusion, an article on the school debate, his first article to appear in print in two years—an article that was prompted by the attack on his competence as a negotiator.

The piece, which first appeared in German, was cast in the form of a letter to the editor of the periodical *Ost und West*. It was a strange, even somewhat anachronistic, exercise. Ahad Ha'am began by making it clear that he had written it by request of the editor who asked him to clarify his attitude toward the language that should be used in the Technicum and its secondary school. But his attitude, he says, is self-evident from the fact that he had walked out of the October Kuratorium meeting. Presumably, then, what the editor really wants is for him to elaborate on the reasons for the action. From the outset his tone is pedantic, plodding: he feels it necessary to correct the editor's own request, to insist that there is a crucial distinction between "how" and "why" he reacted as he did. He speculates further that the editor chose him to comment since the affair has mistakenly been described as pitting Zionist against non-Zionist: "And since you know, Mr. Editor, that I have never accepted the 'political program' of the 'movement' and have never been a member of it—perhaps for this reason you have felt that my impressions of the controversy would be of some value to those who also are not part of the 'movement.'" Judging from this performance, it was little surprise that younger readers found him old-fashioned: the letter (filled with rather cloying asides to "Mr. Editor") is far too studied and self-consciously literary a performance to have impressed them.[41]

In substantive terms, he made his case with considerable skill. He first disputes the notion that either in this controversy or elsewhere in Jewish affairs the major debate is between Zionists and assimilationists. Both of these camps are in fact rather small; most Jews fall somewhere in the middle. They remain concerned about Jewish survival, they devote their Jewish energies to the support of benevolent and philanthropic societies; and their attitudes toward these institutions are friendly but also skeptical. Most feel that philanthropic institutions provide Jews with some small semblance of comfort, but they fear that they cannot do enough to stop the deadening, assimilationist "flood" that they, no less than the Zionists, fear.[42]

Well beyond the Zionist camp, says Ahad Ha'am, the revival of Hebrew in Palestine and the resurrection of the Land of Israel reinforces for most Jews their hope for the future. Here they see emerging people who are "Jews in their language, their learning, their aspirations, and in all aspects of their spirit." This provides them with some greater confidence that the "Guardian of Israel" has not abandoned them. It is not Jewish politics, whether in Palestine or elsewhere, that preoccupy such Jews; it is rather the prospect that the revival there might breathe new life into the dry bones of the Jewish people, as it is one of the few encouraging signs in an otherwise depressing Jewish world.[43]

It is in this context then, argues Ahad Ha'am, that the Technicum debate should be understood. On the surface, the dispute seems odd, for why should there be an objection to the use of German, one of the leading vehicles for culture, at a technical institution? Had the school been established elsewhere, this argument would be persuasive. But to launch such an institution in Palestine, and just when the Hebrew language is beginning to consolidate itself, must be seen for what it really represents: much more than merely a philanthropic venture, it is an institutional advance of crucial importance for the whole Jewish people. Hebraic culture is finally and after enormous effort consolidating itself in Palestinian educational circles. At the moment when such victory appears in sight, there is an attempt to introduce German as the language of instruction in what will be the most important school in Palestine. To do this would mean the introduction of an "alien spirit" which could demoralize the still-tenuous cultural and educational underpinnings of Jewish Palestine. The debate, then, is about far more than either linguistics or even education; it concerns the defense of the Yishuv from alien, potentially demoralizing influences. In the end its resolution is crucial for everyone in the Jewish world, since if it is ignored it can stifle the cultural vitality of diaspora and Palestinian Jewry alike.[44]

The letter, which he wrote not as a Zionist but, as he put it, merely "as *a simple Jew,*" stressed how the debate should not be seen as partisan. Those who hoped to use it for their own political designs, including the Zionists, must be stopped. Tchlenow and others found this argument objectionable: they complained about how he had distanced himself from the nationalist enterprise. He in turn faulted Tchlenow for seeing the controversy as a good way of calling attention to Zionism: "It seems you derive comfort now from the fact that the standing of the Zionist Federation has risen as a result of this battle." This was shortsighted and also self-destructive. Ahad Ha'am would have preferred a compromise with the Hilfsverein. Of the Americans he depended especially on Schechter; as for the Germans, not until late March 1914, and on the eve of still another meeting with them, did he finally despair of their help.[45]

In the end the Americans refused to challenge the Hilfsverein, Schechter's own position on the use of Hebrew in the schools remained equivocal, and the intervention of the Great War ensured that nothing was accomplished until it ended. By late March 1914, with the controversy now essentially behind him, he was complaining again, this time to Klausner, that nothing was new in his life, and that this was unlikely to change since he was on the verge of old age. Throughout the controversy he complained of how it sapped his energy, dominated his time, and robbed him of the opportunity to read, or write, or even think at leisure. Once it ended, though, he admitted that he saw an empty future. Once again, when faced with the prospect of large stretches of free time for scholarly work, he balked. With the outbreak of war and with East European as well as Palestinian Jewry threatened with calamities far greater than they had faced before in modern times, he abandoned any hope for sustained research. It seems, despite the anguish that he felt when word of Russian wartime atrocities reached the West, that he felt somewhat relieved from the pressure of having to sit down and write. His career as a writer had effectively reached its end. There was no such thing as peace, he observed in October 1913 to Ben Hillel Ha-Cohen; the closest he had managed to come are those moments of solitude when all, even feelings of kinship to one's closest friends, are obliterated. As in the past, solitude attracted him again but he also found it profoundly disorienting and frightening.[46]

II

Before his final move to England in May 1908, Ahad Ha'am had been there only once, in the fall of 1893 when he was still at the helm of the Bnei Moshe and sought Western support for it and for the Hebrew journal that he hoped to publish. At the time he was barely known beyond Hebraist circles. The first volume of *Al Parashat Derakhim* had yet to appear; his battle with Herzl (whose movement greatly expanded Jewish nationalism's reach and with it familiarity with Herzl's friends as well as foes) had not started. There was a modicum of support in England for the Hovevei Zion but this, as Ahad Ha'am quickly discovered during his stay in London, was tenuous, superficial, and impossible to mobilize in any meaningful way. The British chief rabbi, Hermann Adler, was standoffish and fearful of the impact that Jewish nationalism might have on Jewish efforts for integration in England; the Anglo-Jewish establishment startled him with its stolid, serenely unbookish conservatism: he claimed that it was simply too painful to speak about Anglo-Jewry. Repeatedly once he settled there, he likened the community to a cemetery—serene, comfortable, dotted with grand artifacts and yet devoid of the requisite inner substance or human tension that makes life bearable.[47]

His first months in London, eased somewhat by his daughter Rachel's presence, were spent in a Bloomsbury rooming house; he chose the location to be near the British Museum which, much to his chagrin, he found little time to use. Soon they located a home in the middle-class Jewish suburb of Belsize Park. It was a fairly standard, turn-of-the-century suburban London house, one of the smaller ones on a pleasant, nondescript street. His wife joined him, they expended much effort furnishing it properly (the English, he told Dubnow, take this sort of thing very seriously), and, by the fall of 1908 he was settled in his new job in the City and accustomed—if also glumly resentful—to his routine as a suburban commuter. The urban noise, the long, dull, crowded daily ride from north London to the familiar, never-exhilarating grind of the Wissotzsky tea firm, the wet weather, all so exhausted him that he found little time to read seriously or write. By day he sat over ledgers in a small, windowless city office; by night he sat, almost always alone, in his large, book-lined study reading newspapers, answering letters (rarely as promptly as in the past), and attempting, without any real success, to start his magnum opus on the ethical and national dimensions of Judaism. Here he wrote "Sakh ha-kol," his article on Montefiore, his brief but critical assessment of the Herzliah gymnasium, his letter for *Ost und West* on the Technicum controversy, and a few other odd pieces. His routine was, as he often complained, lonely, unsatisfying, and infertile.[48]

He found little relief in the local Jewish community. Despite his fame in Hebraist circles—which were rather sparse and intellectually unimpressive here—his was not a name that conjured up much importance for English Jews. As even the *Jewish Chronicle* would remark, in November 1907, this was a community "apparently still at the alphabet stage" of Jewish literacy. Few of his essays had appeared in English before the 1912 one-volume collection edited by Leon Simon and published by the Jewish Publication Society of America, but even after their appearance his residence there had little local impact. In a keenly hierarchical community, his interests were of little concern to the plutocratic elite that still managed to hold sway—despite the rapid transformation of what had been in the 1880s a small, provincial, overwhelmingly middle-class community into a vastly more heterogenous, working-class, and (in numerical terms, at least) East European one by the turn of the century. Moreover, Ahad Ha'am's secular Jewish identity seemed odd, even slightly subversive in a community that defined itself, however tepidly, in religious terms and for whom secularism was politically suspect and alien. The Jewish newspaper of record in London, the *Jewish Chronicle,* had little interest in him despite the fact that the paper was owned by the Zionist Leopold Greenberg who, as a Herzlian stalwart, viewed Ahad Ha'am with some suspicion.[49]

Tellingly, when first interviewed by the *Jewish Chronicle,* in a piece that ran on 13 August 1909, more than a year after he had first settled in London, Ahad Ha'am was asked mostly for information about the radicalization of Russia's Jewish youth—a topic that was justifiably thought to be more interesting to the newspaper's readers than the Jewish nationalism that truly preoccupied him. The interviewer showed neither interest in nor awareness of Ahad Ha'am's work; he could as easily have asked the same questions of any Russian Jew critical of the political excesses of the young. In much the same vein, when his name was noted in passing in July 1908 in the *Chronicle*—where he was

identified as "the famous philosopher Ahad Ha'am"—it was in reference
to a query as to whether Russia should be put to task by the West for
its abuse of Jews. That he now lived in London wasn't mentioned, nor
was any indication given of why he merited attention as a "philosopher."
He wasn't listed among the communal notables in London's *Jewish
Yearbook* (there is, of course, the possibility that he refused the honor)
which included the names of his much younger English disciples, Norman Bentwich and Leon Simon. In his 1909 *Jewish Chronicle* interview,
it was admitted in an introductory note that "English Jews have apparently not been awake to the fact that there has recently been living in our
midst a distinguished guest, who it should have been their delight to
honour." Curiously though, when the newspaper published its monthly
summary of the contents of *Ha-Shiloach,* it never mentioned—not even
in late November 1907 when Ahad Ha'am first arrived here to decide
whether or not a permanent move was sensible—that its founding editor
was in London. The presence of this mordant, shy, secular nationalist
of Russian origins, without much money, without a particularly impressive position, and without a reputation outside Jewish circles or a
body of published work that was read or valued by the Jewish communal
elite made little impression on Anglo-Jewry.[50]

This cannot be entirely traced to the community's philistinism. There
were several scholars of Judaica in this same period who achieved a
greater measure of prominence in England: the Cambridge rabbinic
scholar Solomon Schechter whose appointment at the venerated university was a source of some pride and whose religious inclinations much
more closely meshed with those of the community than Ahad Ha'am's;
and Joseph Jacobs, a man of vast learning and widely diverse interests
such as ethnography, statistics, and fairy tales; his statistical work especially was seen as practical and, hence, worthy of respect. These two
along with a handful of others with serious scholarly interests in Judaism—Moses Gaster, Lucien Wolf, and the Ahad Ha'amists Norman
Bentwich and Leon Simon—made themselves available to the Jewish
community, which listened to them with measured if somewhat distant
attention. They were, as the *Chronicle* often described the young, energetic Simon, of some value as figures who enlivened an otherwise dull
and predictable Jewish scene.[51]

In contrast, and almost from the time of his arrival, Ahad Ha'am made
himself inaccessible. Even under the best circumstances he was reticent,
a man who opened up only with his dearest, oldest friends. In Russia
he had little contact outside his immediate circle; and in London the com-

parable circle was far smaller. Public speaking, he declared, was out of the question although on at least one occasion he did speak for a London Hebraic society: a summary of his remarks that appeared in England's only Hebrew-language periodical, the amateur weekly *Hayehoody,* made his words seem pedestrian and must have confirmed his belief that the audience was unworthy of him. He refused nearly all other invitations. "A vow of silence" is how he would describe the decision. From the vantage point of the English Zionist Federation, run as it was by men faithful to Herzl's legacy, this silence was welcome and Ahad Ha'am's presence in their country unhelpful, although harmless. When urged by Weizmann to attend the 1908 English Zionist Federation meeting held in Manchester soon after his arrival in England, he agreed only if it was understood that he was not to be invited to speak. Briefly and in silence, he sat on the podium; he quickly excused himself and used the time for a much-needed rest. (Indeed, just before the meeting, on 26 January, Weizmann wrote Ahad Ha'am with the assurance that, "Your conditions will be met. No one will know about your arrival. I saw you named in the Press but I declared categorically that you were not coming to the meeting and that in no circumstances would you be speaking there.")[52]

When his voice was heard, as in the 1909 *Jewish Chronicle* interview, it lacked the nuance and authority of his Hebrew, whether because of unperceptive questions or his discomfort with English. He sounded testy ("English Jews can really form no conception of the peculiar mental outlook of their young Russian coreligionists"), rather old-fashioned and conservative ("At the present time, the sexual question is very much in vogue, and the young people think that its discussion is the most vital matter of the moment"), and despairing, with little evidence of his analytic precision. Economic conditions in Russia, he explained, were disastrous; even among the liberals there were few philosemites and emancipation was unlikely for some time to come. His only hope was that Jews might be "imbued with sufficient moral strength to resist their oppression"—to withstand such conditions until they eventually change. It was only Zionism, he explained, that could provide Jews with such spiritual underpinnings, but "this side of Zionism has hitherto been very much neglected" because of the movement's excessive preoccupation with politics and economics. True, some of the basic features of an Ahad Ha'amist perspective could be found here, but without its characteristic acuity or linguistic freshness. Nor did he on this occasion seem to make much effort to impress his listeners; perhaps he was so despairing of their ability to understand Russian Jewish conditions that he spoke in overly simple terms. Few could have understood from the interview why Ahad Ha'am was believed to be, as the *Chronicle* itself intoned, among "the greatest thinkers on the spiritual and intellectual problems which beset the Jews in modern times."[53]

Not all Jews in England here were quite as indifferent to his participation in communal affairs as the leadership of the local Zionist Federation or the Anglo-Jewish elite. The Hebraists of England, the sort who organized the Hebrew-speaking evening that he had addressed and who put out the Hebrew-language weekly *Hayehoody*, naturally hoped that his move would revitalize Hebraic life or, at least, bring them into contact with one of its reigning luminaries. They reached out to him, only to be rebuffed. They impressed him as being much the same self-important, marginally talented, and intellectually derivative maskilim that had beseeched him for attention ever since the 1880s; now, as in the past, he treated them dismissively, mostly with outright indifference. Condescend to them as he might, they were among the very few Jews in England who understood at least some of his frustrations, which resembled their own.[54]

A particularly vivid, and also rather ironic source of evidence for such frustration, is an open letter by Isaiah Wassilevsky, a Manchester-based Hebrew writer who had emigrated from Eastern Europe. He sharply criticized Ahad Ha'am for having denied Hebraists much-needed encouragement by refusing to meet them when he attended the Zionist Federation meeting at Manchester. Ahad Ha'am responded in an exchange that appeared in *Hayehoody* that he had never been a public man but rather was a writer without the sort of communal obligations of which Wassilevsky spoke.

He treated the protest with disdain: he apologized for having been compelled to air publicly his private affairs and explained that the obviously inappropriate criticism was frivolous, even pathetic. Yet Wassilevsky's unusually frank, bitter letter provides a glimpse at what it was like to be a Hebrew intellectual in England, cut off from the more vibrant features of East European Jewry, from English society, and surrounded by a materialistic and vapid Jewish one. Despite its purple, uncontrolled language, it probably reflected some of Ahad Ha'am's own sense of social and cultural displacement, especially in Wassilevsky's charge that from the moment that Hebraists like himself arrive here

we all sit imprisoned in an atmosphere of deceit, shut in by cunning and hypocrisy, with fear of the larger world afflicting even the best of us, and all, almost without exception, are the objects of treachery. We sit among people whose souls are those of prostitutes, whose instincts are those of prostitutes, whose actions are those of prostitutes. The chatter and the various voices that one hears in this place are normally, and quite simply, about how to make money, how to gain honors, and how to earn a living.[55]

Perhaps it was this isolation from Jews and the English alike that helped prompt him in 1910 to venture outside the parameters of Jewish concerns and explore issues of a much more general nature. He produced a series of twenty Hebrew epigrams. Ten of them he published in the Odessa-based Zionist weekly, *Ha-Olam;* he later told its editor that had they made much of a stir he would have sent more. (They did not, perhaps partly because they appeared under his initials.) These new writings suggest an ambivalent desire on his part to reach beyond the Jewish world, an inclination that was self-sabotaged in part by his own stubborn insistence on writing the epigrams in Hebrew. But they show him as thinking deeply about larger issues, probably with a desire to stretch his intellectual reach beyond what was, in England at least, a tightly circumscribed Jewish world. Tellingly, of the twenty epigrams he wrote, the ten he chose to publish were the most personal; the ones whose publication he delayed were mostly glosses on his essays. Hence, not only was he compelled to air his thoughts on issues well outside the realm, strictly speaking, of Jewish life, but—though still circumscribed by the self-imposed limitations of a Hebrew writer—he published only those that revealed the most about his private self. It is interesting in this regard that few recognized the epigrams as his: the discrepancy between his public and private personas, which he traduced in this unusual exercise, was so stark that few saw him in these candid, highly revealing reflections.

He seemed propelled here to speak in an autobiographical voice albeit slightly veiled: "You know," he wrote Dubnow in September 1916, "I am unaccustomed to revealing my feelings transparently. Many believe that I am wholly incapable of even bringing myself to the point of feeling. This is not true. But there is in the depths of my soul something that works against my own inclinations to reveal what I feel in any 'outward' manner." The epigrams represented for him a way of testing the emotional limits of his own responses to himself. In particular, he seemed intent on examining the impact of eroticism, especially sublimated eroticism, something seemingly so out-of-character with the prudish, guarded Ahad Ha'am of the past. In one of them, he writes:

Seneca said: "We are going to die, we move toward death every day." And there is no scene quite so full of pain and happiness as the encounter between two people who had once been close and have been separated for a long time. Each searches for that picture of their friend that they have kept within themselves, and for whom they have yearned for so long, but they find before them someone else, someone who resembles somewhat the person they recall but who is also different: familiar and at the same time foreign. And far greater is the hidden sorrow than the manifest joy.[56]

Does this perhaps refer to an encounter with Tsina Dizengoff for whom he still harbored erotic desire?[57] He describes his meeting a person for whom he has "yearned for so long"; in this particular case the epigram might, in fact, be devoid of sexual inference. Having moved to a place that was far from his closest friends, such ruminations could be attributed to other, much more obvious motivations. Other epigrams, though, were more explicit in their sexual implications:

Even the quiet and tranquil heart expresses with enormous passion the need to break out for a time from the social cage in which it is interned. In moments of rebellion such as these a man is liable to put at risk himself, the honor of his good name, all for which he has worked throughout his life—everything for one taste from the wellspring of life as it emanates from a heart that is free. And people see him and say: "So and so who is so smart, what does he see in such nonsense?" And they conclude, "A man does not sin unless he is possessed by the spirit of foolishness."

Such a view, he contends, is utterly fatuous.

Or:

When the evil inclination senses that one has managed to overcome it, it whispers: "Look, the moment of opportunity is passing you by, and if not now when? Later you will find that you will regret all your days this wasted opportunity that you let slip through your hands." And people do not realize how powerful such whispers are, or recognize the things that we do simply out of fear of the prospect of remorse.

Perhaps the most revealing was an epigram without a semblance of sexual implications that shows Ahad Ha'am to be acutely aware of his own need to appear "small" (as he puts it here) despite his inclinations to the contrary: in other words, it shows how he is fully conscious, and aware even of the psychological aberration, of the often painful lengths to which he goes to act the part of a man of distinction by simulating inconsequence:

If mankind only knew what suffering was felt by the person who, throughout his life, exerts himself and puffs himself up in an effort to appear great in his very smallness. If so, people would no longer envy the man who wears a crown that is, in fact, inappropriate for him but they would say instead with compassion: "Look what burden this poor man had to bear in his refusal to acknowledge his rightful place."

Among the epigrams that remained unpublished were ruminations on the vagaries of assimilation and apostasy written before he had knowledge of Rachel's marriage, and on nationality, where he insists that one cannot understand a nation's character unless one is a member of it, or at least married to one. Some of them were little more than clever turns of phrase: "In general, people talk to say something rather than because they have something to say." Even his reflections on the inadequacies of altruism ("Altruism is but a reversed form of egotism") was a gloss on his just-published essay on Montefiore. The published epigrams were better, more interesting, and more personal.[58]

He called them *remazim* or hints. Perhaps he meant this merely to underline their brevity, to indicate that because of this they could do no more than nod in the general direction of the truth rather than enumerate it more fully. More likely, he meant to indicate that he was engaged here in a form of exposition that held back more than it revealed, a simulated candidness that shed quite intentionally only limited light, but without being self-evidently elusive. The epigrams revealed someone both hungry for confession and coy, eager to be frank about matters public and private but keenly self-conscious about the need to put one's best foot forward. For many years, albeit much less explicitly, this is precisely how he had been writing.

Repeatedly he had demonstrated the need to reveal himself, to unburden himself and not only to those closest to him but publicly to a larger world upon whom he had so successfully imposed the image of what constituted Ahad Ha'am. He dabbled in autobiography but admitted to Dubnow that he couldn't produce more than a few sketches because he found it too painful to tell the truth and yet hated the distortions that crept into his narrative. Instead, and always in veiled forms, he wrote himself into studies of Moses or Maimonides, or, for that matter, the unyielding, exemplary but ultimately destructive "Prophet" pitted (as he argued years before in "Kohen ve-navi") across space and time against the accommodating but politically essential "Priest." This is how he hinted that what the public believed Ahad Ha'am to be was not altogether accurate. Sometimes he was coy; other times shocking, even self-lacerating.

But always, of course, he wrote in the form of hints: usually tangential, easily debatable comments that could be interpreted in various ways; self-characterization embedded in historical description; learned allusions whose misinterpretation attested to the boorishness of those around him and further justified his need for discretion, for hiding what might otherwise be embarrassing or misunderstood. His decision to write, and more importantly to publish, the remazim was consistent with this tension between concealment and self-revelation, the erection of a stolid, seemingly consistent persona and an abiding need to be candid and frank, even at the expense of his reputation or standing.

At the time he wrote these epigrams he seemed reasonably content with his life, despite his misgivings about England, his job, his lack of progress on his study of the underpinnings of Jewish nationalism. To be sure, he was immersed in several aggravating but admittedly energizing communal battles: the Brenner affair and the negotiations over the Technicum curriculum. His visit to the 1911 Zionist congress reminded him how much his teachings had now entered the Zionist mainstream. His home life was comfortable; he presided on Friday evenings over a fairly traditional Sabbath meal although accompanied by after-dinner cigarettes, and soon a youthful entourage including Simon, Bentwich, and occasionally Weizmann interjected into his routine some intellectual vitality. His relationship with his new English-born disciples was warm and often paternal; perhaps because he saw them as newcomers to the Jewish scene, he permitted himself to speak of Jewish nationalism with them in something akin to inspirational terms: writing Norman Bentwich, for example, in January 1914, at a time when there was a good deal of positive movement toward establishing a Jewish university in Jerusalem, he congratulated him on a new job in Egypt and added, "But I hope that we will eventually see you occupying a chair in Jerusalem, once we build the 'third temple' that we expect to see."[59] Elsewhere in letters to Bentwich he tried to combine (often none-too-successfully) an off-handed English jocularity with moral suasion. Writing from Woodhall Spas in August 1915, his style bears neither the fluency nor the wit of his Hebrew, which may also indicate why he failed to make more of an impact on local cultural life:

It is very cruel of you to have written to me in Your usual "Egyptian" way, knowing that in my glorious "Retreat" I have nobody to assist me in deciphering Your hieroglyphs [sic]. But with the assistance of God, which is at present claimed everywhere, I managed to overcome the difficulties, at least, to such an extent as to understand the general meaning of Your card.[60]

In the same letter, and in reply to news that Bentwich would soon be married, Ahad Ha'am tells him that he will be unable to attend the wedding but that he wishes to extend him "harty" (sic) congratulations, albeit "outside the synagogue": "I know You are fully aware what a tremendous responsibility it is now to build up a new house in Israel. But I am sure You will do all in Your power to make Your house a stronghold of Judaism in the *true* sense of the word, and I hope You will succeed." In contrast to his correspondence with Simon, with whom he spoke as an older, experienced peer, to Bentwich he was always the master—tolerant, kind, encouraging, and unquestionably patronizing.[61]

Others would soon join this small, intimate circle. With the outbreak of World War I, Tchlenow and Sokolow, both of whom were based in London beginning in 1915 as representatives of the Zionist movement, would visit the Ginzberg household frequently. (Ahad Ha'am claimed that it was on his advice that they came to London to give an official underpinning to Weizmann's unauthorized forays into wartime Zionist diplomacy.) By now he was very close with Weizmann; his relations with the young Leon Simon were also warm and he would claim, once he moved to Palestine, that his friendship with Simon was one of the few he made in all his years in England.[62] Max Raisin describes the scene at his home on a Friday evening in the summer of 1909: Here Rivka Ginzberg, "a tiny lady, talkative and on her feet most of the time," spoke much more than her husband who, though he "seemingly had so little to say, dominated the gathering." Raisin said the house was brilliantly illuminated by Sabbath candles. (Rivka Ginzberg remained rather observant and, on another occasion, admitted that only once in her life had she lit a fire on the Sabbath, an act prohibited by Jewish law, when it went out in Asher's study and he complained of the cold: "But is there anything that one would not do for one's husband?" she explained in justification.) Raisin added that she served an ample and tasty Sabbath meal, and conversation moved freely over the course of the evening from Yiddish and English to Russian. Ahad Ha'am's "detached smile" enormously impressed Raisin, as did the great care he took in inscribing in Raisin's autograph book an utterly prosaic message ("In memory of our pleasant evening"); this pleasant, attentive man seemed happy with every reason to be so. Raisin was perhaps not too perceptive; in any event, he didn't know Ahad Ha'am very well and was awed by his encounter. But his impressions of Ahad Ha'am's life and his Sabbath social circle suggest that he was surrounded in London with a reasonable degree of comfort and conviviality.[63]

But the book that had haunted him for so long, and in which he would distill his thoughts on the national underpinnings of Judaism, remained unwritten. It appears, in fact, that he never got much beyond writing its outline. He continued to ruminate over it, and even after he moved to Tel Aviv in 1922 he still hoped to write it. When Chaim Tchernowitz visited him soon after the outbreak of the war Ahad Ha'am showed him a sheet or two of paper which, Tchernowitz said, he carried in his pocket as he traveled to work, and that contained the book's outline. The outline, which Tchernowitz describes in his memoirs as "a precise list of the contents of his 'book,' organized and put into subheadings,"[64] was deposited in his archives when they were organized in Tel Aviv and contained the following:

Jewish National Consciousness
A general study of its essence and development from its beginnings and until the present.

1. Awareness of national unity in Israel (tribes, classes).
2. The recognition of national distinctiveness as a product of the actions of a nation.
3. National consciousness as reflected in relations with other nations.
4. National consciousness in terms of its relation to the various prerequisites of nationalism:

   a. the racial element
   b. the religious element
   c. the linguistic and literary element
   d. the legal element
   e. the educational element.

5. National consciousness in relationship to the national ideal of the future.
6. How national consciousness will be actualized in the nation's struggles.
7. The impact of Jewish national consciousness on the social and spiritual beliefs of the nation.[65]

He had claimed in the past that there was little written on nationalism that had particularly interested him in its theoretical implications for Jewry. Clearly now he expected to couch this study in the larger theoretical literature. Earlier he described his scholarly work as an investigation into the ethical dimensions of Judaism; this aspect seems to have receded somewhat by the time he wrote the outline. True, in moments of despair, as in February 1915 when writing to Ben Hillel Ha-Cohen, he bemoaned that he had "neither the will nor the ability" to produce the book. But when he wrote Dubnow a year later (and perhaps because Dubnow's disciplined productivity had always intimidated him) he insisted that he expected, at the very least, to write a series of articles on the national idea in Judaism; it was in this context that he asked Dubnow for the text of his recent lecture on the religious underpinnings of collective life, a topic that intrigued him for many years. He wrote, "I have never, not even once, managed to produce a clear exposition of it." He took extensive notes in this same period for the writing of a study of biblical literary style and prepared on index cards a chapter by chapter list of the more important biblical phrases.[66] But his health deteriorated, his spirits lagged, the war depressed him deeply, and a family tragedy intervened that persuaded him (or so he later claimed) that he had lost the right to teach his people.

He referred to the family tragedy as a "catastrophe." He used the term *hurban* for both the devastations of World War I and his domestic woes. By 1909, his oldest daughter Leah, married to the Haifa dignitary Shmuel Pevzner, was consigned to a sanitarium outside Berlin. Ahad Ha'am's son Shlomo visited her often; their father remained solicitous, but distant. His sister Chana, about whom he rarely spoke, had a history of mental breakdowns, and he seems to have feared that Leah suffered from a hereditary disorder. Periodically Leah would rejoin her husband in Haifa or in London, where he went often for business, only to return to the sanitarium worse off than before.[67]

Much more devastating for him was the marriage in the winter of 1912 of his youngest daughter Rachel to a non-Jewish Russian writer, the radical journalist Mikhail Ossorgin. By all accounts Ossorgin was an affable, humane, and talented man who (after some initial hesitation) was willingly converted to Judaism by a Parisian reform rabbi at the advice of Ahad Ha'am's son, Shlomo, and before Ahad Ha'am was informed of the marriage. Rachel met her future husband in Rome's Russian student colony where the twenty-four-year-old Rachel had gone to study in 1905. They moved in together before Ossorgin, who already was married, divorced his wife. They were married in 1912 in a civil ceremony. Shlomo and Rivka had known of the relationship since 1910, but Ahad Ha'am was told nothing until his son broke the news to him. Indeed, Rachel had returned home from Rome for visits every year, but had not told her father of Ossorgin because she feared his reaction.[68]

When his son gave him the news in June 1912, he broke off relations with Rachel and refused to see her again for some ten years. He told his closest friends about it. As shocking as it was, it was not unprecedented in his circles and intermarriage, even conversion to Christianity, had already touched the immediate families of Mendele, Dubnow, and Ben-Hillel Ha-Cohen. Nonetheless, he refused to be comforted or reconciled with Rachel: when Tchernowitz offered to convert Ossorgin in an orthodox ceremony Ahad Ha'am responded that for nonreligious Jews like himself even after a hundred such conversions a "goy remains a goy." Did he, asked Ahad Ha'am in a letter, "change [by his conversion] his soul from within?" He ruminated bitterly on how similar his plight was to that of the eighteenth-century enlightenment thinker Moses Mendelssohn, several of whose children converted after his death; he insisted that his daughter's act had undermined everything that he stood for. He told Shlomo he would never write again.[69]

To friends who cautioned him to respond more mildly to Rachel's marriage—Smilansky urged him to reconsider cutting her off—he insisted that such flexibility would mean the end of the Jewish people. Jews had managed to sustain themselves for centuries precisely because such marriages were unthinkable. Once the door was opened for the "enemy," he told Smilansky, the Jews would be decimated within a few generations. The fundamental issue was not, as Smilansky had formulated it, whether a Jewish girl could find happiness in such a home. In fact, he insisted to Smilansky, she could not and would come to regret her decision for the rest of her life. Rather the enemy must be stopped for the sake of larger, national reasons since "there can be no mercy when national survival is at stake." As Ahad Ha'am told Thon, whom he praised for having been free from such agony with his own children, there can be no greater accomplishment in such times than to say with confidence that one's children truly belong to you.[70]

Ahad Ha'am started to ruminate on his childrearing practices, about which he had not written much before, reassessing whether he had been a good parent. He had always been aware that he wanted to bring his children to Judaism through love rather than the sort of coercion that he had known as a child. To Shlomo he gave comprehensive Judaic training—teaching him Hebrew before he knew Russian, in fact—and he was kept at home throughout his early years and taught by private tutors in Jewish and general studies. Both Leah and Rachel, however, were introduced to Jewish subjects in a much more haphazard fashion; they were also sent to Russian schools. Years earlier, in 1901, in a reply to a question from a Danzig Hebraist who asked Ahad Ha'am whether he should send his son to a non-Jewish school, Ahad Ha'am outlined at some length the various educational decisions he made for his children: his oldest, Leah, born when he still lived in Gopchitse, was permitted to speak Yiddish so she would not feel alienated from the Jews around her; his priority was for her to feel herself "a part of the community." Eventually she entered Russian schools and excelled. In the case of his son, who was eleven in 1901 when he wrote this letter, he was still tutored at home and examined at the end of each year to ensure that he met the standards of the best local schools. In this way he would be kept at arm's length from the pernicious influences that had ruined so many Jewish gymnasium students.[71]

He seems to have worked out the details with considerable care. At the same time, he had trouble communicating to his children this concern in emotional terms. Asked many years later about his upbringing, Shlomo refused to say much more about what life was like in his father's home than that Ahad Ha'am was usually busy and distant.[72]

The cultlike atmosphere surrounding Ahad Ha'am for much of his life in Odessa, his taxing schedule (as editor, tea executive, and nationalist leader), and, perhaps above all, his lifelong, intense self-absorption meant that he had little time for his children, to whom he behaved with correctness and formality. Perhaps because of his sternly positivist inclinations, he paid little attention to the ritualistic side of their Jewish upbringing. When it was time for Shlomo to celebrate his Bar Mitzvah, for example, Ahad Ha'am failed to make preparations for his son to be called to the Torah as tradition prescribed; it was Bialik who took the boy along with him on the Sabbath morning to a *shtibl*, an informal hasidic prayerhouse, around the corner from the Ginzbergs' house, where Shlomo was initiated into Jewish adulthood and without even the presence of his father. Shlomo recalled the incident years later in a newspaper article about his upbringing, but refused—and in a laconic, cold fashion reminiscent of his father—to comment on it.[73]

The tension between the intense Jewish preoccupations of Ahad Ha'am's entourage, who dominated the family's Friday evenings, and their indifference to religious ritual Shlomo noted rather early on. He first called attention to their Sabbath smoking. Ahad Ha'am had instructed his guests not to smoke in front of the children, and they indulged themselves in the various corners of the large house until Shlomo made it clear that he knew what was happening. Soon the circle was smoking openly until Ahad Ha'am stopped the practice when word spread among local traditionalists. As Ahad Ha'am described his own ritual observance: "In *mitzvot* [the observance of ritual commandments] I did not educate [Shlomo]. In my home we keep the ritual dietary laws and I observe certain ritual practices, especially the Sabbath and festivals (even though I am not careful to avoid all that technically falls under the category of 'work' as defined by Jewish law). The boy learned on his own to sanctify the Sabbath and to honor various religious customs, but I did not compel him to do so."[74]

The religious inconsistencies of their home, where their mother remained observant despite her husband's secularism; their father's distant relationship with his family and his favoring of Leah and Shlomo over Rachel; the unevenness of the daughters' Judaic training, despite his frequent complaints about the inadequacies of Jewish girls' education (an issue the Bnei Moshe addressed when it established special schools for girls)—all these factors may have played some role in influencing Rachel's inclinations. More important, of course, were the collapsing social boundaries in Russian student life between Jews and non-Jews in these years, a phenomenon that Ahad Ha'am had anticipated and much feared.

By all accounts, he grieved for Rachel, but he tended to see what happened primarily in terms of its impact on himself, as his greatest personal and ideological defeat. In his mind, there was little that separated the one from the other. The most important feature of this tragedy, as he told Smilansky, was the way in which this intermarriage—despite Ossorgin's conversion—undermined his ideology which, in turn, weakened Jewry's ability to sustain their lives in diaspora. Despite his deep feelings toward his daughter, he managed to transform a domestic tragedy into a political-cultural one, to make it over in abstract terms as a denial of his authority and his national redefinition of Judaism. As much as he mourned for Rachel, it was his tarnished authority that he seemed to regret most. "Der Staat hat keine Töchter!", the state has no daughters, he sternly lectured Smilansky when urged by him to reconsider his reaction in light of his daughter's happiness. When faced with a choice between the needs of the nation and the desires of the heart, the latter had to be put aside. It was precisely because Rachel was unable to see things this way that she had fallen into this tragedy. He admonished Ha-Cohen in a letter written in October 1912 that if "you and I and people like us" compromise on matters of this sort that determine our people's future "we are leaving it to the simple Jews to make the same decisions for themselves."[75]

At the very heart of his conception of the nation was the recognition that if the Jewish people were to be revived, individual needs had to be subordinated to the collective. His inability to communicate this teaching to his own daughter was the source of enormous pain and self-recrimination. This pain was not merely the product of his distrust for non-Jews, especially Russians; his suspicions were definitely intensified now, leading him to speak with some frequency about his yearning to cut himself off from the gentile world and settle in Palestine. But it was the way in which the marriage undermined the efficacy of his life's work that ate at him. His comparison between his fate and that of Mendelssohn was poignant. In contrast to other maskilic nationalists, he had always deeply admired Mendelssohn while also seeing him as outdated. Much like the conversions of Mendelssohn's children, which symbolically illustrated the failure of the Mendelssohnian haskalah, Ahad Ha'am feared his daughter's marriage signaled that his own school would succumb to a similar fate.

Nevertheless, it is unlikely that it was either Rachel's marriage or Leah's illness that stopped him from writing; even earlier he had ceased to produce much and, in fact, had announced in "Sakh ha-kol" that he had written all that he intended. His comment to Shlomo coincided with his finishing touches on the last volume of *Al Parashat Derakhim*, which he claimed as his last foray into publicistic writing. However, he would continue to ruminate over the writing of a more serious and sustained treatment of Jewish nationalism; Ahad Ha'am was after all carrying about the book outline that Tchernowitz spotted two years after he learned of Rachel's marriage.

In the end, his daughter's decision, as he understood it, implied that a secular identity was insufficiently resilient to sustain Judaism, that an identity shorn of its theology and embedded instead in the tribal, secular attachments endorsed by Ahad Ha'am could not stem the tide of assimilation, intermarriage, and conversion—that is, of national catastrophe. He saw Rachel once more during a trip to Europe in 1923, but essentially their relationship ended. He insisted on reacting to what Rachel did in terms of how it affected him and his ideology; in his mind these were interlinked with his people's future. Never had he felt compelled to pay so dearly for his principles.

III

In early July 1914 Ahad Ha'am was still embroiled in the Technicum controversy, smarting, or so he said, from the celebrations in honor of his twenty-fifth anniversary that had proceeded despite his ritualistic warnings, and preoccupied with producing on Ahiasaf's invitation a Hebrew translation of Pinsker's *Autoemancipation*. Never had he attempted a translation of such length and, particularly in light of his high regard for the pamphlet and its author, he insisted that his publishers send his first few pages to readers who would judge whether they were of sufficient quality. Not surprisingly, when that July his draft was submitted the referees expressed their approval, and Ahad Ha'am continued working through much of 1915 on the forty-page booklet. He was meticulous and extraordinarily slow, but it helped take his mind off news of the war's carnage which was beginning to filter back to the west.[76]

Before word reached him of mass expulsions, pogroms, and other atrocities—which, by mid-1915 had culminated in the dislocation of hundreds of thousands of Russian and Galician Jews—his attention was directed to the war's effect on Palestine. He sensed that the war could prove even more beneficial than the 1908 Turkish revolution whose potential at the time he had overrated. Precisely what Jewish nationalists could do to promote their cause in such circumstances wasn't clear, as he wrote in a letter to Weizmann in November 1914. It was, in fact, precisely at such moments that he was at his best: the current state of affairs, as he came to argue repeatedly, was difficult to assess if only because its fluidity highlighted Jewry's fundamental powerlessness; its dependence upon the goodwill of others could not be more starkly apparent than it was now. Nonetheless he admitted, in his letter to Weizmann, that he sympathized with Weizmann's inclination to create at least an "illusion" that the nationalists were doing something. Insofar as anything could be done nationalists could nurture impressions, remain firm on matters of principle, and prepare for the use of power without currently having much in hand.[77]

In the letter, he suggests circulating a memo to men of influence on the European scene—in particular to Balfour. (Weizmann knew of Balfour's sympathy with the Zionist cause and he started to cultivate him before the outbreak of war.) By working with Balfour and others like him, Ahad Ha'am urged, European opinion could be prepared for a postwar settlement that would take the needs of the Jewish people into account. A week later, in a second letter to Weizmann, he wrote that at this juncture modesty was crucial, especially since Turkey's fate was undecided, and England might not be Palestine's master at the war's end. Jewish nationalists must make it clear to the English that if they do have a hand in the postwar settlement, all that the Jews require at the moment is a guarantee of unhindered Palestinian colonization and cultural work. There is no need to announce the goal of Jewish autonomous existence under the English flag: no doubt, he added, we shall have to contend with the bombast of Zionism's "political" branch that will use every opportunity to declare their intentions to the detriment of the movement. But as important as it is to steer clear from goals that are too expansive, it is essential to avoid those that are too modest: philanthropy, it must be made clear, is not in our interest; nor are policies designed merely to provide succor to the beleaguered Jews of Palestine and Eastern Europe or that see Zionism's goals within narrow, patronizing confines. A principled stance is required, somewhere between philanthropy's minimalism and the maximalism of the classical Herzlians.[78]

Indeed, at a time like this "spiritual Zionism" is precisely what non-Jews best understand. In a letter written early in 1915 to Simon, Ahad Ha'am suggests that he has long been persuaded that they sympathize with it more readily than Jews. Just the other day, he continues, Sokolow and Tchlenow were sitting in his house discussing how to best promote the Zionist case among the English and whether to air our real aspirations, or speak merely of Zionism as a solution to our economic problems. Ahad Ha'am told them that, without doubt, the best tactic is to be as frank as possible about our designs but without saying much about aspirations which, in any event, can't be realized for some time in the future. And divided though English Jews are over Zionism, they must be at least guardedly open with non-Jews about what they believe even if the non-Jews have trouble understanding, since, he insists, it is better to be misunderstood than to speak in inauthentic terms. In other words, again as so often in the past, he had little difficulty exercising evasiveness as long as it didn't require downright inauthenticity. The first year or so of the war found him as he remarked in March 1915, "perched between hope and fear" but still certain, like most of those close to him, that once the carnage ended Palestinian Jewry's position would be "clearer," and probably much better.[79]

Not surprisingly, he found little opportunity for sustained intellectual work in this period, so he spent some time carving out a role for himself as confidant to Sokolow, Tchlenow, and especially the young, increasingly dominant Weizmann. Although he complained to Dubnow in May 1915 that all he wanted now was to flee civilization, to run away from its wretchedness, when he went that August to Woodhall Spa for a cure, he wrote Klausner how difficult it was to abandon "the center of Jewish life" at a time like this.[80]

His "silence" he now justified as a product of his unwillingness to compromise Jewish nationalism at a moment when its aims were best kept to itself. It was impossible to discuss nationalist intentions in Palestine given wartime constraints; East European Jewish affairs were, moreover, all but inaccessible because of Russian censorship and the vicissitudes of wartime communications. By the spring of 1915, mass expulsions of Jews from the Russian provinces of Kovno, Grodno, and elsewhere had been carried out with great haste and ruthlessness. Yet even when the dimensions of the *hurban* in the East came to be known, his reaction was still to insist that silence was the only reasonable course. *Ha-Shiloach* was closed by the Russian authorities along with most other publications in Hebrew and Yiddish. When he heard of this, he told Klausner that it would be best if all the empire's Jewish periodicals were shut down, for their silence would speak more eloquently than words. Telling the truth about Jews, either in Russia or elsewhere, was inconceivable at the moment, either for the muzzled and beleaguered Jews of Eastern Europe or for their supporters in the West: when his friend Tchernowitz called upon the leaders of Zionism to be frank, irrespective of cost, Ahad Ha'am berated him and demanded that Tchernowitz name a country where leaders conducted themselves in this way. If he could identify one, Ahad Ha'am promised to abandon all and move there.[81]

By the time news of wartime Russian Jewry finally reached him his physical ailments began to intensify—pains in his throat, nervous exhaustion, "bad blood," and moments of melancholia so severe that he mused that death would be preferable. Nothing, not even a summer's rest at a "superior house" in August 1915 ("my rest is complete, my medical cure is poor"), or the completion of his translation of *Autoemancipation* eased his mood. In 1915 Jews were permitted to settle (on a provisional basis and only until the war's end) anywhere in Russia except its rural areas, but even this abolition by the Russian government of the Pale of Settlement he inferred as tragic in that it would now be much harder "to maintain the old foundations of Jewish life." With the Palestinian haven being threatened with disintegration, though only a few months earlier it had seemed on the verge of a real breakthrough, and with Russian Jewry being confronted with its greatest challenges while being denied the tenuous security of the Pale, never had things been worse. The dreams he had during the first stages of the war were gone. He could only compare the tumult and horror of wartime life to the terrible period described in classical Jewish literature as immediately preceding the coming of the Messiah; all that was missing, and was unlikely ever to appear, was the Messiah himself.[82]

By the time he finished his translation of *Autoemancipation* in the fall of 1915, there seemed no ready topic to write about. He remained convinced that it would be too dangerous to express openly his opinion about Palestine; he favored an English protectorate of some sort. To criticize the prospective World Jewish Congress seemed futile. In light of the horrors of East European Jewish life, to whom could he now preach his message of spiritual Zionism? There was no one to whom Russian Jews could now turn except God. There was no reason to have faith in humanity's moral sentiments, and, in a letter to Dubnow in late 1915, he claimed that the "silences" he saw in Dubnow's recent articles said much more than his words. Even in England "the land of Spencer and Mill," hateful, illiberal, antisemitic sentiments were now the norm; he probably was referring to the widespread criticisms of Jews being underrepresented in military conscription. For him the hubbub over this issue meshed with the multitude of other hatreds now dominating European affairs.[83]

Any hope there may have been rested with American Jewry; the leading Jews of England he called "fools" for their response was to shut their eyes to the horrors of East European Jewry and their implications. On the whole, the only credible conclusion one could draw from current affairs was that "it is difficult to be alive." To his friend Ben Ami, one of the original Bnei Moshe circle, he said that the sole consolation was that neither of them were likely to survive much longer; they would soon be freed from the "repulsive orgy" surrounding them. Writing letters was now as difficult for him, he claimed in mid-1916, as the splitting of the Red Sea; even his lifelong letter writing habit had suffered because of what he now called his "principled silence."[84]

Despite his mounting despair over the war, his friendship with Weizmann placed him very near the center of Zionist politics. Weizmann, who had lived in England since 1903, came there originally to fill a rather junior academic post in chemistry at Manchester. Ambitious, intelligent, and extraordinarily fluent (eventually also in English), he had great stamina and the ability to elicit the sympathy of those around him, so he quickly climbed the academic ladder of his formidable academic institution: by the beginning of the war he held the post of reader with a good salary, was widely published, and well regarded by colleagues at the university and beyond. He and his wife, Vera, had a fine house and good friends, including non-Jews who welcomed the Weizmanns into their homes with apparent ease and affection. He was a vice-president of the English Zionist Federation and at the center of a group of some of its most intelligent young members, including Simon, Sacher, and Bentwich. The still-young man (Weizmann was forty in 1914) seemed to have found security and some happiness in England. But a modicum of recognition at a provincial English university together with a middle-level leadership position in the unimpressive world of English Zionist politics failed to satisfy him. Working hand in hand with Ahad Ha'am, who for several years before the issuance of the Balfour Declaration in November 1917 was his closest confidant on political affairs, he charted for himself and his movement an ambitious course aimed at nothing less than his own preeminence and a diplomatic breakthrough of incomparable importance for Zionism.[85]

Such success was, of course, at first unforeseen, or, as Ahad Ha'am would later comment in a letter to Weizmann, "thanks to your personal qualities and to favorable external circumstances"; by no means was it apparent in 1914 (or, for that matter, even in mid-1916) that England could be persuaded to produce a document like the Balfour Declaration. Yet Weizmann's persistence, tactical skill, and numerous contacts in government and society proved invaluable. Ahad Ha'am, that tireless foe of diplomatic Zionism, served throughout as his confessor and critic, as a figure of eminence within Jewry who lent the younger man enhanced standing. The friendship was important for both, a safe, familiar, and fertile haven on foreign soil.

It was at first an unequal relationship, with Weizmann a ready disciple—eager to make Ahad Ha'am feel at home in England and protective of his time, his mercurial moods, his delicate health, and (after Rachel's marriage and Leah's hospitalization) his unhappy family life. And it was Weizmann who sought advice from the older, experienced man, who spent evenings at his London home, and who borrowed money from him regularly. As a leader of the Democratic Faction, Weizmann had previously turned to Ahad Ha'am as the movement's emblem of anti-Herzlian culturalist politics but an intimate relationship between the two was only forged when they both lived in England. Before Ahad Ha'am's arrival, Weizmann had gravitated to Moses Gaster, a Romanian born rabbi and scholar, who played a prominent if also highly vituperative role in local Zionist affairs; the erudite, Judaically sophisticated Gaster was, as Weizmann quickly recognized, vastly preferable to the provincial "political" Zionists who dominated the local scene, especially since by 1909 the movement was split down the middle with contesting leaderships divided along mostly personal lines. With Ahad Ha'am's arrival, Weizmann transferred his allegiance from Gaster to Ahad Ha'am who happily found his isolation relieved somewhat by Weizmann's seductive combination of energy, attentiveness, and excessive demands.

It was undoubtedly apparent to Weizmann that a close relationship with Ahad Ha'am was useful on several levels; here, as in most other areas of his life, utility played its role as a guide to sentimental attachment. First, Ahad Ha'am was a practiced hand at Jewish nationalist affairs: his opinions were often astute and informed by learning and a comprehensive theoretical framework that was similar in many respects to Weizmann's. Both were refugees from a richly variegated Jewish cultural and political world who now found themselves in an immeasurably more secure but also dull milieu and where the sort of issues that were of such self-evident importance for Russian Jewry were marginal, quaint, laughably self-important. In addition, Weizmann's association with Ahad Ha'am—which he quickly established publicly by bringing him as his guest to the Zionist Federation meeting in Manchester soon after his arrival in the country—helped consolidate his standing as a Zionist leader with a pedigree that far outdistanced his older, better-established English competitors. And this relationship, carefully nurtured over the course of the next decade, meant that he was in close contact with Ahad Ha'am during the negotiations over the Technicum project. Indeed, at one stage, and when it seemed well on the road to success, Weizmann did his best to steer it in a direction suitable to his research interests so that he might teach at it or, perhaps, even direct it. By the time the Balfour Declaration was issued he had distanced himself somewhat from Ahad Ha'am, exhausted by the older man's bitterness and cynicism, and drawn to other, more powerful and expansive figures in the Jewish world and beyond it. Until then, Ahad Ha'am had probably been his most intimate ally.

Aside from numerous visits to the Ginzbergs' where he frequently spent the night, he proposed to the reticent Ahad Ha'am that they go together on excursions (to Wales, or to London's Franco-British Exhibition of 1908); he watched over Shlomo's short-lived chemistry career when he was briefly a student at Manchester in 1910 and before he returned to philosophy studies in Paris. He befriended Ahad Ha'am's daughter Leah whom he visited in the sanitarium, and later saw to it that Shlomo's wife was hired as an archival assistant by the Zionist movement.[86]

Especially in moments of despair (and Weizmann was little less mercurial than Ahad Ha'am) he came to depend heavily on Ahad Ha'am: "I so wanted to be with you and to be a little refreshed," he writes in February 1909. "I feel dreadful all the time. A terrible sadness and dejection are weighing me down, and sometimes I gasp for breath. It was never in my nature to complain, but it is now, and sometimes I'm ready to kick myself." To be sure, in the same letter he makes it clear that Ahad Ha'am might well hold the key to Weizmann's redemption, namely an appointment to the Technicum. But, still, there is no reason to disbelieve the statement at the end of this letter: "I feel an overwhelming need to have a heart-to-heart talk with a 'fellow man.'"[87]

All the while Weizmann tried to draw Ahad Ha'am into his own schemes: an English-based Palestinian "colonizing company" aided by the son of the chief rabbi was one idea ("What do you think of this?" he asked Ahad Ha'am, in February 1910. "Would you like to try to do something here?"). Weizmann bemoaned what seemed to him to be an excessively cumbersome route to academic promotion at Manchester, his disappointment with Wolffsohn (who, as head of the Zionist movement, spent much of an English trip in 1910 attacking Weizmann), and his hatred for the local Zionist scene. Vigorous, sentimental, uncommonly energetic, and self-centered to a fault, Weizmann was characteristically blunt even in his dealings with his mentor: in a letter written to Ahad Ha'am a few months after he first learned of Rachel's marriage Weizmann inquires, "And how are you feeling? Have you recovered completely?", before launching into a long description of his Zionist and scientific affairs. Still less tactful was his decision in early February 1913 to bring Nora Schuster, a young Cambridge student and family friend for whom he had romantic feelings, to the Ginzbergs' home where he declared his affection at the foot of the stairs as she was making her way to the guest room. The flustered Schuster left early the next morning for Cambridge with Weizmann forced to excuse somehow her sudden, unexpected departure to the Ginzbergs.[88]

By now Weizmann saw Ahad Ha'am as an ideological guide of the first rank: establishing a Jewish university was the project at the top of Weizmann's political agenda until the outbreak of the war. Through that work he had made his first contact with the Rothschilds who would play a crucial role in the Balfour Declaration. His work was influenced by Ahad Ha'amist views on the interrelationship between cultural and political change. The project's apparent viability resulted from a softening of Turkish attitudes toward Jewish land acquisition, a new and sympathetic Smaller Actions Committee, an increase in the size of Jewish migration to the Yishuv, and the success of Palestine's Hebrew secondary schools that prepared students for a university education. When Weizmann explained the rationale for the university at the Eleventh Zionist Congress in September 1913, it was in terms drawn explicitly from Ahad Ha'am: he argued that the university must serve as "guardian of those values which are most precious to the future of the nation; it would cultivate the living Jewish national tongue, it would be a meeting place for all Jewish creative activity in literature, art, and science: In a word, it would be 'the cultural center.'"[89]

No one could claim, he continued, that its establishment would solve the economic problems facing contemporary Jewry. But Zionism does not presume to have "a speedy cure for Jewish poverty." Instead, like Zionism, the university "is the bread of tomorrow": "The university is a stone in this structure of the future, which we mean to set up for the new Jewry in Palestine."[90]

On the eve of the war that brought the university project to a halt, their relationship was as close as it would ever be. Within a year, Weizmann would acknowledge in a report to the Zionist organization's executive committee on his initial discussions with David Lloyd George, Balfour, and others that "although it fell to my share to be the instrument of carrying out the above mentioned work, it is chiefly due to Ahad Ha'am, who every day, at all times, and every moment gave us the advantage of his valuable advice, and his full moral support, and submitted every step to a searching criticism and discussion. Practically nothing was undertaken without his knowledge or consent." In the event that Weizmann passed through London without stopping to visit (increasingly common as the war continued and both his Zionist and scientific duties took on a much higher profile), Ahad Ha'am reacted with hurtful surprise; he had grown accustomed to the younger man's attentiveness, to his seemingly insatiable need for encouragement.[91]

Ahad Ha'am's active role in the diplomatic maneuvers leading to the Balfour Declaration might seem surprising in view of his criticism of Herzlian politics and his aversion for its pretence and half-truths. His well-known insistence on delineating cautiously the boundaries between what could and could not be expected of the Jewish nationalist enterprise seems so out of kilter with these machinations: he became a central member of a group engaged in drawing up maps designating Jewish

Palestine's borders; his close associate Shmuel Tolkowsky produced them. He participated in debating whether it was best to establish a state immediately or for the Yishuv to remain a protectorate of England. These debates took place even before the English moved beyond the borders of Egypt. Ahad Ha'am's group encouraged the English in their belief (untrue, as they well knew) that the masses of Russian Jews were fervently Zionist and could be persuaded to keep Russia in the war if Britain allied itself to their cause. The Balfour Declaration would have been inconceivable without a series of miscalculations by the British, all nurtured by this small circle of Zionists: how much sway Jews had over Russian politics, how much they had in the financial circles of the United States. Ahad Ha'am clashed with Weizmann, as we shall see, over some of the more dubious machinations, but by and large, he found them justified.[92]

Ahad Ha'am never abandoned his inclination to stress caution over action. (Even Weizmann's prewar work on behalf of the Jewish university had unsettled Ahad Ha'am who feared that it might turn the Turks against the Yishuv.) After the Turkish revolution of 1908, however, he was attentive to the changing political character of the region in which Zionism's fortunes appeared increasingly promising. Despite the deep depression of the first few war years when Ahad Ha'am's only comfort was reading, as he wrote Dubnow, *Ecclesiastes* and the ancient Greek satirist Lucian, by early 1917 he, too, was hopeful that a breakthrough was in sight. The sort of diplomacy in which he was engaged suited rather than conflicted with his temperament. Unlike his disastrous diplomatic confrontation with Rothschild several years earlier, it was Sokolow and Weizmann, not Ahad Ha'am, who were publicly active, whereas his own role placed him behind the scenes: and the negotiations were conducted behind closed doors, with powerful and interested negotiating partners and without the populist hubbub that had accompanied Herzl's early forays. He was attuned to how the English as well as the French political elite was preoccupied with gaining whatever small advantage it could over its enemy as the military stalemate dragged on. The otherwise arcane agendas of the small, marginal nationalities thus gained a new visibility in this political climate, especially because the war, with its obscure Serbian origins, had from the outset lent their national aspirations unusual attention.[93]

In contrast to their role during the Herzlian epoch, the Zionists could thus claim to have serious negotiating partners in discussions that were kept under wraps not only from the larger community of Jews but also from the designated leaders of English Zionism (like Cowen and Green-berg who were kept at arm's length during this entire process). This satisfied Ahad Ha'am's sense of propriety, discretion, and elitism. It was not negotiations that he found distasteful; it was when they were fueled by hubris and shadow boxing that he denounced them. These discus-sions instead seemed to him sensible; with solid and clearly defined goals and interested and powerful negotiating partners, and free from the disgraceful self-promotion of the past. During one especially sensitive moment in May 1917, when in reaction to leaks in the *Jewish Chronicle* of their negotiations with the British government, Ahad Ha'am ex-pressed his conviction in a meeting at his home that neither English nor Russian Jews could be trusted with unnecessary information. Few, with the exception of those in the room and a handful of others—Simon, Tolkowsky, Sokolow were in attendance—could be relied upon. If news spread beyond them they risked total defeat. The requisite secrecy of these prolonged negotiations meshed with his longstanding sense of politics; he threw himself into them with great commitment, attending meetings sometimes on a daily basis.[94]

Sokolow and Tchlenow, both members of the Smaller Actions Com-mittee of the Zionist movement, arrived in England where, by early 1917, Ahad Ha'am's home was the primary gathering place for their meetings. Among those who came regularly, for both formal and in-formal gatherings, were his new English entourage (Simon, Bentwich, Israel Sieff, Harry Sacher, and Simon Marks) foreign nationalist leaders working without the sponsorship of the Zionists but with their private political agendas (Vladimir Jabotinsky, Joseph Trumpeldor, Pincus Rut-tenberg), and longtime friends like Weizmann and Sokolow. In such gatherings Ahad Ha'am could be expansive, even amusing: when once in April 1915 the men retired to the study to smoke at the very moment his wife placed the lit Sabbath candles on the table, Ahad Ha'am was inspired to tell the following joke: "A young man who returns from his studies in Germany is walking in his shtetl on the Sabbath with a cigarette in his mouth. His childhood friends turn to him and say, 'Aren't you embarrassed, Yankel? A Jew walking and smoking on the Sabbath!' 'Oh,' he answers, 'I completely forgot!' 'How could you have forgotten that it is forbidden to smoke on the Sabbath?' 'No, that isn't it,' he responded. 'You forgot that it is Sabbath today?' 'No, I forgot I was a Jew.'"[95]

Here, albeit in different form, was the message of "Slavery in Free-dom," that mainstay of his now-familiar arsenal. But the fact that he related it in a smoke-filled room—his study, no less—on Sabbath eve introduced an element of poignancy that could not have been lost on his listeners. Be that as it may, with these men he was able to come out of himself, to talk, to plot, to joke at times, to escape the awful isolation that had been his lot since his arrival in England.

By the spring of 1917, the Jews of Russia had just been emancipated with the February revolution and negotiations with the British entered a decisive stage. Ahad Ha'am threw himself into considerable activity and found himself overwhelmed by a sense of mounting expectation; he reminded his old comrade Barzilai, who spent the war years penniless in Swiss exile, that it was good to be alive at a time like this. Even better times were certain for Palestinian as well as Russian Jewry: "Yes, my friend," he said to Ben Ami, "miraculous are the days in which we live and it is a pity that we experience them only in old age, with the best years spent in misery and sadness." Engulfed at his full-time job at the tea firm, he found himself overwhelmed by his participation on what was now called the Political Committee, headed by Weizmann (until January 1917, and reconstituted in July 1917 under the joint leadership of Sokolow and Weizmann as the London Zionist Political Committee) which required considerable work between its meetings. Disappointment would soon overtake his sense of achievement as it always had but he, too, was briefly swept up by the group's euphoria.[96]

The Palestinian agronomist Tolkowsky, who came to England early in 1915, provides an intimate record in his diary of Ahad Ha'am and the way in which he was seen by those around him. Tolkowsky shows him to be an exceptionally clearheaded and astute analyst but also a man with an odd, often petulant style of imposing his will. He is described as someone who insisted upon frankness while guiding the group in evasiveness and dissimulation. He is shown as someone who demanded to be heard yet was also deeply ambivalent about speaking in unequivocal terms; not surprisingly, he was an object of fascination even for those who found him objectionable (as did Jabotinsky, for instance) in almost every respect.

He was the best-known figure in the group and at those times when their Friday night gatherings were not held at his house, the topic of conversation was often him. In a conversation recorded by Tolkowsky, he tells how at the Weizmanns' London home in April 1917 the conversation turned to the perplexing influence Ahad Ha'am exerted over his English disciples. Their eclectic, inconsistent way of following Ahad Ha'am confused them. Sacher, for instance, was among those who felt strongest that the call for a Palestinian Jewish state should be made without equivocation, a position abhorred by the cautious Ahad Ha'am. More perplexing, as someone in the room asked, was why Ahad Ha'am refused to use his authority to check their rhetorical excesses. Tolkowsky suggested that it was his modesty that stopped him. Vera Weizmann disagreed. She insisted that it was because of his fear of failure, his unwillingness to associate his good name with any cause that stood the chance of disappointment. More important for him than anything else was this good name, and to prove her case she told them the following:

One night when Weizmann was staying overnight at Ahad Ha'am's, he walked in on Weizmann as he was reading a popular French novel which he often did to put him to sleep. "Oh you are reading that. It is most amusing," said Ahad Ha'am. "How do you know? You don't read this sort of thing. How would you know that it is amusing?" Ahad Ha'am: "And who told you that I don't read them?" Weizmann: "Because I have never seen them around your house." Ahad Ha'am: "I read them, and afterwards I burn them." Weizmann: "Why?" Ahad Ha'am: "One has to consider one's immortality."[97]

Few in this group would have ventured the story: Vera was one of the more venomous in the circle and the furthest removed from the nationalist cause and its protective stance toward Ahad Ha'am. But for all of them, working with him in close quarters was trying, especially because his reactions were often theatrical and archaic. Not many of them, though, would go quite so far as Jabotinsky who, sitting a few weeks later in Weizmann's living room, admitted to Tolkowsky that he simply hated Ahad Ha'am. Tolkowsky responded that Ahad Ha'am was worthy of great respect as the man who had at one time in his youth managed to transport himself and a part of the Jewish people to "a state of ecstasy." To Jabotinsky he was "cold and totally devoid of warmth," incapable of honest creation (and, hence, unworthy of the appellation of genius), and equipped only to criticize. Jabotinsky hated the entourage that tended to gather around him on Friday evenings: it was, he said, intolerable—made up of pathetic, pale, "cripples." He admitted that once many years ago, Ahad Ha'am wrote a few good essays, none of which remained relevant. In every other respect as an intellectual and a man he was painfully distasteful.[98]

Others, too, including those far more sympathetic and tolerant than Jabotinsky, found Ahad Ha'am's reactions in this stressful, heady period just shy of intolerable. Tolkowsky tells of an incident at a dinner in June 1917 in honor of Sokolow. He had just returned from a successful diplomatic foray to Paris and Rome where he had managed to come away from the Vatican with a reasonably positive statement of support for Zionist designs in Palestine. Ahad Ha'am was angry at the time with Sokolow and Weizmann over their unwillingness to be as frank as he wished them to be about the course of their current negotiations; when he was asked to give the last of the tributes, he "jumped up in his seat like someone who had just been stung" and stated that since he was not a diplomat he could not really assess the value of Sokolow's diplomatic achievements, the focal point of the evening's festivities. There are others here, he continued, who are themselves diplomats and they can make such judgments. All that he could say was that Sokolow was a vigorous and devoted man. These are traits that are important at this time when diplomatic activity is the focus of so much attention. Unlike "practical work," when diplomacy is anything but entirely successful it leaves no historical trace at all. Commitment is all the more crucial for someone who devotes his time to this sphere since he must always face the likelihood that his work will amount to nothing. Tolkowsky writes: "There was a bit of applause, just enough so as not to embarrass the speaker, but he left a bitter taste in the room." Bitter, lonely (all the more so by 1917 once Weizmann had found for himself a bevy of much more influential allies), he would enter meetings to which he had no intention at remaining merely to announce his various dissatisfactions: Tolkowsky recalled one occasion when he came to a meeting to tell Sokolow that he had tried to contact him unsuccessfully: "Evidently, you have no time for me," he said and walked out of the room.[99]

Petulant, ailing, unable or unwilling to impose his will in a clear-cut manner on those most sympathetic to him, he was also painfully shy in public. When speaking at a London memorial meeting for Tchlenow, who died soon after the Balfour Declaration was announced, he read a prepared text in an unsteady voice that clearly betrayed his lack of confidence. He continued, however, to show his political mettle at times: at the 3 November 1917 meeting of the Political Committee, one of a series of daily meetings held in the immediate wake of the declaration, he provided a brilliant assessment of the document and how best to take advantage of it. The first question to consider, he proposed, was how the group responsible for it wished themselves to be seen: as one special sector of Jewry, or as the brokers for the Jewish people as a whole? The English remain under the impression, he continued, that the declaration was issued for the sake of all the Jews who will, as a result, be swayed to support their side in the war. And they appreciate the difficulty the

Zionists have as a movement divided into two camps. What this means is that the Zionists do not need to support openly the English camp; the English do not expect us to side with them openly nor do they expect the Balfour Declaration to rectify the complicated dilemma facing world Zionism all at once. What he cautioned now, as he had so often in the past, was restraint: the Political Committee must concentrate, until England wins the war, only on Jews in the English orbit; it is only in this orbit that it can make real gains in these uncertain times.[100]

On the Arab question, too, his viewpoint in these discussions was cautious and circumspect, embedded less in morality than political self-interest. Speaking at another November meeting, he argued that Jews have no reason to believe that the English will provide them with a state in a region without a Jewish majority. The idea that they will support Jews controlling towns with an overwhelmingly Arab population is ludicrous. Comparisons between the prospects of Jews and of Armenians, which were rife at the time, were no less fatuous since the Armenian claim was bolstered by a demographic concentration in the region for thousands of years.[101]

The only credible Zionist demand that could then be made was for free immigration: "The only request that we can make is for permission to go there; over the next twenty-five or thirty years everything will change." Especially now that the English must, for the short term, remain attentive to Arab needs, little else is possible: "We must be modest and insist upon only what is absolutely essential. All else that might be set aside will come as a matter of course once we live there." He made no reference to ethical prerequisites, or to the legitimacy of the demands made by the local Arab population. Indeed, as he explained, caution was required because of his belief in the limits of Jewish power, the danger that comes when one overreaches oneself. He seemed to have few doubts at this stage, at least, that Jews would achieve in the future a majority status in Palestine. But until then they must be careful to avoid antagonizing their British sponsors; their efforts must be free from any taint of scandal that could block their future call for a Jewish state. His emphasis on the need for purity in the nationalist enterprise sees the rationale purely in instrumental terms. Perhaps he was being particularly attentive at this point to practical concerns in the wake of the Balfour Declaration. But the meeting was a closed one; the text of his remarks is available only in Tolkowsky's diaries. There is every reason to believe that he was being sincere, and, indeed, his argument is consistent with his essential pragmatism on this issue for many years.[102]

He showed a comparable toughness in a 5 September 1917 letter to Weizmann that helped dissuade him from resigning from the presidency of the English Zionist Federation to which he had been elected earlier that year. The election, of course, had merely formalized the central role he had occupied since the beginning of the war. His threatened resignation was over a disagreement about the wisdom of making public a Zionist decision to refrain from supporting a Jewish Legion in the British army that he claimed put at risk negotiations with the British which were then in high gear. In a brisk, pointed manner Ahad Ha'am warned Weizmann that he would now speak as "an older colleague, who was in the line of battle while you were still in school, and who has almost certainly had some influence, direct or indirect, on your attitude toward Jewish problems." He told Weizmann that the action he contemplated was little less than a "stab in the back" to Zionism. The entire Zionist enterprise would suffer, he warned, and he showed in his analysis of its likely impact his keen grasp of the prerequisites of leadership:

Nobody is absolutely irreplaceable; and if you gave up the job for some reason beyond your control, like a severe illness or some other mishap, that would certainly be very regrettable, and a great blow to the cause but in that case the work would be carried on by others, not completely ruined. On the other hand, if you had from the outset met the authorities as a duly appointed representative of the Zionist Organization (as Sokolow did afterwards), your resignation would not have seemed to the other side so astonishing, because they are familiar with the principle of election, and are used to changes of personnel by which one emissary replaces another. Normally it is not the personality that matters, but the credentials. But your position is exceptional. You took up the job not as the duly appointed representative of some corporate body, but as a private Zionist. Thanks to your personal qualities and to favorable external circumstances, you became in a comparatively short time almost the symbol for Zionism for many people of influence. And suddenly one fine day you announce that you are no longer in the business, that you have resigned! To whom have you handed in your resignation? Who, having chosen you, has the right to accept your resignation? It was circumstance that chose you, and circumstance will release you in due course when complete success or failure makes your job no longer necessary. But until then you cannot leave your post without creating in the minds of those with whom you have negotiated so far a most unfavorable impression of Zionists—and perhaps of Zionism—and nobody will be able to carry on what you began.[103]

Indicative of Weizmann's gratitude to Ahad Ha'am for this and so much else, one of his first acts upon receiving news of the Balfour Declaration was to rush over to Ahad Ha'am's home to tell him the news personally. Tolkowsky, who accompanied Weizmann, records that Ahad

Ha'am was visibly moved, particularly when he realized that Weizmann was telling him first. But even at this moment, which represented in many respects the culmination of his work as a Jewish nationalist, his caution got the best of him. "After a single instant of emotion," relates Tolkowsky, Ahad Ha'am "immediately began to harrass him with questions about its publication, saying, 'It is essential to act with great care and to prepare things effectively before anything is done.'" Ahad Ha'am would later recall the moment differently. In his memoirs, dictated in the last year of his life, he tells: "And on one evening close to midnight, Weizmann came to my house, his face beaming, with a piece of paper in his hands, and he said to me: 'Here it is!' This was the document that has been known since then as the 'Balfour Declaration.' Weizmann had received it only a few hours earlier and he hurried over to show it to me before it was made public. How wonderful and pleasant were those days, the honeymoon of our dreams." Both might well be right; Tolkowsky's version seems more credible, more in keeping with Ahad Ha'am's characteristic pedantry.[104]

Indeed, he showed a similar inability to size up the significance of the Balfour Declaration in his introduction to the 1921 edition of *Al Parashat Derakhim*. It was written after the San Remo Conference, where Britain's control over Palestine was confirmed, but also in the aftermath of the April 1920 Jerusalem riots that left six Jews dead. It was the riots that left the greatest impact on him: there was little confidence here in his assessment of the prospects for Jewish Palestine. He devoted the bulk of his remarks to the difference between the draft adopted by the British and the one that the Zionists would have preferred. The Zionist draft affirmed that Palestine was "*the* national home of the Jewish People" and, he said, had Jewry's historic right to rebuild their nation been accepted it would have undermined any attempt to derail a future Jewish state. Since in the final British version Palestine was merely acknowledged as "*a* national home for the Jewish People," Jewish claims were likely to carry no more weight than those of others with historic links to Israel. The current formulation "makes the land into the common property of a variety of nations," he argued. Under the present arrangement, the best that could be hoped for would be that over time and once Jews prove that their intentions do not threaten the Arabs the possibility of transferring authority over the land to its rightful Jewish owners could be broached. They must therefore demonstrate that they could rule in a decent, orderly fashion.[105]

The Balfour Declaration's achievements, which Ahad Ha'am insisted were much more modest than often believed, were made still more tenuous by the recent Jerusalem riots. This tension could only be exacerbated by any action by Zionists to further alienate and frighten the Arabs; moreover, Jews had to bear in mind that the hopes that they had come to associate with Balfour could well be excessive. Palestine still remained in the hands of foreign masters, and the future of the Yishuv was dependent on their sufferance. To imagine that the internal life of Jewish Palestine could be immediately transformed, as it had to be, while concentrating at the same time on the rebuilding of social and economic infrastructure was expecting too much:

At this great and difficult moment I appear before my readers—perhaps for the last time—and at the beginning of this book repeat once more my old warning for which most of the essays in this book represent a commentary: Do not attempt to reach the goal before the conditions necessary for their attainment are ready; and do not disparage work that is possible at any given time and conditions even if it will not bring on the Messiah either today or tomorrow.[106]

In a footnote he reflected on how in 1891 in "Emet me-eretz yisrael" he had commented on how unlikely it was that Palestine's Arabs would look the other way while the Jews reclaimed the land. In this respect at least, he felt, current events had proven him prescient—as indeed they had. But here, as elsewhere, he failed to say much about the moral ambiguity of Zionism's stance toward the Arabs, the ambiguity implicit in the claim that it was Jews alone who could claim for themselves legitimate hegemony over a land where others constituted the majority: quite explicitly in his new introduction—despite his cautionary remarks about the need for decent and just treatment of Arabs in Palestine—he bemoaned that the final draft of the Balfour Declaration left open the possibility of conflicting national claims. The original draft, which he had had an important hand in writing, was in his mind unambiguous and immeasurably preferable; the pragmatism that remained implicit in his call for good relations between Jews and Arabs in Palestine rendered marginal for him the moral underpinnings of this problem. In this context especially, and in view of the way in which this essay addresses quite directly the Arab problem and its implications, the absence of any discussion of it by him in ethical terms is jarring.[107]

No less jarring was his inability—and in an essay that was likely, as he anticipated, to be among his last—to be more attuned to what the

Balfour Declaration meant for the Jewish world well beyond Zionism. His cautionary remarks were, of course, on the mark: many Jews did see the Declaration as signaling the dawning of redemption, as the immediate prelude to the creation of a Jewish state. Hence there was some reason for concern about the impact this might have on Jews once their expectations were unsatisfied, as they would be. And the Jerusalem riots left the Zionists demoralized and deeply apprehensive. But the acuity of Ahad Ha'am's discussion of the drafts of the Balfour Declaration could not deflect attention from the piece's discordant, sour tone, so out of kilter with the bulk of contemporary Jewish reactions to the Declaration, within the Zionist camp and outside it, and its self-evident importance. Clearly the Declaration's significance was not lost on Ahad Ha'am, who was deeply moved by it; but, much as Tolkowsky had reported, when within moments of learning of the Declaration he roused himself to complain and worry, his performance in this essay was much the same. Often in the past, as for example in "Sakh ha-kol," he had managed to balance encouragement and denunciation in an article that, controversial as it was, was fairer in its recommendations. Now he seemed incapable of this, overwhelmed by the difficulties confronting his people, by the likelihood that they were ill equipped for these tasks ("obviously we have learned nothing," he writes here in connection with the excessive expectations created by Balfour). And all this seemed to mesh for him with his own physical decline which, indeed, he discusses at some length in this essay. Later, when there was widespread disappointment in the Yishuv with the British mandatory government this article was cited for its prescience. At the time it was—and perhaps more so than anything else that he had written before—cranky and ungenerous.

IV

He wrote these musings on the Balfour Declaration at a terrible low point. By the time the new edition of *Al Parashat Derakhim* appeared in mid-1921, Ahad Ha'am claimed that it had been two years since he had read a book, that he had written nothing in this period except for the six-page introduction. There seemed little prospect that his health would improve. He now suffered from chronic insomnia and took sleeping pills nightly; after a while they ceased to have much effect. And the world outside seemed to him to mirror much the same misery: Soviet Russia he described as "hell," England (for which he would long once he left it for Palestine) was for him little more than a "prison," and Palestine could still, he feared, slip through Jewry's hands through Western mendacity, Arab connivance, or the widespread indifference of the Jewish world. On the eve of his departure for Palestine, in late 1921, he wrote to Klausner that he was still unconvinced that Jews were sufficiently committed to the revival of Palestine. And without this commitment, not even an unambiguous declaration in favor of Zionism by a Western power could have secured Jewish claims.[108]

Earlier, in August 1918, he described himself as "sick and yet not sick." He managed to work, to make his way on his own to meetings, to see friends: "What else," he asked plaintively, "can one expect in old age?" Soon his health would deteriorate markedly and he began to complain that he could no longer read books or write a simple letter. All he wished was to be sufficiently healthy to move to Palestine and make some contribution there; by now his desire was to be, as he now put it, "ke-ahad ha'adam" (like any other person).[109]

He would use this term repeatedly. On one level, it meant that, though he had resigned himself to no longer function as Ahad Ha'am, the influential arbiter of Jewish cultural politics, he hoped to be of some benefit to the Jewish revival; but his illness seemed to preclude even this. At the same time, he revealed himself to be keenly and painfully attuned to the difference between what it meant to be *ahad ha'am* and *ahad ha'adam*—the latter representing a fall from grace, a decline to the level of the mundane. And, as was no less true now than in the past, his description of himself defined how others close to him saw him: indeed, depictions of his life in the early 1920s (by Rawnitsky, Bialik, Tchernowitz among others) use the same terms to explain what he now was, and more importantly, what he was not: "He was now no longer Ahad Ha'am," Bialik stated baldly in a funeral oration. Had Ahad Ha'am not said this first, it is unlikely that Bialik would have. In effect, he authorized him to do so. By the fall of 1919, having retired from Wissotzsky's expecting he would spend much of the next year reading in the British Museum in preparation for a book that he might write when settling in Palestine, he took to bed with a relapse of his nervous disorder that now essentially paralyzed him. Several doctors told him that they could find nothing wrong with him; there were others who decided that he was stricken with sclerosis.[110]

He himself attributed his decline to the horrors of wartime: it is amazing, he told Ben Hillel Ha-Cohen in January 1918, that under these conditions everyone did not go mad. He also pointed to the death of his friends (Tchlenow's sudden death particularly stunned him), and he claimed that his retirement from Wissotzsky's caused his health to plummet. He admitted that silence on the literary scene was itself a sign of his illness—a deep, inconsolable sorrow that even the Balfour Declaration could not assuage. By early 1919 when news of the Ukrainian pogroms—which decimated hundreds of Jewish communities and were responsible for the murder of as many as 100,000 Jews—began to sift through to the West, he described himself as shattered. He considered (but quickly discarded the idea because of ill health) joining a Ukrainian-sponsored commission of inquiry that would visit the region and investigate the causes of the pogroms: the destruction wreaked on this area, one with which he was, of course, intimately acquainted, coupled with the possibility that the promises of the Balfour Declaration could still be derailed in postwar negotiations or by Palestine's Arabs—all contributed to his deep depression. How much worse, he now ruminated, it must be for those who were inside the Zionist camp and who found themselves confronted with the prospect of seeing all they spent their lives building shattered beyond recognition.[111]

He emerged from the war "wounded," no less so, he insisted in a letter in June 1919, than those who had seen combat. These "spiritual wounds," he claimed, were unlikely to heal. Had he spent his life training himself in some useful occupation—say in the study of reptiles or insects—he could now cut himself off from the wretched world of men, from the fearful visions of inhumanity that haunted his sleep. True, the Jews themselves, as a nation had not participated directly in the worldwide carnage, but they did not have the opportunity: indeed, whenever he congratulated himself on this score he heard the voice of the Devil who appeared before him and, with his terrible laugh, reminded Ahad Ha'am of his foolishness: "'How,' he asks, 'can you be so certain that you would have acted better than the others if you had been tested?'"[112]

So awful is the postwar world, he claimed, that the normal person lacks the requisite vocabulary to describe the "fury and indignation, the pain and despair." If the Jews really were, as the Bible claims, "the sons of prophets," the only credible response on our part would be to cry out in the voices of an Isaiah and Jeremiah. And we would do this without thought to what this might cost us in diplomatic or other terms. Ahad Ha'am was no less hard on himself than others in this regard: he admitted that he despised his own inability to scream in despair when he learned of the escalating violence in the Ukraine and Poland. Instead, he maintained his silence—which he still defended as a sensible tactic though he considered it also as an "illness"—indicative of his mounting suspicion that anything except complete fury in the face of evil was morally bankrupt. He mused that, in light of the events that have wreaked havoc on contemporary Jewish life, there was the possibility that when Jews finally reclaimed their land they would arrive shorn of their ideals, utterly without hope, broken on the inside. Never since his youthful "Kesavim balim," with its celebration of the unrestrained, mad willfulness of Abraham the Fool, had he shown himself to be quite so torn between the politics of sublimation—by now his trademark on the Jewish political scene—and those of unrestraint.[113]

He took some pleasure in the fact that Weizmann could now address heads of state with a frankness that had been (as Ahad Ha'am put it) inconceivable for Jews for thousands of years. Still, the unruliness of political life in the Yishuv—with the socialist groups Ahdut ha-Avodah and Ha-Poel Ha-Tsair already in the early 1920s constituting by far the largest single blocks—worried him. He continued to think of solutions as if he were a great leader who would bring the disparate forces of Jewish life under some control; with the exception of Weizmann whose presence abroad was essential, no one in Palestine seemed capable of doing this: he insisted that this was the chief problem of Palestinian Jewish life, second only to the growing antagonism of the local Arabs. He surveyed the possible contenders—Ussishkin, Weizmann, a handful of others—but beyond these worthy candidates, the choice seemed meager: "We are poor in human material, and in every direction that we look one feels above all this absence of men. . . . And without 'men,' without this awakening from below, it is difficult for me to imagine how we can overcome the enormous obstacles that are blocking our way." Especially since the scene had become so dominated by "all sorts of sects and parties," each with a conflicting and often dubious platform.[114]

What preoccupied him most, though, was his declining health. He had short spells of vitality and optimism, but on the whole suffered from pains, was tortured by lack of sleep, and obsessed by his inactivity, his almost constant exhaustion, his bitterness. This is nowhere more vividly clear than in a diary he kept for himself on the advice of a London-based Indian healer to whom he turned in desperation in May 1921 for a cure for his insomnia. Nightly for a period of two weeks from 11 May to 25 May, he jotted down in English—so that the healer himself could monitor his sleep habits and the impact of the prescribed cure—how he responded. His reports were detailed and meticulous, with the numbers of hours of nightly sleep recorded, when and how he applied the various oils that the Indian supplied him, and so forth. In their detail, at least, these were characteristic of the man. Needless to say, altogether out of character was the enterprise itself—its irrationalism, the way in which it traduced his lifelong commitment to science.

The entry for Wednesday, 11 May 1921, "Beginning of Hindan [sic] Treatment" reads:

Thoroughly wasched [sic] head with warm water & Cutticura Soap. Wrapped head with Towel and went to sleep, having . . . nothing. Slept very well whole night in bed, with only small interruption.

The following day, though he napped an hour after lunch, he felt "as bad as ever." That night was a restless one, with little more than four hours of sleep until he took half an adalin tablet, despite his application of "Himm-oil" before he went to bed. By Friday he was in communication with his healer, writing him for advice as to how to proceed. Within a week it was apparent to him that he had fallen into a pattern: his oil treatment would be followed by a few hours of sleep after which he had to take a pill—usually one-half of an adalin—to sleep the night. On one night he might sleep well; the next would be "still worse" than he had for weeks. On Monday, 23 May, he experienced an "exceedingly bad day." As he recorded: "At bed time applic. of the oil. Could not get asleep *at all*. At almost 2 took a *whole* tablet of adalin and slept about 5 hours." On the final day of the cure—by now he seems to have despaired that the oils would help him—he had an "awful" night; he could not remember one quite so bad. Nonetheless,

In the evening I saw people and felt much better. At bed time I took nothing but still got asleep very soon and slept about 4 1/2 hours. Afterwards I again got asleep for a couple of hours after having taken 1/2 dose adalin.[115]

This sleeplessness (which only worsened when he moved to Tel Aviv where he was given a house near the Herzliah gymnasium in what was the very center of the new, bustling town), his inability to concentrate, and his lack of energy, all these persisted until the end of his life.

It was in this wretched state that he moved to Palestine. Here for the few last years of his life, despite his infirmities, his bitterness, and his insatiable anger, he managed to recreate something of his original, beloved Odessa circle. He witnessed the birth of the Hebrew University and had a hand in shaping its first, tentative steps as an institution of higher learning. He lived out these last years in the world's first Hebrew-speaking city, Tel Aviv, whose mayor, Meir Dizengoff, one of his former Odessa devotees, looked to him as something of a philosopher king. This new city's main academic institution (the Herzliah gymnasium) saw itself inspired by him; Tel Aviv's first daily newspaper, *Ha-Aretz*, was edited by one of his own men, Moshe Glickson, a devoted follower who wrote the first biography of Ahad Ha'am. At rare moments—but such moments did occur—he could not help but be moved by what he saw here. At such moments he seemed satisfied, as imperfect as it still was. He still couldn't allow for the possibility that conditions here might remain imperfect indefinitely: the foundations were set for the thoroughgoing revival he had predicted, that he demanded was essential if the Jews were to survive and flourish. For Jews merely to survive would mean a rejection of history, of the prophets, of their essential character. He wrote Leon Simon, who had never been to Palestine, in the summer of 1925:

There is really something to see here, my dear friend, if, of course, it represents only a small beginning. And it pains me that you did not manage to come for the opening of the university. One doesn't see a marvelous spectacle of this sort everyday, even among the great and powerful nations. Needless to say, I do not wish to give the impression that all here is good and nice and that there is nothing about which to complain. Ah, there certainly is much to complain about, but when I recall the conditions here thirty, twenty, or even five years ago, I must admit that our lives were not in vain and we labored so that the next generation might come into a worthy inheritance.[116]

Conclusion

In a last conversation with Bialik, shortly before Ahad Ha'am's death, the two discussed the importance of the Sabbath. Ahad Ha'am confirmed his belief in its centrality in Judaism; as he had often expressed, its rejection would be comparable to assimilation. It had to be one of the chief features of the Jewish revival in Palestine and elsewhere.[1]

This conversation, in effect a declaration from Ahad Ha'am's deathbed, may seem incongruent, its message awry for lifelong secularists like Bialik or Ahad Ha'am. Both men shunned the synagogue (whether on the weekday or the Sabbath), and Bialik was spotted smoking cigarettes on the streets of Tel Aviv during his Friday night walks. A story circulated at the time around Tel Aviv about how Bialik was stopped by five youths one Friday evening and asked how it was that he could smoke on the Sabbath. He readily agreed with them, put out his cigarette, and began to speak with considerable eloquence about the significance of the Sabbath in Jewish history. Upon finishing his oration, he turned to the small group, with a smile, and asked: "Do any of you have a cigarette?"[2]

Indeed, the town in which this conversation between Bialik and Ahad Ha'am took place—Tel Aviv was still officially the Hebrew-speaking suburb of Jaffa, though it would soon evolve into an independent city—was itself perhaps the most vivid example of the essentially secular character of their collective vision for the Jewish future. Designed, by and large, by the men of Ahad Ha'am's Odessa entourage, most importantly its future mayor Dizengoff, no provisions were made in its original plans for the location of a synagogue, in sharp (and conscious) contrast to the prerequisites guiding Jewish institutional life through the ages. Instead, at its center was the Herzliah gymnasium, by now widely regarded as the institution that most closely mirrored Ahad Ha'am's cultural priorities. In 1914, about one-third of Tel Aviv's population of two thousand was made up of students. The gymnasium building was vast; it was entered by way of a long, impressive outdoor corridor designed to be reminiscent of the path leading to the temple of Jerusalem: Ahad Ha'am, and others, called it "our *bayit*"—echoing classical Judaism's designation for the temple. Here the future elite of Israel would master the past with its more resonant lessons made into a part of a transformed Judaism. The gymnasium itself would be a beacon for the new city, altogether different as it was from wretched Jaffa, backward-looking Jerusalem, and the East European shtetlach across the seas. This town, Dizengoff explained, would be "clean, beautiful, healthy."

Insofar as Ahad Ha'amist values were to reign on any large scale in pre-state Palestine, it was here in Tel Aviv of the 1920s. Its urban designers, working closely with Dizengoff who in turn sought almost daily advice from Ahad Ha'am, looked toward an eclectic mix of cities, or outstanding sections from various ones, as the models for Tel Aviv: Hampstead Garden suburb (which, of course, Ahad Ha'am knew intimately), the seaside promenade of Odessa, and Vienna's Ringstrasse. It aimed to be, from the beginning and despite the resistance of organized labor, a self-sufficient capitalist empire with its comfortable burghers and literate, urban, Hebrew culture. In the early 1920s many here preferred to speak of it as the Mediterranean Leipzig. It declined assistance from the outside including the sort of support that had sustained the Palestinophile movement from its beginning; even Rothschild's offer to rebuild it after the devastation of World War I was turned down. By the 1930s, 50,000 Jews lived here with 13,000 Hebrew-speaking children attending its municipal schools.[3]

By the mid-1920s, this small seaside city—the first one run by Jews since exilic times—with its straight streets, its few well-laid out promenades (much of the city was rather haphazardly constructed), its liberal, secular government could (and did) point with pride to the fact that secular Zionism's leading philosopher lived here—on a street named after him and a few minutes' walk from the Herzliah gymnasium, a carefully orchestrated act whose symbolic politics was clear and unabashed. Bialik now wandered its streets, though he refused to live up to expectations and, much to the chagrin of some of its younger, more militant elements, spoke Yiddish or Russian, not Hebrew. Dizengoff was its chief figure and maintained close ties and deep devotion to Ahad Ha'am, whose old Odessa circle maintained a remarkably coherent presence in local governmental and cultural affairs. There was even an unsuccessful attempt in these years to revive the Bnei Moshe in Tel Aviv.[4]

Here in a city that resembled something of a cross between an unwieldy fish market and the Ringstrasse, Zionism's many contradictions were to be confronted with particular directness: in this self-styled Hebrew city Jewish nationalism would, and with as much self-consciousness as it would ever muster, negotiate its way between exclusivity and xenophobia, between the need to protect its own and the prospect of hurting others, between a reasonably decent nationalism and an ugly and oppressive one.

To the extent to which Ahad Ha'am elaborated in these years how to institutionalize in Palestine the values of Judaism, he did so in his address at the opening in December 1924 of the Institute for Jewish Studies, the centerpiece of the Hebrew University. He had attended the university's opening ceremony on Mt. Scopus. Soon afterwards, still heady from the impressions of the event, he wrote Simon the letter in which he exclaimed: "One does not see a marvelous spectacle of this sort everyday, even among the great and powerful nations." He could not attend the Institute's inaugural ceremony, but here—in an event even closer to his heart than the opening of the university itself—he made explicit his assumptions about the role that the university's Judaic sector should have on Jewish Palestine and the future of the Jewish people.

He describes himself here as "one of the last remnants of the first generation of rebuilding [binyan]," as someone who can speak with confidence about how the prophecy that from Zion will come forth Torah will indeed be fulfilled in our lifetime. This is the task of this bayit whose future seems now happily secure. It represents a vivid example of how the most brilliant achievements begin with the smallest, most modest deeds, with projects that might appear to possess but the vaguest resemblance to one's ultimate goals. In much the same way the university on Mt. Scopus originated with the small, modest Jaffa gymnasium. It was established with enormous toil; poor, its beginnings tenuous, it won the heart of the Jewish people and launched the first full school curriculum in Hebrew. Who could have predicted that in only thirty years' time one could progress from this rather tentative stage to a Hebrew University? And if the first generation of Jewish nationalists—confronted with the multitude of problems that thwarted them from the beginning of their enterprise—could achieve so much starting with so little, can one even imagine the rewards reaped by the next generation?[5]

Indeed, in Ahad Ha'am's view the ingredients essential for the Hebrew culture he had long envisioned now seemed in place: especially since a significant diplomatic victory had finally been won, it was clearer than ever before (or, so he argued) that such achievements were hollow without the cultural underpinnings that had to be at the heart of the Yishuv's agenda. Despite Balfour, and in view of the absence of a coherent Palestinian Jewish economy or a sufficiently large Jewish population to offset the importance of the local Arabs, it was more essential than ever to firm up the cultural institutions of Palestine: without them new settlers would flee the raw, uninviting surroundings.[6]

He remained vague as always on the basic content of this culture, how it would translate itself into the daily routine of a transformed Jewry: if asked how the civic religion of Israel would look with a secularized Sabbath no longer dictated by Jewish ritual, he would, no doubt, have avoided the question; in any event, he never addressed it directly. He was willing to affirm in his old age in Tel Aviv at least one aspect of what must be at the heart of this new Hebrew culture in a September 1922 letter to the editor of *Ha-Aretz* about the treatment of Arabs by Jews in Palestine. A week before, the newspaper had reported rumors of the killing of an innocent Arab youth by young Jews taking revenge for recent killings in Palestine. Then-editor Leib Jaffe declared in an editorial: "The shedding of innocent blood shakes the foundations of the world. On land soaked with innocent blood, nothing will sprout, our nation's freedom will not arise, and its future will not bloom." Ahad Ha'am wrote to congratulate him and denounce the killing as a travesty of the first order.[7]

Many years earlier, he reminds the editor, in his essay "A Small Consolation," he said something he assumed to be self-evident: "A Jew and blood! Are there two things that are more contradictory than these?" It seemed to him then that was an assumption that no one, save a madman, could question:

For surely what did we rescue from the disastrous destruction of our temple and homeland if not the teachings of our prophets, which we took with us on the long road to exile to illuminate the darkness of our lives in foreign lands? *Our blood was spilled like water in every corner of the world for thousands of years, but we did not spill blood*. We always remembered that the great ethical teachings that our ancestors bequeathed us were the teachings of the future that we were obliged to follow even at the risk of our lives until they became the possession of the whole human race; until the animal within us ceased to rule the lives of the individual and society.[8]

So, Jews had nothing to do with such barbarism and they guarded the teachings of the prophets which they were convinced would in time put an end to the savagery that they, more than most, came to abhor. In fact, they associated their own redemption with the extinction of such violence in all parts of the world: "On that day, this people too would dwell securely in its land and see with its own eyes the great victory, the triumph of its teachings for which it had been slain for thousands of years."[9]

The killing of the Arab boy and the reaction to it in the Yishuv which, he hints, was inclined to excuse the brutality of his Jewish murderers, "filled him with dark thoughts." It forced him to question the basis on which he had built his philosophy of Judaism. All began to collapse within him: "And if these were to collapse, what would I have to show in my old age after a lifetime of toil? Except, that is, for an empty heart and a despairing soul?" If, upon reaching the homeland, the Jews sacrifice the great ethical teachings that had always served to define them, the redemption of the land would have been senseless:

For without these principles—Almighty God!—what are we, and what will be our life in this land that, for its sake, we have made the endless sacrifices necessary for its rebuilding? Is it only to add but another small nation of new "Levantines" in a corner of the Orient that will compete with the other Levantines already there in all their debased practices—in a lust for blood, for revenge, for rivalry, etc.—will this constitute their way of life?

If this is the Messiah, may he come, but may I not live to see him![10]

Until this point, and even in his pioneering statements in "Emet me-eretz yisrael," there had been an air of pragmatism to his ruminations on the Arab problem. Though he believed that no contradiction existed generally between the demands of pragmatism and ethics, never before had he made the argument that the call for a decent treatment of Palestine's Arabs was essential to the future of Judaism; nor had he before suggested that this represented the most crucial test that Jewish nationalism faced as it forged its place in its corner of the modern world. He noted a concrete example, one of the few he would ever mention, of what it meant to transform a modernized Judaism into the civic religion of a future Israel. More than anything else he said about Arabs, this brief, furious letter—and despite its "orientalist" assumptions—stands out as his most intellectually courageous statement. Here, and for the first time, he placed the problem at the heart of his moral universe, and he suggested that unless it was addressed in the Yishuv in the clearest possible terms the resurrection of Zion would be worse than incomplete: it would be fraudulent, a stark departure from all that had separated the Jews from the savagery that had made their lives hell for so long and that they so despised.

His last years in Palestine were unhappy ones. The irony of his situation was not lost on him: here he was surrounded by friends (nearly all those who remained from his old Odessa circle made their home here), and several of them saw him almost daily, particularly Rawnitsky and Bialik. From the vantage point of the Tel Aviv authorities he was probably the city's most distinguished resident; even the British High Commissioner Herbert Samuel sought his advice, sending for him from Jerusalem immediately after Ahad Ha'am's arrival. Samuel, and others in the Mandate administration, read Ahad Ha'am in English translation and were much impressed. (The Simon translation, as Ahad Ha'am wrote his friend proudly in 1922, sold well in Jerusalem bookshops.) They looked to him as a moderating voice in a tense, factionalized Palestine.[11]

Yet Ahad Ha'am complained incessantly of Tel Aviv's heat and noise, of his still-nagging insomnia, of his inability to work or make much of a contribution to public life. He was active in raising funds for the support of Hebrew writers in Palestine, he was one of the directors of the university (though eventually he had to abandon the idea of going to its meetings in damp, distant Jerusalem), and he served from 1924 as a member of the municipal administration—sitting usually in a corner of the room silently smoking cigarettes one after another. He chatted daily with Dizengoff in his office and met during their morning tea break with the teachers of the Herzliah gymnasium. And yet he found himself unable to shake an intense yearning for London. He writes Dubnow, in March 1923:

Yes, for London. Not, that is, for close or dear friends that I left there—there are no more than three or four of these—but, simply for London. For its streets and stores more numerous than its inhabitants, for the dark "City" where I spent many years without either light or air, for the suffocating fog . . .[12]

No doubt, he adds, this is a clear sign of spiritual sickness; such feelings would otherwise be unthinkable. Despite, or because of, their intensity he could make little sense of them.

Nothing that he did here managed to sustain his interest for long. While in the midst of preparing his edited correspondence for publication, his major literary project in these years, he left Palestine for abroad; it was not long after writing his despairing letter to Dubnow. The excuse was a meeting at Wissotzsky's London office; the real reason, to the extent to which Ahad Ha'am understood it, was his abiding attachment to a European urban culture which his raw, ambitious Hebrew utopia couldn't satisfy. He took the opportunity to meet his estranged daughter Rachel in Germany where, somewhat frostily, they renewed their relationship now that her marriage had broken up; in London in September, he beseeched Bialik to accompany him back to Palestine because he missed him deeply but also since his bad health would not permit him to travel unaccompanied. It is telling that he made the arduous trip despite his poor health. That November in Paris he complained about how he still couldn't find someone to accompany him back to Palestine, he begged friends for company, and he dallied in Europe as long as he possibly could. Returning to Palestine, he immediately started to plan his next trip to London the following year; it never took place (and he complained about this until shortly before his death) because his health no longer permitted such exertion. When Max Raisin spotted him in a Mt. Carmel hotel in the summer of 1925, he was "thin and shrunken, he looked even smaller than he was. He held out a tiny hand and smiled his old detached smile which his eyes hardly reflected. . . . I was painfully affected by his appearance."[13]

The suggestion that he edit a selection of his letters for publication was made to him in the summer of 1922, soon after his arrival in Palestine. Alter Druyanow, who was apparently the first of several of his friends to make the recommendation, did so in response to Ahad Ha'am's complaint that there was no role for him in his new Palestinian home; Bialik concurred that the idea was so good that the original plan of one book should be expanded into a two-volume set. Soon Ahad Ha'am, ever attentive to presenting his life's work in a neatly organized fashion, envisioned four volumes to complement the chronological sequence of *Al Parashat Derakhim*. By the summer of 1925, when the project was completed, he had supervised the publication of six volumes, still no more than a fraction of the total number.[14]

The letters were designed to cover his public life. They began with his editorship of *Ha-Shiloach*—it was only then, he claimed, that he began to keep copies of his correspondence—and continued until his move to Palestine. Certain periods of his life were given special weight: his editorship of *Ha-Shiloach*, the Technicum negotiations, his debate with the Nietzschean "youth" surrounding Berdyczewski. His family life was all but ignored (though he permitted a reference or two to his break with his daughter Rachel); any mention of his father, mother, even his wife was fleeting, mostly oblique, and unkind. Several letters spoke of his "weaknesses," mostly his inefficiency as an administrator; but, as he understood, this in its own way was also a source of his strength.

He supervised the project with his characteristic stern efficiency. He hired a secretary—a young, enthusiastic Ukrainian maskil Yochanan Pograbinsky, a recent arrival in Palestine, who was recommended by Rawnitsky. In fact, ever since first spotting Ahad Ha'am at a tour of the encampment for new refugees in Haifa where he lived, Pograbinsky admitted to stalking him, to sitting outside his Tel Aviv house for another glimpse of the esteemed nationalist master. Hired to copy the texts of Ahad Ha'am's edited letters—Ahad Ha'am reviewed daily with Rawnitsky and others the sections that he planned to publish and those that he chose to delete—Pograbinsky performed his task with care, devotion, and (as Ahad Ha'am noted, with pleasure) a promptness rare in Palestinian Jewish life. Later he would be appointed curator of Ahad Ha'am House, which contained the writer's library; Pograbinsky, in this capacity, prepared unpublished work for publication after Ahad Ha'am's death. As curator, Pograbinsky proved to be a loyal, defensive sentinel.

Ahad Ha'am's health began to decline sharply in the winter of 1926, soon after his seventieth birthday, which was celebrated with testimonials that appeared in Jewish publications throughout the world. Despite his almost constant pain, he refused to lie in bed: he dressed daily, and he sat on a chair in his study as friends read to him from daily newspapers. One of the last pictures of him shows him sitting with his old Odessa circle in his study: Bialik and Ben Ami stand in back of him; Rawnitsky sits at his side. Ahad Ha'am is deathly pale, fragile, thin, and meticulously dressed. Unlike the others, he looks away from the camera.

Pograbinsky reports that Ahad Ha'am told him the night of his death that he was convinced he would never awaken from his sleep.[15] He died that morning on 2 January 1927. As was the practice at the time in Palestine, when one of the grand figures of the Yishuv died, thousands of Jews from all parts of the land joined the funeral procession. He was buried in Tel Aviv next to Max Nordau.

On the anniversary of his death Bialik addressed a crowd at Ahad Ha'am's gravesite, a practice that continued for several years. These orations were deeply reverential. In 1929 Bialik declared Ahad Ha'am to be a thinker so original and revolutionary that "it is possible to build based on Ahad Ha'am's work a wholly new world for the nationalist Jew, a new 'prayerbook.'" In subsequent speeches he spoke of Ahad Ha'am as the symbol that all future Jews could unite around, the only true teacher of his generation, the Maimonides of the modern age, a man possessed by "holy fire."[16]

This is what Ahad Ha'am meant for Bialik and others of his generation. By and large, such reverential rhetoric proved unsuccessful in inspiring Jews without Bialik's maskilic past; its traditionalist allusions sounded arcane to the younger Jews of Palestine, its devotion seemed excessive and obsequious.

It is ironic that this proved to be the fate of the greatest internal critic of the Zionist movement. Of course he sought out such reverence, he encouraged it, and with the exception of those he felt were his equals (Dubnow was one of the very few), he believed it appropriate that those around him treat him in this way. But such descriptions of him also served to obscure his most important contribution to Zionism: the way in which he had subjected it to relentless scrutiny even before it won for itself much of a constituency or a Palestinian beachhead.

The fact that Zionism's leading thinker was also its chief internal critic reflects the prominent role played by social criticism in Russian thought; in this respect Ahad Ha'am no less than Lilienblum was a child of Russia's 1860s, with its politicized and utilitarian literary agenda. The Russian Haskalah, too, stressed the importance of social criticism as a source of enlightenment. But the way in which Ahad Ha'am combined the roles of ideological mentor and critic, with a fierceness and consistency that spanned some four decades of the movement's growth, was unique in modern Judaism.

It is not merely that he cautioned against the boastfulness or the seemingly innocent exaggerations of a new national movement. He also had a keen awareness of the cost of redemption: its financial, political, as well as its moral cost. In his view the Jews were marked by a specialness that spanned the ages and whose loss—whether by assimilation or the defensive xenophobia of state building—would mean that mankind itself lost something fundamentally humane and essential. He never ceased to believe that the revival of Palestine was crucial for the survival of the Jewish people. But this belief was tempered by a realization of what it meant to resettle a people dispersed throughout the world in an ancient homeland that was dreadfully poor, already populated, and in the hands of unfriendly powers. Despite the lyricism with which he described the Jewish attachment to the hills of Judea and the Galilee or the view from atop Mt. Carmel, Ahad Ha'am never lost his awareness of the thin line separating illusion from state building, and separating obsession with the impossible from the sober prerequisites of national revival.

That this vision now seems lamentably dated in its Spencerian assumptions, its contingent morality with regard to Arabs, and, of course, in its belief that it was possible to construct one nation's utopia on what was (probably inevitably) disputed territory—this, perhaps, is what seems most apparent when one thinks today of Ahad Ha'am. His belief in the need to reconstruct the cultural underpinnings of Jewish life was, to be sure, *maskilic,* or Jewish enlightenment-inspired in its origins; but it was also astute in its judgment of his people's shortcomings, their accumulated resentments, the wages of exilic life, and its terrible, sometimes crippling, burdens. He imagined with considerable vividness the distortions of a thwarted homecoming—thwarted by unsublimated hatreds, by wrongs too fresh to forget, by resentments too powerful to leave behind even once freedom was (or seemed to have been) won. As I read him daily over the last few years, often turning to him immediately after putting down my morning newspaper, the distance between commitments scholarly and extra-academic would shrink: I would read him, as he himself (and despite his grander pretensions) meant to be read, as a newspaperman reporting the ugly truth to a people he loved, about things he hated, about a land that was wonderful and also terrible, that might bring redemption but also horror, that could well be responsible for freedom from exile but also, at worst, for a moral exile more terrible than the numbing, assimilationist alternative.

At times no doubt he was too sober, too pessimistic, too prone to despair. But he managed to interject into the Jewish nationalist enterprise a heightened sense of its fundamental ambiguity: it could only achieve its extraordinarily ambitious goals if it moderated its appetite, if it muted its tendency to lose itself in its dreams (which he identified as among the curses of exile), if it better faced up to its own limitations and the limits placed upon it by the larger world. And he came to understand with special clarity in the last years of his life in Palestine that perhaps the greatest test it faced was the way in which it treated the "strangers" in its midst. On one level, the success of Zionism would be determined by its ability to galvanize the Jewish people so as to make such strangers a minority in Israel; on another level, though, if it failed to create a society in which an Arab minority could live with dignity, whatever success it achieved would be worse than tainted—it would traduce the Jewish past and render all that Jews had accomplished a mockery. It would mean that the Jews had defiled Zion, had taken hold of what had always been the most treasured feature of Jewish life and distorted it beyond recognition.

Notes

The published work of Ahad Ha'am is reprinted in *Kol kitvei Ahad Ha'am* (Jerusalem, 1956). A selection of his correspondence may be found in *Igrot Ahad Ha'am*, 6 vols. (Berlin, 1923–1925). A later edition—*Igrot Ahad Ha'am*, 6 vols., new ed. (Tel Aviv, 1956–1960)—includes some previously unpublished correspondence. In my book I draw on the original edition of his *Igrot* except for letters that appear only in the new edition. *Pirkei zikhronot ve-igrot* (Tel Aviv, 1931) contains a small selection of unpublished letters. Unpublished correspondence cited in my book may be found among his papers in the Ahad Ha'am Archives at the Jewish National and University Library, Givat Ram, Jerusalem, and in the Central Zionist Archives, Jerusalem. Letters are dated in my footnotes as they appear in his correspondence, sometimes based on the Hebrew calendar.

With a few exceptions, the translations from Ahad Ha'am in this book are my own; I have consulted the translations of others, particularly *Selected Essays of Achad Ha'am* (Philadelphia, 1914), and *Ten Essays on Zionism and Judaism by Achad Ha'am* (London, 1922), both translated and edited by Leon Simon. These pioneering volumes, inspired by Leon Simon's devotion to Ahad Ha'am, frequently take liberties with Ahad Ha'am's texts in their effort to render his ideas attractive to Anglo-American readers.

Notes to Introduction

1. *Igrot Ahad Ha'am,* vol. 3 (Berlin, 1923–1925) (6 July 1904), 186; Israel Friedlaender, "Ahad Ha'am," in *Past and Present: Selected Essays* (New York, 1961), 276. There is an impressive body of biographical literature on Herzl. Among the best studies is the keenly perceptive work by Ernst Pawel, *The Labyrinth of Exile: A Life of Theodor Herzl* (New York, 1989). The sole systematic bibliography of secondary literature on Ahad Ha'am, culled exclusively from Hebrew-language sources, was prepared by Yochanan Pograbinsky, *Kiryat sefer:* 11 (January 1934), and 12 (April 1935).

2. M[oshe] Glickson, *Ahad Ha'am: Hayav ufo'ulo* (Jerusalem, 1928), 2.

3. See, for example, the newspaper articles in *Ha-Aretz* (13 January 1967); *Yediot Ahronot* (14 January 1977); Shlomo Avineri, *The Making of Modern Zionism* (New York, 1981), 112–124. Arthur Hertzberg writes in *Jewish Polemics* (New York, 1992), 87: "Contemporary Israeli writers and intellectuals such as Amnon Rubenstein, A. B. Yehoshua, Amos Elon, and Amos Oz are under [Ahad Ha'am's] influence or, like the Israeli historian David Vital, they write in conscious opposition to his politics."

4. Dan Miron, *Bodedim bemoadam* (Tel Aviv, 1987), 102–103; Hayyim Nahman Bialik, *Devarim she-be'al peh,* vol. 2 (Tel Aviv, 1935), 201.

5. Teresa de Laurentis, "Issues, Terms and Contexts," in *Feminist Studies/ Critical Studies,* ed. Teresa de Laurentis (Bloomington, Ind., 1985), 9.

6. Bialik, *Devarim,* vol. 2: 201.

7. See Gershom Scholem, *Od davar* (Tel Aviv, 1986), 72–73; Susan Lee Hattis, *The Bi-National Idea in Palestine During Mandatory Times* (Tel Aviv, 1970), 19–78; Aharon Kedar, "Brith Shalom," *The Jerusalem Quarterly* 18(1981): 55–85; *Ba-Sha'ar* 22(1979): 60–81; Ya'akov Rabinowitz, a labor-oriented journalist, comments on the use of Ahad Ha'am in binationalist circles in *Gilyonot* 20, no. 9: 105–111. Also see Abraham Schwadron, *Torat ha-tsiyonut ha-akhzarit* (Tel Aviv, 1943/1944). Ahad Ha'am's impact on American Jewish life is evaluated in Baila Round Shargel, *Practical Dreamer: Israel Friedlaender and the Shaping of American Judaism* (New York, 1985), and Meir Ben-Horin, "Ahad Ha'am in Kaplan: Roads Crossing and Parting," *The American Judaism of Mordecai M. Kaplan,* ed. Emmanuel S. Goldsmith, Mel Scult, and Robert M. Seltzer (New York, 1990), 221–233.

8. Aryeh Simon and Yosef Heller, *Ahad Ha'am—:ha-ish po'ulo ve-torato* (Jerusalem, 1955), and Leon Simon, *Ahad Ha'am* (Philadelphia, 1960). An incisive treatment of Ahad Ha'am's thought may be found in Eliezer Schweid's recent *Toledot he-hagut ha-yehudit be-me'ah ha-esrim* (Tel Aviv, 1990). Among the most lively criticisms of Ahad Ha'am can be found in Baruch Kurzweil, *Sifrutenu ha-hadashah: hemshekh o mahapekhah?* (Jerusalem, 1964/ 1965).

9. Krishan Kuman, *Utopia and Anti-Utopia in Modern Times* (Oxford, 1987); *Kol kitvei Ahad Ha'am* (Jerusalem, 1949), 23.

10. Andrzej Walicki, *The Slavophile Controversy* (Oxford, 1975).

Notes to Chapter One

1. Ahad Ha'am, *Pirkei zikhronot ve-igrot* (Tel Aviv, 1931), 76. (Henceforth: *Pirkei zikhronot*.) The three versions of his memoirs in this volume—written or, in the last instance, dictated by Ahad Ha'am—together with his sister Esther Ginzberg Shimkin's richly detailed Russian-language typescript, *Akhad Gaam v dome ego roditelei v derevnie Gopchitse* (4°/791 CZA), represent essentially the only available sources on his early years.

2. *Pirkei zikhronot*, 80.

3. Ibid., 77; Ginzberg Shimkin, "Akhad Gaam," 8–16. For discussions of the wages of status and class tensions in Russian Jewry see Yisroel Sosis, *Di sotsial-ekonomishe lage fun di ruslendishe yuden* (Petrograd, 1919), and Ezra Mendelsohn, *Class Struggle in the Pale* (Cambridge, 1970). Also see the savagely satirical fictional account, Yisroel Aksenfeld's Yiddish novel *Dos Shterntikhl*, analyzed from the vantage point of how it illuminates class tensions in Dan Miron, *Ben hazon le-emet* (Jerusalem, 1979), 177–216.

4. *Pirkei zikhronot*, 77.

5. Ginzberg Shimkin, "Akhad Gaam," 17–18.

6. *Pirkei zikhronot*, 51.

7. Ibid., 55; Ginzberg Shimkin, "Akhad Gaam," 4.

8. Ibid., 3.

9. *Pirkei zikhronot*, 79.

10. Ibid., 49.

11. Ibid., 47. On the Ruzhin dynasty see: Shaul Ginsberg, *Historishe verk*, vol. 1 (New York, 1937), 97–120; A. Litvin, in *Yidishe neshomes*, 6 vols. (New York, 1916/1917); Marcus Moseley, "Jewish Autobiography in Eastern Europe: The Prehistory of a Literary Genre," (D. Phil., Trinity College, Oxford, 1990), 257–258.

12. Ginzberg Shimkin, "Akhad Gaam," 16–18.

13. *Pirkei zikhronot*, 42–43.

14. Ibid., 43.

15. Ibid., 49–50.

16. Ibid., 65.

17. *Pirkei zikhronot*, 54; on his mother's death, in 1908, see the letter in 4°/791/1309, CZA.

18. *Pirkei zikhronot*, 44–45.

19. Ibid., 47–48.

20. His study schedule as an adolescent is outlined in his *Pirkei zikhronot*, 80–87.

21. See the introduction by Emmanuel Etkes to Isaac Ber Levinsohn, *Teudah be-yisrael* (Jerusalem, 1977), 3–19.

22. Steven J. Zipperstein, *The Jews of Odessa: A Cultural History, 1794–1881* (Stanford, 1985), 9–21.

23. *Pirkei zikhronot*, 88.

24. Ibid., 53.

25. It was, in fact, Ginzberg, not his tutor, who misquoted the passage that, contrary to what he remembered, is not the same in tractate *Pesakhim* 49b as in *Shabbat* 129a.

26. *Pirkei zikhronot*, 2–3. Ginzberg Shimkin corrects her brother's version of the events leading to his marriage—one of the very few passages in her memoir that explicitly contradicts his account—in "Akhad Gaam," 31.

27. Ibid., 31–33.

28. *Pirkei zikhronot*, 45–47.

29. Ibid., 4–5. On Russian university entrance examinations see Patrick L. Alston, *Education and State in Tsarist Russia* (Stanford, 1969), 98–99.

30. *Pirkei zikhronot*, 6–8.

31. Ibid., 7, 85.

32. Ibid., 77.

33. Ginzberg Shimkin, "Akhad Gaam," 33.

34. Chaim Tchernowitz, *Masekhet zikhronot*, (New York, 1945), 80.

35. *Kol kitvei Ahad Ha'am*, 115.

36. Ibid., 116–117.

37. Ibid., 120.

38. *Pirkei zikhronot*, 8.

Notes to Chapter Two

1. Jonathan Frankel, *Prophecy and Politics: Socialism, Nationalism and the Russian Jews, 1862–1917* (Cambridge, 1981), 49–132; Shulamit Laskov, *Ha-Biluim* (Jerusalem, 1979).

2. Yosef Goldstein, *Ben tsiyonut medinit le-tsiyonut ma'asit* (Jerusalem, 1991), 13–19; Yehuda Slutsky, *Itonut ha-yehudit-rusit be-me'ah ha-esrim* (Tel Aviv, 1978), 9–45.

3. There is little scholarly work on Leon Pinsker. Still reliable is Alter Druyanow, *Pinsker u-zemano* (Jerusalem, 1953). David Vital's treatment of him is superb, see *The Origins of Zionism* (Oxford, 1975), 109–132.

4. Ibid., 153.

5. Mordecai Ben Hillel Ha-Cohen, *Olami*, vol. 2 (Jerusalem, 1927), 99–100; as Shmuel Ettinger and Israel Bartal write of the Hovevei Zion in *The Jerusalem Cathedra*, vol. 2 (1982), 217: "It became the movement of a few Hebrew writers, a few rabbis, several intellectual circles, including some young students, and some of the bourgeois class."

6. For a description of these pre-Kattowitz deliberations, from a perspective squarely within Ahad Ha'am's camp, see Abraham Elijah Lubarsky's letter in *Ha-Shiloach* 6, no. 5 (November 1899): 476–477.

7. *Ha-Melitz* 1883, no. 89: 1409; Shulamit Laskov, ed., *Ketavim le-toledot hibat-tsiyon ve-yishuv erets yisrael*, vol. 3 (Tel Aviv, 1988), 376, 497.

8. *Ha-Shiloach* 6, no. 5 (November 1899): 476–477.

9. *Pirkei zikhronot*, 9; Yosef Klausner, "Asher ben Yeshayahu Ginzberg," *Luah Ahiasaf* 11(1903): 258–259.

10. The quotes are drawn from the translation of *Autoemancipation* in *Road to Freedom* (New York, 1944), 83–84, 86.

11. I rely in my account of these events on a series of memoirs written by Joshua Eisenstadt, or Barzilai whose descriptions are substantiated by primary sources, including Ahad Ha'am's letters and Bnei Moshe publications and protocols. Among these memoirs are: "Zikhronot yamim rishonim," *Ha-Olam*, esp. no. 28 (1914): 2–5; "Eikh na'asoh Asher Ginzberg le-Ahad Ha'am?", *Ha-Shiloach* 30(1914): 302–305; "Bnei Moshe," *Ha-Toren* 2(January/June 1914): 113–120; and the fragment quoted in Shmuel Tchernowitz, "Le-toledot venei moshe u-manhigah," *Ha-Aretz* no. 2116 (1926), found in Bialystok among the papers of an associate of the religious Zionist leader Shmuel Mohilever. Shmuel Tchernowitz's *Bnei Moshe u-tekufatam* (Warsaw, 1914), the only full-length monograph on the group, retains its value. The Central Zionist Archives holds protocols of Bnei Moshe meetings. I learned much from Yishai Arnon, "Mishnatah u-pe'ulah shel agudat 'venei moshe' be-eretz yisrael (1889–1897)." (Master's thesis, Bar Ilan University, 1983); though it relies uncritically on Ahad Ha'am's own assessment of himself, its reconstruction of the political trajectory of the Palestinian Bnei Moshe is impressive. Informative is Esther Stein-Ashkenazi, "Agudat 'venei moshe,' merkazah ve-varsha, u-zikatah le-tenuat hibat zion," *Ha-Tsionut* 11(1986): 29–64. An erudite overview of the Bnei Moshe may be found in Joseph Salmon's "Ahad Ha'am and Bnei Moshe: An 'Unsuccessful Experiment'?", in *At the Crossroads: Essays on Ahad Ha-am*, ed. Jacques Kornberg (Albany, New York, 1983), 98–105, and his *Dat ve-tsiyonut* (Jerusalem, 1990), 204–251.

12. *Ha-Shiloach* 6, no. 5: 476–47; Tchernowitz, *Masekhet zikhronot*, 89; Barzilai, "Eikh?," 302–303; Tchernowitz, *Bnei Moshe*, 11–12.

13. Tchernowitz, *Masekhet zikhronot*, 88–89. A useful source of bibliographical information on Ahad Ha'am's entourage is S. L. Tsitron, *Leksikon tsiyoni* (Warsaw, 1924); also see Efraim Talmi, *Leksikon tsiyoni* (Tel Aviv, 1981).

14. A vivid description of this circle may be found in Simon Dubnow, *Kniga zhizni*, vol. 1 (Riga, 1934), 245–256.

15. Tchernowitz, *Masekhet zikhronot*, 74; Dubnow, *Kniga zhizni*, vol. 1, 248–252.

16. Barzilai, "Eikh?," 302–305; and Barzilai's reconstruction of the Bnei Moshe's prehistory in *Ha-Toren* 1:113–120.

17. *Der Yidisher Veker* (Odessa, 1887).

18. Barzilai, "Eikh?," 302.

19. See Tchernowitz, "Le-toledot."

20. Ibid.

21. See Tchernowitz, *Bnei Moshe*, 169–170.

22. This text was among the archival papers published though curiously never previously used in work on Ahad Ha'am, in Reuven Brainin, *Ketavim nivkharim* (Merhavyah, 1965), 499–500. Ahad Ha'am mentions in his memoirs that Dawidowicz was a tutor of his sister Chana, see *Pirkei zikhronot*, 65–67. For information on him see Ha-Cohen, *Olami*, vol. 3: 39–40, and the eulogy in *Luah Ahiasaf* 6 (1898): 346–347. Barzilai mentions in his article ("Eikh?," 303) that Dawidowicz was among those who came to Ginzberg's in this period, and

he identifies him as one of the founders of a society promoting the use of the Hebrew language who at the time of his Friday evening visits "was still a writer for *Voskhod* and a thoroughgoing opponent of the Hibbat Zion."

23. See the chronological reconstruction of Yosef Goldstein, "Le-toledot masa'o ha-rishon shel Ahad Ha'am: Emet me-eretz yisrael?," *Cathedra* 46 (1987): 91–108.

24. The greeting to Fin appeared in Ha-Melitz, no. 24 (28 September 1888). It is reprinted, with introductory notes, in *Ha-Po'el ha-tsair* (10 April 1955): 11. Also see Barzilai, "Eikh?," 305.

25. Ginzberg's correspondence with Zederbaum is published in *Pirkei zikhronot*, 177–186. Lubarsky's role is discussed in Barzilai, "Eikh?," 304–305.

26. *Pirkei zikhronot*, 177.

27. Ibid.

28. Ibid., 179.

29. Ibid., 183.

30. *Kol kitvei*, 11.

31. Ibid.

32. Ibid., 12.

33. Ibid.

34. See Ha-Cohen, *Olami*, vol. 3, 7; For Lilienblum's reply to "Lo zeh ha-derekh" see *Kol kitvei Moshe Leib Lilienblum*, vol. 4 (Odessa, 1910), 157–164.

35. Simon and Heller, *Ahad Ha'am*, 28.

36. See Emmanuel Etkes, "Ha-G'ra ve-ha-haskalah: tadmit u-metsiut," *Perakim le-toledot ha-hevrah ha-yehudit bi-yeme ha-benayim uba-'et ha-hadashah mukdashim le-prof. Ya'akov Katz* (Jerusalem, 1980); Eli Lederhendler, *The Road to Modern Jewish Politics* (New York, 1989). On the secularization of traditional Jewish leadership motifs see Ruth Wisse, *I. L. Peretz and the Making of Modern Jewish Culture* (Seattle, 1991).

37. *Pirkei zikhronot*, 11.

38. Onkelos renders the passage:

ואמר אבימלך מה דא עבדת לנא כזעיר פון שכיב דמיחד
בעמא עם אתתך, ואיתתא עלנא חובא.   (אונקלוס)

39. I have noted elsewhere, in "Ahad Ha'am's Politics," *Jewish History* 4, no. 2 (Fall 1990): 95, that the index cards—prepared by Ahad Ha'am in anticipation of the writing of (an unwritten) book on the literary style of biblical texts—lists biblical passages chapter by chapter; the card devoted to Genesis 26 skips line 10 without mention. In his article in *Ha-Toren*, Barzilai takes issue with (what he sees as) Ahad Ha'am's contention in his essay on the Bnei Moshe that the group was a failure, but does not object to the way in which Ahad Ha'am describes his own involvement in its prehistory.

For a sustained discussion of the role of pen names in East European Jewish literary life in this period, see Dan Miron, *A Traveler Disguised* (New York, 1973), 16, 155–165. Miron is primarily interested here in analyzing the utilization of pen names in Yiddish literature but in an aside he reflects on their role in Hebrew (p. 273): "For a Hebrew writer of the time, employing a pen name was usually a matter of decorum. His real name, of Germanic or Slavonic origin, was not regarded as worthy of being incorporated (as the author's signature) into the pure biblical Hebrew text. . . . It was not, however, his intention to conceal his personal identity [as was true for Yiddish] and to disassociate himself from his literary work, and therefore he made every effort to retain in his pen name a part of his real name or an indication of it . . ."

40. *Kol kitvei Ahad Ha'am,* 437.

41. Tchernowitz, "Le-toledot." Stein-Ashkenazi places the Bnei Moshe within the context of other self-consciously elitist Jewish nationalist groups of the period, see "Agudat," 29–30. Yosef Goldstein evaluates these conflicting versions in *Ahad Ha'am,* 90–96.

42. Tchernowitz, *Bnei Moshe,* 16–47.

43. For a collection of addenda to "Derekh he-hayyim," along with other documents, see Ahad Ha'am Archives, 1882, JNUL.

44. *Igrot Ahad Ha'am,* vol. 6 (28 Elul 5649), 84.

45. Tchernowitz, *Bnei Moshe,* 26.

46. A. Friedenberg, *Zikhrones fun a tsionistishn soldat* (Brussels, 1938), 34–35.

47. Eliyahu Ze'ev Levin-Epstein, *Zikhronotai* (Tel Aviv, 1932), 81.

48. For the 1891 edition of "Derekh he-hayyim," circulated internally by the Bnei Moshe, see Ahad Ha'am Archives 1882, JNUL.

49. Ibid., 8.

50. Ibid., 7.

51. *Kol kitvei,* 19.

52. Ibid., 21–22.

53. Ibid., 22.

54. Moshe Smilansky, "Zikhronot me-eretz yisrael," *Ha-Omer* 1 (1907): 1–3.

55. Tchernowitz, *Masekhet zikhronot,* 70–72; also see this author's *Pirkei hayyim* (New York, 1954), 132–133.

56. *Ha-Melitz* no. 80 (5 April 1890).

57. Bialik describes his first encounter with Ahad Ha'am's writings in *Igrot Hayyim Nahman Bialik,* vol. 1 (Tel Aviv, 1937–1939), 119–122. His subsequent relationship with Ahad Ha'am, and its impact on his literary production as Hebrew's "national poet," remains the subject of controversy. Dov Sadan's stark criticism of Ahad Ha'am's impact on Bialik is conveniently reprinted in Gershon Shaked, ed., *Bialik: yetsirato le-sugeha bi-re'i ha-bikoret* (Jerusalem, 1974), 16–19. A new, essential study is Dan Miron, *Ha-Peredah min ha-ani he'ani* (Tel Aviv, 1986), 95–107. Also see David Aberbach, *Bialik* (London, 1988), 53–55.

58. Tchernowitz, *Masekhet zikhronot,* 74. The Bnei Moshe's disdain for card playing is stated explicitly in "Sefer takanot" (Warsaw branch, no date), A35/9/1, CZA.

59. Goldstein, *Ahad Ha'am,* 207.

60. *Igrot Ahad Ha'am,* vol. 6 (25 Teveth 5653), 119.

61. A4°791/54, Bnei Moshe Collection, CZA.

62. *Shene hezyonot* (Warsaw 1891).

63. Ibid., 27–29.

64. Ibid., 27.

65. Lilienblum's article was published in *Ha-Melitz* no. 32 (7 February 1892) and no. 35 (11 February 1892). Ahad Ha'am's reply in *Ha-Melitz*

appeared in no. 55 (5 March 1892), no. 57 (9 March 1892), no. 59 (11 March 1892), and no. 60 (12 March 1892). It was one of the very few he wrote that he chose not to reprint in *Al Parashat Derakhim;* he explained that he was embarrassed by its vituperativeness. It seems likely that it was more than its intemperate prose that embarrassed him, but also the way in which Ben Avigdor made so vividly clear the hero worship that was at the heart of the Bnei Moshe's agenda, especially in its earliest stages.

66. "Sakh ha-kol," Ahad Ha'am Archives, 1882 JNUL.

67. Tchernowitz, *Bnei Moshe,* 62–78.

68. Ibid. 143–144.

69. The document is printed in "Sakh ha-kol"; see especially its concluding paragraph, p. 28. Ussishkin would repeat much the same recommendation at the 1902 Russian Zionist congress at Minsk, see *Tazkir Lopukhin,* trans. Yael Harussi (Jerusalem, 1988), 139. Also see Tchernowitz, *Bnei Moshe,* 30.

70. Letter dated 18 Iyar 5652, A4°791/1916 Bnei Moshe Collection, CZA.

71. See Tchernowitz, *Bnei Moshe,* 141–155. Its achievements are discussed, with a particularly detailed description of its Palestinian work, in Levin-Epstein, *Zikhronotai,* 79–111, and passim. For a recent study of the founding of the Bnei Moshe's Jaffa library Sha'ar Zion, see Dov Schidorsky, *Sifriyah va-sefer be-eretz yisrael be-shilhe ha-tekufah ha-'oto'manit* (Jerusalem, 1990), especially 79–85.

72. To the extent to which its political agenda was enumerated clearly—and, of course, its secrecy was itself meant to obscure this (arguably, even from much of its own membership)—see, in particular, the first addenda to "Derekeh he-hayyim" in "Sakh ha-kol," 10–15. Also see *Ha-Tsefirah* (20 November 1890).

73. Tchernowitz, *Bnei Moshe,* 29–30; Ha-Cohen, *Olami,* vol. 3, 80–83.

74. These events are summarized in Arnon, "Mishnatah," i-xvii.

75. See *Pirkei zikhronot,* 14–16. For a detailed reconstruction of this trip see Goldstein, "Le-toledot," 91–108. Tchernowitz, *Masekhet zikhronot* tells (p. 144) how it was Lilienblum's task to record Ahad Ha'am's book-length oral reports.

76. *Kol kitvei Ahad Ha'am,* 23.

77. *Igrot Ahad Ha'am,* vol. 6 (5 Adar 5651), 87.

78. Arnon, "Mishnatah," 26–78. On the Moscow expulsion see *Evrei v Moskve* (Berlin, 1904).

79. Goldstein, "Le-toledot," 96–103. On spiraling land prices in Palestine in this period see Neville Mandel, *The Arabs and Zionism Before World War I* (Berkeley, 1976), 8–9. Ahad Ha'am's insistence was long-standing that the only way to build Jewish Palestine was on a money-making basis. See the letter dated 24 Sivan 5652, A4°791/1916, Bnei Moshe Collection, CZA. Also see Ruth Kark, "Rehishat karka'ot ve-hityashvut haklait be-eretz yisrael bi-tekufat Tiomkin," *Ha-Tsionut* 9(1984):179–194.

80. For a set of vivid reminiscences of the troubling impact that Ahad Ha'am's apparent cynicism during this trip had on one Palestinian Jewish settler—in this instance Moshe Smilansky who would emerge as one of his lifelong stalwarts—see Smilansky, "Zikhronot me-eretz yisrael," 3–9. On the Tiomkin controversy see Ahad Ha'am's letters, written in Odessa, dated 8, 17,

23 Tevet 5652, A4°791/1916, Bnei Moshe Collection, CZA. He criticizes bitterly the Jaffa branch's bookkeeping in a letter to it dated 21 Sivan 5652, 4°791/1916 and, on 21 Av 5652, makes it clear that he intends to monitor closely its activities.

81. *Kol kitvei Ahad Ha'am*, 23–24.

82. Ibid., 24–25.

83. Ibid., 25.

84. Ibid., 26.

85. Ibid., 24. Yosef Gorny, *Zionism and the Arabs, 1882–1948* (Oxford, 1987), 27–77; Israel Kolatt, "The Zionist Movement and the Arabs," *Studies in Zionism*, vol. 5 (April 1982), especially 129–136. Also see Derek Penslar, *Zionism and Technocracy: The Engineering of Jewish Settlement in Palestine, 1870–1918* (Bloomington, Ind., 1991), 1–37, and Gershon Shafir, *Land, Labor, and the Origins of the Israeli Palestinian Conflict, 1882–1914* (Cambridge, 1989).

86. *Kol kitvei Ahad Ha'am*, 30.

87. *Igrot Ahad Ha'am*, vol. 6 (19 Teveth 5651):87.

88. *Ha-Melitz* (6 August 1891) and (9 August 1891). Levinsky wrote several articles in this period criticizing Ahad Ha'am: see Yosef Klausner, *Yotsrim u-vonim*, vol. 1 (Tel Aviv, 1925), 278–279.

89. *Ha-Melitz* (4 July 1891) and (5 July 1891). Also see Ussishkin's diary of his trip in *Sefer Ussishkin* (Jerusalem, 1933), 24–69.

90. For a discussion of the (repeated and frustrated) search within Hovevei Zion circles for strong leadership see Steven J. Zipperstein, "Heresy, Apostasy and the Transformation of Joseph Rabinovich," in *Jewish Apostasy in the Modern World*, ed. Todd Endelman (New York, 1987), 206–231.

91. *Igrot Ahad Ha'am*, vol. 6 (29 Elul 5651), 89.

92. *Igrot Ahad Ha'am*, vol. 3 (28 March 1905), 99–100.

93. See chapter 5.

94. *Kol kitvei Ahad Ha'am*, 91.

Notes to Chapter Three

1. *Igrot Ahad Ha'am*, vol. 1, new ed. (May 1896): 95. (This letter is dated by Ahad Ha'am with only the month and year.)

2. Patricia Herlihy, *Odessa, 1794–1917* (Cambridge, Mass., 1986); *Kitvei E. L. Levinsky*, vol. 2 (Odessa, 1913), 494–502.

3. Zipperstein, *The Jews of Odessa*, 70–95.

4. Seltzer, "Ahad Ha'am and Dubnow: Friends and Adversaries," *At the Crossroads*, 63–64.

5. Tchernowitz, *Masekhet zikhronot*, 6.

6. Tchernowitz, *Pirkei hayyim*, 161.

7. Quoted in *Nationalism and History: Essays on Old and New Judaism by Simon Dubnow*, ed. with introd. by Koppel Pinson (Philadelphia, 1958), 14.

8. *Igrot Ahad Ha'am,* vol. 4 (14 February 1908): 10.

9. For a detailed examination of this three-way debate—between Ahad Ha'am, Lilienblum, and Dubnow—see Shlomo Breiman, "Ha-Pulmus ben Lilienblum le-ven Ahad Ha'am ve-Dubnow," *Shivat Zion* 1 (1950): 138–68.

10. Dubnow, *Kniga zhizni,* vol. 1, chap. 26.

11. Ibid.

12. *Kol kitvei Ahad Ha'am,* 64.

13. Ibid., 65.

14. Ibid., 67.

15. Ibid., 68–69.

16. *Igrot Ahad Ha'am,* vol. 4(19 February 1910), 119.

17. *Pirkei zikhronot,* 55–56.

18. *Ha-Melitz* no. 80 (14 April 1889); no. 81 (16 April 1889).

19. Ibid.

20. Ibid.

21. Ibid.

22. *Kol kitvei Ahad Ha'am,* 2.

23. Ibid., 46.

24. Ibid.

25. Ibid., 88.

26. Ibid., 89.

27. Ibid.

28. Tchernowitz, *Masekhet zikhronot,* 79–86.

29. Ehud Luz, *Parallels Meet: Religion and Nationalism in the Early Zionist Movement, 1882–1904* (Philadelphia, 1988), see especially 27–133.

30. Ze'ev Glickson, *Zikhronot* (Tel Aviv, 1946), 47.

31. Eli Lederhendler, "Interpreting Messianic Rhetoric in the Russian Haskalah and Early Zionism," in *Studies in Contemporary Jewry,* vol. 7 (New York, 1991), 21.

32. Ibid., 21–22.

33. See Salmon, *Dat ve-tsiyonut,* 204–251.

34. Ibid., 207–209; Yehoshua Kaniel, *Hemshekh u-temurah* (Jerusalem, 1981).

35. Ahad Ha'am Archives 1883, JNUL.

36. Ibid.

37. This lithographed broadside is headed: "Fire Surrounds the Four Corners of the House of Israel." Ahad Ha'am Archives 1883, JNUL. Also see A. R. Malachi, "Milhemet ha-yishuv ha-yashan be-Ahad Ha'am," *Ha-Doar* no. 37(24 Elul 5616).

38. Tchernowitz, *Bnei Moshe,* 120–121.

39. Ibid., 111–125.

40. B[oris] Brandt, *Khanukah: istoricheskii ocherk* (Warsaw 1890), 3.

41. Ibid., 5.

42. Tchernowitz, *Bnei Moshe,* 134–136.

43. Ibid., 78, 95, 97–98.

44. Luz, *Parallels Meet,* 84.

45. *Kol kitvei Ahad Ha'am,* 52.

46. Ibid.
47. Ibid., 53.
48. Ibid.
49. See Pines' "open letter" to Ahad Ha'am, A 109/33, CZA.
50. Herbert Spencer, *The Principles of Sociology*, vol. 2, 3d ed. (Westport, Conn., 1975), 321; *Kol kitvei Ahad Ha'am*, 83.
51. Ibid., 83–84.
52. Ibid., 85.
53. Ibid., 85–86.
54. *Igrot Ahad Ha'am*, vol. 3 (14 January, 1907), 275.
55. *Kol kitvei Ahad Ha'am*, 70–71.
56. Ibid., 71.
57. Ibid., 72.
58. Alan Mintz, "Ahad Ha'Am and the Essay: The Vicissitudes of Reason," *At the Crossroads*, 6.
59. Ibid., 9.
60. *Kol kitvei Ahad Ha'am*, 75–76.
61. Ibid., 76.
62. Ibid., 77.
63. Ibid., 78.
64. *Pirkei zikhronot*, 17–21.
65. *Kol kitvei Ahad Ha'am*, 31–2.
66. Ibid., 32–34.
67. Ibid., 34.
68. *Igrot Ahad Ha'am*, vol. 1, new ed. (29 November 1896), 154.
69. Ibid., vol. 6 (6 Kislev 5652), 95.
70. Ibid., vol. 6 (23 Kislev 5652), 96–101.
71. Ibid., vol. 6 (11 Adar 5652), 108–109; ibid., vol. 6 (23 Nisan 5652), 110–111.
72. Ibid., vol. 6 (24 Kislev 5652), 100.
73. Ibid., vol. 6 (27 Nisan 5652), 34–35.
74. See Yosef Goldstein, "Ma'amado shel Ahad Ha'am ad bo Herzl be-re'i mishpat divah neged Margalit," *Zion* 52, no. 4 (1987): pp. 471–487.
75. *Igrot Ahad Ha'am*, vol. 6 (5 Elul 5652), 113–114; Tchernowitz, *Masekhet zikhronot*, 126–140.
76. Ibid., 13–19.
77. Goldstein, "Ma'amado," 475–477.
78. Ibid., 475–482.
79. Ibid., 482–487.
80. *Igrot Ahad Ha'am*, vol. 6 (8 Tishre 5655), 141; ibid., vol. 6 (16 Kislev 5655), 142; ibid., vol. 6 (24 Adar 5655), 146–151.
81. *Kol kitvei Ahad Ha'am*, 448–449.
82. Tchernowitz, *Bnei Moshe*, 141–155.
83. *Igrot Ahad Ha'am*, vol. 6 (24 Kislev 5657); 163–164.
84. See *Kol kitvei Ahad Ha'am*, 437.
85. For example, *Igrot Ahad Ha'am*, vol. 5 (20 April 1913); 39–40.
86. *Kot kitvei Ahad Ha'am*, 449.

Notes to Chapter Four

1. Slutsky, *Itonut*, 203–267.

2. Robert Alter, *The Invention of Hebrew Literature* (Seattle, 1988), 13. There were four Hebrew dailies published in the Russian empire by the mid-1880s, see Gershon Shaked, *Ha-Sifrut ha-ivrit, 1880–1980*, vol. 1: *Ba-Golah* (Tel Aviv, 1977), 26.

3. See Miron, *A Traveler Disguised*, 1–33.

4. *Ha-Shiloach* 17 (1905): 417–422; "Kievskaia guberniia," *Evreiskaia entsiklopediia*, vol. 9, cols. 513–514; Slutsky, *Itonut*, 12–13.

5. Miron, *Bodedim bemoadam*, 352–353.

6. *Kol kitvei Ahad Ha'am*, 184.

7. *Igrot Ahad Ha'am*, vol. 6 (24 Kislev 5657), 163.

8. Ibid., vol. 6 (13 Kislev 5654), 134.

9. This period in his life, and in particular Ahad Ha'am's (at first abortive) attempts at launching a Hebrew periodical, are traced in Yosef Oren, "Ahad Ha'am ve-M. Y. Berdyczewski: tehilat ha-hitkatvut (1891–1896)" (Master's thesis, Tel Aviv University, 1982). On his conversations with Ludvipul about the prospective journal, see Oren, "Ahad Ha'am," 23–26.

10. Ibid., 35.

11. Ibid., 37–38.

12. Ibid., 37.

13. *Igrot Ahad Ha'am*, vol. 6 (19 Teveth 5654), 134–136.

14. *Pirkei zikhronot*, 25.

15. See *Igrot Ahad Ha'am*, vol. 6 (11 Elul 5653), 124.

16. Ibid., vol. 6; *Pirkei zikhronot*, 21–25.

17. Ibid., 23.

18. Ibid., 24.

19. *Igrot Ahad Ha'am*, vol. 6 (21 Tishre 5654), 129.

20. *Pirkei zikhronot*, 25.

21. *Kol kitvei Ahad Ha'am*, 104.

22. Ibid., 105.

23. Ibid., 106.

24. Ibid.

25. Simon, *Ahad Ha-am*, 118–119; *Otsar ha-yahadut: hoveret le-dugma* (Warsaw, 1906).

26. See his letter to Eliezer Kaplan, 9 April 1895, A35/3, CZA. For a detailed account of *Ha-Shiloach* see Ali Mohamed Abd El-Rahman Attia, "The Hebrew Periodical *Ha-Shiloach* From 1896 to 1919 and Its Role in the Development of Modern Hebrew Literature" (Ph.D. diss., School of African and Asian Studies, University of London, 1979).

27. *Kol kitvei Ahad Ha'am*, 125–126.

28. Ibid., 127.

29. Repeatedly he attempted to characterize his readership: *Igrot Ahad Ha'am*, vol. 1 (13 January 1897), 58; ibid., vol. 2 (27 September 1901), 253;

ibid., vol. 4 (22 July 1909), 94. He was keenly self-conscious about his tasks as an editor: See *Igrot Ahad Ha'am*, vol. 1 (20 November 1898), 292–296; ibid., vol. 2 (24 March 1901), 208–210; ibid., vol. 3 (1 June 1902), 47–48.

30. Ibid., vol. 1 (6 January 1897), 57.

31. *Kol kitvei Ahad Ha'am*, 127.

32. Ibid., 127–128.

33. *Igrot Ahad Ha'am*, vol. 1, new ed. (13 January 1897), 166–167.

34. See Attia, "The Hebrew Periodical," 92–104.

35. *Igrot Ahad Ha'am*, vol. 2 (15 October 1899), 100.

36. Ha-Cohen, *Olami*, vol. 3: 32, 45.

37. Ibid., 48–49. *Igrot Ahad Ha'am*, vol. 1 (22 February 1898), 190; Ahad Ha'am's rather offhanded treatment of an aspiring writer is captured vividly in Jacob Fichman's memoiristic *Sofrim be-hayehem* (Tel Aviv, 1942), 28–31.

38. *Ha-Melitz* no. 160 (21 July 1905) and no. 161 (23 July 1905).

39. Miron, *Bodedim bemoadam*, 333–367; Arnold J. Band, "The Ahad Ha-Am and Berdyczewski Polarity," *At the Crossroads*, 49–59.

40. Moseley, "Jewish Autobiography in Eastern Europe," 69–80.

41. See Menahem Brinker, *Ad ha-simtah ha-tveryanit* (Tel Aviv, 1990).

42. *Kol kitvei Ahad Ha'am*, 252–253.

43. Ibid., 258.

44. See Nachman Drosdorff, *Ahad Ha'am* (Holon, 1962), 78.

45. *Kol kitvei Ahad Ha'am*, 254–255.

46. Ibid., 254.

47. Ibid.

48. Ibid., 302.

49. Ibid., 303.

50. Goldstein, *Ben Tsiyonut*, 20–29. On Ahad Ha'am's first impressions of Herzl see Vital, *Zionism: The Formative Years*, 24–35, and passim.

51. *Igrot Ahad Ha'am*, vol. 1 (9 May 1898), 217; ibid., vol. 1 (24 May 1898), 226; ibid., vol. 1 (31 October 1898), 285; ibid., vol. 2 (13 February 1899), 34; ibid., vol. 2 (22 March 1899), 59–60; ibid., vol. 2 (13 January 1901), 190. Also see Shmuel Werses, *Haskalah ve-shabta'ut* (Jerusalem, 1988).

52. *Igrot Ahad Ha'am*, vol. 1 (29 July 1897), 122.

53. See Yosef Goldstein, "Herzl and the Russian Zionists: The Unavoidable Crisis?," in *Studies in Contemporary Jewry*, vol. 2 (Bloomington, Ind., 1986), 208–213; Michael Heymann, "Herzl ve-tsiyonei rusiya," *Ha-Tsionut* 3(1973): 56–99.

54. Leib Jaffe, *Bi-Shelihut am* (Jerusalem, 1968), 21.

55. *Kol kitvei Ahad Ha'am*, 276.

56. *Igrot Ahad Ha'am*, vol. 1 (7 October 1898), 276–277.

57. Ibid., vol. 1 (1 September 1897), 125–126.

58. *Kol kitvei Ahad Ha'am*, 460.

59. Ibid.

60. Ibid., 275.

61. Ibid.

62. Ibid.

63. Ibid.

64. Ibid., 276.

65. The articles by Slutsky and Shor appeared, respectively, in *Ha-Melitz,* no. 279 (17 December 1897), and *Ha-Melitz,* no. 289 (30 December 1897); also see *Igrot Ahad Ha'am,* vol. 1 (23 January 1898), 110, and Vital, *Zionism: The Formative Years,* 8. On Ahad Ha'am's article, see Ha-Cohen, *Olami,* vol. 3: 76–77.

66. Ibid., 77–78.

67. *Kol kitvei Lilienblum,* vol. 4: 247–255.

68. Ibid., 254.

69. *Igrot Ahad Ha'am,* vol. 1 (28 January 1898), 175.

70. *Kol kitvei Ahad Ha'am,* 135.

71. Ibid.

72. Ibid., 136.

73. Ibid., 137.

74. Ibid., 138.

75. Ibid., 140.

76. *Igrot Ahad Ha'am,* vol. 1 (24 May 1898), 226; ibid., vol. 1 (31 October 1898), 285; ibid., vol. 2 (13 February 1899), 34–35; ibid., vol. 2 (22 March 1899), 34, 59–60.

77. Ibid., vol. 1 (20 April 1898), 210; also see Vital, *Zionism: The Formative Years,* 36.

78. See the summary of the meeting (written by Tchlenow) in S. Eisenstadt, ed., *Yehiel Tchlenow: pirkei hayyav* (Tel Aviv, 1937), 104–115.

79. Ibid., 113; Ha-Cohen, *Olami,* vol. 3: 81.

80. Eisenstadt, *Yehiel Tchlenow,* 114–115.

81. Jehuda Reinharz, *Chaim Weizmann: The Making of a Zionist Leader* (New York, 1988), 71–73. For indications of Ahad Ha'am's enhanced standing in Zionist circles in this period see: *Sionistskoe dvizhenie sredi evreev'* (Odessa, 1900); Joseph Klausner, *Dukhovnyi sionizm' i ego glavnyi predstavitel'* (St. Petersburg, 1901); Salomon Schiller, "Smolensky und Achad Haam," *Die Welt* no. 39 (1901): 6–8; Salomon Schiller, "Achad-Haam als Historiosoph," *Die Welt* no. 42 (1901): 9–10; ibid., no. 43 (1901): 6–7; ibid., no. 45 (1901): 7–10.

82. On the role of culture as an issue in the Second Zionist Congress, see Michael Berkowitz, *Zionist Culture and West European Jewry Before the First World War* (Cambridge, 1993), chaps. 2–3.

83. *Igrot Ahad Ha'am,* vol. 1 (27 July 1898), 255; ibid., vol. 1 (1 August 1898), 256; ibid., vol. 1 (28 January 1898), 175.

84. Quoted in Almog, *Zionism and History,* 106.

85. See Chaim Weizmann, *Trial and Error,* 36–37.

86. Israel Klausner, *Oppozitsyah le-Herzl* (Jerusalem, 1960), 7; Leonard Stein, ed., *The Letters and Papers of Chaim Weizmann,* vol. 1 (London, 1968), 52. (Henceforth: Weizmann, *Letters and Papers.*)

87. Kornberg, "Ahad Ha-am and Herzl," in *At the Crossroads,* 117.

88. Klausner, *Oppozitsyah,* 11, 16.

89. Ibid.

90. Ibid.

91. Norbert Elias, *The History of Manners* (Oxford, 1978), 5–6. On the formulation of the idea of "culture" see Christopher Herbert, *Culture and Anomie: Ethnographic Imagination in the Nineteenth Century* (Chicago, 1991).

92. Weizmann, *Letters and Papers*, vol. 1: 85.

93. Alex Bein, ed., *Sefer Motzkin* (Jerusalem, 1939), 8–9.

94. Ibid.

95. Vital, *Zionism: The Formative Years*, 192–195, also see Ben Halpern, *Brandeis, Weizmann, and American Zionism* (New York, 1987), 13–26.

96. See Klausner's comments in *Oppozitsyah*, 5.

97. Quoted in Weizmann, *Letters and Papers*, vol. 1: 414.

98. *Kol kitvei Ahad Ha'am*, 295.

99. Ibid.

100. Ibid.

101. Ibid., 296.

102. Ibid.

103. Ibid., 297.

104. Ibid., 298.

105. *Igrot Ahad Ha'am*, vol. 1 (8 March 1898), 195–196.

106. Klausner, *Oppozitsyah*, 28, 33, 66–67; *Igrot Ahad Ha'am*, vol. 1 (19 September 1898), 268.

107. Vital, *Zionism: The Formative Years*, 370–371.

108. *Kol kitvei Ahad Ha'am*, 150.

109. Ibid., 151.

110. Ibid., 152.

111. Ibid., 153.

112. Ibid., 189. On the close relations between the school and the Bnei Moshe see Arnon, "Mishnatah," 36–45.

113. *Kol kitvei Ahad Ha'am*, 190.

114. Ibid., 191–194.

115. Ibid., 193–204.

116. Ibid., 204–206.

117. Ibid., 208–210.

118. Ha-Cohen, *Olami*, vol. 3: 99–104; *Igrot Ahad Ha'am*, vol. 2 (22 June 1900), 124.

119. Ibid., vol. 2 (20 June 1899), 82. For a guide to late nineteenth- and early twentieth-century notions of illness see Edward Shorter, *From Paralysis to Fatigue* (New York, 1992).

120. *Igrot Ahad Ha'am*, vol. 2 (15 July 1899), 128.

121. Ibid., vol. 2 (12 August 1899), 89.

122. Ibid., vol. 2 (18 July 1900), 130; ibid., vol. 3 (13 March 1902), 25; ibid., vol. 3 (16 September 1902), 71.

123. Ibid., vol. 2 (12 August 1899), 89. On his relationship with Tsina Dizengoff see Joseph Klausner, *Darki likrat ha-tekhiyah ve-hage'ulah* (Tel Aviv, 1955), 71.

124. *Igrot Ahad Ha'am*, vol. 2 (12 January 1899), 18.

125. Klausner, "Asher ben Yeshayahu Ginzberg," 254–255; Tchernowitz, *Masekhet zikhronot,* 10–11; Barzilai, "Eikh?", 303.

126. See Tchernowitz, *Pirkei hayyim,* 182.

127. *Igrot Ahad Ha'am,* vol. 2 (16 January 1899), 20.

128. Ibid., vol. 2 (7 February 1899), 28.

129. Ibid., vol. 2 (22 April 1899), 71.

130. Ibid., vol. 2 (9 May 1899), 72; ibid., vol. 2 (20 June 1899), 82; ibid., vol. 2 (26 June 1901), 234; ibid., vol. 3 (13 March 1902), 25.

131. Shimkin Ginzberg, "Akhad Ga'am," 34.

132. *Igrot Ahad Ha'am,* vol. 1 (24 August 1896), 8.

133. Ibid., vol. 1 (3 May 1898), 215.

134. Ibid., vol. 1 (12 May 1898), 219.

135. See Tchernowitz, *Masekhet zikhronot,* 93–96.

136. *Igrot Ahad Ha'am,* vol. 3 (15 December 1902), 89–90.

Notes to Chapter Five

1. *Igrot Ahad Ha'am,* vol. 3 (24 January 1904), 161–162; ibid., vol. 3 (14 August 1906), 248; ibid., vol. 4 (10 October 1910), 152.

2. Ibid. vol. 3 (24 January 1904), 162.

3. Ibid., vol. 2 (21 September 1900), 154.

4. Ibid. 3 (24 January 1904), 162.

5. Ibid. vol. 3 (2 April 1906), 225.

6. See Vital, *Zionism: The Formative Years,* 4–44.

7. The best source for this confrontation is Shulamit Laskov, "Hovevei tsion be-ma'avak im Rotshild al penei ha-yishuv," *Ha-Tsionut* 12 (1987): 29–71. The Hovevei Zion's preparations for the meeting are described in *Ha-Melitz* nos. 40–41 (1901).

8. Laskov, "Hovevei tsion," 29–36.

9. Israel Kolatt, "Po'alei ha-aliya ha-rishona," in *Sefer ha-aliya ha-rishona,* vol. 1, ed. Mordekhai Eliav (Jerusalem, 1981), 360–367.

10. See *Divrei ha-bikoret* (Odessa, 1900).

11. Laskov, "Hovevei tsion," 35–42.

12. See *Ha-Melitz* no. 41 (3 April 1901).

13. Ibid.

14. See Laskov, "Hovevei tsion," 45–46. Goldstein's interpretation of Ahad Ha'am's involvement differs somewhat with both Laskov's and my own. See Goldstein, *Ahad Ha'am,* 276–281. He sees Ahad Ha'am as politically outflanked and (characteristically) unrealistic. This may have been true but Goldstein does not take into account sufficiently how closely identified Ahad Ha'am was with this project, at least before the delegation's departure for the meetings in Paris with Rothschild.

15. Laskov, "Hovevei tsion," 53–55.

16. Ibid., 56.

17. See, for example, Sokolow's (rather typically) mild account of the encounter in *Ha-Tsefirah* no. 110 (31 May 1901): 64.

18. *Igrot Ahad Ha'am*, vol. 2 (18 June 1901), 232.

19. See *Kol kitvei Ahad Ha'am*, 164–172.

20. Ibid., 172.

21. Ibid.

22. Ibid., 172–173.

23. Weizmann, *Letters and Papers*, vol. 1: 150.

24. *Igrot Ahad Ha'am*, vol. 3 (24 August 1902), 68.

25. See *Kniga zhizni*, vol. 1, chap. 38; *K voposu o natsional'nom' vospitanii* (Odessa, 1903), iii–vi.

26. Steven J. Zipperstein, "Transforming the Heder: Maskilic Politics in Imperial Russia," in *Jewish History; Essays in Honour of Chimen Abramsky*, ed. Ada Rapoport-Albert and Steven J. Zipperstein (London, 1988), 95–96; also see Lederhendler, *The Road to Modern Jewish Politics*, 112–119.

27. See Tchernowitz, *Masekhet zikhronot*, 86.

28. *K voposu*, iii–vi.

29. Ibid., iv.

30. A full version of his remarks are published in *K voprosu*, 12–30. A typescript draft of the lecture with handwritten amendments by Ahad Ha'am may be found in the Ahad Ha'am Archive, JNUL 1889. The citations below are drawn from his edited Hebrew-language version in *Kol kitvei Ahad Ha'am*, 410–414.

31. Ibid., 410.

32. Ibid.

33. Ibid., 411.

34. Ibid.

35. Ibid., 413.

36. For Ahad Ha'am on his expectations for the Minsk conference, see *Igrot Ahad Ha'am*, vol. 3 (11 August 1902), 65–66, and (11 August 1902): 66–67.

37. See Moshe Kleinman, "Kenesiyat ha-tsiyonim be-Minsk," *Luah Ahiasaf*, vol. 10 (1902); Mordekhai Nurock, *Ve'idat tsiyunei rusiyah be-Minsk* (Jerusalem, 1963/1964), especially Israel Klausner's introduction, 15–16; Moshe Cohen, "Ahad Ha'am be-kenesiat Minsk," *Netivot*, vol. 1 (1913): 11–13.

38. Ibid., 12–13.

39. See chapter 6

40. See Nurock, *Ve'idat*, 64–65.

41. *Tazkir Lopukhin*, 133–154.

42. *Kol kitvei Ahad Ha'am*, 176.

43. Ibid.

44. Ibid.

45. Ibid.

46. Ibid.

47. Ibid., 181–182; Nurock, *Ve'idat*, 67–77.

48. *Igrot Ahad Ha'am*, vol. 3 (5 October 1902), (8 October 1902), (10 October 1902), 76–78.

49. Goldstein, "Herzl and the Russian Zionists," 208–226.

50. The controversy over *Altneuland* is summarized in Pawel, *The Labyrinth of Exile*, 467–474, and in Shulamit Laskov, "Ha-riv al odot Altneuland," *Ha-Tsionut* 15 (1990): 35–53. Also see Jacques Kornberg's introduction to *Altneuland, Old-New Land* trans. Lotte Levensohn (New York, 1987); Ya'akov Oved examines *Altneuland* in the context of nineteenth-century utopias in *Zmanim* 2, no. 5 (1981): 70–83.

51. See Berkowitz, *Zionist Culture*, chaps. 3–4.

52. *Kol kitvei Ahad Ha'am*, 317.

53. Ibid.

54. Ibid., 320.

55. *Die Welt*, (13 March 1903); see Weizmann, *Letters and Papers*, vol. 2: 270.

56. Ibid., 270–271; On Ahad Ha'am's reaction to Nordau's article, see *Igrot Ahad Ha'am*, vol. 3 (30 March 1903), 100–102.

57. *Voskhod* no. 12 (1903), cols. 8–12; *Budushchnost'* no. 12 (1903): 223, 237–238; *Der Fraynd* no. 55 (11 March 1903); *Ha-Melitz* no. 107 (11 May 1903); also see Mathias Acher [Nathan Birnbaum], *Ein Denker un Kampfer der Jüdischen Renaissance* (Berlin, 1903).

58. *Voskhod* no. 28 (1903), cols. 4–9.

59. Ibid., pp. 9–10.

60. See *Kitvei Levinsky*, vol. 2: 4–46.

61. For example see ibid., 12–14.

62. On Levinsky see the memorial volume in his honor: *Ha-Shiloach* 23, no. 6 (December 1910).

63. Weizmann, *Letters and Papers*, vol. 2: 356.

64. Shlomo Lambroza, "The Pogroms of 1903–1906," in *Pogroms: Anti-Jewish Violence in Modern Russian History*, ed. John Klier and Shlomo Lambroza (Cambridge, 1992), 191–247.

65. Ibid., 195–212; William C. Fuller, *Civil-Military Conflict in Imperial Russia, 1881–1914* (Princeton, 1985).

66. Dubnow, *Kniga zhizni*, vol. 1: 376–377.

67. *Igrot Ahad Ha'am*, vol. 3 (29 April 1903), 115.

68. See Frankel, *Prophecy and Politics*, 133–170; I examine some of these themes in "Old Ghosts: Pogroms in the Jewish Mind," *Tikkun* (May/June 1991).

69. *Igrot Ahad Ha'am*, vol. 3 (24 May 1903), 124; also see ibid., vol. 3 (16 May 1903), 120 and (31 May 1903), 125.

70. Ibid., vol. 3 (16 May 1903): 120–121.

71. On this fact-finding mission of Bialik, see Chaim Shorer, *Ha-Pogrom be-kishinev bi-melot 60 shanah* (Tel Aviv, 1963), 29–49, and Hillel Barzel, *Shirat ha-tehiyah: Hayyim Nahman Bialik* (Tel Aviv, 1990), 245–282; *Eduyot nifge'e kishinev, 1903: ke-fi she-nigbu al yede H.N. Bialik ve-haverav* (Tel Aviv, 1991). Mintz's discussion may be found in *Hurban* (New York, 1984), 129–154.

72. See David Roskies, *Against the Apocalypse* (Cambridge, Mass., 1984), 88–91.

73. Dubnow, *Kniga zhizni*, vol. 1: 379–380.

74. *Kol kitvei Ahad Ha'am*, 501–502.

75. Ibid.

76. Ibid. Also see *Igrot Ahad Ha'am*, vol. 3 (18 June 1903), 17.

77. Pawel, *The Labyrinth of Exile*, 498–499.

78. Raphael Patai, ed., *The Complete Diaries of Theodor Herzl*, vol. 4 (New York, 1960), 1544.

79. On the Uganda Affair see Michael Heymann, *The Minutes of the Zionist General Council: The Uganda Controversy* (Jerusalem, 1970), and Vital, Zionism: *The Formative Years*, 267–347.

80. Ibid., 348–364.

81. *Igrot Ahad Ha'am*, vol. 3 (31 August 1903), 136.

82. Ibid., 138.

83. Ibid., 139. Also see *Kol kitvei Ahad Ha'am*, 340–341.

84. *Kol kitvei Ahad Ha'am*, 341.

85. *Igrot Ahad Ha'am*, vol. 3 (6 July 1904), 186.

86. Ibid., vol. 3 (27 September 1903), 140; ibid., vol. 3 (29 October 1903), 148; ibid., vol. 3 (24 January 1904), 162.

87. Ibid., vol. 3 (27 September 1903), 140.

88. Ibid., vol. 3 (15 February 1904), 169.

89. Ibid., vol. 3 (18 September 1906), 259.

90. *Kol kitvei Ahad Ha'am*, 342.

91. Ibid., 343.

92. Ibid., 343–345.

93. Ibid., 345.

94. Ibid., 346.

95. Ibid., 346–347.

96. Quoted in Frankel, *Prophecy and Politics*, 147.

97. Ibid., 148.

98. See Hans Rogger, *Russia in the Age of Modernisation and Revolution, 1881–1917* (London, 1983), 209.

99. Weizmann, *Letters and Papers*, vol. 2: 305; Slutsky, *Itonut*, 30–31; Alexander Orbach, "Zionism and the Russian Revolution of 1905: The Commitment to Participate in Domestic Political Life," in *Studies in the History and Culture of Eastern-European Jewry*, vol. 24/25 (Bar Ilan University, n.d), 7–23.

100. See his letter to Dubnow: *Igrot Ahad Ha'am*, vol. 3 (3 April 1905), 200–202.

101. Ibid., vol. 3 (13 January 1906), 196.

102. Ibid., vol. 3 (24 April 1906), 231; ibid., vol. 3 (10 May 1906), 240.

103. Ibid., vol. 3 (3 April 1905), 201.

104. Ibid., vol. 3 (3 June 1906), 241–242.

105. For Dubnow's comments see "Uroki starshnykh dnei," *Voskhod* nos. 47–48 (December 1905); also see Frankel, *Prophecy and Politics*, 136–138, and Slutsky, *Itonut*, 94–97.

106. *Igrot Ahad Ha'am*, vol. 3 (3 April 1905), 200–202.

107. Quoted in Slutsky, *Itonut*, 94–97.

108. Ibid.

109. *Igrot Ahad Ha'am*, vol. 3 (23 April 1906), 230. Also see ibid., vol. 3 (12 November 1905), 211–212; ibid., vol. 3 (15 November 1905), 212–213; ibid., vol. 3 (4 February 1906), 219.

110. *Kol kitvei Ahad Ha'am,* 403. On the Czernowitz conference see *Di ershte yidishe sprakh-konferents* (Vilna, 1931), and Joshua A. Fishman, "Attracting a Following to High-Culture Functions for a Language of Everyday Life: The Role of the Tshernovits Language Conference in the Rise of Yiddish," *International Journal of the Sociology of Language* 24 (1980): 45–73.

111. *Kol kitvei Ahad Ha'am,* 104. On what was his fairly mild, albeit patronizing, attitude toward Yiddish—in contrast to the Yiddishist movement, which he roundly condemned—see *Igrot Ahad Ha'am,* vol. 3 (10 May 1906), 240–241, and ibid., vol. 4 (27 December 1908), 54–55; see also Zalmen Zylberczweig, *Ahad Ha'am un zayn batsiung tsu yidish* (Los Angeles, 1956). The background to post-1905 Jewish linguistic debates in David E. Fishman, "The Politics of Yiddish in Tsarist Russia," *From Ancient to Modern Judaism: Essays in Honor of Marvin Fox,* vol. 4, ed. by Jacob Neusner, Ernie Frerichs, and Nahum Sarna (Atlanta, 1989), 155–171.

112. *Kol kitvei Ahad Ha'am,* 405–406.

113. *Igrot Ahad Ha'am,* vol. 4 (24 February 1910), 124.

114. Ibid., vol. 4 (17 April 1910), 131.

115. See Jonathan Frankel's introduction to Sophie Dubnov-Erlich, *The Life and Work of S.M. Dubnov,* trans. Judith Vowles, ed. Jeffrey Shandler (Bloomington, Ind., 1991), 16.

116. Robert M. Seltzer, "Simon Dubnow: A Critical Biography of His Early Years," (Ph.D. diss., Columbia University, 1970).

117. Seltzer, "Ahad Ha-am and Dubnow: Friends and Adversaries," *At the Crossroads,* 60–72.

118. See *Kniga zhizni,* vol. 1, chap. 26.

119. *Igrot Ahad Ha'am,* vol. 3 (21 May 1906), 283–284.

120. *Igrot Ahad Ha'am,* vol. 3 (26 November 1906), 269. It is unlikely that Dropsie College would have offered him the position even if he had pursued it with greater seriousness; his secular Zionism, it seems, put off its leadership, as Ahad Ha'am had expected it might. For a time, though, he was intrigued: see his letters to Lubarsky in *Igrot Ahad Ha'am,* vol. 3 (25 April 1905), 207, ibid. vol. 3 (30 April 1906), 235–237, and ibid., vol. 3 (8 July 1906), 244. On his travels in these years, especially those connected with his job at Wissotzsky's, see his detailed record of trips taken between 1903–1909, Ahad Ha'am Archives 1875, JNUL.

121. *Igrot Ahad Ha'am,* vol. 3 (2 April 1906), 225–226. Here, in a letter to his dear Odessa friend Jehuda Leib Grazovsky, he writes that he had for several years consciously distanced himself from Palestinian affairs both because he had so little to show for his past efforts and also because he hoped to produce a literary project that did not have the "smell of the marketplace." In the letter he explains that the "pressures of everyday life"—in other words, the pull of Russian politics—have forced him to change his course; his stance toward Palestine-based politics has now changed, he adds.

122. On Ben Zion and his journal see Nurit Govrin's detailed monograph *Ha-Omer: tenufato shel ketav-et ve-aharito* (Jerusalem, 1980).

123. *Igrot Ahad Ha'am,* vol. 3 (26 November 1906), 269, and (September 9 1906), 253–255.

124. *Kol kitvei Ahad Ha'am,* 379.

125. Ibid., 379–380.

126. Ibid., 380.

127. Ibid., 381.

128. Ibid., 383.

129. See Dubnow, *Kniga zhizni,* vol. 2, chap. 50. Also see *Kol kitvei Ahad Ha'am,* 433–436.

130. Miron, *Bodedim bemoadam,* 361–367.

131. Ibid.

132. See the probing discussion in Menachem Brinker, *Ad ha-simtah,* and, also by Brinker, "Brenner's Jewishness," in *Studies in Contemporary Jewry,* vol. 4 (New York, 1987), 232–249. Ben Zion himself recognizes the differences between the *Ha-Omer's* (potential) readership and that of *Ha-Shiloach* and discusses this in the editorial to his first issue; see Govrin, *Ha-Omer,* 4. Also see Yosef Gorny, "Hope Born Out of Despair," *The Jerusalem Quarterly* 26 (1983): 84–95.

133. Ben Zion is quoted in Govrin, *Ha-Omer,* 43–46; Anita Shapira, *Berl,* vol. 1 (Tel Aviv, 1981), 45–68; Zohar Shavit, *Ha-hayyim ha-sifrutiyim be-eretz yisrael, 1910–1933* (Tel Aviv, 1982). On Ahad Ha'am's departure from Odessa see *Ha-Olam* (27 May 1908), 291–292.

134. Simon, *Ahad Ha-am,* 209; Govrin, *Ha-Omer,* 121–122.

135. Another study by Govrin, *Me'ora Brenner: Ha-Ma'avak al hofesh ha-bitui* (Jerusalem 1985), provides essential background information. Several of the articles I quote are reprinted in its appendix.

136. *Igrot Ahad Ha'am,* vol. 4 (23 February 1909), 61.

137. *Kol kitvei Ahad Ha'am,* 377.

138. Ibid.

139. Stanley Nash, *In Search of Hebraism: Shai Hurvitz and His Polemics in the Hebrew Press* (Leiden, 1980), 158–167.

140. See Govrin, *Me'ora Brenner,* 134.

141. Ibid., 134–135.

142. Ibid., 139.

143. Ibid.

144. Brinker, "Brenner's Jewishness," 239.

145. Govrin, *Me'ora Brenner,* 30.

146. Yitzhak Bacon, *Brener be-London: tekufat "ha-me'orer" (1905–1907)* (Beersheva, Israel, 1990), 34.

147. Govrin, *Me'ora Brenner,* 31–35.

148. For the transcripts of this meeting see ibid., 160–164.

149. See Abraham Kustitski, *Be-terem he'ir ha-boker* (Jerusalem 1987), 396–397.

150. Govrin, *Me'ora Brenner,* 184–188.

151. See his letter reprinted ibid., 189–190. For Ahad Ha'am's essay "Torah mi-zion," see *Kol kitvei Ahad Ha'am,* 406–409.

152. *Igrot Ahad Ha'am,* vol. 4 (26 December 1911), 253–254.

153. *Pirkei zikhronot,* 39.

154. *Igrot Ahad Ha'am,* vol. 4 (17 August 1908), 26–28.

155. *Pirkei zikhronot,* 27.

156. Kustitski, *Be-terem*, 396–397; also see Israel Kolatt, "Ideologia u-met-siut bi-tnuat ha-avodah be-eretz yisrael" (Ph.D. diss., Hebrew University, 1964), and Shafir, *Land, Labor, and the Origins of the Israeli-Palestinian Conflict*, 45–90.

157. *Igrot Ahad Ha'am*, vol. 5 (12 February 1914), 160–161, and ibid., vol. 4 (12 January 1910); 114–115.

158. *Kol kitvei Ahad Ha'am*, 424; *Pirkei zikhronot*, 41.

159. Kustitski, *Be-terem*, 396–397; Yosef Aharonovich, "Al ha-'Sakh ha-kol,'" *Ha-Po'el Ha-Tsa'ir* no. 16 (5672): 3–6.

160. *Kol kitvei Ahad Ha'am*, 421.

161. Ibid., 423.

162. Ibid., 424–425.

163. Ibid., 428.

164. Ibid., 437.

165. *Igrot Ahad Ha'am*, vol. 5 (20 April 1913), 39–40.

166. *Kol kitvei Ahad Ha'am*, 355.

167. Ibid., 363.

168. Ibid., 363–364.

169. Ibid., 364.

170. Ibid., 392–394.

171. Ibid., 366.

172. Leon Simon, *Studies in Jewish Nationalism* (London, 1920), 78. Bialik would echo similar sentiments—albeit with a greater insight into his mentor—in his address on Ahad Ha'am's seventieth birthday in 1926: "He always manages to overcome the 'I.' Nonetheless, and despite his own will, it is precisely his individuality that we encounter when we read his words: the greatness of man, the power of his personality." *Devarim*, vol. 2; 192.

Notes to Chapter Six

1. A large, interesting body of literature exists on the crisis of "Ahad Ha'amism"—much of it, in fact, more interesting than the interpretive work on Ahad Ha'am himself: see, for instance, Miron's superb *Bodedim bemoadam*. A full and perceptive discussion of this literature may be found in Nash, *In Search of Hebraism*. *Netivot* (1913) in which Ben Avigdor's bitter assessment of Ahad Ha'am appeared offers a vivid example of how controversial Ahad Ha'am had now become. Not only does it include the unusually lengthy (and, for the Hebrew press at least, uncharacteristically vitriolic) article by Ben Avigdor, but Ahad Ha'am is used as a foil at the beginning of Lachower's (mostly positive) review of the contributions of Berdyczewski (see p. 138): "Ahad Ha'am," writes Lachower, "is a man of opinions, Berdyczewski is a man of ideas." Shai Ish Hurwitz's article criticizes the use of cultural categories when applied to the building of Palestine (pp. 300 and passim). And elsewhere in the volume, *Ha-Shiloach*—which continued to be seen, of course, as part of Ahad Ha'am's

stable long after he retired as editor—is cited as a prime example of cultural irrelevance (p. 322).

2. Vital, *Zionism: The Crucial Phase*, (Oxford, 1987), 35–85. Louis Lipsky records his impressions of Ahad Ha'am surrounded by his entourage at the 1913 Zionist Congress in *Memoirs in Profile* (Philadelphia, 1975), 132: "Ahad Ha'am was shy in speaking. . . . I remember him at the caucus. He was silent throughout, listening, with his head absorbing the Russian words of his disciples and indicating no immediate reaction."

3. Ben Avigdor, "Ahad Ha'am u-venei moshe," *Netivot* 1 (1913).

4. *Ben Avigdor le-hag yovlo* (Warsaw, 1916).

5. Ben Avigdor, "Ahad Ha'am," 243–244.

6. Ibid., 240.

7. Ibid., 247–248.

8. Ibid., 248.

9. Ibid.

10. Ibid., 267.

11. Miron, *Bodedim bemoadam*, 354–355.

12. Ibid., 355–365.

13. See *Igrot Ahad Ha'am*, vol. 5 (16 August 1913), 77–79.

14. *Ha-Shiloach* 30 (1914): 193–194.

15. Ibid., 195–196, 211, 272, 294–296.

16. See especially Bernfeld's essay, ibid., 195–205.

17. Ibid., 197.

18. Ibid., 247.

19. Ibid., 295.

20. Ibid., 296.

21. See *Din ve-heshbon shel ha-ve'idah la-safah ve-la-tarbut ha-ivrit be-Berlin* (Berlin 1910), especially 25–32.

22. Ibid., 25–27; Nash, *In Search of Hebraism*, 287.

23. *Din ve-heshbon*, 30.

24. David Frischman, "Konferensiyah," in *Ketavim*, vol. 8 (Warsaw 1931), 42–43.

25. On the impact of Ahad Ha'am on Magnes: Arthur Goren, "Between 'Priest and Prophet'," in *Like All the Nations? The Life and Legacy of Judah L. Magnes*, ed. William M. Brinner and Moses Rischin (Albany, 1987), 57–68.

26. Ibid., 60–61; Arthur Goren, ed., *Dissenter in Zion* (Cambridge, Mass., 1982), 10–11.

27. "The Harmonious Jew," *The American Hebrew* (25 January 1907): 311.

28. Ibid.

29. *Ha-Shiloach*, 30 (1914): 297.

30. On the debate over Haifa's Technicum see Weizmann, *Letters*, vol. 5, 289; Ismar Elbogen, *A Century of Jewish Life* (Philadelphia, 1945), 307–308; Ha-Cohen, *Olami*, vol. 5, 72–73; Isaiah Friedman, "The Hilfsverein der deutschen Juden, the German Foreign Ministry and the Controversy with the Zionists, 1901–1918," in *Leo Baeck Institute Yearbook*, vol. 24 (1979): 291–319. Moshe Rinott, *Hevrat ha-ezra li-yehudei germanyah bi-yetsirah ube-ma'avak*

(Jerusalem, 1971). More recently, see Rinott's discussion of educational trends in Jewish Palestine between 1882–1918, and in particular his treatment of the "language war," in Kolatt, ed., *Toledot,* 621–714. See Ahad Ha'am's own summary for Dubnow, *Igrot Ahad Ha'am,* vol. 4 (14 February 1908), 8–10. An example of Ahad Ha'am's pragmatic stance on the role of religious instruction in schools, see Igrot Ahad Ha'am, vol. 4 (28 February 1908), 14.

31. Reinharz, *Chaim Weizmann,* 375.

32. Ahad Ha'am mapped out his own understanding of this prolonged debate in a letter to Paul Nathan, see *Igrot Ahad Ha'am,* vol. 5 (28 September 1913), 81–86. Nathan's original involvement in the project is described by Rinott, *Hevrat,* 184–187.

33. Weizmann, *Letters, and Papers,* vol. 5: 108.

34. Rinott, *Hevrat,* 187–190.

35. *Igrot Ahad Ha'am,* vol. 4 (28 September 1908), 36–7, (24 October 1908), 46, and (17 January 1909), 56–57; ibid., vol. 5 (25 November 1913), 118–121.

36. Rinott, *Hevrat,* 189–193.

37. *Igrot Ahad Ha'am,* vol. 5 (28 September 1913), 83.

38. Ibid., vol. 5 (7 October 1913), 90–93, (8 October 1913), 93–95; (5 November 1913), 104–5; (6 November 1913); 105–106; (9 November 1913), 106–107. On what came to be known in Jewish Palestine as the "language war" also see Rinott, *Hevrat,* 206–210.

39. See, for instance, *Igrot Ahad Ha'am,* vol. 5 (13 November 1913), 102, and (23 December 1913), 133–137.

40. Ibid., vol. 5 (23 December 1913), 133–137, and (4 November 1913), 103.

41. *Kol kitvei Ahad Ha'am,* 456.

42. Ibid.

43. Ibid., 456–457.

44. Ibid., 457–458.

45. *Igrot Ahad Ha'am,* vol. 5 (23 January 1914), 144–147, (31 January 1914), 151–155, (2 February 1914), 155–156, (9 February 1914), 159–160, and (26 July 1914), 196–197.

46. Ibid., vol. 5 (8 October 1913), 94.

47. Ibid., vol. 3 (17 December 1907), 290, (18 December 1907), 291–292; ibid., vol. 4 (2 January 1908), 1; ibid., vol. 3, (28 January 1909), 60, ibid., vol. 3 (20 December 1907), 292.

48. On his routine at Wissotzsky's see his letter to Ha-Cohen (9 May 1909), 4°/1068 Ahad Ha'am Archive, JNUL. I thank Shulamit Laskov for bringing it to my attention. Glimpses at the various issues confronting Ahad Ha'am in the tea trade are provided in letters written to him by Abraham Eliyahu Lubarsky: see, for instance, the letter he writes from New York, where he ran the Wissotzsky office, to Ahad Ha'am (still in Odessa) on 3 September 1906, Ahad Ha'am Archive 522, JNUL.

49. Stuart A, Cohen, "Anglo-Jewry and Zionism: The Initial Confrontation, 1895–1900," *Michael* 6 (1986): 49–74. Also see Eugene Black, *The Social Politics of Anglo-Jewry* (Oxford, 1988), 1–35; Lloyd P. Gartner, *The Jewish*

Immigrant in England, 1870–1914 (London, 1960); David Cesarani, ed., *The Making of Modern Anglo-Jewry* (Oxford, 1990), especially Bryan Cheyette's excellent article, "The Other Self: Anglo-Jewish Fiction and the Representation of Jews in England, 1875–1905," 97–111. The *Jewish Chronicle* mentions Ahad Ha'am once in 1908: On 3 July 1908, p. 8, under the heading "Ahad Ha'am's Advice"—and where he is identified as a "famous philosopher"—he is asked whether claims against Russia in respect to the empire's antisemitic record should be pressed vigorously abroad. That he now lived in England was not mentioned in the newspaper until its August 1909 interview.

50. *Jewish Chronicle* (13 August 1909): 12.

51. On the "Wanderers" see Norman Bentwich, *Wanderer Between Two Worlds* (London, 1941). For a good example of how Leon Simon was treated, see *Jewish Chronicle* (18 March 1908): 19: "No-one expected a team guided by Mr. Leon Simon would prove altogether devoid of restiveness. For Mr. Simon thinks for himself, he has a point of view, he is, in short, unconventional." For a litmus test of how controversial this circle of young Jewish nationalists (which included both Simon and Bentwich) were, see the dispute generated by Norman Bentwich's article "Zionism at the universities," *Jewish Chronicle* (26 March 1909): 22. No fewer than twenty-five Anglo-Jewish grandees signed a letter of protest, and the Chief Rabbi sent along one of his own: see *Jewish Chronicle* (26 April 1909): 11–13.

52. See the summary of his appearance before the London Hebraist "Hevrat shel agudat sifrut ha-ivrit" in *Hayehoody* (12 February 1908): 12, which captured his arguments without their usual suppleness; indeed, it made them sound like a rather mechanistic social darwinism. The speech is better summarized in *Ha-Olam* no. 7 (19 February 1908): 106–107. In January 1909 he participated in a public forum in London together with the visiting Hebrew writer Reuven Brainin, see *Jewish Chronicle* (8 January 1909): 30. On his trip to Manchester, see Weizmann, *Letters and Papers,* vol. 5 (26 January 1908), 76.

53. *Jewish Chronicle* (13 August 1909): 12.

54. See his comments on what he saw as England's "narrow-minded," even bigoted Jewish nationalists: *Igrot Ahad Ha'am,* vol. 4 (3 July 1908), 19.

55. *Hayehoody* (20 February 1908): 4–5; Ahad Ha'am's reply appeared 27 February 1908, 4–5.

56. A handwritten list of twenty remazim may be found in the Ahad Ha'am Archives 1875, JNUL. The ten published originally in *Ha-Olam* no. 36 (1910) are reprinted in *Kol kitvei Ahad Ha'am,* 455–456.

57. See Klausner, *Darki likrat ha-tekhiyah,* 71.

58. Ahad Ha'am Archive 1875, JNUL.

59. *Igrot Ahad Ha'am,* vol. 5 (18 January 1914), 142.

60. A 4°/791, Ahad Ha'am Archive, JNUL.

61. Ibid.

62. *Igrot Ahad Ha'am,* vol. 6, new ed., (13 January 1925), 265.

63. Max Raisin, *Great Jews I Have Known* (New York, 1952), 8–14; Shmuel Tolkowsky, *Yeman tsiyuni medini* (Tel Aviv, 1981), 7.

64. Tchernowitz, *Maskehet zikhronot,* 97–98.

65. Ahad Ha'am Archive, 1875, JNUL.

66. *Igrot Ahad Ha'am*, vol. 5 (June 1914), 180–181.

67. *Igrot Ahad Ha'am*, vol. 4 (3 September 1912), 289; Weizmann, *Letters*, vol. 7, 189.

68. Isaac Remba, *Banim akhlu bosar* (Tel Aviv, 1973), 164; Tchernowitz, *Masekhet zikhronot*, 100; also see letter dated 29 October 1912, 4°/791/1916, CZA.

69. Tchernowitz, *Masekhet zikhronot*, 100; Yosef Goldstein summarizes the reactions of Ahad Ha'am to his daughter's marriage in an article in *Ha-Aretz* (19 April 1989), 14; see also *Remba, Banim,* 168–169.

70. Ibid.

71. Ibid., 173; *Ha-Olam* no. 21, (25 May 1928): 386–387.

72. *Davar* (5 May 1965): 12.

73. Ibid.

74. Remba, *Banim,* 174–175; Tchernowitz, *Maskehet zikhronot,* 84–85.

75. *Igrot Ahad Ha'am*, vol. 5 (7 January 1913), 2; A°/791/1916, CZA.

76. *Igrot Ahad Ha'am*, vol. 5 (5 April 1914), 169, (15 June 1914), 191–192, (5 November 1915), 232–233, and (15 October 1916), 275–279.

77. Ibid., vol. 5 (15 November 1914), 203.

78. Ibid., vol. 5 (22 November 1914), 203–205.

79. Ibid., vol. 5 (12 January 1915), 206, and (8 March 1915), 215.

80. Ibid., vol. 5 (28 April 1915), 218–219, and (16 August 1915); 222–223.

81. Ibid., vol. 5 (5 July 1915), 220, (8 July 1915), 220–221, (27 August 1915), 223, and (20 February 1916), 250.

82. Ibid., vol. 5 (13 July 1915), 221 (27 August 1915), 223, and (3 September 1915) 225.

83. Ibid., vol. 5 (3 September 1915), 225–226, (5 November 1915), 232–233, and (20 January 1916), 246–247.

84. Ibid., vol. 5 (9 February 1916), 247–248, (1 September 1916), 267, and (5 September 1916), 269.

85. See Reinharz, *Chaim Weizmann,* 233–288; Devorah Barzilay-Yegar, "Crisis as Turning Point: Chaim Weizmann in World War I," *Studies in Zionism* 6 (1982): 241–254.

86. *Igrot Ahad Ha'am*, vol. 5 (5 September 1917), 315–316; Weizmann, *Letters and Papers,* vol. 5: 82, 236, 315; vol. 8: 94.

87. Weizmann, *Letters and Papers,* vol. 5: 101–102.

88. Ibid., vol. 5: 196, 200, 331; vol. 6: 377.

89. Ibid., vol. 6: xv–xxi; Reinharz, *Chaim Weizmann,* 387.

90. Reinharz, *Chaim Weizmann,* 388.

91. Weizmann, *Letters and Papers,* vol. 7: 212.

92. See Barzilai-Yegar's introduction to Tolkowsky, *Yoman* (Tel Aviv, 1981), ix–xx.

93. *Igrot Ahad Ha'am*, vol. 5 (31 January 1917), 291; Vital, *Zionism: The Crucial Phase,* 121–166.

94. Tolkowsky, *Yoman,* 63.

95. Ibid., 6.

96. *Igrot Ahad Ha'am*, vol. 5 (6 April 1917), 298–300; Jehuda Reinharz, "The Balfour Declaration and Its Maker: A Reassessment;" *Journal of Modern History* 64, no. 3: (1992): 455–499.

97. Tolkowsky, *Yoman*, 54–55.

98. Ibid., 69.

99. Ibid., 123, 291.

100. Ibid., 199, 219, 272.

101. Ibid., 269.

102. Ibid., 219–220.

103. *Igrot Ahad Ha'am*, vol. 5 (5 September 1917), 315–317.

104. Tolkowsky, *Yoman*, 190; *Pirkei zikhronot*, 60–61.

105. *Kol kitvei Ahad Ha'am*, ix.

106. Ibid., x.

107. Ibid.

108. *Igrot Ahad Ha'am*, vol. 6, new ed. (13 July 1921), 169, and (27 October 1921) 176–177.

109. Ibid., vol. 6 (6 August 1918), 112, and (6 October 1918) 118.

110. See, for example, his use of the term to describe himself before the outbreak of the War: *Igrot Ahad Ha'am*, vol. 4 (10 December 1912), 300.

111. *Igrot Ahad Ha'am*, vol. 6, new ed. (6 February 1918), 98–99, (27 February 1918), 100–101, (30 April 1918), 105–106, and (12 September 1919), 150.

112. Ibid., vol. 6 (8 June 1919), 138.

113. Ibid., vol. 6 (18 July 1919), 144–145, and (27 August 1919), 147–149.

114. *Igrot Ahad Ha'am*, vol. 6, new ed. (28 April 1919), 131–133.

115. Ahad Ha'am Archives, 1875, JNUL.

116. See *Pirkei zikhronot*, 156.

Notes to Conclusion

1. See Shlomo Shva, *Hozeh berah* (Tel Aviv, 1990), 256.

2. Ibid.

3. On Tel Aviv, see Alter Druyanow, *Sefer Tel Aviv* (Tel Aviv, 1936); Mordecai Naor, ed., *Tel Aviv berishita, 1909–1934* (Jerusalem, 1984); Ruth Kark, *Yafo: Tsmikhatah shel ir, 1799–1917* (Jerusalem, 1984); Yosef Katz, "Ideology and Urban Development: Zionism and the Origins of Tel Aviv, 1906–1914," *Journal of Historical Geography* 12, no. 4 (1986); 402–424; S. Ilan Troen, "Establishing a Zionist Metropolis: Alternative Approaches to Building Tel Aviv" (typescript, forthcoming: *Journal of Urban History*). I am indebted to Professor Troen for providing me with a copy of this article in advance of publication, and also to Arnold Band for calling my attention to it.

4. Ha-Cohen, *Olami*, vol. 4: 158.

5. *Kol kitvei Ahad Ha'am*, 464.

6. Ibid.

7. Leib Jaffe's editorial appeared in *Ha-Aretz* on 29 August 1922; Ahad Ha'am's letter was published three days later and is reprinted in *Kol kitvei Ahad Ha'am*, 462.

8. Ibid.

9. Ibid.

10. Ibid.

11. *Pirkei zikhronot*, 96.

12. *Igrot Ahad Ha'am*, vol. 6, new ed. (28 March 1923), 252.

13. Raisin, *Great Jews I Have Known*, 16.

14. On the criteria used for editing his correspondence, see *Igrot Ahad Ha'am*, vol. 6, new ed. (7 July 1922), 240–241. For an account of work on this project, see Yochanan Pograbinski.

15. Ahad Ha'am's last days are described in Pograbinsky, *Me-zikhronotai*, 7–8.

16. Bialik, *Devarim*, vol. 2: 201.

Glossary

The entries listed below give only the particular meaning of a term as used in the text.

aggadah: homilectical sections of rabbinic literature.

Ahdut ha-Avodah: a socialist Zionist association and the dominant party in the Jewish labor movement in Palestine from 1919–1930.

aliyah (aliyot): Jewish immigration to Palestine.

Alliance Israélite Universelle: international organization based in Paris and founded in 1860 for the purpose of defense, charity, and education of less fortunate Jews.

American Jewish Committee: founded in 1906, devoted to protecting the civil and religious rights of Jews internationally.

beit midrash (batei midrash): study house.

Bildung: German for self-improvement or education.

Bilu: a Palestine-oriented youth movement founded in 1882; an acronym from "Bet Ya'akov, lekhu ve-nelkha," "House of Jacob, come and let us go" (Isaiah 2:5).

Blood libel: accusation that Jews use the blood of Christians for ritual purposes.

Bnei Moshe: semi-secret nationalist society led by Ahad Ha'am.

Bund: the General Jewish Labor Union in Russia and Poland, founded in 1897.

Duma: the parliament created in the wake of the 1905 revolution.

Elijah the Gaon of Vilna: the outstanding eighteenth-century rabbinic figure and the emblem of antihasidic, Lithuanian-based, traditionalist Judaism.

galut: exile from the land of Israel.

goy: gentile, non-Jew.

halukah: financial aid by Jewish communities elsewhere to help support Jews in the Land of Israel.

Hannukah: the winter festival commemorating the victory of the Maccabees in 164 B.C.E. over Antiochus of Syria.

Ha-Poel Ha-Tsair: the Young Workers' Party, founded by labor Zionists and populists in 1905.

Hasid (Hasidism): a follower of hasidism, a religious movement of East European derivation stressing mysticism and prayer.

Haskalah: the Jewish enlightenment movement.

heder: a traditional Jewish primary school in which the curriculum consists primarily of the study of the Bible and commentaries, and some rabbinic texts.

herem: excommunication.

Hilfsverein der deutschen Juden: German Jewish organization founded in 1901 and dedicated to improving conditions of Jews in Eastern Europe and the Near East.

hurban: catastrophe.

Jewish Colonization Association: typically known as the ICA, founded by Baron Maurice Hirsch in 1896.

kabbalist: devotee of the most influential system of Jewish mysticism, the Kabalah.

Karaite: a follower of a Jewish sect of medieval origin that denies the talmudic-rabbinic tradition; in modern times, Karaites disassociated themselves completely from normative Jews.

kloyz: house of worship or study.

kvutzah (kvutzot): a cooperative or communal labor group in Palestine.

Maccabees: family that led the second century B.C.E. Jewish revolt against the Syrians.

maggid: a preacher.

Maskil: an adherent of the Haskalah.

masoret: tradition.

melamed (melamdim): a teacher of basic religious studies, generally in a heder.

Midrash Rabbah: compilations of a homiletical and exegetical character.

Mikveh Israel: oldest Jewish agricultural settlement in Palestine; founded in 1870 by the Alliance Israélite Universelle.

Mishna: codification of postbiblical Jewish law redacted approximately 200 C.E. by Judah ha-Nasi.

mitnaged (mitnagdim): a rabbinically oriented, traditionalist opponent of hasidism.

Moses Maimonides: seminal twelfth-century Jewish philosopher and author of *The Guide to the Perplexed* and many other rabbinic and philosophical works.

Moses Mendelssohn: German-Jewish enlightenment thinker (1729–1786).

musar: nineteenth-century Jewish religious movement with roots in Eastern Europe that stressed the primacy of ethical behavior and devotion.

Pale of Settlement: fifteen provinces of western and southwestern Russia officially designated for Jewish settlement.

Pharisees: those in pre-exilic Jewry who emphasized the oral as well as the written law.

pilpul: form of talmudic study characterized by close—and, according to its critics, excessive—attention to textual subtleties.

Poalei Zion: the Workers' of Zion, Marxist Zionist party founded in 1906–1907.

pogrom: an anti-Jewish riot.

Purim: springtime festival commemorating the rescue of the Jews of Persia from destruction as related in the Book of Esther.

rebbe: a hasidic master.

Sabbatai Sevi: seventeenth-century false messiah.

shemitah: the biblical practice of leaving the Land of Israel fallow every seven years.

shofar: ram's horn.

shtetl: small town in Eastern Europe.

Shulchan Aruch: standard code of Jewish law.

Slavophiles: a school of thought originating in the nineteenth century and inspired by romantic nationalism that emphasized Russian, rather than Western, intellectual, social, and economic development.

Society for the Promotion of Enlightenment Among the Jews of Russia: known by its Russian acronym OPE; founded in St. Petersburg in 1863 and devoted to promoting educational and cultural activities.

Sukkoth: Jewish autumn festival commemorating the dwelling of the Israelites in tents during their wanderings after their exodus from Egypt.

Talmud: compendium of Jewish law and related literature codified between the second and sixth centuries.

talmud torah: a communally funded traditional elementary school primarily for the indigent or orphaned.

tefilin: phylacteries worn by adult males at weekday morning prayer.

Temple Mount: the area of Jerusalem containing the Temple compound.

Tisha B'Av: fast day commemorating the destruction of the two temples of Jerusalem.

Torah: the Five Books of Moses; Jewish law and doctrine.

tref: not Kosher.

tsadik: a rebbe.

tzizit: a ritual garment with fringes worn by men outside the synagogue as well as during prayer.

Uganda Plan: British offer to Herzl to settle Jews in East Africa that precipitated a fierce debate in Zionist circles.

Wailing Wall: the western wall of the second temple which survived its destruction.

Wissenschaft des Judentums: the "Science of Judaism" school of Jewish scholarship, which first appeared in Germany between 1810–1820.

Yavneh: rabbinic center after the destruction of the Second Temple of Jerusalem in 70 C.E.

yeshiva: a school for advanced study of the Talmud and related texts.

yichus: genealogy, pedigree, or other forms of personal or familial distinction.

Yishuv: the Jewish population of pre-state Israel.

Yochanan ben Zakkai: a leading rabbinic figure in first-century Judaism.

Select Bibliography

Archival Sources

Ahad Ha'am Archives, Jewish National and University Library, Jerusalem (JNUL)
Central Zionist Archives, Jerusalem (CZA)
Kressel Collection, Oxford Centre for Postgraduate Hebrew Studies

Newspapers and Journals

Articles that appeared in the following periodicals are not cited separately in the bibliography:
Der Fraynd
Der Yidisher Veker
Die Welt
Luah Ahiasaf
Ha-Aretz
Ha-Doar
Ha-Melitz
Ha-Po'el Ha-Tsa'ir
Ha-Olam
Ha-Omer
Ha-Shiloach

Ha-Toren
Ha-Tsefirah
Hayehoody
Jewish Chronicle
Kaveret
Netivot
Pardes
Voskhod
Yediot Ahronot
Zmanim

Secondary References

Aaronsohn, Ron. "Shlavim be-hakamat moshavot ha-aliyah ha-rishonah uve-hitpathutan." In *Sefer ha-aliyah ha-rishonah,* ed. Mordekhai Eliav. Jerusalem, 1981.

———. "Tokhnit Netter-Rotshild: tehilat pe'ulato ha-yishuvit shel ha-baròn be-eretz yisrael." *Cathedra* 44 (1987).

Aberbach, David. *Bialik.* London, 1988.

Abramov, Zalman. *Perpetual Dilemma: Jewish Religion in the Jewish State.* New York, 1976.

[Aharonovich, Yosef]. *Kitvei Yosef Aharonovich,* 2 vols. Tel Aviv, 1941.

Almog, Shmuel. *Zionism and History.* New York, 1987.

Alter, Robert. *After the Tradition.* New York, 1969.

———. *The Invention of Hebrew Literature.* Seattle, 1988.

Alston, Patrick L. *Education and State in Tsarist Russia.* Stanford, 1969.

Anderson, Benedict. *Imagined Communities: Reflections on the Origins and Spread of Nationalism.* London, 1983.

Appiah, Kwame Anthony. *In My Father's House: Africa in the Philosophy of Culture.* Oxford, 1992.

Armstrong, John A. *Nations Before Nationalism.* Chapel Hill: 1982.

Arnon, Yishai. "Mishnatah u-pe'ulah shel agudat 'venei moshe' be-erets yisrael, 1889–1897." Master's thesis. Bar Ilan University, 1983.

Ascher, Abraham. *The Revolution of 1905.* Stanford, 1988.

Attia, Ali Mohamed Abd El-Rahman. "The Hebrew Periodical *Ha-Shiloach* from 1896–1919 and its Role in the Development of Modern Hebrew Literature." Ph.D. diss., School of African and Asian Studies, University of London, 1979.

Avigdor, Ben. *Mi-sefer zikhronotai.* Warsaw, 1919.

Avineri, Shlomo. *The Making of Modern Zionism.* New York, 1981.

———. *Arlosoroff.* New York, 1989.

Bacon, Yitzhak. *Bialik ben ivrit le-yidish.* Beersheva, 1987.

———. *Brener be-London: tekufat "ha-me'orer". (1905–1907).* Beersheva, Israel, 1990.

Bartal, Israel. "Ha-lo yehudim ve-hevratam be-sifrut ivrit ve-yidish be-mizrah eropah ben ha-shanim 1865–1914." Ph.D. diss., Hebrew University, 1980.

Barzel, Hillel. *Shirat ha-tehiyah: Hayyim Nahman Bialik*. Tel Aviv, 1990.

Barzilay-Yegar, Devorah. "Crisis as Turning Point: Chaim Weizmann in World War I." *Studies in Zionism* 6 (1982).

Becker, Ya'akov. *Yosef Klausner*. Tel Aviv, 1947.

Bein, Alex, ed. *Sefer Motzkin*. Jerusalem, 1939.

———. *Theodor Herzl*. New York, 1962.

Ben-Arieh, Yehoshua, and Israel Bartal, eds. *Ha-Historiah shel eretz yisrael: shilhei ha-tekufah ha-Ottomanit*. Jerusalem, 1983.

Ben-Artsi, Yossi. *Ha-Moshava ha-ivrit be-nof eretz yisrael. 1882–1914*. Jerusalem, 1988.

Bentwich, Norman. *Wanderer Between Two Worlds*. London, 1941.

Benyamin, R., ed. *Sefer Ussishkin*. Jerusalem, 1933.

Berdyczewski, Micah Joseph. *Ma'amarim*. Leipzig, 1921/1922.

Berkowitz, Michael. "Art in Zionist Popular Culture and Jewish National Self-Consciousness, 1897–1914." In *Studies in Contemporary Jewry* 6 (New York, 1990).

———. *Zionist Culture and West European Jewry Before the First World War*. Cambridge, 1993.

Bernstein-Kohen, M., ed. *Sefer Bernstein-Kohen*. Tel Aviv, 1946.

Biale, David. *Gershom Scholem: Kabbalah and Counter-History*. Cambridge, Mass., 1979.

Bialik, Hayyim N. *Devarim she-be'al peh*, 2 vols. Tel Aviv, 1935.

———. *Igrot Hayyim Nahman Bialik*. Tel Aviv, 1937–1939.

———. *Ketavim genuzim shel Bialik*. Tel Aviv, 1971.

———. *Kol kitvei H. N. Bialik*. Tel Aviv, 1961.

Billington, James H. *Mikhailovsky and Russian Populism*. Oxford, 1958.

Black, Eugene. *The Social Politics of Anglo-Jewry*. Oxford, 1990.

Brainin, Reuven. *Ketavim nivkharim*. Merhavyah, 1965.

Brandt, Boris. *Khanukah: istoricheskii ocherk*. Warsaw, 1890.

Brinker, Menahem. "Brenner's Jewishness." In *Studies in Contemporary Jewry*, 4 (New York, 1987): 232–249.

———. *Ad ha-Simtah ha-tveryanit*. Tel Aviv, 1990.

Brinner, William M., and Moses Rischin, eds. *Like all Nations? The Life and Legacy of Judah L. Magnes*. Albany, 1987.

Brym, Robert J. *The Jewish Intelligentsia and Russian Marxism*. London, 1978.

Burstein, Moshe. *Self-Government of the Jews in Palestine Since 1900*. Tel Aviv, 1934.

Carlyle, Thomas. *On Heroes, Hero Worship and the Heroic in History*. New York, 1905.

Deich, Lev Grigorevich. *Rol' evreev v russkom revoluitsionnom dvizehenii*. Berlin, 1923.

Der Yidisher Verker. Odessa, 1887.

Di ershte yidishe sprakh-konferents. Vilna, 1931.

Din ve-heshbon shel ha-ve'idat la-safah ve-la-tarbut ha-ivrit be-Berlin. Berlin, 1910.

Drosdorff, Nachman. *Ahad Ha'am.* Holon, 1962.

Druyanow, Alter. *Sefer Tel Aviv.* Tel Aviv, 1936.

———. *Pinsker u-zemano.* Jerusalem, 1953.

Dubnov-Erlich, Sophie. *The Life and Work of S.M. Dubnov,* trans. Judith Vowles, ed. Jeffrey Shandler. Bloomington, Ind., 1991.

Dubnow, Shimon. *Kniga zhizni,* 2 vols. Riga, 1934, vol. 3, New York, 1957.

Eduyot nifge'e kishinev, 1903 ke-fi she-nigbu al-yede H.N. Bialik va-haverav. Tel Aviv, 1991.

Ehrenpreis, Marcus. *Ben mizrah le-ma'arav.* Tel Aviv, 1953.

Eisen, Arnold M. *Galut.* Bloomington, Ind. 1986.

Eisenstadt, S. ed. *Yehiel Tchlenow: pirkei hayyav u-fe'ulato.* Tel Aviv, 1937.

Elbogen, Ismar. *A Century of Jewish Life.* Philadelphia, 1945.

Elias, Norbert. *The History of Manners.* Oxford, 1978.

Emmons, Terence. *The Formation of Political Parties and the First National Elections in Russia.* Cambridge, Mass., 1983.

Etkes, Emanuel. "Ha-G'ra veha-haskalah: tadmit u-metsiut." *Perakim le-toldot ha-hevrah ha-yehudit bi-yeme ha-benayim uva-et ha-hadashah mukdashim le-prof. Ya'akov Katz.* Jerusalem, 1980.

———. "Mishpahah ve-limud torah be-huge ha-'limudim' be-lita be-me'ah ha-19." *Zion* 51 (1986).

Evrei v Moskve. Berlin, 1903.

Febvre, Lucien, and Henri-Jean Martin. *The Coming of the Book.* London, 1976.

Feiwel, Berthold. *Judenmassacres in Kishinew.* Berlin, n.d.

Fichman, Jacob. *Sofrim be-hayehem.* Tel Aviv, 1942.

———. *Alufei ha-haskalah.* Tel Aviv, 1952.

———. *Kitvei Ya'akov Fichman.* Tel Aviv, 1959.

Fishman, David E. "The Politics of Yiddish in Tsarist Russia." In *From Ancient to Modern Judaism: Essays in Honor of Marvin Fox,* vol. 4, ed. Jacob Neusner, Ernst Frerichs, and Nahum Sarna. Atlanta, 1989.

Fishman, Joshua A. "Attracting a Following to High-Culture for a Language of Everyday Life: The Role of the Tshernovits Language Conference in the Rise of Yiddish." *International Journal of the Sociology of Language* 24 (1980).

Frankel, Jonathan. *Prophecy and Politics: Socialism, Nationalism, and the Russian Jews.* Cambridge, 1981.

Friedenberg, A. *Zikhrones fun a tsionstishn soldat.* Brussels, 1938.

Friedlaender, Israel. *Past and Present: Selected Essays.* New York, 1961.

Friedman, Isaiah. *The Question of Palestine, 1914–1918.* London, 1973.

Gartner, Lloyd P. *The Jewish Immigrant in England, 1870–1914.* London, 1960.

Gellner, Ernest. *Nations and Nationalism.* Oxford, 1983.

Ginsberg, Shaul. *Historishe verk,* 3 vols. New York, 1937.

Glickson, Ze'ev. *Zikhronot.* Tel Aviv, 1946.

Glikson, Moshe. *Ahad Ha'am hayav u-fo'ulo.* Jerusalem, 1928.

Goldsmith, Emmanuel S., Mel Scult, and Robert M. Seltzer, eds. *The American Judaism of Mordecai M. Kaplan.* New York, 1990.

Goldstein, Yosef. "Ahad Ha'am veha-histadrut ha-tsiyonit be-reshitah." In *Mile'at,* vol. 2. Tel Aviv, 1984.

———. "Ha-Ma'avak ben haredim le-hiloni'im al demuto shel ha-tenuah ha-tsiyonit, 1882–1922." *Yahadut Zemanenu* 2 (1985).

———. "Some Sociological Aspects of the Russian Zionist Movement at its Inception." *Jewish Social Studies* 48, no. 2 (Spring, 1985).

———. "Ha-Heder ha-metukan be-rusyah ke-basis le-tenuat ha-tsiyonit." *Iyunim be-hinukh* 45 (June, 1986).

———. "The Attitude of the Jewish and Russian Intelligentsia to Zionism in the Initial Period." *Slavonic and East European Review* 64, no. 4 (October, 1986).

———. "Herzl and the Russian Zionists: The Unavoidable Crisis?" In *Studies in Contemporary Jewry,* vol. 2 (Bloomington, Ind., 1986).

———. "Jabotinsky and Jewish Autonomy." *Studies in Zionism* 7, no. 2 (Autumn, 1986).

———. "Le-toldot masa'o ha-rishon shel Ahad Ha'am: emet me-erets yisrael?" *Cathedra* 46 (1987).

———. "Ma'amado shel Ahad Ha'am ad bo Herzl be-re'i 'mishpat divah' neged Margalit." *Zion* 52, 4 (1987).

———. *Ahad Ha'am: Biograpfiah.* Tel Aviv, 1992.

———. *Ben tsiyonut medinit le-tsiyonut ma'asit.* Jerusalem, 1991.

Goren, Arthur A. *New York Jews and the Quest for Community: The Kehillah Experiment, 1908–1922.* New York, 1970.

———. *Dissenter in Zion.* Cambridge, Mass., 1982.

Gorny, Yosef. *Zionism and the Arabs, 1882–1948.* Oxford, 1987.

Gottschalk, Alfred. "Ahad Ha'am, the Bible and the Bible tradition." Ph.D. diss., University of Southern California, 1965.

Govrin, Nurit. *Mikhah Yosef Berdits'evski.* Tel Aviv, 1973.

———. *Ha-Omer: tenufato shel ketav-et ve-aharito.* Jerusalem, 1980.

———. *Me'ora Brener: ha-ma'avak al hofesh bitui.* Jerusalem, 1985.

Greenbaum, Yitzhak. *Ha-tenuah ha-tsiyonit be-hitpathutah,* 3 vols. Jerusalem, 1949.

Ha-Cohen, Mordecai ben Hillel. *Olami,* 5 vols. Tel Aviv, 1927–1929.

Halkin, Simon. *Modern Hebrew Literature.* New York, 1950.

Halpern, Ben. *A clash of Heroes: Brandeis, Weizmann, and American Zionism.* New York, 1987.

———. *The Idea of the Jewish State.* Cambridge, Mass., 1961.

Harcave, Sidney. "The Jewish Question in the First Duma." *Jewish Social Studies* 6 (1944).

———. "The Jews and the First Russian National Election." *American and Slavic East European Review* 9, no. 1 (1950).

Harris, Jay. *Nachman Krochmal: Guiding the Perplexed of the Modern Age.* New York, 1991.

Herzl, Theodor, Old-New Land, trans. Lotte Levensohn. (New York, 1987).

Hurwitz, Shai. Ha-Hasidut ve-ha-haskalah. Berlin, 1911.

Jaffe, Leib. Bi-Shelihut Am. Jerusalem, 1968.

Janowsky, Oscar I. The Jews and Minority Rights, 1898–1919. New York, 1966.

Jewish Leadership in Modern Times: A Symposium. Cambridge, Mass., 1988.

K voposu o natsional'nom' vospitanii. Odessa, 1903.

Kaniel, Yehoshua. Hemshekh u-temurah. Jerusalem, 1981.

Kark, Ruth. "Rehishat karka'ot ve-hityashvut haklait hadashah be-erets yisrael be-tekufat Tiomkin." Ha-Tsionut 9 (1984).

————. Yafo: Tsmikhatah shel ir 1799–1917. Jerusalem, 1984.

Kartun-Blum, Ruth, ed. Ha-shira ha-ivrit bi-tekufat hibbat zion. Jerusalem, 1969.

[Katsnelson, Berl], Kitvei B. Katsnelson, 12 vols. Tel Aviv, 1945–50.

Katz, Yosef. "Ideology and Urban Development: Zionism and the Origins of Tel Aviv, 1906–1914." Journal of Historical Geography 12, no. 4 (1986).

————. Ha-yozma ha-pratit be-vinyan eretz yisael bi-tekufat ha-aliyah ha-sheniyah. Ramat Gan, 1989.

Kaufman, Yehezkiel. Golah ve-nekhkar, 2 vols. Tel Aviv, 1961.

Kedar, Aharon. "Brith Shalom." The Jerusalem Quarterly 18 (1981).

Klausner, Joseph. Dukhovnyi sionizm'i ego glavnyi predstavitel'. St. Petersburg, 1901.

————. Akhad-Gaam: ego dukhovnyi sionizm'. Odessa, 1905.

————. Historiyah shel ha-sifrut ha-ivrit ha-hadashah, 6 vols. Jerusalem, 1930–1950.

————. Darki likrat ha-tehiyah veha-geulah, otobiografyah, 1874–1949. Tel Aviv and Jerusalem, 1955.

Klausner, Israel. Opozitsiyah le-Herzl. Jerusalem, 1960.

————. Mi-katavits ad bazel. Jerusalem, 1965.

Kleinman, Moshe. Demuyot ve-komot. Paris, 1928.

Klier, John, and Shlomo Lambroza, eds. Pogroms: Anti-Jewish Violence in Modern Russian History. Cambridge, 1992.

Kolatt, Israel. Ha-ikarim veha-poalim al ha-Avodah ha-ivrit. Jerusalem, 1964/1965.

————. "The Zionist Movement and the Arabs." Studies in Zionism 5 (1982).

Kornberg, Jacques, ed. At the Crossroads: Essays on Ahad Ha-Am. Albany, 1983.

Kuman, Krishan. Utopia and Anti-Utopia in Modern Times. Oxford, 1987.

Kurzweil, Baruch. Sifrutenu ha-hadashah: hemshekh o mahapekhah? Jerusalem, 1964/1965.

————. Ben hazon le-ven ha-absurdi. Jerusalem, 1966.

Kustitski, Abraham. Be-terem he'ir ha-boker. Jerusalem, 1987.

Lachower, Fishel. Rishonim ve-aharonim. Tel Aviv, 1934/1935.

————. Bialik: Hayyav vi-yetsiratav, 2 vols. Jerusalem, 1950.

Laqueur, Walter. *A History of Zionism.* London, 1972.

Laskov, Shulamit, ed., *Ketavim le-toledot hibat-tsiyon ve-yihsuv erets yisrael,* 5 vols. Tel Aviv, 1982–1988.

———. *Ha-Biluim.* Jerusalem, 1979.

———. "Ha-riv al odot Altneuland." *Ha-Tsionut* 15 (1990).

———. "Hovevei tsiyon be-ma'avak im rotshild al pene ha-yishuv." *Ha-Tsionut* 12 (1987).

Laurentis, Teresa de, ed. *Feminist Studies/Critical Studies.* Bloomington, Ind., 1985.

Le-hag yovlo Ben Avigdor. Warsaw, 1919.

Lederhendler, Eli. *The Road to Modern Jewish Politics.* New York, 1989.

———. "Interpreting Messianic Rhetoric in the Russian Haskalah and Early Zionism." In *Studies in Contemporary Jewry,* vol. 7 (New York, 1991).

Levin, Shmarya. *Childhood in Exile.* New York, 1929.

———. *Youth in Revolt.* New York, 1930.

———. *The Arena.* New York, 1932.

———. *Igrot Shmaryahu Levin: mivhar.* Tel Aviv, 1966.

Levin-Epstein, Eliyahu Zeev. *Zikhronotai.* Tel Aviv, 1932.

Levinson, Isaac Ber. *Teudah be-yisrael.* Jerusalem, 1977.

[Lilienblum, Moshe Leib], *Kol kitvei Moshe Leib Lilienblum,* 4 vols, Cracow, 1910.

Lipsky, Louis. *Memoirs in Profile.* Philadelphia, 1975.

Litvin, A. *Yidishe neshomes,* 6 vols. New York, 1916/1917.

Luz, Ehud. *Parallels Meet: Religion and Nationalism in the Early Zionist Movement, 1882–1914.* Philadelphia, 1988.

Mandel, Neville. *The Arabs and Zionism before World War I.* Berkeley, 1976.

Manuel, Frank E., and Fritzie P. Manuel. *Utopian Thought in the Western World.* Cambridge, Mass., 1979.

Maor, Yitshak. *Ha-tenuah ha-tsiyonit be-rusyah.* Jerusalem, 1973.

Margalit, Elkanah. *Ha-Shomer ha-tsa'ir.* Tel Aviv, 1971.

Meisel, Nachman. *Y. L. Perets: zayn lebn un shafn.* New York, 1945.

Mintz, Alan. *Hurban.* New York, 1984.

Mintz, Mattityahu. *Ber Borokhov.* Tel Aviv, 1976.

Miron, Dan. *A Traveler Disguised.* New York, 1973.

———. *Ben Hazon le-emet.* Jerusalem, 1979.

———. *Ha-peredah min ha'ani he-ani.* Tel Aviv, 1986.

———. *Bodedim bemoadam.* Tel Aviv, 1987.

Moseley, Marcus. "Jewish Autobiography in Eastern Europe: The Prehistory of a Literary Genre." D. Phil., Trinity College, Oxford, 1990.

Motzkin, Leo, ed. *Die Judenpogrome in Russland,* 2 vols. Cologne, 1910.

Naor, Mordekhai, ed. *Tel Aviv bereshita, 1909–1934.* Jerusalem, 1984.

Nash, Stanley. *In Search of Hebraism: Shai Hurvitz and His Polemics in the Hebrew Press.* Leiden, 1980.

Nordau, Max. *Zionistische Schriften.* Berlin, 1923.

Nurock, Mordekhai. *Ve'idat tsiyonei rusiyah be-Minsk.* Jerusalem, 1963/1964.

Oren, Yosef. "Ahad Ha'am ve-M.Y. Berdyczewski: tehilat ha-hitkatvut (1891–1896)." Master's thesis. Tel Aviv University, 1982.

Patterson, David. *The Hebrew Novel in Czarist Russia*. Edinburgh, 1964.

Pawel, Ernst. *The Labyrinth of Exile: A Life of Theodor Herzl*. New York, 1989.

Penslar, Derek. *Zionism and Technocracy: The Engineering of Jewish Settlement in Palestine, 1870–1918*. Bloomington, Ind., 1991.

Pinson, Koppel, ed. *Nationalism and History: Essays on Old and New Judaism by Simon Dubnow*. Philadelphia, 1958.

Pograbinsky, Yochanan, *Me-zikhronotai al Ahad Ha'am*. Tel Aviv, 1937.

Pomper, Philip. *Peter Lavrov and the Russian Revolutionary Movement*. Chicago, 1972.

Poppel, Stephen M. *Zionism in Germany, 1897–1933: The Shaping of a Jewish Identity*. Philadelphia, 1974.

Porath, Yehoshua. *The Emergence of the Palestinian-Arab National Movement. 1918–1929*. London, 1974.

Portugalov, G. M., et al. *Ukazatel' literatury o sionizme*. St. Petersburg, 1903.

Raisin, Jacob S. *The Haskalah Movement in Russia*. Philadelphia, 1913.

Raisin, Max. *Great Jews I Have Known*. New York, 1952.

Rawidowicz, S[himon], ed. *Sefer Sokolov*. Jerusalem, 1943.

———. *Sefer Shimon Dubnow*. London, 1954.

Rawnitsky, Yehoshua. *Dor vesofrav*. Tel Aviv 1926–1937.

Reinharz, Jehuda, "The Balfour Declaration and Its Maker: A Reassessment," *Journal of Modern History* 64, no. 3, 1992.

———. *Fatherland or Promised Land*. Ann Arbor, 1975.

———. *Chaim Weizmann: The Making of a Zionist Leader*. New York, 1985.

Reizen, Zalmen. *Leksikon fun der yidisher literatur, prese un filologye*, 4 vols. Vilna, 1926–1929.

Remba, Isaac. *Banim akhlu bosar*. Tel Aviv, 1973.

Rinott, Moshe. *Hevrat ha-ezra le-yehude germanyah bi-yetsirah ube-ma'avak*. Jerusalem, 1971.

Rodrigue, Aron. *French Jews, Turkish Jews: The Alliance Israélite Universelle and the Politics of Jewish Schooling in Turkey, 1860–1925*. Bloomington, Ind., 1990.

Rogger, Hans. *Russia in the Age of Modernisation and Revolution, 1881–1917*. London, 1983.

Rosenbloom, Noah. "Ahad Ha'am ve-ha-yeda ha-histori." *Sefer ha-yovel li-khevod Shalom Baron*, vol. 3. Jerusalem, 1974.

Roskies, David. *Against the Apocalypse*. Cambridge, Mass, 1984.

Rotenstreich, Nathan. *Al Ahad Ha'am*. Jerusalem, 1956.

Rubenstein, Arieh. "Tefisat ha-'kultura' be-mishnat Ahad Ha'am." *Melila*, vol. 1. Manchester, 1940.

Sadan, Dov. *Avnei bohan*. Tel Aviv, 1951.

Salmon, Joseph. *Dat ve-tsiyonut*. Jerusalem, 1990.

Schama, Simon. *Two Rothschilds and the Land of Israel*. New York, 1978.

Schechtman, Joseph. *The Jabotinsky Story: Rebel and Statesman,* vol. 1. New York, 1956.

Schidorsky, Dov. *Sifriyah va-sefer be-erets yisrael be-shilhe ha-tekufah ha-otomanit.* Jerusalem, 1990.

Scholem, Gershom. *Od davar.* Tel Aviv, 1986.

Schwadron, Abraham. *Torat ha-tsiyonut ha-akhzarit.* Tel Aviv, 1943/1944.

Schwartz, Solomon, ed. *Ussishkin ve-igerotav.* Jerusalem, 1949.

Schweid, Eliezer. *Ha-yahid: olamo shel A. D. Gordon.* Tel Aviv, 1970.

———. *Toledot he-hagut ha-yehudit be-me'ah ha-esrim.* Tel Aviv, 1990.

Seltzer, Robert M. "Simon Dubnow: A Critical Biography of His Early Years." Ph.D. diss., Columbia University, 1970.

———. "Coming Home: The Personal Basis of Simon Dubnow's Ideology." *AJS Review* 1 (1976): 283–301.

Shaked, Gershon, ed. *Bialik: Yetsirato le-sugeha bi-re'i ha-bikoret.* Jerusalem, 1974.

———. *Le-lo motsa.* Tel Aviv, 1973.

Shamir, Ziva. *Ha-Tsartsar meshorer ha-galut: al ha-yesod ha-amami bi-yetsirat Bialik.* Tel Aviv, 1986.

Shapira, Anita. *Berl,* 2 vols. Tel Aviv, 1983.

Sharet, Y, ed. *Igrot B. Katznelson, 1900–1914.* Tel Aviv, 1961.

Shargel, Baila Round. *Practical Dreamer: Israel Friedlaender and the Shaping of American Judaism.* New York, 1985.

Shavit, Ya'akov, ed. *Ha-Historiyah shel eretz yisrael.* Jerusalem, 1981.

Shavit, Ya'akov, and Ya'akov Goldstein, eds. *Leksikon ha-ishim shel eretz yisrael, 1799–1948.* Tel Aviv, 1983.

Shavit, Zohar. *Ha-hayyim ha-sifrutiyim be-eretz yisrael, 1910–1933.* Tel Aviv, 1982.

Shorer, Chaim. *Ha-Pogrom be-kishinev bi-melot 60 shanah.* Tel Aviv, 1963.

Shorter, Edward. *From Paralysis to Fatigue.* New York, 1992.

Shva, Shlomo. *Hozeh berah.* Tel Aviv, 1990.

Simon, Leon. *Studies in Jewish Nationalism.* London, 1920.

———. *Ahad Ha'am.* Philadelphia, 1960.

Simon, Leon, and Yosef Heller. *Ahad Ha'am: ha-ish, po'ulo ve-torato.* Jerusalem, 1955.

Sionistskoe dvizhenie sredi evreev'. Odessa, 1900.

Slutsky, Yehuda. *Itonut ha-yehudit-rusit ba-me'ah ha-esrim.* Jerusalem, 1978.

Smith, Anthony. *Theories of Nationalism.* New York, 1983.

Sokolov, Nahum. *Sefer zikharon.* Warsaw, 1889.

Sosis, Yisroel. *Di sotsial-ekonomishe lage fun di ruslendishe yuden.* Petrograd, 1919.

Spencer, Herbert. *The Principles of Sociology,* 3d ed., 3 vols. Westport, Conn., 1975.

Stein-Ashkenazi, Esther. "Agudat 'venei moshe,' merkazah be-varsha u-zikatah le-tenuat hibat tsiyon." *Ha-Tsionut* 11 (1986).

Talmon, Jacob L. *The Unique and the Universal.* London, 1965.

Tazkir Lupokhin, trans. Yael Ha-Russi. Jerusalem, 1987.

Tcherikower, Elias. *Yehudim be-ittot mahapekhah*. Tel Aviv, 1957.

Tchernowitz, Shmuel. *Bnei moshe u-tekufatam*. Warsaw, 1914.

Tchernowitz, Chaim. *Masekhet zikhronot*. New York, 1945.

———. *Pirkei hayyim*. New York, 1954.

Tobias, Henry J. *The Jewish Bund from its Origins to 1905*. Stanford, 1972.

Tolkowsky, Shmuel. *Yoman tsiyoni medini*. Tel Aviv, 1981.

Tsamriyon, Tsemah. *Shloshah hogim: Rambam, Mendelsohn, Ahad Ha'am*. Tel Aviv, 1979.

Tsitron, Shmuel. *Dray literarishe doyres*, 4 vols. Vilna, 1920–1928.

———. *Toldot hibat tsiyon*, vol. 1. Warsaw, 1945.

Vital, David. *The Origins of Zionism*. Oxford, 1975.

———. *Zionism: The Formative Years*. Oxford, 1982.

———. *Zionism: The Crucial Phase*. Oxford, 1987.

Walicki, Andrzej. *The Slavophile Controversy*. Oxford, 1975.

Weisbrod, Robert G. *African Zion*. Philadelphia, 1968.

Werses, Shmuel. *Haskalah ve-shabta'ut*. Jerusalem, 1988.

Wisse, Ruth. *I. L. Peretz and the Making of Modern Jewish Culture*. Seattle, 1991.

Wolfe, Bertram. *Three Who Made a Revolution*. Boston, 1948.

Zenzipper, Arye [Rafaeli]. *Pa'amei ha-ge'ula*. Tel Aviv, 1951.

Zipperstein, Steven J. *The Jews of Odessa: A Cultural History, 1794–1881*. Stanford, 1985.

———. "Heresy, Apostasy and the Transformation of Joseph Rabinovich." In *Jewish Apostasy in the Modern World*, ed. Todd Endelman. New York, 1987.

———. "Transforming the Heder: Maskilic Politics in Imperial Russia." In *Jewish History: Essays in Honour of Chimen Abramsky*, ed. Ada Rapoport-Albert and Steven J. Zipperstein. London, 1988.

———. "Ahad Ha'am's Politics." *Jewish History* 4, no. 2 (Fall 1990).

———. "Old Ghosts: Pogroms in the Jewish Mind." *Tikkun* (May/June 1991).

Zylbercweig, Zalman. *Ahad Ha'am un zayn batsiung tsu yidish*. Los Angeles, 1956.

Index

Abramowitsch, Shalom Jacob. *See* Mendele Mocher Seforim
L'Activité mentale (Pauhlan), 77
Adler, Hermann, 277
Africa, Uganda Plan (1903), 194, 206–215 passim, 253
Agnon, Samuel Joseph, 232
Agriculture, Palestine, 126, 201; Ahad Ha'am's visits, 59–60, 95, 158, 246–251; Bnei Moshe's Rehovot, 54, 59, 64, 95, 175; Brenner Affair and, 242, 243, 244; funding, 54, 95, 125, 173–174, 175; Ginzberg family/Ahad Ha'am considering move into, 17, 19, 95; grape industry/wine production, 59–60, 111, 246; Herzl and, 155; Hovevei Zion's projects, 59, 86, 155; kibbutz, 250; labor, 174, 175, 242–250 passim, 270; Rothschild and, 95, 155, 158, 173–176
Agudat Moshe, 98
Ahad Ha'am, xvii-xxiv, 18, 19–20, 33–66, 154, 171–172, 193, 252, 303–308; as *ahad ha'adam*, 311; and Ahad Ha'amism, 31, 244, 258; beaten by a policeman (1907), 68, 226; biographies of, xx–xxi, 38, 315; criticized, 56, 62–65, 84–85, 87, 94, 120, 123, 135–137, 146–147, 172–173, 197, 231, 248, 259–267, 303–5; death (1927), xviii, 323; early years (*see*

Ginzberg, Asher); and emotional expression, 135–136, 282, 290; eroticism in epigrams, 282–283; as European, 28–29, 146, 261; finances, 28, 98–99, 108, 110, 115–116, 164–169 passim, 179, 252–253; friendship, 50–51; as "harmonious Jew," xxiv, 268; as *Ha- Shiloach* editor, 108–127, 166–169, 170, 171, 179, 213, 322; and honesty/secrecy, 38, 52, 56, 63, 294, 302; illnesses, 99, 115–116, 158, 161–163, 165, 227, 233, 269, 295, 310–314, 322, 323; impersonality, 257; irony, 126–127, 190; job (*see* Wissotzsky tea company job); leadership, 31, 38–42, 45, 50–51, 64–66, 98–99, 101, 120–121, 171, 266–267; London home, 70, 169, 170, 172, 234–235, 244–245, 269, 277–314 passim; morbidity, 178–179; name's meaning, 41; "opportunism," 146; pen name, xviii, xxv, 33, 40–41; political skills, 56, 65–66, 97–98, 104, 120, 189–190; romanticism, 231, 247; secularism, 11–12, 48–49, 80, 123, 239, 268, 278, 292; seventieth birthday, 323; sixtieth birthday, 257; skepticism, 146, 172; solitude, 276–277; Tel Aviv home, 287, 314–315, 317–319, 321–323; writing aspirations, 171;

369

Designer:	U.C. Press Staff
Compositor:	Braun-Brumfield, Inc.
Text:	10/13 Galliard
Display:	Galliard
Printer:	Braun-Brumfield, Inc.
Binder:	Braun-Brumfield, Inc.